Heartfelt Greetings

From Nazi-Occupied Norway

Compiled by:
Barbara Peterson Schutte, American Falls, Idaho
Karen Peterson Fisher, Bow, Washington
Teresa Peterson Miller, Snohomish, Washington

Editor: Teresa Peterson Miller

Profits of book sales will be donated to non-profit organizations
Compilers and editor did not and will not receive remuneration

Newspaper clippings from personal family collections, except where noted.

Cover Design & Page Layout: Tony D. Locke, MM

We would be amiss if we did not share the "silver lining" as we buckled down in the quiet of our homes during the Global Pandemic of COVID-19, which greatly adjusted our lifestyles early in 2020 and continuing into 2021. Truly, this change in our lives helped to provide the time in the preserving of this history. We thank our dad, Carl Peterson (Sophie's brother), for cherishing these documents in a special drawer at his home, instilling in us that these are to be valued treasures. And our utmost thanks to the author, Aunt Sophie, for all her letters, journaling, and gems that she carefully preserved for us. And mostly, we thank our God for preserving Sophie during this time and giving us the opportunity to share her story. We sisters have enjoyed meeting together through Zoom meetings, text messages, FaceTime Messenger, and e-mails as we discussed and toiled over the project that we feel God has placed in our midst for a time such as this. Many, many hours have been spent over our keyboards typing up the letters and the journal entries, coupled with researching and correspondence. It has filled our time with meaning, learning, admiration, love, and appreciation for those who have gone before us and who we continue to go forward with. Often, it has caused our hearts to be filled with thanksgiving while wishing we could converse with the special loved ones who in some way or another partook in this journey but are no longer with us here on earth. We hope you enjoy the preservation of Sophie's Story as well as the future benefits and appreciation of this piece of true history.

Barbara

Karen

Teresa

HeartfeltGreetings3@gmail.com

This book is dedicated to the memories of

SOPHIE PETERSON JOHNSON

Our beloved aunt who lovingly connected with our extended family in Norway and endured with faith the challenges of wartime while preserving the memories for us to appreciate.

CARL ELMER PETERSON

Our father, Sophie's brother, who honorably and faithfully served in the Army Corps of Engineers of the United States of America during WWII.

ACKNOWLEDGEMENTS

Randi Kiester

This book would not be complete without the help we have received from our cousin, Randi Egelandsdal Kiester. Randi, in her patience, perfection and perseverance, has carefully translated the Norwegian letters for this project. She met Barb many times through FaceTime, toiling over the sometimes almost illegible letters that were written on poor quality or aged paper. Her familiarity with the dialect from the Egersund and surrounding region was of enormous help when confusion arose. Also, her knowledge of the area and our Norwegian family assisted us immensely when statements needed some clarification. We also want to express our heartfelt appreciation for the numerous hours she sacrificed out of her busy schedule to help with the maps which involved the placement of the many towns and farms that Sophie traveled to. Randi was born in Egersund, Norway, but has resided in the U.S.A. since 1997. She is the daughter of Sophie's first cousin, Gudrun (and Karl) Egelandsdal Thorsen, and is married to Jeff Kiester. Randi is a knitting designer, sharing the Norwegian culture and her gifts of design with the world, and you can find her at Randi.k.design on Instragram and/or *www.ravelry.com/designers/randi-k-design.*

Thank you, Randi, for the time you have generously given to preserve this story. You are appreciated more than you will ever know. And thank you, Jeff, for your explanations when clarification was asked of you during the translation process and for giving up time with Randi while she did this important work.

Rolf Mong

We are also very thankful for the help of our cousin, Rolf Mong, who resides in Mong, Egersund, Norway, for answering an enormous number of emails with questions about the family of Peder Mikal Pedersen Omdal including their spouses, their children, the areas where they lived, and questions about the Rodvelts, the Mongs, the Vagles, the Maulands, and others. Rolf also helped translate some words and names Sophie used, identified some of the people in pictures Sophie had saved, and he wrote a wonderful history of the family farms at Omdal and Grødem, as well as essays about the history of the Ladies' Aid group. Rolf also wrote about the geographical and topographical aspects of the Egersund and nearby areas. He translated some Norwegian letters for us. We are so grateful!

Rolf's mother, Thelma Rodvelt Mong, became a very close friend of Sophie's and was also a first cousin of hers. You will find her mentioned quite often in the book.

Rolf, we really appreciate you and your valuable help! And to Marit Elisabeth, Rolf's wife, we extend our heartfelt appreciation for her support while Rolf assisted us with our questions.

Arild Stein Thorsen

With interest, purpose and devotion, our cousin, Arild Stein Thorsen from Egersund, responded to numerous e-mails as we searched for information about our family in Norway. We very much appreciate his provision of the Eikelandsdal family tree which enabled us to familiarize ourselves with the cousins and their families on Sophie's mother's side. When requested, he faithfully continued to provide us with contact information assisting us to carry on our research. His generosity with his time and knowledge is very much appreciated. Thank you, cousin Arild, and to your wife, Hildur.

Stuart Omdal

We are thankful to Stuart Omdal, our American-born cousin, a retired professor of education from the University of Northern Colorado, for his suggestions, counsel, and help with editing.

Family and Friends

We acknowledge and express thanks to the MANY OTHERS who have contributed information about persons mentioned by Sophie, her experiences, and the preserved history that are contained within the pages of this book. They brought forth information that was appreciated and beneficial such as newspaper articles from cousins, memories shared of family gatherings with Sophie, etc. Numerous avenues of communication via email, messenger, penned letters and telephone, as well as encouragement from extended family and friends helped us with the completion of this project.

Karen and Barbara also want to acknowledge Teresa Peterson Miller for her leadership in this project. She was a great organizer of the many files that required attention to prepare for publication. Also, we thank our husbands for their patience, willingness, and understanding as we persevered to complete this time-consuming project. Thank you, Bob Schutte, Jerome Fisher, and Greg Miller. You are appreciated more than you know.

Heartfelt Greetings and THANKS to All!

Barbara, Karen & Teresa

PREFACE

This young lady, Sophie Peterson of Bow, Washington, U.S.A., being the author and main character of this nonfiction book, was born in America in 1906. At 33 years of age, Sophie decided to take a year off from teaching primary school and travel to the beloved country of Norway, the previous home of her father and mother who had immigrated to America in 1903 and 1905, respectively.

After traveling from Seattle, Washington, U.S.A. and taking a North Cape boat tour of Northern Norway, Sophie was introduced to her relatives. This book begins with her arrival on the family farm in southwest Norway on July 31, 1939, from whence she meets many aunts, uncles, and a grandfather whom she had never met before. Her wonderful connections with and love for family convinced her to tarry in the much-loved country of Norway, rather than risk crossing the Atlantic in war-time. She had planned to stay a year, but it would be almost five years before she returned home to America, due to the unexpected Nazi occupation of Norway and her sudden arrest and transport to three different prison locations.

This book contains her preserved diaries and letters; and reveals the many feelings and facts related to the happenings in Norway and the impact of WWII and post war challenges.

Norway

NORTH CAPE
Hammerfest
Trollfjord
Vardø
Kirkenes
Tromsø
FINNMARK
Finnsnes
TROMS
Narvik
LOFOTEN
Bodø
NORDLAND
Trondheim
Kristiansund
Molde
Ålesund
Sogndal
Lillehammer
Bergen
HARDANGER
Sauda
laugesund
Oslo
Stavanger
Sola
Sandnes (Vagle, Gandal)
Klepp (Bryne)
Ålgård
Nærbø
Sirevåg
Egersund
Moi
Sogndal
Jossingfjord
Flekkefjord
Kristiansand

Towns and Farms Visited by Sophie

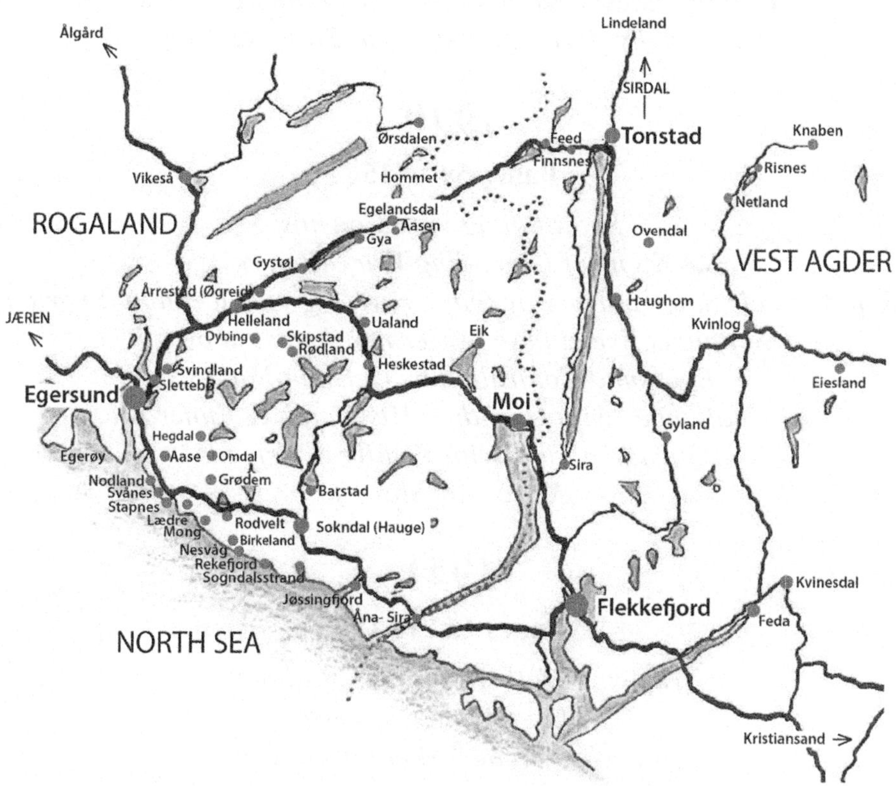

Dotted line marks the border between Rogaland and Agder counties

Dotted line marks the border between Rogaland and Agder counties

TABLE OF CONTENTS

Family

Names in *italics* were not used by Sophie in her writings.

Only the offspring that were alive when Sophie's diaries and letters were written are included.

Sophie's Parents

Tollag Olaus Severin Pedersen Omdal: Born June 2, 1884 in Omdal, Egersund, Rogaland, NORWAY. Died May 17, 1965 in Bow, Skagit County, Washington, USA. Tollag was born to Peder Mikal Pedersen Omdal and Taline (Tollaksdatter Mong) Omdal.

Christine Mikkelsen Eikelandsdal or Egelandsdal: Born July 6,1881 in Egelandsdal, Heskestad, Rogaland, NORWAY. Died March 3,1962 in Mt. Vernon, Skagit County, Washington, USA.
Christine was born to Mikkel Karlson and Rakel Serina (Salvesdatter Bjørnstad) Eikelandsdal

Tollag and Christine were married November 22,1902 in Rogaland, NORWAY. They went by the last name of Peterson after arriving in America.

Family of Mikkel Karlson and Rakel Serina (Salvesdatter Bjørnstad) Eikelandsdal

Blood relative is named first in each line.

Valborg (Mikkelsdatter Egelandsdal) and Tollef Olson Gya
Lisabeth (Gya) and Theodor or Ted Halvorson
Ragna Sofie (Gya) and Karsten Moi, Arvid Eyvind, Vegard, Kirsten Synnøve
Ole and Asgjerd Gya
Ingrid Torgine (Gya) and Torvald Lindeland, Torleiv, Torbjørg, Bjørn
Mikael and *Astrid* Gya
Martin Olai and Marie Gya
Olga (Gya) and Jonas Øveland, Torlaug
Valborg (Gya) and Albert Espeland
Tor and *Lillian* Gya

Martha (Mikkelsdatter Egelandsdal) and Ole Eiesland
Oskar and Selma Eiesland
Magnus and *Anna Bø Eiesland*, Olav
Ingrid and *Johan* Eiesland

Johannes and *Torlaug* Eiesland
Thor and *Carrie* Eiesland
Øyvind and *Martha* Eiesland
Rakel Eiesland

Teoline Kristine (Mikkelsdatter Egelandsdal) and Johan Teodor Tønnesson Gystøl
Amanda Gystøl
Rakel Sofia (Gystøl) and *Nikolai* Egelid, Olav, Jens, Laura, Olga, Torlaug, Sigrun
Anna (Gystøl) and Magnus Steiestøl
Maria (Gystøl) and *Martin Jørgen* Halvorson
Torvald and Konstanse Gystøl, Tora
Martin and *Ingrid* Dybing
Jon and *Abigae*l Gystøl, Johan
Anton Emil Gystøl
Gunder Tanderup Gystøl
Tyra Johanna (Gystøl) and Jakob Gyland
Asbjørn Olav Gystøl

Berthe Tobine (Mikkelsdatter Egelandsdal) and Andreas Torgerson Østrem
Martin and Martha Østrem, Arvid
Thorvald and Marta (Teodorsdatter Ramsland) Østrem, Bjørg, Inveig, Aslaug Tordis
Anders Moldetved and Kristine Østrem, Arnfinn, Torgunn
Anna or Anne Berte Østrem
Sigurd Rudol*f* and Signy (Ollestad) Østrem, Tønnes Andreas, Arvid, Britt
Randi Margrethe (Østrem) and Joseph Skipstad, Josefine, Bertha, Hjørdis, Kjetil, Jan Reidar
Fredrik and Jenny (Revsland) Østrem
Bergit (Østrem) and Alf Skåra, Alf
Alf Bottolv and Sigfried (Slettebø) Østrem
Tor Mikal and *Gerda* Østrem
Gudrun (Østrem) and *Odd* Ellingsen

Christine (Mikkelsdatter Egelandsdal) and Tollag Olaus Severin (Pedersen Omdal) Peterson
Peter and Margery Leona (Warfield) Peterson
Sophie (Peterson) and Birger Kon Johnson
Martin and Margaret (Frost) Peterson, Jeanne; and when widowed, Margaret married Howard Graff
Tora (Peterson) and Sigurd or Sig Freestad, Torvald or Siggy
Torval Cornelius Peterson

Oscar Severin and Eileen (Tenneson) Peterson, Judith or Judy, Stanton or Button, Dennis or Mac, Roger or Joe
Theodora Ragna or Teddy (Peterson) and Christian (Chris) Lawrence Hansen, *Christian*, David
Carl Elmer and Alice June (Boe) Peterson, Carlene, Barbara, Karen, Keith, Teresa
Melvin Norris and Wanda (Loop) Peterson, Marvin, Wayne, Cheryl, Polly
Clarence Peterson

Karl Mikkelson and Anna (Gabrielsdtr Espetveit) Egelandsdal
Mikal Karlson and Tomine Egelandsdal, Tordis
Ragna Sofie (Egelandsdal) and Trygve Hetland, Ivar, Torbjørn, Korbjørn
Tyra (Mikkelsdatter Egelandsdal) and Tønnes Tunheim, Kirsten, Irene
Gudrun (Egelandsdal) and Karlemann or Karl Thorsen, Anna Karin, Arild Stein, Randi
Astrid (Egelandsdal) and Gjert Skadberg, Kåre
Agnes Sophie (Egelandsdal) and Øivind Berentsen, Hans
Gunnar Egelandsdal
Karstein Egelandsdal
Sigmund and *Gunnlaug* Egelandsdal

Semine (Mikkelsdatter Egelandsdal) and Ommund Torgerson Østrem
Anna Bertha (Østrem) and Magnus Aarrestad, Svein, Liv
Rakel Serina (Østrem) and Abraham Øgreid, Anna Kjerstina, Jostein, Sylvi, Olav
Torger and Malene Østrem, Ove, Sigbjørn
Mikael and Minnie Kristina (Teodorsdatter Ramsland) Østrem, Tor Olav, Ingveig
Olav and Berta Østrem, Anne Elise
Sanna (Østrem) and Harald Peersen, Håvard
Margrethe (Østrem) and Einar Sørdal, Leif Magne
Trond Magne and *Alida* Østrem

Family of Peder Mikal Pedersen and Taline (Tollaksdatter Mong) Omdal

Blood relative is named first in each line.

Tollag Olaus Severin (Pedersen Omdal) and Christine (Mikkelsdatter Egelandsdal) Peterson
See list of descendants above under Christine (Mikkelsdatter Egelandsdal) and Tollag Olaus Severin (Pedersen Omdal) Peterson

Peder (Pedersen Omdal) and Ellen Martine (Martinsen Stapnes) Peterson
Tilda Margaret (Peterson) and *Bert* Hansen
Martin Theodor Peterson

Palmer Edwin and *Myrtle Edna (Penix)* Peterson
Mynor Peter and *Margery (Morris)* Peterson
Ernest or Ernie John and *Beatrice (Staffanson)* Peterson
Myrtle Theodora (Peterson) and *John Milton* Allgire
Esther Pauline (Peterson) and *Ernest Arnold* Boe
Marie Eleanor (Peterson) and *Claude Donald* Geiger

Helene (Pedersdatter Omdal) and Andreas Emil Rodvelt
Tora Rodvelt
Thelma Petrea (Rodvelt) and Sivert Hovland Mong, Rolf, Brit Helene
Mikal and *Berit (Mong)* Rodvelt
Alf Henry and *Jean Aileen (Østebrød)* Rodvelt
Petter and *Selma (Raugstad*) Rodvelt

Lars Mikal Pedersen and Berthea or Thea (Vagle) Omdal
Petter and *Klara* Omdal
Henrik or Henne and *Agnes* Omdal

Anne Marie Pedersdatter Omdal

Petter Theodor Pedersen Omdal Grødem

Descendants of Per Larssen and Marta (Svendsdatter Lædre) Omdal
Aunts, uncles and first cousins of Sophie's father.
Sophie mentions these relatives many times in her writings.

Lars Pedersen and Helen (Grødeim) Omdal

Svend Pedersen and Berte Gurine (Mong) Omdal
Louisa or Lovise Marie (Svendsdatter Omdal) and 1) Andreas or Andrew Johnson, and 2) Tom Jakobson Hadland
Nels Tobias Svendsen and Sina Marie (Nesvåg) Omdal, Bertha, Sigve or Sig
Elisabeth Marie (Svendsdatter Omdal) and Kristian or Chris Marius Mikkelsen Rodvelt
Peder Martin Svendsen and 1) Inga Marie (Berntsen) Omdal, and 2) Anna Gurie (Berntsen) Omdal, and 3) Clara Marie (Boe Hansen) Omdal
Selma Bertine (Svendsdatter Omdal) and Little Lars Bovitz Omdal

Severin Pedersen Omdal

Marie Pedersdatter Omdal

Jonas Pedersen and Engel (**Jacobsdatter** ***Mong) Omdal***

Peder Jonason Omdal
Jakob Jonason Omdal
Lars Jonason Omdal Mong
Hans Jonason and Kristine Mong

Helene (Pedersdatter Omdal) and Johan Svarteberg

Peder Mikal Pedersen and Taline (Tollaksdatter Mong) Omdal (Sophie's grandparents)

See previous Eikelandsdal section for list of their offspring.

Elias Pedersen and Ingeborg Helene (Nilsdatter Mong) Omdal

Infant Eliasdatter Omdal
Lars Herman Eliasen and Jenny Ruth (Johnson) Omdal, Roy Ernst
Nils Emil Eliasen and Elisabet Marie or Maria (Jørgensdatter Omdal) Omdal
Peder Johan Eliasen Omdal
Martine Eliasdatter Omdal
Ingvald Emil and *Johanne* (Stapnes) Omdal
"Little Elisabet" Marie Omdal

Tollef Pedersen and 1) Serine (***Reinertsdatter Grødeim*****) Omdal, and 2) Sille (Larsdatter Omdal) Omdal**

Paul Martin (Tollefson) and Rakel Omdal, Magnhild
Karl Johan (Tollefson) and Henrietta or Hattie Josephin (Johnson) Omdal, Carlton
Gjertine (Tollefsdatter Omdal) and Erling Larsen Omdal
Reinart Tollefson Omdal
Marta (Tollefsdatter Omdal) and Nils Stapnes

Elisabeth Omdal

Dear Reader,

The following is a combination of diaries and letters that were preserved by Sophie (Peterson) Johnson and her relatives, written during her time in Norway and thereafter. Many of the letters were written in the Norwegian language and have been translated into English. These treasures of inscriptions are recorded in chronological order. There are times when events are repeated, as Sophie records her experiences in her diaries and shares the same encounters and happenings via her penned letters to family at home.

The diary entries are printed in regular font, and the letters are *italicized.* When the editors added names, words, notes or explanations, an effort was made to change the font from regular to italics, or in the case of letters, from italics to the regular font. At times we gave the full name of a person for clarification.

To enhance your experience as you travel with Sophie vicariously throughout the beloved homeland of both of her parents, you may greatly benefit by familiarizing yourself with the following:

- Maps
  Pages x - xi
- Family
  Page xiv - xix
- Geographical & Topographical Aspects of the Egersund Region
  Page 304
- History of Omdal & Grødem
  Page 307

We hope and pray that you enjoy these preserved treasures, and that they will strengthen your love and support for family and others, during trying times and always. May your life be enriched by reading this book.

Sincerely and with Heartfelt Greetings!

Barb, Karen & Teresa

1939

Sophie Settles in Grødem – Meets Father's Family
Meeting Mother's Family near Egelandsdal
Sophie Writes Letters to Home – Sharing About Travel & Family
Britain & France Declared War on Germany
Sophie Contacts American Consul, Effects of War Felt
Ocean Mines Affect Fishing, Shrimping & Travel
Electricity Arrives in Grødem, Radio & News

July 31, 1939 - Monday

The city *(Stavanger)* is old, with crooked, narrow streets, but interesting. Shopped for silver all day. Out to Sola in the evening. Rainy, but nice drive. The country was interesting, with stone walls and small farms. Sola has a modern, up-to-date summer resort.

August 1, 1939 - Tuesday

Breakfast in room at hotel. Bought raincoat for $6.00.

2:35 p.m. - Took train from Stavanger, arriving at Egersund at 5:00 p.m. Checked in at Victoria Hotel and telephoned Onkel Petter. We all took a taxi out to Grødem, met Onkel Petter and Tante Anne *(brother and sister, both unmarried)* and Bestefar (*Grandfather*) all for the first time. Returned to Egersund for the night.

Sophie's Grandfather Peder Mikal Pedersen Omdal

August 2, 1939 - Wednesday

Pearl and Verna Urmey and I shopped for pottery at Fayancefabrik. They use clay from England and the molds are baked three times - two hours, then fifty hours, then the third time longer, then enamel dipped, painted, enameled again, and baked. Red paint turns to gold - brown turns blue, design comes through the coat of enamel.

Noon - Pearl and Verna left by train. I met Tante Helene *Rodvelt* and Elisabeth Birkeland *Nesvåg (sister of Bergitte Birkeland Jacobson in Bow, WA, U.S.A.)* then took

Mathilde Grødem, Tante Anne Marie Omdal, Sophie Peterson, Alf Henry Rodvelt, Sivert Hovland Mong at Omdal.

Tante Anne Marie Omdal, Sivert Hovland Mong, Onkel Petter Theodor Omdal Grødem with hay on his back, Mathilde Grødem

the bus out to Grødem at 1:00 p.m. Onkel Petter met me at the road *(still a very long walk to the farm).*

August 3- 4, 1939

Helped in the hay. Onkel Petter made me a new red rake. They cut the hay by hand and spread it out to dry. When rain comes, they put it up in shocks. The next day, they spread it out to dry. When dry, they haul it into the barn on a small wagon drawn by one small horse or carry it in on their back.

We eat six times a day. Onkel Petter killed the fatted calf. I talked to Onkel Lars on the phone, also to Tante Helene *(both are siblings of Tollag, Sophie's father).*

August 5, 1939 - Saturday

Worked in hay when weather permitted. Picked berries and cleaned them for juice and pudding. Churned butter and got ready for company in the evening. By 8:00 p.m. company had arrived - Onkel Lars and Tante Thea and their son Petter; Andreas and Tilde Mauland and their son Sven of Stavanger; three other young people from Vagle; Thelma Rodvelt; her boyfriend Sivert Mong; Tante Helene and Onkel Andreas Rodvelt and their sons, Mikal, Petter, and Alf Henry. Everyone stayed overnight. Some slept in the barn on the hay. Great time. Nice to meet all the relatives.

August 5, 1939

Dear Parents and Siblings,

I must write this in pencil because I do not have any ink. Right now, I'm at Grødem and it is really pretty here. We arrived in Egersund on August 1st, and we stayed at a hotel as I did not want to bring strangers (Pearl and Verna) *to Grødem for overnight. I talked to Onkel on the phone and told him that we would come out there for a while. However, we went back to Egersund in the evening, as Pearl and Verna had to travel the following day. The next day, I took the bus back to Grødem.*

I met Tante Helene in town. Thelma works at the Old Folks Home in Egersund. Bergitte Jacobson's sister was with Tante Helene and she was disappointed with Karen and Oskar Holt

(from Bow, WA), *because they had left without telling them they were leaving. She said that she had wanted to go with them and meet Bergitte. She also had some reading glasses that she wanted to send with them to give to Ole Birkeland. However, she was able to send them with Pearl. Pearl is supposed to give them to you, and you can give them to Ole.*

Grandpa is doing fairly well. He is sitting up in his chair most of the time.

Yesterday, I spoke with Onkel Lars on the telephone. Tonight, they are all coming to gather here on the farm at Grødem and will stay until Sunday. There will be nine from Jæren. Thea's sister and her husband (The Maulands) *are also coming. Sivert is picking up Thelma with his car, along with Tante Helene and Andreas and the boys from Rodvelt. So, we will have a full house and I have no idea where all of them are going to sleep.*

Mathilde Grødem was here and helped with the hay. Sivert Mong was here one day, and I also have been out raking and gathering the hay in piles. I was sure that my arms would be stiff and sore after the first day, but I didn't notice anything of that sort. They had just started working with the hay before I arrived. There has been a lot of rain. Sivert will come over and help next week.

Thank you for the letter that I just received. Did you receive the $7.00 that I sent you to pay for the suitcases? I just wonder if you received it, as you had not mentioned it in the letter. I am so happy to hear that you finally have gotten new wallpaper in your bedroom. Just bring down my bed and use it.

Yesterday they slaughtered a calf, so it will be a big party here tonight and tomorrow.

I have already gotten to know several from the nearby farms. In town, I met Martin Østrem's brother Sigurd, Tante Berthe, Sina Birkeland's brother, and many others that I cannot recall the names of.

You should see how nice they have improved the house here. Almost each of the rooms are newly painted, with new linoleum in the kitchen, hallway, and dining room. Also, new curtains, and several new chairs. They have decorated it quite special.

*They still have not gotten electricity, but I think it will happen soon. Onkel says that the first thing they are getting is a radio - so that they can listen to what kind of weather is expected the next day. In the garden are yellow cherries, blackberries, gooseberries, and red currants - and they are all ripe. But they are so busy with the hay now, that I'm afraid a lot of it is going to go to waste. Onkel showed me some apple trees that Papa (*Tollag*) had sent home. They are growing very well and producing apples. Onkel said that they produced some large apples last year also. It is coffee time here now, so I will continue after Tante Helene and Onkel Lars have been here - we are expecting them in just a minute.*

Sunday night:

Well, now I have met Onkel Lars and Thea's oldest boy Petter, Onkel Andreas and Tante Helene, their twins Petter and Alf Henry, their daughter Thelma and son Mikal, and Tilde and Andreas Mauland.

Their oldest boy, Sven, drove the car; they have a new 1939 Ford with a radio - and it is something great. Grandpa was able to listen to the sermon from Oslo on the radio this morning - but I do not know how much he understood. It has been so nice to meet everybody, and we have had a great time

1939

Friends and Family from Vagle, Rodvelt, and Stavanger came to Grødem to welcome Sophie

today. We took a lot of pictures over by the waterfall, and I hope that some of them will be good. I got to talk to Peder Johan Omdal from Stavanger - he dropped by for just a while on his way to Vatland.

Next week, Thelma is on vacation days - so I am going to Rodvelt to be there a few days. The week after that, Lars at Vagle is taking vacation days - so I will go and be there with them. He wanted me to visit when he had a chance to be home. He lives near Stavanger. After that, I will go to Ragna's at Moi and I suppose at that time, I will meet more of my family on Mother's side.

Mathilde sends her greetings. She is here and she helps Anne a lot. There must be someone in the house with Grandpa all of the time. Grandpa, Anne, and Petter also send their greetings. If anyone asks about me, please tell them that I enjoy it very much here at Grødem. I have not been to Omdal yet, but we are supposed to go over there one evening soon.

Live well.

Heartfelt Greetings from Sophie

P.S. You should have seen the beautiful rake that Petter made me, and he painted it red. Write to me soon and tell me how you are all doing, and also all the news.

August 6, 1939 - Sunday

Slept late and had breakfast at 10:00 a.m. Listened to the church service on Sven's radio, especially for Grandpa's sake, but he could not follow along.

Strange but true - in the afternoon everyone goes off and takes his afternoon nap. Coffee later. When company goes home, everyone follows them out to the main road. I rode out with Sven and walked back. Half hour each way. Thunder and lightning in the night.

August 7 - 8, 1939

It rained all week - farmers got no work done. One night, Mathilde, Petter, and I took a walk to Myran *(farm)* at Omdal. I have met most of the neighbors. I like it here very much.

My cousin, Martin Dybing, was injured in the storm on his bicycle.

August 8, 1939

Dear Theodora, Chris, and David,

I have finally settled down here at Grødem and like it fine. Really, it is just beautiful with all the high mountains, waterfalls, lakes, and valleys. I wish you could see it.

In July, the North Cape trip was decidedly the highlight of my travels thus far. The weather was just perfect, and we saw the midnight sun in all its glory for two nights. One night when we should have seen it, it was cloudy. The other nights were light all night. The sun would go below the horizon for an hour or more the farther south we went, but we couldn't think of going to bed until 3 or 4 in the morning on the whole trip. Every night there was some form of entertainment on deck, and the Captain was right in the midst of it. Everyone was just crazy about the Captain. He did everything he could to make people feel at home and have a good time, and there was a very nice crowd on board. You know, it often happens that people do not get to see the Midnight Sun on these trips; it all depends on the weather. If it is cloudy, of course you don't see it, but the Captain said this was one of the best trips he had had from the standpoint of the weather and people on board. Everyone had a swell time.

We got some swell Midnight Sun pictures. You'll have to drop in on Pearl when she gets back and see the pictures. I got some dandy Lap pictures with their reindeer.

Pearl has a copy of all my pictures as well as hers, and I have one of each of hers. It was a trip I'll never forget. It was a sight to see the sun come down and stop quite a distance above the horizon and after seven minutes go up again. We took a number of other pictures at midnight.

Did I tell you we climbed to the top of North Cape? The boat stopped, and a smaller boat from the Cape came out and took the passengers to land, where those who wanted to could scale the high rocky mountain. It took four hours to go up and come down. It was a hot climb even if it is the northern-most point in Norway.

At Vardø, I met Sig's brother Isak (Friestad)*; he came down to the boat. I told the captain I was meeting a friend there and to make the stop as long as possible. The captain paged him for me, or I wouldn't have known who he was or he me. He's a nice-looking chap. He took me up to his apartment which was very nice, but I couldn't stay long, as the boat stayed only a half hour. So, we surely talked a blue streak. He doesn't like it very well there, and I don't blame him. It is a fish town, and it is very cold as it is very far north. No trees, not a cow in the countryside, and too cold. They did have a few goats, however. It seems that after two years he will get a promotion. The winters must be terrible, dark day and night. No matter what time of night the boat came into any town along the way, the whole town would be down at the dock. People just don't sleep at night, or perhaps a few hours, and then they nap in the daytime. When you ask anyone when they do sleep, they'll say, "Oh, in the wintertime".*

We were a whole day at Trondheim on the way down. Olaf, Sig's other brother there, came to the boat and took us sightseeing. We visited the famous old Dom Kirke built in 1172 of beautiful architecture and sculpturing. It has gone through fire and whatnot in its time. It has been under reconstruction for seventy years and will not be finished for thirty more years. The work is very minute and precise, but beautiful. We climbed to the top of the tower (172 steps), from which we got a lovely view of the city and harbor. Out in the middle of the harbor stands an 11th Century old underground prison on a small island. It is now used as a bathing resort. We did not go out, however, as time did not permit. We had dinner at their house. I marvel at Olga's good humor and disposition, being disabled. She still has a lot of personality and character. Of course, she gets nowhere, but I guess she keeps the telephone busy. Her folks live in Haugesund, and she calls home to her mother whenever she wants. It costs her nothing, as Olaf has charge of the lines. She had just had a half hour's conversation with her mother the night before we were there.

At our next stop, we stayed in Stavanger a day and a half and shopped, or rather Pearl and Verna did the shopping. By the way, you must see the lovely souvenirs Pearl has accumulated. I haven't gotten so many, and only very small things. Egersund is a 2 ½ hour train ride from Stavanger, but I didn't realize that Grødem is only one Norwegian mile from Egersund. We got a hotel in Egersund. As soon as I found out how close it was to Grødem, I telephoned Onkel Petter and told him I was here and was coming out for the evening. We got a taxi to take us out, and the taxi driver was well acquainted with the folks here, so he came in and visited too, until we were ready to go back to town for the night. So that's how I first met Grandfather, Onkel Petter, and Tante Anne. Grandpa doesn't get around very much. He just sits in his chair most of the time. He doesn't see very well. He uses two canes, and then he barely makes headway. Someone has to be with him. He continually asks Tante Anne what I think. She says he's afraid I won't stay long enough, but I tell him he doesn't need to be afraid of that. Onkel Petter seems younger than I had pictured him in my mind. He's 39 and is he lots of fun! He can think of the craziest things. Sometimes I laugh until I cry. Mathilde, a half sister of Gus Grødem, is staying here helping Tante Anne and if she isn't the life! She and Onkel Petter are a two ringed circus by themselves. Tante Anne is a little quieter. She has had to work hard in her day, and Grandpa and Petter both seem to depend on her.

The day the girls left we also visited the Egersund Fayancefabrik porcelain and pottery factory which certainly was interesting. Pearl and Verna each got some pieces of pottery made there. I was glad they got to come out that evening, so now they can picture where I am.

I shall see if I can give you a picture of the place. There are only two houses at Grødem. They stand about two yards apart on a sloping green space on a hillside. There are high hills on both sides and in back, but in front the land slopes down to a large lake. On a clear day, we can easily see the North Sea in the distance. To the right and in the back is a huge waterfall where the city built a dam, and down below the hill is the powerhouse. There is a lake at the back of the dam.

The water from the lake comes over the dam, over the falls, and down the hill into the lake in front of us. You can hear the roar of the falls constantly, but one becomes accustomed to it. One sees other smaller falls down the mountainsides. This is a beautiful time of the year with heather and other wildflowers in bloom everywhere. My first impression was, "what a lonesome place this is going to be", but you'd be surprised how close people live in spite of the fact that you don't see their houses. We can see one of the houses of Omdal from here - the only other house in sight. People drop in every day from goodness knows where. They say they live on the other side of this or that hill. One of these days I'm going to climb these mountains and see what lies on the other side.

I've met a lot of people already. You know, people here have lots of time. When anyone goes by on the road, they always stop to chat awhile, and of course I am quite a curiosity, so they all come in to "helse paa Amerikaneren" (greet the American). *Nobody here waits for an introduction. He walks right up to you, shakes hands with you, and tells you who he is. It's quite different from what we are used to, but nice. People are very sociable.*

Last Friday, Onkel Peter killed the fatted calf in preparation for Saturday and Sunday. Saturday night, Onkel Lars and Tante Thea, Mr. and Mrs. Mauland, and their 22-year-old son (Sven) drove out from Stavanger in Mr. Mauland's car. Four young people, one being a cousin of ours, came by bus and train from Vagle. Cousin Thelma and her boyfriend came out from town, and Onkel Andreas and Tante Helene, their son Mikal and their twins (Petter and Alf Henry) *who are 11 years old, all came. It was fun meeting relatives, and everybody is just grand to me. Onkel Lars is surely lots of fun too. They all took to me just like a mother hen would to her baby chicks.*

We all sat up until 2:00 Saturday night talking, and then they insisted I translate the English news which came over the radio in the car. Sven, the boy who drove the car, speaks some English, so when I got stuck for a word, he would help me out. And I do get stuck many times. He is going to Germany to study this fall and will be there three years; he is a very bright chap and very interesting. They all stayed overnight and all-day Sunday. People slept in every room in the house, and some slept on the hay in the barn. They are not so particular.

The farmer's chief worry here is to get his hay in, which is a slow process, as their hay fields consist of small patches here and there on the hillsides. Everything is done by hand. First, they cut it with the scythe, then someone with a rake spreads it out evenly to dry. When it is dry on the top, it is turned over to dry on the other side. When it is perfectly dry, it is put in shocks and later loaded into a little two-wheeled wagon drawn by a little half-pint horse to the barn. Horses over here are much smaller than in the U.S.A. If the hay field happens to be near the barn, Onkel Petter carries it on his back. If the weather is good, the process doesn't take so long, but we've had a lot of rain the last two days. It always seems to clear up in the afternoon, however, but not long enough for the hay to dry. You should see the fancy rake Onkel Petter made for me - a beautiful red one. You should see me make the hay fly.

Thelma was here today. She is Tante Helene's daughter, and she works at the Old People's Home in town. When she

Thelma Rodvelt became a close friend of Sophie's

has her vacation next week, I'm going to spend a few days at Rodvelt. Then I think I'll go and see Ragna a while. I also found out, after I had been in Stavanger, that I have several cousins in town. Had I known it, I should have looked them up.

You can tell Mother that Tomine, the wife of Onkel Karl's oldest boy Mikal Egelandsdal, *is in a sanitarium with TB and is quite sick. They have a little girl; someone else is taking care of her. I haven't seen them yet.*

I have been expecting my trunk from Stavanger. The people who were here Sunday said they'd take care of my trunk there and send it to Egersund, which saves me a trip. I surely need my old shoes. I still think I shall get some rubber boots because when it rains here, it pours.

We eat six times a day here - only five times for me, as I'm not up for their first breakfast which they have at 6:00 a.m. The second breakfast is 9:00 a.m. - the time I get up. Dinner is at 12 or 1:00 p.m., coffee at 2 or 3:00 p.m., and again at about 5:00 p.m. The supper may be anytime from 8 to 10:00 p.m. Well, I must close. Everyone is going to bed. Everyone says I must "hilse" to you. Write soon.

Love, Sophie

P.S. Sorry to hear you have not been well. What is the trouble? Please write, and let's hear how you are getting on.

August 13, 1939 - Sunday

We went on a trip to meet cousins today including to Egelandsdal where Mother's old home is. I met three of Mother's sisters and her one brother that day. Home again late.

August 14 - 15, 1939

11:00 a.m. - Took train to Ualand. Dinner at Sigurd Østrem's. Went for a morning walk and stayed overnight. The next morning, we walked over to Anders Østrem's. Had dinner and coffee. In the afternoon, we took the train to Årrestad, met by Torger *Østrem's* wife *Malene*. Went in and visited her in the new house and had coffee again. Then we went over to Tante Semine and Onkel Ommund's at *Årrestad*. Nice place, nice visit. Coffee again. Stayed until dark. Rakel *Øgreid* and Bertha *Aarrestad* came over for a short time. Tante Semine and Bertha walked a ways home with us. Walked in the moonlight to Helleland. Lovely walk. Home by 11:00 p.m.

August 16, 1939

10:30 a.m. - Left Østrem's. Arrived at Egersund 11:00 a.m. Visited Berntine Skadberg *(Aunt Ellen Peterson's sister)* and girls. Watched the process of making fish balls and fish pudding. Shopped for yarn, etc. Took bus out to Grødem, arriving at 2:30 p.m. Went out to Omdal to work in hay the rest of the day. Worked in hay at Omdal the rest of the week.

August 19, 1939

9:30 a.m. - Alf, Tante Anne and I walked to Rodvelt. Tante Helene met us on the way - a good hour's walk.

August 19, 1939 - Saturday

Dear Parents and Siblings,

How are you at home? Everybody is good here and they are working to get the hay in because of the nice weather we have had this week. Last week it rained very hard. The rain washed out the road in several places.

I have to tell you about the trip we took last Sunday. We rented a car with a chauffeur. It was Anne, Petter, Thelma, Mikal, Sivert, and me in the car. First, we went to Andreas Østrem's at Helleland. They knew we were coming because we phoned a few days earlier. We were there for dinner. I enjoyed being there. Anna was home on vacation from Stavanger where she works at the Indre Missions Hotel. Tor and Gudrun and Alf were home, and Anders and Sigurd and their families came right after dinner. They have a large, beautiful car. Both of them live at Ualand and they are married to sisters. Anders has two children - Arnfinn and Torgunn, and Sigurd has a boy - Tønnes, two years old. It was nice to meet Tante Berthe. She looks very young. After dinner, we went over to Dybing, and the Østrem family all went to Gya. We all met at Gya later. Amanda was home when we came but had to leave for Sandnes before we left. She's working on a farm there. Tyra, the youngest girl, was home also and one of the boys. They lost a boy, Anton, in April; he died of pneumonia. I guess you have heard about it. It has been very hard for them all.

Poor Tante Teoline, she looked very tired, worn out and thin. She looks like she's the oldest of all your siblings. We had coffee and food there, and afterwards we went out and looked at the foxes and at the high hill behind the house where you see far and wide. It was very nice up there with a lot of blueberries, lingonberries and bog bilberries. We couldn't stop at Dybing for long because we were on our way to Gya. When we came to Gya, Tante Valborg and the family were gone to Egelandsdal. Anders went after them and they all came back home except for Tante Valborg. She was going to come with the car later on. I got to meet a whole flock of young people, all of them my cousins, but I can't remember their names right now.

Since Tante Valborg didn't come, we drove to Egelandsdal, and on the way there we meet Torger Østrem and his wife Malene, and Tante Valborg was with them. We stopped there on the road and Valborg wanted to go with us back to Egelandsdal so she could chat with me a little bit. Because of that, I got to meet Onkel Karl and Tante Anna and the girl, another Tyra, that is home and the youngest boy, Sigmund. Gudrun and Astrid are in Egersund where they work. Mikal has a farm a little distance out of Egersund at Svindland. I haven't met any of them yet. Mikal's wife, Tomine, has been sick at the Sanitarium for a long time with TB. She is better now and will supposedly be home this fall. They have a little girl, Tordis, that stays with Onkel Karl. I liked it very much in Egelandsdal, but we couldn't stay there very long. It was late

evening before we left. The others all went on to their homes except for me. Tante Anna asked me to stay a few days; she was going to be away on Wednesday. I didn't have any extra clothes with me, but I still stayed over.

I think we did pretty good in one day. It was just enough time to meet them. Next time I will stop longer with each of them. Tante Valborg looked really good. She had lots of pep. I got to see the large mountains at Gya and Melk Aanen (Milk River). *It was nice. They own everything on that side of the river or stream, so they are really busy, but they are all prospering well. None of them are married except Lisabeth Halvorson, now in Squamish, B.C., and Ragna. I have not seen Ragna yet. They are expecting a baby, so I was thinking it best to visit later when she has gotten it.*

On Monday, Anna and I took a train to Ualand, and we stayed with Sigurd and Anders until Tuesday. Then we took the train to Årrestad and went to visit Tante Semine and Onkel Ommund. We met Bertha and Rakel. Bertha has two children, Svein and Liv, and Rakel has three children, Anna Kjerstina, Jostein, and Sylvi. I saw there was a liveliness in Rakel. Torger has built a nice new house just before you come up to Semine's house. Both Bertha and Rakel live at Årrestad. They were all doing well.

I forgot to say that one of the Dybing boys (Martin) *is in the hospital. Two weeks ago, when we had the bad weather, he was on the road close to Gya. A stone mass came down and a large stone fell on his leg, and he fainted. Someone in a car found him lying there and took him to Egersund to the hospital. He was better Sunday, but I haven't heard anything this week.*

Today it is Saturday. This week we have been working in the hay at Omdal. I've been working two days. They finished today.

Tonight, Tante Anne and I are going to Rodvelt. I haven't been there yet. I will stay there a few days while Thelma has vacation. I was invited downtown Egersund to Berntine Skadberg's. Berntine's place is really nice. I stopped in and visited her on Wednesday when I came from Helleland. You have to tell Aunt Ellen (Berntine's sister in Bow, WA, U.S.A.) *that I was there and watched while they made fish balls. I sat there and ate as she cooked them.*

I have waited so long now for the big suitcase. I don't understand why it hasn't arrived yet.

I bought yarn and I'm going to start to make a sweater with long sleeves. I can tell I will need some clothes with long sleeves.

I am already invited to Andreas Østrem's family for Christmas.

*I have been to Rodvelt a few days now. One day Thelma and I were at the wetlands and picked red currants and then we went on a boat trip to Mong. Yesterday we went to Herman Mong's (*brother of Nels Mong in the U.S.A.) *and got mackerel. He had gotten many that day. Tonight we are going to Barstad.... to fish. We are going with Torvald Rodvelt (he has a car) and some other young people. We are bringing the coffee pot with us. I think I need to stop. Write soon and tell me everything new.*

On September 26, Tante Helene and Andreas are celebrating their Silver Wedding. Mathilde and I are going to help with baking.

How is Theodora?

Heartfelt Greetings, from Sophie

August 20, 1939

Dinner, nap, ride to Sokndal and Nesvåg. Had a picnic on the rocks on the North Sea. The sea was beautiful and calm, with a lovely sunset on the water. Met Andreas Nesvåg. Visited Tomine *Nesvåg*, sister of Sina *Nesvåg Omdal (in Bow, WA, U.S.A.),* and Gurina. Stood out and looked out to sea, a beautiful sight. Stopped in at Andreas's home. Home late - lovely day. Stayed over with Thelma.

August 21, 1939

Tante Anne went home to Grødem in the morning. Edith, a cousin of Thelma's, arrived from Stavanger. In the afternoon, we went to Myran, Omdal, to pick currants. Went for a boat ride afterwards. Sivert Mong took berries home for us on his bicycle.

August 22, 1939

Went to Mong for mackerel.

August 23, 1939

Went fishing in evening to Barstad. Not a bite. Edith, Thelma, Sivert, and I picked solbær *(black currants*) until the sun went down. Coffee and lunch on rocks, then rode home.

August 24-25, 1939

Took the bus home to Grødem in the afternoon. Stopped at Hausan where Petter, Anne, and Mathilde were working in the hay.

Had a letter from Mother. Elisabeth Omdal was at Grødem doing some baking. The next day, Elisabeth helped with making doughnuts.

August 26, 1939

5:00 p.m. - Onkel Petter, Anne, Helene, Sivert, Thelma, Sivert's father Tarald Mong, and I started out to Vagle. Arrived about 9:00 p.m. Had coffee and lunch late in the evening. We sat up late and talked.

August 27, 1939 - Sunday

Thelma, Sivert, Tarald, and I went to Høylands Church at Sandnes. Had dinner, then went back to Sandnes stadium to a football game played by teams of girls. Other interesting sports - horse racing, bicycle racing, short and long-distance running.

August 28, 1939

Onkel Lars has a vacation, so he took me over to Klepp to visit Sig Freestad's (Note: Sig changed the spelling of his name after moving to America.) folks, Ole Rasmusen and Atelia Dybing Friestad. Øystein was home. We stayed till 9:00 p.m. and were back home at 10:00 p.m. Nice walk. I am going back next week and will stay with them.

August 29, 1939

In the afternoon, Lars, Thea, and I went over to a neighbor's. We watched them cut oats with hay mower, then the girls and men tied it up in bundles by hand.

Onkel and I took a walk to the top of the mountain where we got a good view of the farms below, Sandnes to the right, Stavangerfjord and North Sea straight ahead. The view was beautiful. We ate hazelnuts and gabbed. Went back to the house and visited with Marit and her mother, Martha

Skadsem, who is Thea's sister. Went home about 6:00 p.m.

August 30, 1939

Took the train to Stavanger to visit the Maulands. Tilde Mauland met us at the train. We went down to shop first and did a few errands. Had dinner with the family at the Promenade Café. Good dinner, then went home for coffee. Grand, big home, lovely furnishings, impressed by lovely hand paintings on walls. Lovely bronze head sculpture of Tilde. After a rest period, we went for a drive in their car to - 1) Lighthouse, 2) Lista - Summer resort *two hours from Stavanger,* 3) Hummeren Hotel - Eating place, 4) Husmor School *(Housewife School)*, 5) Sola. Enjoyed lunch and music - too early in the evening for any crowds. Lovely beach, ideal swimming, white sandy beach, also tank *(pool?)*. Sven was the only one who went in. They took us home to Vagle. I met the grandparents. A lovely time and nice day.

August 31, 1939

Lars hauled in the oats. I washed a few clothes, not much of anything. Lars's son Petter started back to work at the factory.

September 3, 1939

War was declared. *(Britain and France declared war on Germany, after invasion of Poland by Hitler.)* I wrote to the American Consul.

Amanda *Gystøl*, from Dybing, came over for dinner. After dinner, I borrowed a bike and went to Sandnes to visit Martin Østrem. It was my first cycle trip in Norway. No traffic was on the highway, as people cannot buy gas. All sales on gas is government controlled.

Sven *Mauland* and Petter *Omdal* came to accompany me home. We got back to Vagle just before dark. Went to Marit Skadsem's to see all the lovely handwork done at Husmor School. Beautiful weavings.

September 4 - 7, 1939

Monday afternoon - started out for Friestad's at Klepp. Thea walked partway with me. I borrowed Henne Omdal's suitcase.

It was too wet and rainy on Tuesday and Wednesday to do anything, so I stayed indoors. On Thursday, Ole Friestad and I went to Håland *village (near Bryne)* to see Ingvald Omdal, Papa's first cousin. I visited his school the next day; we had a very nice visit there. Lovely location, near Sola Airport and the ocean. A German doctor and his son lie out there in his boat - he refuses to go back to his country.

Left Håland at noon on Friday - got back to Klepp in the afternoon.

September 4, 1939

Dear Theodora,

How's everything over there? It seems like a long time since I heard from you. Maybe I have a letter at Grødem? I haven't been there for over a week. I am here at Vagle with Onkel Lars and like it well here. I would like to stay here longer, but I am due at Sig's folks' place today. She asked me to spend a few days with them, and then Sig's sister, Randi Olfel from Anda, asked me to spend a few days there. Lars and I walked over to the Ole Friestad's last week, so it isn't so far from here - about an hour's walk, but I'm getting good at walking distances and like it fine. Onkel Petter called up from Grødem the other day, long distance, to hear if I wasn't coming home soon. No matter where I've been or how long, it is always nice to get to Grødem. We really have a good time there.

Thea Omdal, Henrik Omdal, Sophie, Målfrid Skadsem, Tilde Mauland

Onkel Lars has had his vacation the last two weeks. Lars has taken me someplace almost every day. We are not far from Stavanger, and Tante Thea's sister, Tilde, lives there.

The Maulands have a wholesale business of electrical goods. Their oldest son was to have gone to Germany to study. He had his passport and everything, but of course he can't go now on account of the war. He speaks German and English as well as Norse. He's a great help to me in my language difficulties. He's been out here on the farm much of the time. When we were in town, he and his folks took us out to dinner. Then we went back to their home for siesta and afternoon coffee which is usually served about an hour after dinner. Coffee is never served <u>*with*</u> *dinner. Then, they took us for a ride to three different summer resorts with lovely bathing beaches. We also visited a "husmor"* (housewife) *school, a school where girls may go and learn to keep house and do lovely fancy work, etc. One of the girls here in the neighborhood has just finished a course of five months there, and the lovely things she's made - it's just unbelievable. I just couldn't believe they were handmade. They weave such fine, lovely materials, and the needlework is so intricate that I don't think I would tackle it myself - it puts American needlework to shame. There is a "husflid"* (handicrafts) *school in Stavanger where they teach handwork. I would love to go myself if it were just for a month or two, but I don't want to be tied down for five months. Well, I guess I got off the track. We also visited the Sola Airport which is supposed to be the best in the land. Just two weeks ago, we saw German planes returning from an exhibition there. The Germans have some strange-looking little planes with hardly any wings they call "Chasers". They go like lightning. Now that war has broken out, they have ordered soldiers out to guard the airport, as they fear Germany may want to take it. It's a fine halfway mark between Germany and England. Well, I'm off the track again. The ride ended up at the Sola Summer Resort, a huge hotel near the airport on the North Sea. The sand is so pretty and white, and it's a very popular place. We had coffee and lunch there in the evening. They told us at the hotel that business was poor on account of war conditions, and a party from*

England had canceled their reservations. They cater especially to foreigners. Yesterday I heard they had had orders to close their doors.

We certainly feel the effects of the war already, and only yesterday was war really declared. Everything is tightening up. I had thought Norway wouldn't feel anything, but conditions here have changed much the last two or three days. People who own private cars cannot buy gasoline. Only trucks, buses, and taxis can operate. However, people can travel very conveniently, as there are trains and buses which make good connections with most all points. The Maulands (the people I mentioned) had to store their car away and come out on the train Saturday.

People cannot buy more than just so much sugar, flour, and coffee for each family. However, it's enough to get along on for daily use. But it's too bad for those who haven't put up their jams and jellies. They can't buy sugar for that now. People cannot buy coal, only wood. All Norwegian ships have been ordered into port at home here, or if out, into neutral port, to await further orders. I don't believe Norway will be drawn into war, but they are preparing themselves, and they are watching the food supply as there is bound to be a shortage. The bakery truck has quit delivering on account of the lack of gas. The milk delivery trucks in town have also quit for the same reason. I had thought I'd send this letter by airmail, so you'd hear sooner since the war broke out, but now I just heard they've called in all airplanes, mail and otherwise. So, you see, I'm right in the midst of a lot of excitement. They've been announcing over the radio the last two days that all American citizens must get in touch with the nearest American Consul. So, I immediately wrote him at Bergen. I don't know how he will advise me, but I feel it is much more dangerous to try to come home than to remain, especially since the terrible disaster this morning when the British ship sank. I don't feel I've been here half long enough, either.

I went into town Saturday, especially to see the Consul, only to find out there was none in Stavanger. We have two cousins, sisters Anna and Bergit Østrem, who work in a hotel in town, so I visited there. Anna just takes care of the telephone calls and helps serve dinner once in a while, so she had lots of time to talk. We had afternoon coffee in one of the vacant hotel rooms overlooking the open public market. All the farmers bring their fruit, vegetables, flowers etc. to the marketplace to sell them. Everything is very cheap. I bought a huge bouquet of lovely asters to take home for ten cents. You can get ½ dozen lovely hot house roses for 25 cents. It's very interesting to see how people come and bargain, and the whole market square is packed with people until 2:00 when everyone clears out at once, and the street cleaners wash the place up after them.

My trunk finally arrived Friday night, September 1. The boat was a long time on the way. It was lucky I happened to be in town the next day and just walked into Mauland's shop when they stood with my papers ready to go down and get it out of the customs. You see, they had promised to look after my trunk when it came in. I was so glad Sven went ahead with it, as he's well acquainted with the officers down there, as they get many things for their business from other countries, and it goes through the customs. I was sure mad at one of the officers. He had to see every blessed thing. We had to pile everything out and then had a time putting it back again. He was going to charge duty on those tablecloths and all those little things that were new. But Sven talked him out of it, so it ended up with my paying $1.00 duty on the face creams and powder. The rest went duty free.

Yesterday, Amanda Gystøl who does housework at Sandnes came out to Onkel Lars's, and after dinner, she and I rode bicycles into town to see Martin Østrem who is the telegraph operator. He is also a cousin of ours. They have a lovely house in town. It was a half hour's cycling, and it went swell for me, as there were no cars on the road, as they can't get gas to run them. In the evening, Sven Mauland and Petter Omdal, Lars's oldest boy, age 19, came after me on their cycles. It's lots of fun cycling. Everybody does it here.

You can pass this letter on to Mother and can say I'm staying until it's safe to travel, even if it takes two years.

Love to all, Sophie

P.S. Write soon and tell me how everything is at home. I am at Sig's folks' now and was getting ready to mail this, and Sig's mother says I must greet you all from them.

September 8 - 10, 1939

Øystein walked with me from Klepp to Anda where I met Arne and Randi Olfel and Ane Friestad. The Mission Society met at her house Friday night. On Sunday, Randi and I went to Stavanger to the China Mission autumn meeting. We heard excellent speakers. At noon, we had dinner at the hotel; Anna Østrem served us, then we went out in the country to Johan Friestad's, and met his wife too. I also met two of Tante Semine's children, Sanna and Mikael Østrem. Their father Ommund is in Rogaland Hospital. I went home on the train. Lars, Sven and Petter were there to meet me. We walked home in the rain to Vagle.

September 11, 1939

I stayed over Monday night at Vagle, then took the train to Egersund. On Tuesday at 10:00, I took the bus to Grødem. Onkel Petter met me at the highway with horse and wagon to carry my trunk. I stayed home *at* Grødem the rest of week. On Friday night, Petter and I called on Mandius Omdal Hausan and his housekeeper, Anna.

Grandpa is getting more and more feeble each week.

September 13, 1939

Dear Mother and Father and Siblings,

Thank you for the letter that I received today. It was nice to get a letter from Father also. I had a letter from Theodora today also. I'm happy to hear that everything is well at home. Father asked if I understood what he wrote. Yes, go ahead and write in Norwegian; I can understand everything. I even understood the few English sentences he wrote.

I've been gone for a couple of weeks now. I was visiting Vagle for a week and I had a lot of free time. One day Onkel Lars and I went to Ole Friestad's, and we went to Stavanger several times. Another day we went to visit the Mauland family. They left their business and took us on a car trip. Another day I visited Anna Østrem who works at Indre Missions Hotel in Stavanger. When I had been one week at Lars's, I went to Ole Friestad's and stayed there until Thursday. Atelia, Sig's mother, is pretty bad with asthma, but she is doing all the housework herself. Ane, the oldest girl, was with her sister Randi. Thursday afternoon, Ole and I went to Håland and visited Ingvald Omdal, (the brother of Lars and Jenny Omdal of Bow, WA, U.S.A). *I stayed overnight and visited the school the next day. On Friday, when I came back to Friestad's, Øystein, their youngest, followed me to Anda where Randi and Arne Olfel live. I stayed there Friday night and Saturday. Sunday there was a big gathering in Stavanger. It was a fall meeting for the China Mission, and there were a lot of people and good speakers. The speakers were two men that Randi knew from China. I didn't stay with Randi very long, so I had to promise to come back and stay several weeks later.*

Last Sunday, I met Tante Semine and Onkel Ommund Østrem's daughter, Sanna, who is in Stavanger learning to be a nurse. She said that her father was admitted to the hospital in Stavanger. He has an ulcer in the stomach, they say. And Martin Dybing of Teoline is still in the hospital in Egersund. Supposedly he gets stiff knee. That's bad.

Sunday, September 3, when visiting Lars, Amanda came bicycling before dinner. In the afternoon, we borrowed another bicycle, and we biked into Sandnes and visited Martin Østrem. It looks great at their place.

Today I had a letter from Bergit, sister of Anna Østrem, and she invited me to come there Saturday this week so that she and Olga Gya of Tante Valborg can come with me to visit Ragna at Moi. I have not been there before. Ragna just had a little baby named Arvid.

I just received the suitcase. I sent it on to Egersund, and I just got it home yesterday. So now I had better start giving out the gifts. The dress for Tante Anne fits, but I don't think Tante Helene can get into hers. It looks very small, so I'm afraid it will be for Thelma when I look at the size.

Grandfather is the same as before. There has to be someone with him at all times. He calls for Anne all day, but he doesn't want anything. He just wants to make sure she is there. Poor Tante. She has lost a lot of weight this last winter; we can see it on her clothes. Bestefar barely lets her sleep.

You asked how I was with money; I'm still doing fine. I have $300.00 left, and I don't get to use so much here at the countryside. I actually think it's quite cheap to travel here. But I hope you don't forget my life insurance policy. I think it is due very soon. Don't forget it. Please.

Do you notice differences from the war? We notice it quite a lot here. People don't get to buy gasoline for their cars. It's only buses and trucks that get to buy gas. The buses don't go as often as before. The Sokndal bus went three times a day between Egersund and Sokndal before, but now it goes only once a day because they don't have enough gas. People only get to buy one kilo (2.2 pounds) *of sugar, and one pound of coffee for each person a week. And they do not get as much white flour as they want either. They have called on soldiers to guard along the ocean and several to guard at Sola, Norway's best airport. If German or English airplanes fly over Norway, Norway can take them down, because war countries are not allowed to fly over neutral countries. It was quite hectic here a few weeks ago, but it is quieter now.*

We are going to get electricity at Grødem soon, and Petter says that the first thing he will get is a radio.

Live well and greet everyone that's asking for me. I like it here very much. And Grandfather, Anne, and Petter are greeting you all. Hello to my brothers, Carl and Melvin.

Heartfelt Greetings, Sophie.

September 16-18, 1939

9:30 a.m. - Took bus to town *(Egersund).* I got my suitcase, did a few errands, and called on Astrid Egelandsdal who works at Berntine Skadberg's, had coffee, and then took the train out to Moi. Olga and Bergit got on at Helleland. I enjoyed a very nice visit with Ragna and Karsten Moi. They have a baby boy, *Arvid*, one month old. We visited Karsten's furniture factory. On Sunday I met Thor Egeland, a cousin to my cousin at Egelandsdal. On Monday I called at their home.

September 19, 1939

Today was Petter's birthday. I got home at 2:30 p.m. It was a hot walk from the highway. We had a crab feast in the evening - twenty crabs. I gave Onkel cuff links. I had baked a birthday cake, so we had hot chocolate and cake afterwards.

September 24, 1939 - Sunday

Tollef and Serine Omdal's daughter and husband, Nils and Marta Stapnes, came over for dinner. My first Sunday at Grødem since I arrived.

September 26, 1939

Today was Tante Helene and Andreas Rodvelt's Silver Wedding Day.

September 27, 1939

Dear Theodora,

Today is such a perfectly gorgeous day; I thought I'd sit out here on the steps and write. The lake in front is so still, you can see the reflection of the mountains and trees in it. I never get tired of looking at it. This morning when I got up, I took my Kodak and climbed that steep, rocky mountain in back of the house to get a better view of the lake and ocean. Every little distance I'd stop and think to myself, "My, this would make a swell picture", but then I thought, "Well, the farther up I go the more of the ocean I can see", so I kept going, but the joke was on me. When I got almost to the top and turned around, it had clouded over just that quick, and I got caught in a shower. I snapped a picture anyway and hurried back to the house. When I got back, the shower was over. I'm going up again. I should get a lovely picture from up there. I shall send you one when I do, just to give you a better idea of what it looks like here.

Thanks so much for the pictures of David. They were all good. I show them to everybody. They surely think he's some boy. I'd like one of the others too, if you can spare them. I'll have some more snaps ready to send home next time I write.

Today, Onkel Petter and I are going fishing. Two others are going along. We have to go quite-a-ways, so I'll borrow a bicycle. We're going to fish for "berggylt". That's supposed to be a kind of fish, but I have never seen one yet. We will go to Mong and fish in the North Sea.

The fishermen around here are going to have a hard time this winter. I was talking with Sivert Mong, Thelma Rodvelt's boyfriend who fishes for a living. This time of the year, they generally fish for mackerel and sell all they get to Germany, but this year they can't market them, so there's no reason to fish. They also fish for shrimp, but this year they can't do that either, as there are mines laid out all along the coast, five hours out where they fish for shrimp. Several big boats have run on mines right along the coast here. One boat struck a mine out from Stavanger. They could see the blaze out on the sea. The Germans are patrolling the water so that English boats don't reach Norway with goods. Just yesterday, they sank a cargo of coal out from Bergen. They generally take the crew off and then sink the cargo. Two days ago, in the evening, a boatload of people from Sweden came in to Egersund. The Germans had sunk their boat, but a Norwegian boat took the passengers. No country which is in war is allowed to come into any neutral harbor. If they do, the neutral country takes them. A number of German boats have gone on the rocks purposely, close in along the coast here so they don't have to fight. They are kept prisoners here until the war is over. German planes have landed out at Sola near Stavanger and given themselves up rather than fight.

When I was over at Klepp, I went over to Håland and visited Ingvald Omdal and his school. He is Lars Herman Omdal's brother (from Bow, WA, U.S.A.) *and teaches in a two-room school. I stayed one night with them and visited the school in the forenoon. Ingvald took me out to the ocean just a little distance from the school. All along the coast, on the higher peaks, you could see soldiers on guard.*

How are conditions over there? You should have good times with prices up. I hope the U.S.A. doesn't ever take part in the war. I don't know how I'll ever get back home, but I'm not going to start worrying about that yet.

Last week, I was up at Moi where Ragna Moi lives. She's a cousin, you know. Her husband, Karsten, and his oldest brother, Emil Moi, own a furniture factory, and do they put out some lovely furniture! They're streamlined and up to date in every way. It is not a large factory, only ten men working, but they put out a lot of stuff. Moi is an interesting little town, busy with factories. There are four furniture factories, one clothes hanger factory, one clothes pin factory, and three leather goods factories where they make gloves, leather purses, and bags. Next time I go over, I'm going to get a purse and a pair of gloves. They're so much cheaper at the factory, they say. I am invited to spend the New Year's holidays there. I have already been invited out for the Christmas holidays with Onkel Andreas Østrem. But Onkel Petter says I can't go.

Onkel Petter was 40 years old last week. We had a crab

feast on his birthday. Of course, all the neighbors were in. We had twenty crabs. Later in the evening we had hot chocolate and cake.

Continued on Friday, September 29, 1939

Well, we went fishing, just three of us - Petter, Sivert, and me. We got eighteen in all. I caught four myself, but any dunce can catch a fish here; there is such an abundance. We rowed out quite a distance to some high rocks out from the main shore. It got kind of rough and beastly cold, so we didn't stay long. It was fun anyway.

I want to ask you if you'll do something for me. When you and Tora have read the McCall's magazines, will you send them to me? I saw that Arne and Randi (Friestad) *Olfel get the National Geographic magazine sent to them. His brother sends them, and they don't cost much. Wait till you get about three magazines and send them in one bundle. It surely would be nice to have something to read. I read a little Norwegian, but it would be nice to have something English. There was something else too. They like to have me bake cakes, cookies, pies, etc. here, and I don't have any recipes with me. I have just been going by guess so far. I wonder if you'd copy some good standard recipes and send them to me. I'd like that Soft as Silk recipe for white cake, also a yellow cake, a chocolate cake, a spice cake, and a fruit cake recipe (not too expensive). I would also like an overnight cookie recipe and any other good, but not too fancy, cookie recipes.*

I'm going to bake Tante Helene's and Onkel Andreas's silver wedding cake. They're having the reception on October 8. I will have to make a wild guess again. I made a big batch of spritz cookies for her yesterday.

Tomorrow, Petter and I are going to Vagle to Onkel Lars's. Tante Anne would go too, but someone has to stay with Grandpa; someone has to be with him all the time. He wants Anne beside him. He's just like a child. He's gotten feebler since I've been here.

Hope you are steadily getting better. Do you have someone with you now? It seems like there have been a lot of people sick around there this summer and quite a few deaths. I had a very interesting letter from Olga Benson the other day.

Your letter was also very newsy. Write soon again. I'm glad you didn't turn any of my letters into the newspaper as you mentioned. If you had, I don't think I'd write you again - because when I write, I like to just ramble. If it went into the paper, it would surely be picked to pieces grammatically. So please don't do anything like that. Well, write again soon - a nice long one like last time. When you copy those recipes, just stick them in between the pages of the magazines when you send them. Call Mother and tell them all hello. Hello to Christie and David. Petter and Anne both say to greet you from them.

Love, Sophie

P.S. Find out if Dad sent in my life insurance premium will you? He promised he'd look after it for me, but I'm afraid he might forget about it. Will you check up on that? I surely don't want it to lapse. Thanks.

September 30, 1939

6:00 p.m. - Took train to Vagle, accompanied by Tante Helene and Onkel Petter. Met Frøken Anna Ålvik on the train. *(Note – Anna was a schoolteacher in Mong, and she and Sophie became good friends.)* Also, we met Peder Johan Omdal's oldest son on the train. We got to Ganddal about 7:00 in the evening. Had dinner and all kinds of good things to eat.

October 1, 1939 - Sunday

Went to church and sat from 10:00 a.m. until 2:00 p.m. There were 155 confirmants. I was tired and sleepy, and for the first time since I came to Norway, hungry. I went home by bus, but the bus had trouble halfway. I rode the rest of the way on a truck; it was a cold ride. Onkel Lars carried me over the swamp, as I had on my holey shoes. The pork dinner sure tasted good. Henrik Vagle *(Thea's brother)* is so funny. We took pictures after dinner, then music and dancing until late. After they all had gone home or gone to bed, Sven, Onkel, and I sat and talked late into the wee hours.

October 2, 1939 - Monday

Onkel Petter and Tante Helene left on the 10:00 a.m. train. Later we walked over to Heien with Mathilde (*Grødem*) and visited until noon. Then Marit walked home with me and stayed for dinner. We helped Onkel Lars sort potatoes, then baked some cakes. They turned out good. I stayed over for the week.

October 4, 1939

I took the train to Stavanger. Sven Mauland met me at the train depot, and I went home with him for dinner. Tilde helped me shop for a hat. I finally found one. We had hot chocolate and sandwiches at a café. In the evening, Sven and I went out to see Peder Johan Omdal, but he was not home. We walked downtown and called on Anna Østrem. She served us refreshments and coffee, and we sat and talked until about 10:00. We did the town before going home. I stayed overnight at Maulands.

October 5, 1939

8:00 a.m. - I took the train back to Vagle. Tilde came with me. We helped Onkel Lars finish sorting potatoes. I baked another cake. Tante Thea and I went for a walk over to the old folks, *Henrik and Martine Vagle*, and then to the factory to see Onkel Lars work. Onkel walked home with us. We had coffee and lunch and went to bed.

October 6, 1939

Onkel walked to the station with me. I got to Egersund about noon and did some shopping, then went straight to Rodvelt and baked cakes for the silver wedding celebration.

October 7, 1939

Thelma, Mathilde, Hans *Rodvelt Andersen*, and Elisabeth (*Rodvelt) Rimestad* came on the noon bus. We had a big dinner in the evening with twenty guests. The tables were decorated nicely, and the dinner was very good. Everybody sat up until 4:00 in morning. Coffee and lunch and fruit was served every few hours. Frøken Ålvik and I slept together on a little divan. I don't know where the others slept, if they did.

October 8, 1939

I am very disappointed that Onkel Lars didn't come. I slept until noon and had breakfast in bed. These dinner guests came from town today: Hans Andersen (*he had moved to Cape Town, South Africa in 1902*), Kristian Rodvelt and family, and Lars Grødem. Hans (the family calls him The African), and I took a walk over to his old home. We visited with his relatives awhile. Got back in time to say "adjø" (*good-bye*) to guests from town.

Hans Rodvelt Andersen, Mathilde Grødem, Helene and Andreas Rodvelt

October 9, 1939 - Monday

I helped clean up and move furniture, then took the bus home to Grødem in the evening. Anne came to meet me.

October 11, 1939

Tante Anne and I went to Stapnes for the day. We had dinner at Johanna Lædre's. Later we went to Marta and Nils Stapnes' and had coffee. Marta went along with us to visit Aunt Ellen Peterson's brother, Lars Stapnes, and we had coffee again, then we went to Selmer Stapnes' and family *(Petter Stapnes from Bow, WA, U.S.A.'s folks and family).* We walked home in the dark; it was cold and windy. We walked at least eight miles that day.

Oh yes! Grødem got electricity last week and a fine new radio.

October 12, 1939

Helene Rodvelt and Hans came to Grødem to dinner. Anna Ålvik came later on her bicycle and stayed for the evening. We had "sjelde paa von" *(leftovers?)* for supper, and trout for dinner. Got New York on the radio.

October 14, 1939

Tante Anne and I went to town *(Egersund).* We had lunch with Mathilde. Later we visited Sille and Grandonkel Tollef *Omdal* and his twin Grandtante Elisabeth. I saw Tante Anne to the bus at 6:00 p.m. and met Mikal Egelandsdal. I went to Skadberg's store until they were ready to go home, and then stayed with Berntine until Wednesday.

October 15, 1939 - Sunday

Berntine's daughter, Anna, and I went to church. *Tønnes Friestad's daughter,* Else Marie, was baptized. Church in evening, then walked to Årrestaddal.

October 16 - 17, 1939

I had dinner with Tønnes Friestad in Egersund, then went out to Svinland to Mikal Egelandsdal's at 5:00 p.m. There was no bus on account of gas control, so I took a taxi. Tomine, his wife, just out of the sanitarium, is not too strong. Mikal has hired a girl to do work. I stayed overnight. I went back to town on the 10:00 a.m. bus and had lunch with Mathilde.

I went to a party for Thelma Rodvelt at Mrs. Knute Lædre's apartment. We laughed ourselves sick, ten girls in the party, playing games. Geography game was good. I lost the front part of a crown.

October 18, 1939 - Wednesday

Got up, had a good bath, and went to the dentist in Dybing. I got my tooth fixed for three kroner and had dinner at Berntine's. After dinner, I went to Johan Rodvelt's. I also visited the graves of Aunt Ellen (*Stapnes*) *Peterson's* mother *(Theodora Jakobsdatter Stapnes),* Elen Johnson's mother, and Sina Birkeland's mother and father *(Sofie Jacobsen Stapnes and Ludwig Omdal Stapnes.)*

I also visited my cousin Gudrun *Egelandsdal* - she has her own apartment. Her sister Astrid and I had coffee with her. They both went to the depot with me, as I was going to Årrestad to see Tante Semine.

October 19-20, 1939

There was a heavy frost. I sat by the fire Thursday and Friday and knit on a sweater but did not get it finished.

October 21, 1939 - Saturday

I took the noon train to Moi. Ole Gya and Tor came later in the evening.

October 22, 1939 - Sunday

We went to church. Baby Eyvind Arvid Moi was baptized. I was his cap-godmother. We had dinner at the Tourist Hotel in the afternoon, and then had a nice walk. There was much company in the afternoon. Little Valborg and I went to a show in the evening. We saw "Charlie McCarthy, Detective".

October 23-26, 1939

We baked cakes. On Tuesday we had a ladies' party. Ragna *Moi* decorated the cakes beautifully and served lovely sandwiches. Painters came Wednesday. Thor and Emma called in the evening. We shopped Thursday.

October 25, 1939

Dear Parents and Siblings!

It has been a long time since I've heard anything from you, but maybe I received and missed a letter now that I am at Moi. I have been thinking for a long time that I need to write, but every day passes so fast, and I have traveled a lot from place to place. This month I have traveled very much.

October 1st I was at Vagle for the confirmation of Henne, the youngest son of Lars and Thea, so I stayed there for a week, and I also took a trip into Stavanger. I stayed with the Mauland family that night. They are very nice to me. I went over to Peder Johan's one evening, but they were not

Henrik Omdal.

1. Klara Vagle Quale 2. Margrethe Kvål 3. Berthea (Thea) Omdal 4. Henny Quale 5. Henrik Vagle, Sr. 6. Martine Vagle 7. Helene Omdal 8. Marit Skadsem 9. Målfrid Skadsem 10. Johan Øvestad 11. Lars Mikal Omdal 12. Magnhild Øvestad 13.? 14. Marie Vagle 15. Jonas Vagle 16. Olga Vagle 17. Henrik Vestly 18. Andreas Mauland 19.? 20. Mathilde Mauland 21. Petter Omdal 22. Henrik Omdal 23. Martin Skadsem 24. Petter Vagle 25. Kristoffer Vestly 26. Henrik Vagle 27. Henrik Vagle, Jr. 28.? 29. Petter Theodor Omdal Grødem 30. Henrik Mauland

home, so I will have to see them the next time I'm in town. Every time I'm in Stavanger, I go to Anna Østrem's for coffee. She is so nice.

I went to Tante Helene and Onkel Andreas's Silver Wedding celebration. It lasted three days. I made and decorated a wedding cake with the bride and groom on the top and they thought it was marvelous. There were over twenty guests during Saturday evening and Sunday.

Do you remember Hans Rodvelt Andersen, brother of Theodora and old Petter Rodvelt? He has been living in Africa for thirty years and right now he is home visiting. It is a bit hard for him to speak Norwegian after so many years; he's not much better than me. But it was nice to get to speak English with him, and he knows English better than Norwegian. He has a large family in Africa and has gotten a pension from the railroad company there. He's your age. Tante Helene and he plus the teacher in Mong were visiting us at Grødem the week before last. He remembered Bestefar Per Larssen Omdal very well. I have gotten to know the teacher in Mong, and we spend a lot of time together.

You won't believe how fun it has been at Grødem now with electricity and radio. Tante Anne got an iron from the headmaster a long time ago. It is great having a radio because Grandfather loves to listen to the sermons, and when he hears a hymn, he starts singing. He is sitting up more now since they got the radio. He thinks it is not "too bad". When we got electricity and lights he said, "Yes, that is something." He is so pleased.

The weather has been so great, so we have gotten the potatoes and everything in a long time ago. It went well. Sivert Mong has helped a lot since he cannot fish anything in shallow water because of the war. The mines are laying so close to the shore, and it is dangerous to go out and fish. They can't sell any fish anyway, because they used to sell to Germany.

Tante Anne and I went to Stapnes, and we visited Johanna Lædre for dinner. She is Ella Hansen's cousin (Ella was living in Bow, WA, U.S.A). In the afternoon we visited Marta Stapnes, (sister of Karl Tollefson in Bow, WA, U.S.A.). *They have a beautiful view over the ocean from their house where they live. It was interesting to see so many large boats pass that close to land. The boats stay inside from where the mines are lying. Then we visited Lars and Ellen's brothers. All is well with them. At the end of that evening we visited Selma Stapnes at Petter Stapnes' family home. It was a lot in one day, and we walked many miles. We were not home until about 9:00.*

On Saturday before last, Tante Anne and I went to Egersund. She bought fabric for a coat. As we were in town, we visited with Mathilde and Lars Grødem, Sille and Grandonkel Tollef, and Grandtante Elisabeth. I have finished knitting a sweater with long sleeves and it is both pretty and warm. I can feel it is much colder here than at home, so I have bought woolen stockings and woolen underwear. I have never worn that heavy clothing before, but I can feel that it is necessary.

I stayed a few days in town. I stayed with Berntine Skadberg from Saturday night until Wednesday. I know the town pretty well now and know where people live. One day I went to Mrs. Tønnes Friestad's, and one day I visited Svinland where Mikal Egelandsdal lives. I met him in town for the first time, so he invited me home. His wife had just come home from the sanatarium. She's doing better, but she needs to rest a lot every day. Their little girl, Tordis, is staying at Onkel Karl's.

One day Berntine and I and Maria Mong (Lars Stapnes' wife's sister that lives in Bergen) *visited the mother and father* (Bertine Berntsdatter Mong Aase and Johan Theodor Rodvelt Aase) *of Karen Martinson, Tina Boe and Ben Johnson. It's very nice to get around and meet people. We couldn't stay long that afternoon because I had to reach the 5:00 train that evening. But I know the way now, so I will go over and visit another time.*

I'm staying here a few more days and then I will go back down to Tante Semine's. It will probably be almost Christmas before I can go back to Grødem again, because there are still so many to visit here. I haven't met all my cousins yet, but I will meet more as time passes. Astrid of Onkel Karl works at Berntine's, and Gudrun is working in the decorating department at the Fayancefabrik Pottery Factory, so we visited them in the afternoon when she was finished working.

I met Martin Dybing in town also. He was in the hospital a long time with that leg that was crushed. He can bend the knee pretty well now but walks very carefully. It is a miracle that the knee didn't get stiff. Most of the muscles were cut, so there is not a lot of strength in the leg. It was very sad. He is as charming as anyone can be. Amanda Gystøl will be home soon, and at that point I will go and stay with them for a while.

The dresses that you sent for Tante Helene and Thea didn't fit, but the one for Anne fit well. I believe they are going to alter Helene's dress for Thelma.

They are painting and wallpapering the living room and the bedrooms here. It is a new house and very nice. Karsten Moi is so busy at the Furniture Factory that he doesn't have time to do it himself. So today there are two men working. All the furniture in the house - beds, tables, overstuffed chairs, sofa, and everything else he has made himself. He is very talented.

I should have told Aunt Ellen Peterson *that I visited Berntine and that I went to Stapnes, but you have to let her know that I will try to write another letter. Berntine has a great new house; it's probably one of the nicest ones in town.*

How are you all at home? Please greet Bertha and Sina Omdal (in Bow, WA, U.S.A) *and everybody from me.*

Did you get the old Dalerne (newspaper)*? I wasn't sure if you cared for them but if you do, I can collect a few and send more over. How is Bovitz Omdal doing? Many here are asking about him.*

Ragna and Karsten are sending their greetings. She had a letter from her older sister Lisabeth in Squamish, B.C. Canada yesterday. It had been censored in England. I haven't had a letter from anyone at home since the war started, so you have to write me. It's been quite a while. How are Peter and Margie and the children? Is Martin staying up in Alaska this winter? I have not heard anything from him.

Heartfelt Greetings, Sophie

P.S. I have put on weight, so the black suit is too small. I'm afraid the rest of the clothes will be too small soon.

October 27 - 28, 1939

Visited Emma and Thor Egeland. We had the best lefse, supper, etc.

Bought some good warm house shoes and socks. Ragna went to the station with me. I took the train to Årrestad. Olav Østrem came home from Nærbø that evening. He and Mikael *Østrem* are ordered out on neutrality guard duty - Mikael to Kristiansand and Olav to Madla in Stavanger. They will be gone 45 days.

October 29, 1939

In the morning I got eight letters from home and friends - it's fun getting so much mail at once, but then it has been a month since I had mail.

In the afternoon, Bertha Aarrestad and her husband Magnus and their two children came - one boy, Svein and one girl, Liv. Also, Rakel and her husband Abraham came and their three children, a girl, Sylvi, a boy, Olav, and a baby girl, Anna Kjerstina. Anna and Bergit Østrem came over from Helleland.

October 30 - November 1, 1939

Olav Østrem and Mikael Østrem left for their respective posts of duty. I took a snap of them as they were ready to leave.

On Monday and Tuesday, I wrote letters all day to my sister Tora, Ruth Bradley, Pearl Urmey, Yvonne Halsey, Leta Schlicht, and Evelyn Oakland. On Wednesday we went to town on the 10:00 a.m. train. I bought some silk crochet thread and yarn for mittens and visited Berntine Skadberg and the sisters - Astrid and Gudrun Egelandsdal. I had coffee with Mathilde and talked with Andrew Thompson's brother, Kristian Mikkelson, and his father, Torkel Mikkelson, at his shop. Met Margrethe downtown. We took the same train home. Astrid and Gudrun came to the station with us. Met Kristine Østrem, wife of Anders, on the train and enjoyed her company all the way home.

October 30, 1939

Dear Tora, Sig, and Little One,

Was I glad to get a stack of eight letters all at once yesterday! Yours was one of them. I hadn't had a letter from home for about a month. I was beginning to think everyone had forgotten me, but I guess the mail had been held up somewhere, as I noted some or most of the letters had been five weeks or more on the way.

I am at Tante Semine's and Onkel Ommund's, a short distance out from Egersund by train. They have eight in the family. The three oldest are married but live quite near. Two boys left this morning to report on "Neutrality Guard Duty" as they call it - one to Fort Madla near Stavanger and the other to Kristiansand. They are calling all boys their age (20 - 25) *for a period of 45 days, regardless of what work they are doing. A number of schoolteachers, I hear, have been called also. When the 45 days are up, a new group goes out.*

Going back to this family - they have one girl, Sanna, in nurse's training in Stavanger and the two youngest, a boy, Trond Magne, and a girl, Margrethe, at home. Onkel Ommund has been in the hospital in Stavanger for six weeks with ulcers of the stomach. He came home last Saturday and is much better.

Last week I was at Moi with cousin Ragna. A week ago she wrote me that she was going to have the baby baptized, and she wanted me to be one of the witnesses. So, of course I went. I love it at Moi; it has such lovely scenery. I had the experience of being "Hue godmor" or "Cap-godmother". I stood alongside Ragna when she held the baby Arvid, and when the preacher was ready to baptize, I took the cap off the baby and later placed it back on. I had never seen it done that way before, but it went fine.

Ragna and Karsten have a lovely new house. He and his brother, Emil, have a furniture factory, so he had made all the furniture in the house, and it's every bit so much or more modern than over there (in the U.S.A.). *Moi is a strange little town with so many factories. The people just seem to be talented in the line of woodwork. There are also purse and glove factories. I wanted to get me some gloves, but when we got there, they had just shipped out their best styles, and I was not satisfied with what was left, so I didn't get any. It was interesting to watch the people at work. I have also worn my purse ragged by daily use, so we went to the Purse and Bag Factory. I got me a big thing. I wasn't exactly satisfied with the style, but it is a dandy big one. We watched them at work too.*

A few weeks ago (the time goes so fast, it seems like the other day), I spent four days in Egersund. I had intended to spend only Saturday and Sunday with Berntine. She has quite a thriving business - grocery and fish store. Doing very well; it has good location in the new Post Office, and they have just moved into a lovely new home - one of the nicest in town.

While I was there, I called on Tønnes Friestad one day and had dinner with them. The two oldest girls are working outside the home, so I didn't get to meet them. They have some lovely children. I am going back again and spend the weekend with them sometime. I also went out to Svinland where Mikal, the oldest son of Onkel Karl lives. Mikal is tall and very good looking. I find I have a lot of handsome cousins; it surely is fun meeting them all. It is funny how they all make you feel right at home and as if you had known them a lifetime.

Gudrun, one of Onkel Karl's daughters, is a painter in the Fayancefabrik in Egersund. She paints designs on dishes. A sister of hers, Astrid, does housework for Mrs. Skadberg where I stayed. Gudrun has an apartment, so I have a standing invitation there when I come to town.

While I was in town those days, I also visited with Mathilde, a good friend of Tante Anne. She was at Grandpa's most all summer. She is a half-sister of Gustav Grødem and Inga Vatland. I always like to go there; she is so much fun. Then I called on Karl Tollefson's father, Tollef Omdal, who is also Grandpa's brother. He's married to Bovitz Omdal's older sister Sille. I also visited a sister of Grandpa's who is also in town - Elisabeth Omdal. They all make so much fuss over one. I guess it's because they are old, and they appreciate when one calls on them.

I also visited Karen Martinson's folks. They were so glad to see someone who knew Karen, Ben Johnson, and Tina Boe (their children in Bow, WA). *Berntine* (Aase) *had tears in her eyes. Johan* (Rodvelt Aase) *just scolded me for not coming before now.*

I got to talk to Andrew Thompson's father and brother in the shoe store. Mathilde and I went in to use the telephone. Mathilde is related somehow, so she introduced me. They wanted to know about Andrew. I said I hadn't seen him for a long time, so when you write, please tell me if he has work, and how he is getting along. They say he never writes.

Tante Anne gave me goods for a new dress. It is the prettiest black wool material, just like heavy silk - very expensive too, so I'm almost afraid to let anyone sew it for me, but I should like it made for Christmas. Maybe I'll take a trip into Stavanger and have a dressmaker there sew it. Clothes here don't have quite the style and fit - that is, generally speaking. But I know a lady - Tante Thea's sister in town; she is a snappy dresser, so I'll get her to recommend a dressmaker.

It's fun to get into town once in a while after being in the country. I like to have an excuse so I can go see Onkel Lars who lives near Stavanger. When I was there last month, I said I didn't think I would get back until after Christmas, but now I'm already aching to go back for a week. We have such good times. I've gotten acquainted with so many in the neighborhood there too.

Andreas Aase, Karen (Aase) Martinson, Ben C. Aase Johnson, Berentine (Tina) Aase Boe

I didn't tell you about Tante Helene and Onkel Andreas's Silver Wedding. They feasted and celebrated for three days. Many people can't celebrate without wine, etc., but there wasn't any such there. The first night nobody went to bed before 4:00. I was one of the first to hit the hay; I was so tired. Then, everyone stayed overnight. Anna Ålvik and I slept together on one of those little narrow single beds. I had breakfast in bed the next morning. There were twenty people in the party. I baked the wedding cake and decorated it with a miniature bridal couple on top. They thought it was pretty nice.

It is beginning to get wintry and cold. There is frost every night, so I have invested in some warm woolen underwear socks. You just can't wear only silk socks here - it is too cold. I have chilblains on my toes now, and it's just because I didn't give up and wear warmer socks before. I learned my lesson. I have the warmest house shoes. You'd laugh if you saw them, but they are just the thing; I never freeze in my feet with them on. They are all of a half inch thick padded wool.

You asked something about war, etc. Yes, there are sea battles not so far out, with torpedoing and mine explosions. Now and then, passengers from torpedoed boats, or those rescued after going on a mine, are brought in. It is really terrible to think of. A couple weeks ago, a German airplane with one wing shot off by the British came inland near where Sina Nesvåg Omdal used to live. No one had been killed or injured. There are many air battles on the North Sea. It's almost everyday news, but German or British planes and ships cannot come into land here. If they do, they are immediately taken as prisoners and held until the war is over.

You asked about food rationing. The only food that is rationed is coffee, sugar, and some restrictions on certain kinds of flour. But most people buy their bread, and they can get all the bread they want. People can get along very well with the sugar they are allowed (of course there isn't enough to can with or make jam or jelly), and unless they are awfully strong coffee drinkers, they get enough of that too. We use an awfully lot at Grødem - it just barely reaches. I have a food rationing card in my name also. But I'm sure they get enough coffee, now that I'm not there.

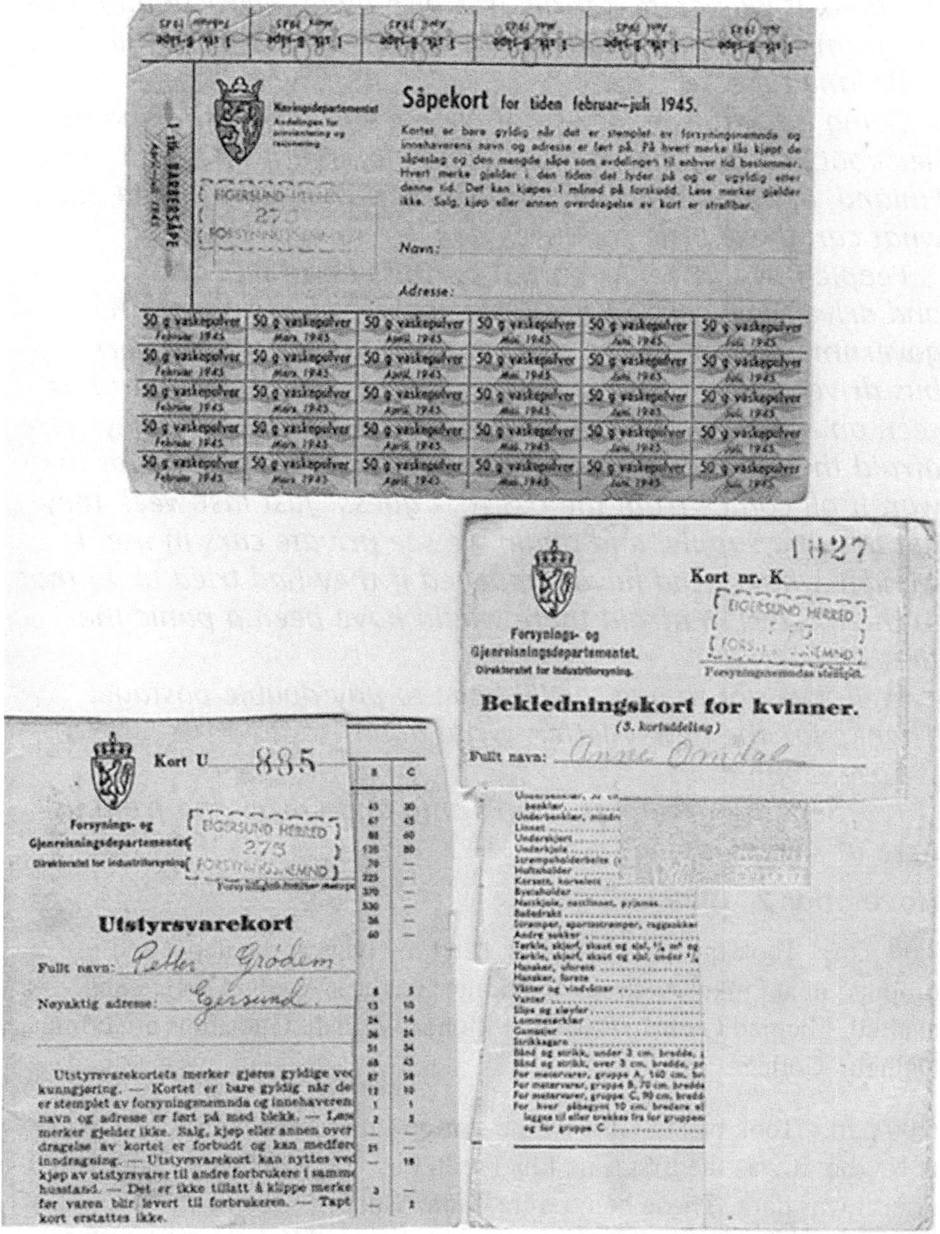

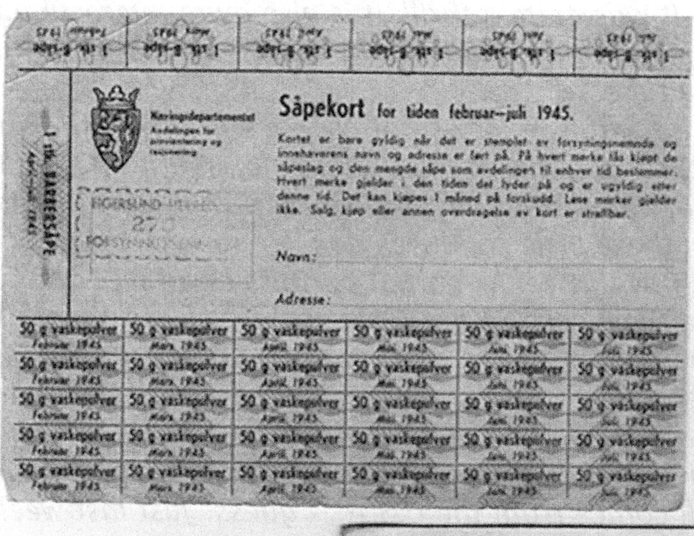

Såpekort for tiden februar–juli 1945.

Næringsdepartementet
Avdelingen for rasjonering

Kortet er bare gyldig når det er stemplet av forsyningsnemnda og innehaverens navn og adresse er ført på. På hvert merke fås kjøpt de såpeslag og den mengde såpe som avdelingen til enhver tid bestemmer. Hvert merke gjelder i den tiden det lyder på og er ugyldig etter denne tid. Det kan kjøpes 1 måned på forskudd. Løse merker gjelder ikke. Salg, kjøp eller annen overdragelse av kort er straffbar.

EIGERSUND HERRED
273
FORSYNINGSNEMND

Navn:

Adresse:

50 g vaskepulver Februar 1945	50 g vaskepulver Mars 1945	50 g vaskepulver April 1945	50 g vaskepulver Mai 1945	50 g vaskepulver Juni 1945	50 g vaskepulver Juli 1945
50 g vaskepulver Februar 1945	50 g vaskepulver Mars 1945	50 g vaskepulver April 1945	50 g vaskepulver Mai 1945	50 g vaskepulver Juni 1945	50 g vaskepulver Juli 1945
50 g vaskepulver Februar 1945	50 g vaskepulver Mars 1945	50 g vaskepulver April 1945	50 g vaskepulver Mai 1945	50 g vaskepulver Juni 1945	50 g vaskepulver Juli 1945
50 g vaskepulver Februar 1945	50 g vaskepulver Mars 1945	50 g vaskepulver April 1945	50 g vaskepulver Mai 1945	50 g vaskepulver Juni 1945	50 g vaskepulver Juli 1945
50 g vaskepulver Februar 1945	50 g vaskepulver Mars 1945	50 g vaskepulver April 1945	50 g vaskepulver Mai 1945	50 g vaskepulver Juni 1945	50 g vaskepulver Juli 1945

Kort nr. K 1027

Forsynings- og Gjenreisningsdepartementet.
Direktoratet for industriforsyning.

EIGERSUND HERRED
273
FORSYNINGSNEMND
Forsyningsnemndas stempel.

Bekledningskort for kvinner.
(5. kortutdeling)

Fullt navn: Anne Omdal

Kort U 885

Forsynings- og Gjenreisningsdepartementet
Direktoratet for industriforsyning

EIGERSUND HERRED
273
FORSYNINGSNEMND

Utstyrsvarekort

Fullt navn: Petter Grødem

Nøyaktig adresse: Egersund

Utstyrsvarekortets merker gjøres gyldige ved kunngjøring. — Kortet er bare gyldig når det er stemplet av forsyningsnemnda og innehaverens navn og adresse er ført på med blekk. — Løse merker gjelder ikke. Salg, kjøp eller annen overdragelse av kortet er forbudt og kan medføre inndragning. — Utstyrsvarekort kan nyttes ved kjøp av utstyrsvarer til andre forbrukere i samme husstand. — Det er ikke tillatt å klippe merke før varen blir levert til forbrukeren. — Tapt kort erstattes ikke.

They have a swell new radio at Grandpa's. When the electric lights came less than a month ago, Onkel Petter had to have a radio, and it surely is nice to get the current war news three times a day. Grandpa also enjoys it. I can get New York direct. One afternoon at 3:30 p.m., I tuned in and got a breakfast club program from Schenectady, New York. It was released over the N.B.C., so I imagine that you hear the same program at home. It was quite a thrill. It is also quite interesting to hear programs and music from all the European countries and hear their languages.

Going back to war news - of course Norway is shaking in her boots on account of Russia and Finland. If Russia jumps on Finland, of course Norway and Sweden will help Finland, but what can these little countries do?

People have just now gotten permission to buy gas and drive their cars again. A short time after I came, the government stopped the sale of gas to all but taxi drivers, bus drivers, and transfer trucks. Not a private car was to be seen on the road. There was a shortage of gas, and they were afraid they wouldn't be able to get enough on account of the war. It all comes from the U.S.A., I guess. Just last week they got in a big supply, and again we see private cars in use. I wonder what would have happened if they had tried to do that in the U.S.A. I'm afraid there would have been a panic the first day.

Well, I've got to quit, or I'll have to pay double postage. Thanks for the newsy letter. Write again soon.

Love, Sophie

P.S. Sending greetings from Tante and Onkel and from us here at Årrestad.

November 2, 1939

3:00 p.m. - Took train to Helleland. I left my bags at the depot and dropped in at Onkel Andreas and Tante Berthe's. We had coffee and chatted. I helped Gudrun Østrem with her English. Gudrun is attending Dalheim College.

6:00 p.m. - Took bus to Gya. At the station I met Martin Gya who works at Nærbø. It was the first time I had seen him. I got to Gya at 7:30 p.m. after it was dark. Those home were Tante Valborg, Olga, Ole, Mikael, Martin, and Tor. Little Valborg was at Anders and Kristine Østrem's.

On Friday and Saturday, the wind was so strong, most everyone stayed in the house all day. Friday was their Thanksgiving Day.

November 5, 1939 - Sunday

Martin *Gya's* girlfriend, Marie, spent Saturday night. We did nothing special. Each of the boys has his own farm to which they are doing a lot of improving. They rebuilt the house and built a new barn, but no electricity yet.

Onkel Karl Egelandsdal was over yesterday.

I stayed at Gya all week and it was rainy and stormy the whole time. Olga taught me to knit doilies, so I worked on that all week. Tante Valborg carded and spun wool most of week. The days were very dark. They see no sun until February on account of the high mountains. Olga gave me a beaded front for peasant costumes. Tante Valborg gave me homespun yarn for "Selbu" mittens. I shall knit them myself. The boys milk ten cows and have 85 sheep.

November 11, 1939

Saturday night I took the bus to Egelandsdal. Olga walked out to the bus with me. Tyra met me at Egelandsdal. It was dark and rainy when we got there.

November 12 - 18, 1939

I slept late, as usual. It snowed hard but melted soon. It's very interesting to see Mother's old home place, although the old houses are torn down and new buildings have taken their place.

Onkel Karl's family includes Tante Anna, Mikal and his daughter Tordis who is staying here, Ragna Hetland - married to Trygve from Helleland and their two children Ivar and Torbjørn, Tyra Tunheim - home ill and has her child Kirsten with her, Gudrun - a painter at Fayancefabrik, Astrid, who does housework in town and is engaged to Gjert Skadberg, Agnes Berentsen who is married and lives in Ualand, Gunnar, Karstein - age 17, and Sigmund - age 15.

I stayed a week at Onkel Karl's. Didn't do much, as the weather was bad. Finished knitting a centerpiece and crocheted a collar and a doily. On Friday I went to Aasen, and on Saturday I took the bus to Hetland.

November 12, 1939

Dear Theodora,

I received your letter of September 27 just two weeks ago but didn't answer right away, as I had just written you then. I had eight letters in one shipment. Was it nice! I hadn't had any mail for a month before. I'm sure it had been held up somewhere.

I am at Onkel Karl's now at Egelandsdal. I got here last night from Gya where I had spent a little more than a week. Gya, you know, is Lisabeth Halvorson's (in Squamish, B.C.) *hometown. Their father Tollef died when the children were small, so Tante Valborg surely had a hard time in those days. They were a family of nine children, all grown up now, and they have worked themselves up and are considered well off. The four boys work together so harmoniously - the oldest one is the boss. Now they have three farms to work. They are tearing down the old buildings on these older farms, and when they get married, they're building new houses. One of the boys is seldom home, however, as he is a carpenter and works for a contractor. He was home last week, and so I got to meet him. There are still a few cousins I haven't met yet.*

In this family are 1) Lisabeth in Squamish B.C., 2) Ragna - married to Karsten Moi, 3) Ingrid, married to Torvald Lindeland, 4) Ole, 5) Mikael, 6) Martin, 7) Tor, 8) Olga who is your age, just home and has worked in Stavanger the last six years, and 9) the youngest girl is Valborg - age 20.

Olga taught me how to knit those pretty silk centerpieces. Remember, like the one you use on your dining room table. It really isn't difficult; I have almost finished one. I have several different patterns. Tante Valborg spun wool yarn while I was there. Of course, I had to try. I don't have the knack - the yarn got either too thick or too thin. Tante Valborg gave me enough of her home-spun yarn to knit myself some mittens. They're going to be white and black with reindeer pattern. The black wool is natural from their black sheep.

So, you are going to move into town - that's swell. Can I come and live with you when I get back? I could pay you the board money instead of paying house rent elsewhere - if you have room. What are you going to do for a dining room table if you sell the set? If you can't use it, I surely hope Dad buys it from you. You'll have to build up a good fence to keep David off the highway. That's the thing that worries me. You'll have to take his picture in his new suit, so I can see him and see how he has grown since the last pictures I got.

You asked if I got you anything in the other countries. I didn't get much, as I planned to get most of the things in Norway, and I understood you to say you wanted a piece of weaving, so I've been saving your money for that, but if you wanted something else, just let me know. I can get a smaller piece of weaving and perhaps a piece of silver - how will that be? I got some crystal individual salt and pepper shakers and matching candlestick holders in Sweden for you, Tora, and myself. That's about all I have gotten besides the spoons, but I hope to get more things here.

I've seen some of the most interesting weavings. There is a school near one of our tantes at Helleland where they teach all kinds of handwork as well as college subjects. One of her girls goes there, and they said when the term is up around Eastertime, I could use their looms and they'd show me how. I'm going to bring back a piece I've made myself, and I wish you could see some of the lovely weaving. The girls at the school weave their own coat material, one of the requirements of the course.

I thought it would be easy to find pretty silver brooches, but there aren't very many really pretty ones. Pearl gave me a beauty. We both saw it at the same time, and we both wanted it. But I told her to buy it, as I'd be here in Norway and would have a long time to look around. However, she found another one she liked, so she gave me this one and I haven't seen any like it since. You, no doubt, have seen all her things by this time.

Today has been the first day of snow and it has been snowing all day. The hilltops are white.

Two days later - Tuesday

Today it is just pouring down rain. The snow didn't stay long. All the little creeks are just foaming and running over.

I finished the centerpiece yesterday and started on a collar for my blue knit, using the same light silk thread.

I haven't been in Grødem for a month now. There are so

many relatives to get around to, I figure I can make it back for the two weeks before Christmas. Then I don't know what I'm going to do about Christmas. I promised the Østrems I'd come there, but Onkel Petter says I can't go. Maybe I'll stay home at Grødem and go to the Østrems the day after. The whole week between Christmas and New Year's is Christmas here, you know.

When you get this, you will be in your new house, I suppose. I surely hope you like it. You'll have to write and tell me all about it.

I don't seem to have anything to write this time. If I don't write again soon, I want to wish you all a very Merry Christmas and also a Happy New Year. The family here sends their best regards.

Love to all, Sophie

November 14, 1939

Dear Parents and Siblings,

I guess I'll write English this time, so the kids can read it too. Not that I have anything special to write. I came up here to Egelandsdal Saturday night on the bus. It has been raining ever since, except one day it snowed, but it didn't stay on long. Today all the creeks are rumbling and tumbling down the hillsides everywhere. I guess Mother can picture how it looks when it's pouring down rain. Up until last week, we had beautiful weather with sunshine every day, but frosty. I haven't been home at Grødem for a month. Of all the places I've been, I still like Grødem best. It's nice here at Egelandsdal too, but the weather is too miserable to enjoy it.

I had an awfully good time in Gya, but it was so dark there all day with those two high mountains! It starts getting dark there at 2:30 in the afternoon.

Tante Valborg is doing fine. She had a painful arm last winter and supposedly did nothing, but she is fine now. Olga mostly cleaned and took care of the house and Tante Valborg spun yarn. Olga is the only girl that lives at home at Tante Valborg's house. Ingrid is married and has two children, Torleiv and Torbjørg, and lives at Lindeland. Little Valborg is at Sigurd Østrem's house at this time because Signy is expecting another baby. Also, Mikael and Tor, the youngest of the boys, are at home and they are all busy. Martin is a carpenter at Nærbø, but he was home Saturday and Sunday while I was there. Everybody at Gya is so nice. The boys work so well together. They have built a new livestock building and upgraded the house, so now they have very large, nice rooms. They are tearing down the houses on the new farm that the boys bought. Martin is supposedly soon getting married, and he is talking about building a house. They have 10 cows and 85 sheep.

Torvald has taken over Johan Gystøl's farm at Dybing, and they have enlarged the house, they say. I have not been there since they built, but I will go there next week. Amanda is back home now. Martin Dybing's leg is almost healed now.

I guess I forgot myself. This was supposed to be English. Here at Onkel Karl's, everyone is fine. They sure have a time with the two little girls, Tyra's daughter and Mikal's Tordis. Both are two years old. Tyra's Kirsten is the limit. She's so quick to bite and slap the other one. Neither one of them mind. Tante Anna Egelandsdal has something to holler about now.

Tyra and the three boys are the only ones of Onkel Karl's at home. Ragna is married and has a new house at Helleland. I have not met her yet. She has two children, Ivar and Torbjørn. Tomine, Mikal's wife, is not very healthy.

They have been threshing around here the last week. Onkel Karl helped thresh at Delbert in Aasen today. I'm invited over there one day this week.

I met Mama's old boyfriend Ole Bakke. He was so excited they said because he got to meet Christine's daughter. He still lives in the same place.

Onkel Ommund Aarrestad is home again and is much better; he was in the hospital six weeks. Anders Østrem's wife Kristine is in the hospital too. She has to have an operation for a tumor. Tante Semine is not very strong, although she looks well. She sits and knits and crochets almost all day. She has knit sixteen sweaters this last year and I don't know how many bedspreads.

I won't get back to Grødem before the 2nd week in December. I guess I'll have to spend Christmas day at Grødem, and then go to Andreas Østrem's the second day of Christmas.

I am sending a few snapshots you may like to see.

You, Carl and Melvin (Sophie's brothers), *might write me a note when you find time or don't have anything else to do. Tell me the latest gossip, etc. Melvin, are you still dating Wanda Loop? How does the old Ford run? You two could have a lot of fun over here with your cousins; there are so many boys just your ages. Some of them are on duty as Neutrality Guards right now. They are all some pretty nice fellows; I sure wish you could meet them. One of the boys here just bought himself an accordion, so we have lots of music, or noise, I should say, as he is just learning.*

How is my brother *Martin and his house coming along? I suppose there will be a lot of changes by the time I get home.*

Write, all of you.

Love, Sophie

P.S. Onkel Karl says "Hello" to all at home.

November 19 - 24, 1939

Helleland – Tante Berthe

On Sunday afternoon, Berthe and Andreas Østrem went to Stavanger to a funeral. Bergit and I went to the bus station with them and then to cousin Sofie Egelid's who lives near the station. They have four children - Jens, Laura, Torlaug, and Olga Alice. They lost a boy, Olav, of twelve to pneumonia three years ago, after an appendicitis operation.

I knitted two small doilies on Monday and Tuesday. On Tuesday night, Onkel Andreas and Tante Berthe came home. On Wednesday forenoon, Bergit and I took Sigurd Østrem's bus up to Skipstad where we visited Randi *Skipstad.* Her husband Joseph is an American. I got patterns for curtains. On Thursday afternoon, Ragna Egelandsdal Hetland came. Her husband, Trygve, has been in America. Bergit has been swell, taking me around to meet people.

On Friday afternoon, I moved over to Dybing. Those at home were Tante *Teoline* and Onkel *Johan Gystøl,* Torvald, Amanda, Tyra, Jon, and Martin. Gunder is on Neutrality Guard duty.

November 25 - December 1, 1939

Saturday it snowed all day. Saturday night there was moonlight and so we all went to a bazaar. It was a good long walk, and it had snowed pretty hard, so it was difficult to walk home. Got home at 2:00 a.m.

We made tallow candles one night and I learned to braid a belt. Also, I knit several doilies. I stayed a whole week *in Dybing*. Martin Dybing went to town with me. One day we went to see Knut Birkeland's home.

November 26, 1939

Dear Everybody at Home,

I am back at Dybing. It is Sunday afternoon. Everybody is resting or taking a nap after dinner, but I slept so late this morning that I cannot take a nap now. I visited with Tante Berthe for almost a week, and I came back here Friday. Andreas and Ommund and their wives went to Stavanger a few days for the funeral of the husband of one of their sisters. It has not been long ago since their oldest sister in Stavanger died. I stayed home with Bergit when Andreas and Berthe were in town. Onkel Ommund is still not good. He can't stay up for a whole day yet. They say it's probably an ulcer in the stomach, but I don't know. I'm afraid it could be cancer. It was cancer that his sister and brother's sister died of.

The week I stayed at Helleland I got to meet three more cousins that I had never seen before. One day we visited Skipstad where Tante Berthe's daughter Randi lives. She has four children now - three girls, Josephine, Bertha, Hjørdis, and one boy, Kjetil. The two oldest are in school and they are very smart. Another day we visited Ragna Egelandsdal Hetland. They have a large beautiful new house and a shop. It's all very nice. They have two boys. The eldest is Ivar, five years old, and the second, Torbjørn, is a twin and he is two years old. The other twin, Kolbjørn, died when he was seven months old. We also visited with Sofie Gystøl Egelid.

They are all very nice here at Dybing. Amanda had just arrived home from Sandnes where she has worked this summer. Tyra, the youngest one, is going to housewife school in January. Tante Teoline looks much better now than she did this summer. They tell me to greet all of you. Valborg of Aasen is also greeting you.

You won't believe how nice it is in Dybing now with the new house. Well, it is almost new, and I think that they needed it. They have four large rooms downstairs and a lot of room upstairs.

While I was at Helleland, I got the letter that Father wrote me. Also, a letter from Theodora.

You asked me what the Consul said when I checked in. He just said he needed the number on my passport and my name. That was all. I guess I can stay as long as I want to. If the ocean is still turbulent this summer, I think I'll stay a bit longer. It may be too bad if I miss school. It's been so great here. I'm so spoiled now. It's great with peace and quiet and nothing to stress over. I sleep and eat well - I think probably too well.

We hope that Norway is not going to be pulled into the war. Yesterday there were several German airplanes over Sola, the large airport in Stavanger, but they flew pretty high. But the airport is built in a way that if some other country wants to take it, they can just blow it up.

I visited Grandonkel Tollef and Grandtante Elisabeth (twins). It's been almost two months since I was last there. I visited one time later also, but Tollef and Sille were at Omdal. I will pop in the door when I'm back in town again. I'm going to Grødem at the end of this week.

I've been traveling so much lately that it feels good to be home again. It's been six weeks since I was at Grødem last. I might just stay there for Christmas since I just visited Tante Berthe.

So Bovitz Omdal (in Bow WA, U.S.A.) *has died. He went fast. How will it be with Selma and the family? I have thought of them often. And Alfred Hansen - is his wife, Mildred, still sick, or is she feeling better? How is Teddy Mae? You have to let me know how it is with Mrs.* (Valborg) *Rasmussen.*

I'm assuming that Theodora and Chris have moved into their new house. I am happy that Martin has started his.

Thank you so much for the Mt. Vernon Herald. It was probably expensive, but it was very nice to get.

Thank you so much for sending payment to New York Life Insurance. I will see if I can get the little check cashed. If not, I can sign it and I'll send it home to you. I will first try in Egersund to see if I can get it cashed there. I still have money (strange enough).

I won't send anything home for Christmas; I'd rather bring something when I return. If I do not write any other letter before Christmas, have a merry and blessed Christmas and Happy New Year.

Greetings from everyone that received a gift from you.

Heartfelt Greetings, Sophie

December 2, 1939

I went back to Grødem. On Sunday, Thelma *Rodvelt* and her brother Mikal were over for dinner. On Tuesday she came again and stayed until Friday. We made "stoppedekke" *(patchwork quilt).* Thelma sewed dresses for Tante and herself.

December 10, 1939

Onkel Lars and family and Sven Mauland came over for the weekend.

December 17, 1939 - Sunday

Tante Helene and Frøken Ålvik came for dinner. Tante Anne and I walked home with them in the moonlight.

December 17, 1939

Dear Theodora,

Thanks a million for the letter, magazines, cookbook, and all. Mail surely takes forever to arrive.

Three days later - I started this when everyone was taking a nap Sunday afternoon, but they didn't nap long enough. Tante Helene and the teacher from Mong came Sunday for dinner and stayed all day. I enjoy Miss Ålvik very much; she is very interesting.

I had a letter from Mother yesterday saying Martin is married to Margaret. I suppose they'll soon be moving into their new home. How is it coming along? How is your house coming? You'll have to write a detailed description of it. Mother also said you were not feeling too well again. Why don't you let everything slide to give yourself a good rest? We're right in the midst of Christmas cleaning and baking. I did all the baking - three kinds of cookies, doughnuts, fattigmans bakkels, a fruit cake, and a kringle. Of course, Tante Anne made lefse.

There's more work with Grandpa than a child. Of course,

he's too weak to go anyplace. He can barely walk across the floor by himself.

I had a bunch of letters and Christmas cards today too - seven of them, and two lovely hankies - one from Leta in Montana and one from Ruth Bradley. I got a Christmas card signed by nineteen L.D.R. (Lutheran Daughters of the Reformation) *girls. I have had several letters from Agnes Benson. She types them and does a swell job of it.*

I didn't send a single Christmas present. I thought the same as you; I'll bring some little things home with me instead. I have knitted some lovely centerpieces I'm giving to Tante Helene, Tante Anne, and Tante Thea. I am bringing some of them home too.

Onkel Lars and family were here a week ago Saturday and Sunday. I am going over to spend a couple weeks with them again the latter part of January. They're so blame swell and grand to me. I thoroughly enjoy myself over there. Onkel Lars can't see why I can't settle down and stay in Norway. Tante Thea and I are going to spend a week in Stavanger with her sister.

I enjoyed my six weeks visit with Mother's side of the family. Now there are only four cousins I haven't met - that is, besides the family of one of Mother's sisters whom I'll not get to visit until spring.

I am going to town tomorrow morning and coming home at noon by bus. Thelma Rodvelt just called up and said she was going too. She's getting married sometime while I'm here and asked me to be a bridesmaid; that means a new dress. I haven't had my black one made yet.

Onkel Petter is trying to make some wooden shoes. People wear them around on the farm, but he's just messing the house up with shavings for us to clean up. The men folks burn me up. The women do the housework, milk the cows, and take care of the horses, cows, and chickens, feeding them and watering them. You see, all animals stay in the barn all day - all winter long. The men go hunting and fool around. Sometimes they chop wood and sometimes not. The woman on the farm is a slave, in my opinion. I have a hard time keeping my mouth shut sometimes. There are a few places where the men milk the cows, but not generally speaking.

Skiing isn't in swing yet. We've had a very mild winter so far. However, the little kids started skiing a long time ago when I was up in Egelandsdal. I am buying ski pants and the rest of an outfit. I may bring a pair of skis home with me. My money is holding out swell. It's surprising how little it takes when one is out in the country.

You'll have to call Mother and say "hello" to everyone at home. I am afraid I shan't get a letter written home until after Christmas.

Best greetings to Christie and David.

Love, Sophie

P.S. Sure was glad to get the recipes and magazines, and it's swell getting the Mt. Vernon Herald.

December 23, 1939

Decorated the Christmas tree today. Mathilde and Lars Grødem came.

December 25, 1939

Christmas Day - went to church in Egersund. Oanes preached.

We had dinner at home. Grandtante Sille and Grandonkel Tollef, their daughter - Gjertine Omdal, Thelma *Rodvelt,* and Sivert *Mong* came in the afternoon. Thelma and Sivert stayed overnight.

December 26, 1939

Christmas Fest at Stapnes. Walked there in an hour. Very nice Fest.

December 28, 1939

Walked to Rodvelt with Anne and Mathilde and had dinner. The decorations were festive. We left the party at 11:00 p.m. and got home at midnight.

December 29, 1939 - Friday

I spent the afternoon at Pintlo *(name of farm in Omdal that had belonged to Grandonkel Tollef)* with Martine and Elisabet *Omdal,* then I attended an evening party at Hausan *(another farm at Omdal that had belonged to Grandonkel Jonas and Grandtante Engel)* with Mandius and Anna (*his housekeeper*). We were served supper and fruit and nuts.

December 30, 1939 - Saturday

Got up at 7:00 a.m. and had a bath. Took the bus into Egersund and the train to Moi. In the evening, Torvald Lindeland, Olga and Valborg Gya came.

December 31, 1939 - Sunday

Today was the last day in the old year of 1939. It is interesting to see old and young alike on skis. Went to the New Year's Eve party which included music and a three-act play. Lunch was served at tables, and we were all given paper caps. I met some interesting males. The singer took me home. Dancing started at 12:00 a.m. with Olga and Valborg.

1940

Snow Skiing with Cousins
Signs of Impending War, Altmark
Sophie Feels Safer in Norway than Traveling via Ocean to America
Sophie is Eyewitness to German Invasion by Air
Egersund Controlled by German Forces
Challenges with Grandpa, His Death & Funeral
Spending Time with Family & Friends
More War Stories

January 1, 1940 - Monday

I slept until about 2:00 p.m. and had breakfast in bed and a late dinner.

Olga and Valborg were here at Moi for the weekend and went home Tuesday on the 4:00 train. I saw them off. I bought skis Tuesday night. Karsten went over and helped me pick them out. I paid 33 kroner plus 3 kroner for stocks *(poles).*

Lots of good clean sports here for children. Children as young as five years old seen skiing. Skating is a very popular sport also, and tobogganing. There has been snow since Christmas.

I knit myself ski mittens, socks and a cap for my ski outfit. The yarn used was spun by Tante Valborg.

I spent one afternoon with Ragna at Karsten's sister's.

January 2 - 11, 1940

Dina *Moi* served a lovely lunch. One day, Emma Egeland and Marie came over for the afternoon. In the evening, their husbands (*Tor and Martin*) came over for supper.

On the Sunday after New Year's, we went to the Christmas Fest given by the Scouts - a Finland benefit. Everybody went around the tree and sang. The main program consisted of a talk by a Scout leader. There were a number of short skits and plays. The orchestra played several times.

I practiced on skis several times, but the snow is not very good.

January 7, 1940 – Moi

Dear Parents and Everybody at Home,

It seems like it has been a long time since I've written to you. However, I did get your letter in good time before Christmas. It is so funny - some letters take just a short time to come here, and others take much, much longer. The letter that Tora wrote November 9th, I received just a couple days before Christmas. I am sure I still have Christmas mail that is on the way. At the Post Office in Egersund, they are telling me that there will be nothing else from America until the boat is back on January 17th.

I spent Christmas at Grødem. I really felt that I had to be there (wanted to be there), *and we had a very nice Christmas together. We got snow Christmas Eve, and even more during the Christmas week. On Christmas morning, Tante Anne and I went to church in Egersund; we got a lift from someone from Mong that had a bus. All in all, we were thirty people from Mong, Rodvelt, Grødem, Stapnes, etc. The whole family of Helene and Andreas were also in church. Mathilde made dinner when we were in church. She and her father, Lars Grødem, were with us the week of Christmas. The 2nd day of Christmas we went to a Christmas festivity in Stapnes. It was a really nice Christmas party, and there were a lot of people. The 3rd day of Christmas they brought hay from Omdal. On Thursday, Mathilde, Tante Anne, and I went to Rodvelt for dinner. We walked in the snow. I am so happy that I brought the high boots, and I have used them a lot now in the snow. In the evening, we walked back home from Rodvelt in full moonlight and weren't home until midnight. Grandpa was still up and waiting. He never wants to go to bed before Anne comes home. He's been pretty calm lately, so Anne has been able to get out more.*

On Friday, we went to Pintlo in the afternoon and spent the evening with Mandius Hausan.

We had a very nice Christmas tree at Grødem. Petter found a tree, and I got the decorations and decorated it. Thelma and Sivert were also together with us during a couple of the Christmas days. So, it was a lot of fun with Mathilde, Petter, and Thelma. Sivert is a bit quieter. Thelma is not at all quiet. I like her; she is kind.

For Christmas, I got silver candle holders from Tante Anne and Tante Helene. I didn't expect anything, because earlier I had gotten that beautiful dress fabric. Thelma and Sivert bought me a beautiful silver spoon. I had knitted some pretty silk centerpieces like the ones you got from Amanda another year. I gave one to Helene, one to Anne, and one to Thelma. I gave Grandfather some really nice house shoes/ slippers. He is so proud of them that he doesn't want to take them off when he goes to bed. He says they are so good and warm. For all of your siblings, Mother, I sent each of them a large box of chocolates. That has to be enough. I sent Tante Martha (Eiesland) *a large tablecloth together with a letter for*

Christmas. I told her that I will come and see them this spring. It's impossible to get to Haugesund until then. Selmer Stapnes wrote to them and told them not to wait for me until then.

Paul Rodvelt (Ben, Karen, and Tina's first cousin) *has come home. I saw him at the Christmas tree party in Stapnes, but I didn't talk to him.*

At the time being, I have been at Moi visiting Ragna and Karsten for a whole week. I came up here for the New Year's Eve party that he (Karsten) *was part of. He plays in a brass band, and he was also acting in a play. Olga and Little Valborg Gya were here for a few days.*

Well, I bought myself some skis. I have only been out skiing a few days. I'm not very good yet, but it will be fun when I master it better. I got the best kind of skis with bindings and poles for only $9.00. A man here at Moi made them for me. I have knitted some Selbu mittens (traditional Norwegian mitten pattern) *using the nice yarn that I got from Tante Valborg, and the socks are almost finished. I am also going to knit a Norwegian hat, with the same pattern as the mittens.*

It is so pretty here at Moi. All the hills are white and covered with snow. I've never seen children have so much fun as they have here. Children not more than five years old are skiing. Here there is also ice, so when they are tired of skiing, they are ice skating. Almost all grownups and larger kids have some kind of a sled, with long runners and a seat in front which they scoot like a scooter (kick sled) *and go lickety-split*

down the streets.

It is fun to see them go whipping by. There are some swell hills. In some places they get a good start and go a half mile. Kids are all dressed warmly in ski pants, sweaters, and ski shoes - boys and girls alike. I just wish the kids over there (in the U.S.A.) *could see the fun they have here. It's amazing to see how well those little kids handle skis. They do not need poles. They just go sliding along, jumping corners, etc.*

Ragna wants me to stay here awhile and practice on my skis, as there is a little more snow up here. Then I promised Rakel (a daughter of Tante Semine) *that I'd spend a week with her before going back to Grødem. Onkel Lars was home two weeks before Christmas, and I'm going over to them the last part of this month and spend a couple weeks. I will spend some time in Stavanger with Anna Østrem and Tante Thea. I am also going to spend a week with Andreas and Tilde Mauland, so I'm still going strong. It sure is a great life.*

Ragna just now showed me an old blanket that she had gotten from Grandmother (Rakel Serina Salvesdtr Eikelandsdal). *I'm supposed to ask you if you can remember it. It is red and blue, and all the colors are woven into it. She says that you were carried in it at your* (Christine Egelandsdal's) *Christening. She really appreciates it. It's pretty, and the colors are just as fresh and clear as it used to be. She tells me to greet you all. How is Theodora? Please greet Martin and Margaret. I will write to them soon.*

They are still doing Christmas tree parties here. There was a party at Omdal New Year's Day and a party at Nils Omdal's at "Der Oppe" (name of the farm - it means Up There) *at Omdal the Saturday night before New Year's but at that time I had left.*

Right now, we are about to put the little one in a baby sheepskin bunting bag and go for a stroll. This afternoon we are visiting Thor and Emma Egeland.

Live well, all of you, and greet everyone around you. I will write Aunt Ellen (Peterson) *soon. Thelma and Sivert got engaged at Christmas.*

Heartfelt Greetings,
Sophie

January 12, 1940 - Friday

I took the train to Årrestad after spending two enjoyable weeks with Ragna and Karsten. I got to Årrestad about 5:30, then went to Malene and Torger's and chatted awhile. He showed me his prize silver fox fur. It is surely a beauty. His Tante bought it for 70 kroner.

Malene walked over to the folks' place with me. Onkel Ommund was just coming home from work. Mikael was home from training at Kristiansand. Margrethe and Trond Magne were the only others home. Did nothing special in the evening. Torger came over and chatted.

Tante Semine had had a bad spell just before Christmas but is much better again.

January 13, 1940 - Saturday

Årrestad – Slept late as usual. Did some crocheting for Tante on a bedspread.

January 14, 1940 - Sunday

Torger was over with his skis before I was through eating. Got my skis on and Trond Magne and we spent a couple hours skiing. I got some good coaching.

In the afternoon, Tanta and I went to Øgreid. Mikael (*Østrem*) took us on the sleigh. I took my suitcase along to spend a week there. Rakel and Abraham have three children.

January 15, 1940 - Monday

A storm came up, and it turned very cold, colder than they could remember. Elsa, their *hired* girl, fractured her ankle on the way home from choir practice that night and had to stay at Onkel Ommund's overnight.

January 16, 1940 - Tuesday

I got up and helped Rakel with the kids and to hang up the clothes that Elsa had washed the day before. Mikael brought Elsa back in the afternoon. She could only do such work as could be done sitting down.

I had a fire in the bedroom heater, so I was cozy and warm.

Made waffles.

January 17, 1940 - Wednesday

Abraham and his dad went to a funeral of a teacher who died of pneumonia - a cousin of theirs.

We all had coffee with Grandmother *Jørgen* Øgreid. What a job to get the kids to bed. It was always 10:00 before they were all in bed. Impression – spoiled kids!

January 18, 1940 - Thursday

I helped Rakel with work and darned socks. Margrethe came over in the afternoon, so I decided to go home with her instead of waiting until tomorrow. I gave Anna Kjerstina the cap I had knitted, and she was thrilled to pieces.

It took us a half hour to walk back; it's quite difficult walking in snow.

January 19, 1940 - Friday

Got up at 9:00. It had snowed about 16 inches, so I surely was glad I came home yesterday. I would have been snowed in up at Øgreid.

Strangest weather phenomena. It turned dark at 9:30 until after 10:30, but it was only a thunderstorm coming up. After thunder and lightning, snow fell heavily. It gradually grew light.

In the afternoon, Trond Magne and I took skis to Bertha Aarrestad's. The skis were so slippery on account of greasing them, that I simply could not stand up on them. I finally decided to carry them.

We had coffee and a cozy time chatting all afternoon. Bertha showed me her paintings, which were excellent. Carried skis home.

January 20, 1940 - Saturday

Onkel Ommund took me to the Orrestad Station.

Got to town before 11:00. Stopped to chat with Berntine and Anna in Egersund. Berntine always stuffs a couple bars of candy in my purse.

Met Lars Grødem and Grandonkel Tollef downtown.

January 21, 1940 - Sunday

I have a cold, so I'm not practicing on skis, but Onkel Petter uses them every day.

Wrote letter home. Neighbors came over for the afternoon.

January 21, 1940 - Grødem, Egersund

Dear Folks and All,

It hasn't been very long since I last wrote, but I thought I'd scribble a few lines before I write some other letters. When I got back yesterday, I surely had a good big stack of letters and Christmas cards. I had been gone three weeks. I had eighteen letters and cards, so I sat all afternoon reading my mail. Then I had a whole stack of Mount Vernon Heralds and Burlington Journals. It surely was nice to have so much mail at once, but I hadn't gotten any since a day or so before Christmas. Strange enough though, I got Mother's letter before Christmas, but Dad's letter which was sent November 25th didn't get here until the other day.

I had a nice visit at Moi; I stayed two weeks. Then I came down to Tante Semine's and stayed from Friday until Sunday. There was snow, so Mikael, one of the boys, took Tante and me to Øgreid in a sleigh to visit Rakel who is married to Abraham, son of Jørgen. Rakel has three children; the oldest is three years, the next one is three months older than David Lawrence (Hansen), *and the youngest is seven months old, so maybe you don't think she has her hands full. She has a steady girl* (hired help), *and then her husband is awfully good to help around the house. I stayed with them until Thursday. Thursday night it snowed all night, and it would have been almost impossible to get through the next morning, so I was glad I got back to Østrem's before the snow came. There was at least a foot and a half of snow up there, but we have about a foot here. They say it is unusual to have so much snow in this part of the country.*

Tante Semine had a spell just before Christmas when she had to be in bed awhile. It is her heart. She has high blood pressure, you know. I guess she had worked too hard. She seems to be OK now, but she doesn't do much work. She crochets and knits most of the time.

There was so much snow, that Onkel Ommund took me to the station at Orrestad on his little "dresin" (railway hand car)

Onkel Ommund at Orrestad train stop

that he rides up and down the tracks on. He seems to be much better but is still on a diet.

I guess I told you about getting skis. I have been having lots of fun trying to learn, but I caught a cold the other day, so I haven't been out on them for a couple of days. Onkel Petter tried them this morning, but he went out behind the barn to a run so I couldn't see if he took any spills or not.

Well, I got to town before noon and met Lars Grødem downtown, so I just had to go up to Mathilde's and have a cup of coffee. I was lucky to get a ride home after I got off the bus. Erling Omdal was out at the highway with horse and sleigh. So, I traveled by "dresin", train, bus, and sleigh to get home. I sure am glad I have my high-top leather boots; they are just the thing to wear in the snow.

Grandpa thought I had stayed away an awfully long time. He was sure I was dead since I didn't come home sooner. You know, he's quite childish sometimes. He had said to Petter to look in the newspaper and see if my name was listed among the dead. Really, he was serious! He was so glad when I came home "at du kom atte levanda" ("that you came back alive").

I've been laughing all day about something. I just have to tell you about it. Tante Anne had wrapped a hot brick in paper and put it in Grandpa's bed to keep him warm one cold night.

After everybody had gone to bed, he let out a terrible cry for help. He wanted to know what that was in his bed. "Der er ell I bagen min!" ("My butt is on fire!"), *he exclaimed. When Tante Anne looked, it had partly burned through the paper, so I guess it was hot as fire alright. Sometimes he says the funniest things. He's really been awfully good since before Christmas; he sits up most all day. For a while every night he'd want to go to Omdal. He wanted to go home and go to bed. Then he was pretty good for some time, but tonight he started again, but we told him there was too much snow, so he's quieted down again. One night when he was fussing and telling us to get ready to go home to Omdal with him, I said, "You are at home; this is home. Look at the pictures on the wall and see if this isn't home". He looked around and laughed and said "Ja, du er god, men du kan aldrig imbella meg dette er heima."* ("You are good, but you can never convince me that this is my home.") *It is just something that seems to come on at night when it's time to go to bed.*

When the radio is too loud, Grandpa says, "Ikke la masjinen blasa sa hart" ("Don't let the machine blow so hard.")

Well, I should greet you so much from Tante Semine, Onkel Ommund, Rakel, and Bertha. I was over to Bertha's Friday. I went over on my skis.

I asked Bestefar (Grandfather) *if I should "helse" to Tollag and he said "Ja" right away and then he said, "Ka slags helsing ska det va?"* ("What kind of greeting should it be?") *So, he isn't very clear at night, but he'll be OK in the morning (I mean... better). I've gotten so used to seeing him like this, that I think he isn't so bad. He is a lot better than he was in November and part of December.*

Well, I must quit if I'm going to get any other letters written tonight. Greetings to the newlyweds. I am actually going to write them one of these days. Grandpa just asked me if Tollag still has that watch he gave him. I told him you had it, and he seemed quite satisfied. Anne and Petter send their "helsen" (greetings).

Love, Sophie

January 22, 1940 - Monday

Doctored a cold. Went to Ladies Aid.

Younger Women of Ladies' Aid; Anne Marie Omdal – middle of back row

Older Women of Ladies' Aid; Ingeborg Omdal – left front row; Taline (Mong) Omdal – left back row

January 23, 1940 - Tuesday

Today was my birthday. Anne wanted to invite company over for the evening, so I baked a cake and cookies. In the afternoon, Thelma Rodvelt came to spend a few days.

In the evening, Anna and Mandius, Maria and Johan, Thelma and Sivert,

Mikal and I had a party. We stayed up late after the rest had gone. Sivert, Mikal, and Thelma stayed. We had lunch again after 12:00 and "sprit" *(alcohol)* for our colds.

January 24, 1940 - Wednesday

Stayed in bed all day with a cold and headache.

Thelma sewed and mended for Tante Anne.

January 25, 1940 - Thursday

I helped Thelma get started on a silk centerpiece.

I worked on my cap. Grandpa is worse again. He is not clear much of the time, and he needs lots of care. Poor Tante Anne is quite all-in as she does not get any sleep at night with caring for Grandpa.

January 27, 1940 - Saturday

Maria *Lædre's* sister came to Grødem to stay with her while her husband is out fishing.

January 29, 1940 - Monday

Went to Ladies Aid at Pintlo. Maria Lædre and I went. Anna was there. It was pretty difficult walking in snow. Anna and I decided to go to Stavanger soon.

January 30, 1940 - Tuesday

Spent Tuesday evening at Maria's for coffee and knitting.

January 31, 1940 - Wednesday

Went over to Hausan to see Anna. I decided not to go to Stavanger, as I would rather Tante Anne go somewhere for a much-needed rest, as she has not been sleeping lately. Some nights she's up with Grandpa every hour. I told Anna I wouldn't be going to Stavanger until after fishing.

February 1, 1940 - Thursday

Onkel bought himself some skis.

February 2, 1940 - Friday

I got up early and cleaned house. At 8:30, Mandius and Anna stopped in on their way to meet the first bus to town.

Erling Omdal also went out with the sleigh.

February 3, 1940 - Saturday

I got up early again. Nothing special but Saturday work.

February 4, 1940 - Sunday

Late dinner, then a nap. Started to write letters but got none written. Johan and Maria Lædre came over.

Later in the evening Elisabet and Martine *(daughters of Elias Omdal)* came over from Pintlo.

February 5, 1940 - Monday

Tante Anne tried to get away to Rodvelt, but it was late in the day before she got ready, so she decided to wait until tomorrow. Ladies' Aid at Nils Omdal's in the evening. Esther came home from the hospital today.

February 6, 1940 - Tuesday

Tante Anne finally got ready and went over to Rodvelt's to have a few days' vacation and rest. She left about 5:00 in the afternoon. Of course, Grandpa didn't want her to go and fussed a lot. He is so helpless now that he can do nothing for himself. He is so clear out of his head.

I slept down on the divan so that I could hear Grandpa at night. I put a big chunk in the heater, so I had a fire all night. Got to bed at 1:30. Got up a couple times during the night to see about Grandpa.

February 7, 1940 - Wednesday

Mathilde Grødem had her appendix out today. Doing nicely.

Got into the swing of housekeeping, looking after Grandpa. and feeding the calf and chickens. Onkel Petter took care of the other animals; milked, etc. Thelma came in the afternoon. We got supplies from town. Four sleighs went out to the highway to meet the truck.

Grandpa slept swell all night until 6:00 in the morning. I stoked the fire.

Got up and swung coffee pot at 7:30.

Coffee again at 11:30. Sivert came to see Thelma and stayed until 1:00.

February 8, 1940 - Thursday

My sister Theodora's birthday. Grandpa was awfully fussy in the forenoon but OK in the afternoon. Thelma's boyfriend came again so I got no letters written tonight either.

Hot chocolate at midnight. Got up only three times for Grandpa. Kept fire going all night. Washed clothes.

February 9-10, 1940 - Friday

Grandpa was fussy again all day. Nothing to do but ring Anne and ask her to come home. She came home about 9:30.

At 10:00 on Friday, I went over to Maria's for coffee. Elisabeth and all the Omdal ladies were there. Heading home at 12:00, as I stepped out of Maria's house, I slipped on the ice and fell backwards - hitting my head on the porch. I was sure I had fractured my skull. I felt so sleepy and weak for an hour after. I surely felt rotten. I have a nice big bump on the back of my head and a blue bruise on my elbow. I felt rotten all day on Saturday, and my back is bothering me again.

February 18, 1940 – Grødem, Egersund

Dear Olga,

Thanks so much for your nice long letter and Christmas card and the lovely hankie. I got half of my Christmas mail in the middle of January, and it is still coming. I got two Christmas cards last week, so you see how fast mail travels these days. You'll perhaps get this this spring or early summer.

I am still enjoying myself as much as ever. It has been pretty quiet since the middle of January. I haven't gone anywhere hardly, as it has been so beastly cold. I was just glad to have a warm, cozy place to stay. Everything is frozen up. There is a chain of lakes from Grødem out to the ocean, and they are all frozen over, so they ride with horses and sleighs. It would be grand skating, only there is too much snow on it.

All the schools are closed, as they couldn't heat the buildings with the amount of fuel allowed. They've had to ration coal again as there is a shortage due to the fact that few coal shipments get here. Most of them are sunk before they reach Norway. I am surely glad we are out in the country and have plenty of wood to burn. It has turned milder just the last two days, and it is a relief. I haven't been out on my skis as much as I would like, either, on account of the cold. But I had a swell run this morning. You can't imagine how much fun it is. Onkel Petter and Onkel Lars's two boys from near Stavanger and another cousin and I were out today. I surely wish I could take the hills the way they do. They say skiing is good until after Easter as a rule, so I still have lots of time to practice.

I was to a silver wedding last night for Nils Omdal and his wife – he is Lars Omdal's brother. We had a lovely dinner, then coffee, lefse and cakes later in the evening, and still later a fruit course. At 3:00 in the morning she wanted to cook hot chocolate, but we decided (some of us) we'd better call it a day and go home.

This morning they got a fresh batch of guests for dinner. More guests were invited for this afternoon, and tonight they're winding up with a party for all the kids, so it isn't done in one evening as at home. I believe the reason for it is that houses are not large enough to accommodate a large number of guests at a time.

We had some excitement this noon here. We heard the hum of airplane motors and when we looked out, there were three planes coming toward land. First thing we knew, another large plane came from the opposite direction and the three turned and fled. Soon there were several chasing these three out of sight. We heard the hum of motors a long time. We heard no shots, however, so we presume it was just Norwegian coast guard planes preventing either German or English fliers from flying over Norse territory. It has happened (previously) *that we've heard shots and then heard about air battles taking place along the coast hereabouts.*

By this time, you will have heard of that German boat, the Altmark, with the English prisoners which England took the other day. It isn't far from Sokndal. Thelma Rodvelt, a cousin, and I are planning to take the bus out and see what's left. There was excitement here when that happened. I talked with a lady who saw the whole thing. I wish we were a little closer to the ocean so we could see everything.

Uncle Petter and the boys left this noon on a ski trip up in the hills. They wanted me to go along. It's dark now and they're not back yet, so I'm sure glad I didn't go along. I bet they won't be so frisky when they get back as when they left. Uncle Lars's boys are staying a couple weeks and I'm going back with them when they leave. I have an awfully good time over there.

Well, Olga, how have you been? Are you getting a good rest? I surely wish you could have been here too. All fall I slept until 9:00 every morning. This winter I've been getting up at 8:00 to help Tante, as she has so much work to do with the cattle and all. You see, all the animals have to stay in the barn all winter, so there is much work feeding, watering (warm water), and cleaning to do.

I am sorry you didn't get to San José as you planned. Do you plan to go later? Do you have any plans for next year? I doubt very much that I'll be back this year. I would like to spend another year, but I do hate to give up my job.

You said something about me being in the danger zone. Not at all. I'm as safe here as at home, but I don't know how safe it would be crossing the Atlantic. People are traveling all the time, so I guess it's safe too, but I would just as soon not take a chance. What do you think? There are a lot of places I want to see yet, and I have an aunt in Flekkefjord whom I haven't seen yet. Everybody is so perfectly grand to me, and I don't think I've worn out my welcome yet.

Where are your relatives, Olga? I may have seen some for all I know. What are their names and addresses? I may have an opportunity to call on them if I happen to be in the vicinity. I was in Sokndal once, but only on a through trip.

This is the season for herring fishing, but there is little fish. They believe the extreme cold has had something to do with it. There are 350 fishing boats which go out from Egersund every morning and come in in the evening with their catch. I have been wanting to get into town and see everything, but have been having one cold after another, but I am going tomorrow, nevertheless. Aunt Ellen's sister called and asked me to come in and stay a few days with them and they'll show me around. There is a factory where herring oil is made, purified, etc. Berntine surely is grand. She lost her husband when the three girls were little, so she's had a hard struggle of it, but is surely doing fine. She has a "fish ball" business and grocery store. She has three clerks besides herself and they are awfully busy. They just moved into a new house this fall, very modern and American-like.

There surely was a lot of traffic out to Sokndal today. They had funeral services for the seven Germans from the Altmark.

People here are furious to think that they got this far without Norway preventing them.

Well, write when you can. I hope this finds you and your mother (Clara Boe) *and all in the best of health. Greet your mother and family.*

Love, Sophie

February 20, 1940 - Tuesday

Thelma and I went to town to see sild *(herring)* fishing. Not much doing. Shopped a little. Saw a show with Kristian, Thelma, and Sivert. Went for a walk first. Also met Paul Rodvelt for the first time. Stayed with Berntine that night. Snowed eighteen inches during the night.

February 21, 1940 - Wednesday

Went home with Thelma and stayed a whole week. Helped her sew and knit a few things for her trousseau. On Saturday, we took the bus out to Sokndal and Jøssingfjord, a very picturesque fjord. The road winds down the steep mountainside overlooking the fjord to the town below, which is an iron mining and smelter industry town. The fjord is very narrow. The "Altmark" *(ship)* was still grounded, its back stuck up on ice. Germans on deck; some down below working to get her off. Got a number of snapshots.

(Note – The Altmark was a German ship carrying 299 British POW's through Norwegian waters. The POW's were survivors after naval battles between German and English vessels. British destroyers pursued the Altmark and forced it to seek refuge in the Jossingfjord in southwest Norway where it was run aground on February 17 and boarded by the British. Hand-to-hand combat ensued and seven Germans were killed. The POW's were rescued. Hitler and the Wehrmacht had been planning to occupy Norway because they questioned the continuation of Norway's neutrality in the war. Due to the Altmark incident and Norway's cooperation with the British, albeit reluctant and limited, the Germans quickened their plans and occupied Norway on April 9, 1940.)

February 24, 1940 - Saturday

Thelma and I went for a walk to Mong. We visited Anna Ålvik and enjoyed fruit and nuts while she got ready to go with us. Enjoyed a lovely view over the ocean. Took some snaps. On the way home, we stopped at the schoolhouse and enjoyed tea, chocolate and lunch. We talked until a late hour and then walked home.

February 25, 1940 - Rodvelt, Egersund

Dear Theodora,

I received your letter the other day that was written just after Christmas. It was nice to hear how you all spent Christmas.

It seems like I just wrote to you - maybe I'm writing too often. Every time I get in the mood to write letters, I always begin by writing to someone at home first. I wrote Melvin and Carl yesterday and sent a little knitted doily to Pearl for her birthday. It won't get there for her birthday, however, as I sent it so late. I found out I could send it in a large envelope, same as a letter. So, I shall send you, Tora, and the sisters-in-law each one as soon as I get them made.

I hope Mother is much better after her asthma spell. I told the boys (Sophie's brothers) *to help her as much as they could. Do they do a lot of chasing around? Does Melvin still go with the same girl? How about Carl? Is he going to finish the course he started in airplane building?*

Yesterday, Thelma Rodvelt and I took the bus out to Jøssingfjord and saw the "Altmark".

There probably wasn't so much "to do" about it over there, but it was quite an excitement here. We talked to an old lady, Anna Larsen, who lives there. I guess the people were nearly frightened out of their wits when they heard the shooting. Some ran out and buried themselves out of sight in snow drifts. Many took their children and ran to the hills for life. This lady showed us where they found a wounded German lying outside their front gate. The ship is still there, and the crew is still on the boat. They were working to get the boat off the ground. I don't know what their plans are. The Norwegian Marines are on guard in the fjord, while more ships are standing guard at the mouth of the fjord. I took six pictures. I will send you one if they turn out good, and they should.

Today it is beautiful out. The boys have been out skiing and jumping, but I don't have my skis along with me here. The snow is pretty hard and slippery, as it has rained the last few days, and last night it froze again. If we get some fresh snow again now, it will be swell.

I went to see the men fishing for herring, but they are not having much luck yet, as it has been too cold. A lot of floating ice is coming down from the north which is detrimental to fishing. Oh yes, we saw a torpedo chaser yesterday. It is a funny looking boat built for speed. The sailors posed for us with coffee cups in their hands.

Today - as I started to say back there - we are going for a walk out to the seacoast. I want to see if I can get some scenery pictures.

When I wrote to the boys, I said Grandpa was worse, but he has turned much better again the last few days, Tante Anne says. I have been here about a week now. When Petter and

Sophie Peterson in Norse War Zone; Recent Letter Tells of 'Safe Feeling'

A Burlington grade school teacher visiting in Norway, who wrote friends here a few weeks ago that she felt "perfectly safe" in Norway and had decided to extend her stay for another year, perhaps had changed her mind with this week's rapid-fire events in Europe's war.

Sophie Peterson, who was granted a year's leave of absence so she could visit relatives in Norway, was located at Egersund, on the tip of Norway closest to the British Isles, when she wrote Arthur H. Towne Feb. 26. Egersund is midway between Bergen and Oslo on the coast where the heaviest fighting has been reported.

While Miss Peterson's letter advised her superintendent that she was giving up her position for an extended visit in Norway, Towne indicated this week that the school board would hold her position open pending word in the near future that Miss Petersn could and would return to America before fall.

Grave concern for the safety of thousands of Americans stranded in the Scandinavian countries was felt this week, and Miss Peterson evidently is in one of the "hot spots."

Supt. Towne granted permission for publication of the letter, with its numerous interesting comments, as follows:

"Grodem, Egersund
Feb. 26, 1940

"Dear Mr. Towne:

"After much consideration I have decided to extend my visit in Norway another year. However I do regret giving up my position but hope you receive this in ample time to secure another primary teacher.

"The months have certainly passed quickly and I know I shall not be ready to come home this summer. My relatives have certainly made my stay here interesting and enjoyable. As I don't expect to make the trip again I've decided to make the most of it while I am here.

"At first I found the language a little difficult but am getting along very nicely now. I often meet people who speak English however.

"Many people have written and asked if it weren't risky to stay in Norway. I don't think so. I feel perfectly safe.

A few staple foods such as sugar, flour and coffee are rationed but that was done to control prices and prevent people from stocking up. Everyone has all they need and more. Coal is also rationed due to a shortage since so much is sunk by the Germans. Prices on all goods have gone up considerably.

"We are quite near the coast and I often have the opportunity to go out and watch the many boats from all over the world pass by daily. They go near enough land to be identified. People who live right on the coastline sometimes witness sea battles. We can hear the shots from home. I think that's close enough.

"Sunday we witnessed three planes attempting to fly over Norwegian territory. The coast guard plane started after them and the three planes, presumably British or German turned and fled out to sea.

"The 'Altmark' affair has caused a lot of excitement here. The Jossingfjord is not very far from here. We went out and saw the 'Altmark' the other day. It was still grounded but they are gradually getting it back out in the water. The crew is still on the boat. I took a few pictures of it.

"We talked to an old lady who lives there and she said everyone was frightened when they heard the shooting. Some ran out and buried themselves in snow drifts, others ran to the hills. This lady found a wounded German lying outside her front gate.

"Everyone is wondering what will happen next. We saw the graves of the seven Germans who were killed on the Altmark and the floral wreaths which Hitler sent.

"We have had a very severe winter. I have enjoyed the snow and skiing. I just wish the children over there could see the good times these Norwegian children have skiing, skating and tobogganing. It is common to see little five year olds out on skis. They surely do have fun.

"My best wishes to Mrs. Towne and David. Greet the faculty.

Sincerely,
Sophie Peterson."

Henrik Omdal go back to Vagle, I shall go along and spend a few weeks there. They surely have been having fun skiing. You'll have to go home and see the picture I sent of Onkel Petter and three of our cousins on skis. I haven't had my picture taken on skis yet. Maybe I shall sometime, so you can see my ski outfit. I like my ski pants. They are of gabardine, nicely made.

Thelma is busy sewing and embroidering for the coming wedding which I expect will take place in May at Grødem. I have been helping her with some sewing this week. She is a kick; I wish you could meet her. She'd get along well in the U.S.A. with her wit and humor. She picks up all kinds of English phrases and songs and springs them on me.

Well, we're ready for the hike now. I will finish this when I get back.

Continued Monday evening:

It was too late when we got back to write. The Mong schoolteacher and Thelma's beau went along, and then on the way back Miss Ålvik asked us in for tea, and so the evening went too. I got some boat pictures again.

Today we've been to Ladies' Aid. It's not a very big society - only six there - just the ladies in the Rodveltgard. Tomorrow, Thelma, another girl, and I are taking a walk to a place called Birkeland, also out by the ocean.

You know, I spoke of the silver fox. Well, the one Mikael picked out for me I didn't like. I thought it was too large, so I'm sending it back, and I may not get one after all. Well, nothing to write.

All my love to Chris, David, and you,

Love, Sophie

March 10, 1940 - Sunday, Grødem

Dear Mother, Dad and All,

I received your letter of January 18 last week. I should continue my practice of writing Norwegian, but I think I'd better write the language everyone can read.

Tante Helene and the twins (Petter and Alf Henry Rodvelt) *came over yesterday afternoon and stayed until this evening. They just went home. We're having snow showers today, however, it melts as soon as it comes down. We finally got mild weather. Most of the old snow has melted - just the biggest snow drifts are left.*

There is a "Minde (Remembrance) *Fest" today in Stapnes in memory of Emisar Gustav Svånes who died a couple weeks ago. I heard him speak at the Jule Fest in Stapnes during Christmas. It was his son who conducted funeral services for the Germans who were killed on the Altmark. Of course, there was a German preacher there too. We saw him on the bus one day. I am glad I got to see the Altmark before it left. It left on Wednesday and nobody tried to stop it. I am sending a couple pictures I took out there. I told Theodora I'd send them to her, but since I happened to write home first, I'll send them in this letter.*

I spent over a week at Rodvelt and helped Thelma sew. I guess the wedding will be here at Grødem in May.

Petter and Henrik Omdal were here over two weeks. Onkel Lars telephoned several times for them to come home, or they would still be here. I had planned to go home with them, but there's so much to do here, that I thought I'd help with the house cleaning and Paaske (Easter) *baking before I go. We cleaned and scrubbed in the living room. It was a big job to clean the ceiling. These funny heaters surely do dirty up the place and make a lot of work. We've had to carry all the water all winter. Housework here in Norway is inconvenient and heavy. I will appreciate the conveniences in American housekeeping when I get home.*

I guess I'll stay another year. After seeing people taking life easy and as it comes, I've caught the same attitude and can't be hurried.

You can tell Sigurd Stakkestad that I plan to go to Haugesund either the latter part of May or early June. Then I have yet to go to Fjotland, and I want to see Flekkefjord and Kristiansand too. As long as everything and everybody at home are OK, I might as well be here. If only this war would stop.

I am glad to hear that Martin and Margaret have a nice house.

Grandpa is about the same. He looks well and is heavy and strong except for his head. If only he weren't out of his head so much. He imagines all kinds of things, and his mouth keeps going all the time when he isn't asleep, so it's pretty tiresome. I asked him if I should greet Tollag from him and he said "yes". That was all he said.

The fishermen are still out trying their luck at herring fishing but they are not having very much luck. Last week, some boats went up to Haugesund and caught a little. This weekend, Herman Mong, Sivert Mong, and others went to Ålesund.

A lot of farmers are running short of hay, as they hadn't expected such a long hard winter. Some are selling some of their cattle, as they don't have enough hay, and it is awfully high-priced right now. Onkel Petter took a trip to Lista last week and was gone three days - to buy hay. They have to pay nine cents a kilo (two pounds) there at Lista, but it is sixteen cents a kilo here. Many are shaving the bark off of young trees and feeding it to the cattle to save on hay. Sivert Mong is taking his fishing boat to Lista to get some hay when the fishing season is over.

Is Carl still home? Is he going on with the airplane course he started? Thanks, Carl, for the little note you sent on that card. You can write again – a little more. I'll have to quit this scribbling and write some other letters while it's quiet. Grandpa's gone to sleep, and Tante Anne is taking a nap too. I have a pile of 28 letters to answer. It surely is nice to get them, but I just can't keep up answering them.

Greet Bertha, Sina, Martin and Margaret, Theodora, Eileen, and any others you see.

Love, Sophie

P.S. Tante Helene and Andreas said to "hilse" when I write. Anne and Petter also say "hello".

March 13, 1940 - Wednesday

Laying down of arms between Finland and USSR.

March 15, 1940 - Friday

Spent a couple weeks at Grødem helping with housecleaning. Scrubbed everything high and low and did a lot of baking before I went to Ganddal.

March 16, 1940 - Saturday

Took the bus into town. Walked in deep snow out to the bus. Took 11:00 train to Ganddalen. Petter *(Lars and Thea's son)* was there to meet me, and he carried my baggage.

In the evening, Marit, Kristoffer, and Marie *(cousins of Petter and Henne)* were over.

March 19, 1940 - Tuesday

Tante Thea baked bread and worked to get the boys off to Sauda on Påske Tur *(Easter Tour).*

March 20, 1940 - Wednesday

In the morning at 9:30 we got a taxi to drive us to Stavanger where we took the boat "Sand" to Sauda. Left Stavanger at 12:00 noon and got to Sauda at 5:00. It was a lovely trip. Sven was at the dock to meet us. Lots of snow. Took us almost two hours to walk to Svandal where we were to stay with Maulands. First thing, after we got there, we had dinner which surely tasted good after the climb. The boys came up on skis, but I walked. We had four rooms at our disposal. Tilde and I shared one of them.

March 21, 1940 - Thursday

Slept until 8:00. Breakfast. Fixed lunch for boys to take on ski trip. Started up to Djuvsbotnen *(cross-country ski area)* at 9:30 after the boys had greased and gotten our skis ready. It was a lovely, sunshiny day.

Tilde and I went only halfway and came back and fixed dinner. Tilde went down to the boat to meet Mr. Mauland, Kristoffer, Olga and Jonas *(Vagle).* Everyone brought lots of eats. There was a lovely moon out, so a few of us went skiing again in the evening.

March 22, 1940 - Friday

Everybody got ready for a full day. We fixed loads of sandwiches which each packed in little belt sacks. We went clear to the top of the mountain - a three-hour climb on skis.

At 12:00 we heard Easter services out in the open, after which we spent some time running those swell, long, sloping hills. It took two hours to go down. It was a strenuous day. I wrenched both knees and fell on a rock. I went to bed tired that night and sore all over. I was not able to go out the next day. Perfect weather - we all got lovely tans.

March 23, 1940 - Saturday

I stayed inside today, but I tried skiing in the evening a little. My knees still gave in. I wrote several letters. It was a cloudy day.

March 24, 1940 - Sunday

Today was Easter Sunday. After breakfast, we fixed lunch and started out for the top of the mountain for a slalom run.

There were four races today - three boys' classes and one for girls. Henne Omdal came in third place in the boys' group.

Had dinner at about 3:00.

The snow was perfect for skiing. I took out alone again. I got so that I could take the steep hills without taking spills.

Those in our gang: Mr. and Mrs. Mauland, Sven and Henrik Mauland, Petter and Henne Omdal, Jonas and Olga Vagle, Kristoffer Vestly, and myself. Kristoffer was laid up for the rest of the day with a sprained ankle. Most everyone had bruises, banged up knees, and wrenched joints, but no bones broken.

March 25, 1940 - Monday

Got ready to leave Sauda after a five-day vacation. Olga, Tilde, and I walked. The rest skied down. Took St. Suithun boat which held at least 600. The boat was packed. Two other boats took skiers down to Stavanger. We had a cabin, and we ordered coffee and cakes. Got to Stavanger about 5:00. It was a five-hour trip. Mr. Mauland got off the boat first, ran home, got his car, came back and picked us up and took us home to Vagle. Some kids took the train. We had coffee and lunch at the old folks' *(Martine and Henrik Vagle)*. Everyone was well satisfied, and all had a beautiful coat of tan.

March 26, 1940 - Tuesday

Everyone slept late and got rested up after the vacation.

March 27, 1940 - Wednesday

Stayed at Onkel Lars's until April 13. I did most of the housework and helped with cooking while Tante Thea worked outside. It was fat days for the boys. Thea got up, milked and did all the work outside; took care of pigs and chickens. Boys got up about 9:00 - then didn't do much. Petter spent some time on his correspondence course. Some days he worked in the woods and hauled out fertilizer.

Sophie

One day I baked cream horns and cinnamon rolls which turned out swell.

Tante Thea and I went to Sandnes one day to buy yarn for a dress. I bought yarn and knit a Peer Gynt sweater. I knit it in a week. I did not get it embroidered, as war came on, and I didn't get to town to have it stamped.

March 23, 1940 - Sauda Mountains

Dear Theodora,

I guess it is your turn to write, but I'm not particular. I wish you could see where I am now! I'm up in the Sauda Mountains on a ski trip. Onkel Lars called up to Grødem and asked if I didn't want to go along on a skiing party, and of course I was thrilled at the chance. Onkel's two boys and another family rented a cottage up here. Other friends have joined too, so now we are ten in all. We have four rooms and do our own cooking. We came up on a boat Wednesday; it took 5.5 hours, and we are staying five days. It seems to be the custom for everyone to head out on skiing trips over the Easter vacation. There are scads of people up here. Hotels and cabins are all filled up. Nearly all private families have taken in guests. This is a small industrial town. There is an American-owned smelter here which employs quite a number of men. It surely is a beautiful place with these big snow-covered mountains surrounding the valley we're in.

Good Friday, yesterday, we climbed to the top of the mountain where we listened to Easter services. It took us slower ones two hours to get to the top and two hours to get down. I can't take those steep hills on a run like the kids do. "Henne", as we call Henrik, tears down in fifteen minutes. There surely are a lot of what I'd call experts up here - I just stand and marvel at the way they do it. There are hills after hills, one slope after another, so the good ones go just miles in a straight run.

I wrenched my knee yesterday, so I have been laid up today, but just couldn't keep from going out a little for a few runs in the moonlight. I didn't stay out long, as I want to try and make it to the top again tomorrow, as they are having a big meet with prizes for the best ski runners and jumpers. A couple of the boys in our gang are going to try their luck.

They've been babying and greasing up their skis tonight, so they'll be in good shape tomorrow. Henne and his cousin from town are the two reckless ones. They're going to enter the jumping contests. Everyone is getting a beautiful coat of tan.

A week later – Sunday, March 31, 1940

Everybody got back home Monday night after Easter with no bones broken but a lot of sore limbs. It surely was a swell trip. I have been here at Onkel Lars's since. I started on another sweater jacket. It's called a Peer Gynt Jacket with embroidery on each of the front pieces. They are all the go here. I have only worked on it one day and got one of the front pieces done, so I don't think it will take long. Then I was in town with Tante Thea yesterday and I saw some lovely yarn I just couldn't resist buying. You know, I had planned to knit me a black dress. Well, since I dyed my pink one black, I'm going to make this a light dress. Here's a sample of the yarn. The whole dress comes to $3.50, and it's the very best yarn. Onkel Lars teases me; he says when I get it finished, he guesses I'll dye it black too. Have you been doing any knitting? What's everybody been doing all winter? I suppose you are kept occupied with David.

Thanks for the magazines - they came yesterday. I also got a stack of newspapers, so I have been reading all day today. Surely is nice to have the McCall's to turn to for a story now and then.

I forgot to tell you our cousin Henrik (Henne) took third prize in the boys' class in the ski run downhill, and that the two first ones were natives of Sauda, born on skis, and who have taken many prizes before. They knew the hill, while it was the first time Henne had entered, so we thought he did very well. I took a snap of him as he came down the hill but haven't had them developed yet. I am sending a snap Onkel Petter took of me at Grødem in the last snow. The snow is practically all gone now.

What do the folks think of me staying on another year? I don't know how long ago I wrote home - I can't keep track of the letters I write, so if I don't get a letter off to them tonight, you'll have to give them my best regards. Is Carl still home? Maybe I've asked before, but I am wondering if he is going on with the course he started.

Petter, Onkel Lars's oldest boy, is taking a correspondence course preparatory to entering a military school. He applied last fall, but was not accepted, so he's trying again. People here cannot just decide to go to a school. They take an entrance exam; if they don't pass the requirements, they study and try again. Schools don't take just anyone, only those with best standing. Schools are smaller, and when they are filled, they turn the rest away, keeping only those with highest credentials.

How is Mrs. Carl Hansen (Sofie, mother of Chris Hansen)*? How do you like living in town? Guess I won't get my job back, now that I'm staying away longer, so I probably won't get to live with you after all.*

Well then, tell the folks hello. Greet the Hansens, also Ruby and Einar Knutzen, and of course, Chris and David.

Love, Sophie

April 7, 1940 - Sunday

Grandma Martine Vagle's Birthday - 72 years old. Went over for the evening. Maulands were there.

April 8, 1940 - Monday

I went to Stavanger by train at 2:30. Stayed with Anna Østrem at Indre Missions Hotel. A friend of hers and I went to see News on film. I had dinner with Anna; we sat and talked, and I started several letters which were not finished as it is impossible for mail to get through now. Made plans for tomorrow as Anna was to be free. We were worried about the critical situation of Norway. England had just laid out mines in Norwegian territorial waters, and we had just read that a fleet of fifty German ships were on their way to Norway.

April 28, 1940 - Tuesday

On April 9, we woke up at 7:30 to the sound of low-flying airplanes and terrible shooting and bombing. As we rushed from one window to another, we saw a number of German planes flying low over town, so low we felt the vibrations inside the building. As Anna and I stood and watched one plane, it dropped eight or nine bombs - huge things which landed in the street; a few buildings were slightly damaged, although the bombs did not explode. It was explained later that they were only to frighten people. At this time, there was continued bombing and shooting in the harbor nearby, which resulted in the Norwegians sinking a German commercial transport ship loaded with coal on the top deck. Underneath the deck, these ships had soldiers, all kinds of ammunition, cannons, horses, everything needed to carry on war.

Of course, we were all quite upset at this. We listened in on Oslo *(on the radio).* The Germans had come in there. The radio was controlled by Germans. The Germans explained to people that they had taken Norway under their protection only while the war lasted which "sounded" very nice. I decided to get out of town as quickly as possible. One of the men at the hotel had been down to the depot. It was controlled by the Germans. People were hurrying out of town as quickly as they could pack a few things with them. He reported that only citizens of Norway and Germany were allowed to travel by train. Consequently, that left me out. What was I to do? I remembered that the Maulands might be moving out to Vagle, so I called there. Sure; I could drive out with them. If I hadn't caught that ride, I'd have had to walk, which would have taken two or three hours. Then I couldn't have taken my suitcase with me, so I was more than grateful for that ride. The Maulands were taking silver and other valuable household goods out to her folks'. Sven stayed in town to help the Red Cross, and now he can't get out of town, as the Germans refuse to let any men from age 18-45 leave town. I surely hope he will be safe. They have a bomb-proof cellar or room. This same day, a German boat had come into Egersund, flying the Norwegian flag at 4:00 or 5:00 in the morning. They arrested all Norwegian sailors or soldiers in uniform, took over banks, the post office, the telegraph, the railroad depot, and made themselves at home in houses where owners were not at home. They set up headquarters at one of the churches. The Marshal ordered the police force to take off their uniforms and forced them to go under their command.

The Germans knew where everything in town was that they needed, as spies had furnished all that information. It was soon learned that some trusted citizens in town had turned out to be spies - proven by their disappearance the day the Germans came to town. The Germans went to the courthouse and got a list of all those who owned cars and trucks so that when they wanted a car or truck, they just took it... or else. They took bicycles from children as well as grownups. At first, they forced owners to drive the cars, but after a chauffeur near Oslo drove over a bank killing himself and twenty Germans, they decided to do the driving themselves.

Going *(remembering)* back to Stavanger, Germans filled the streets at about 11:00, one hour after I had left. One fellow Onkel Lars knew was shot on the spot when he refused the Germans his car. They walked into stores and took cigarettes, chocolate, etc. without paying. Those who did pay did so with German money which was not worth anything. They started to raid the food supplies from storehouses which they sent by air back to Germany. In the meantime, Norwegians were driving and hauling out flour and food as fast as they could, storing them way out in the country. They kept hauling out until the supply was exhausted. The Germans grabbed all the butter and canned stuff to send back to Germany.

There is great activity in the air every day. One day, forty planes within a few minutes passed over our house at Vagle, transporting troops, then taking back food *(to Germany)*.

Refugees from Sandnes arrived out in the country on Saturday. Larsine *(Omdal)* Sirevåg, her son, mother-in-law, brother-in-law, and his wife came out to stay at Onkel Lars's. Many had left homes and slept in schoolhouses on the floor. Many slept out in the open. When Germans came to the Sandnes depot, they were seen taking out a map from their pockets, looking at it a few minutes, then going downtown to the place without asking any directions. They took over banks, post offices, RR *(Railroad)*, everything.

We saw the English bombard Sola, the airport near Stavanger. Not a great deal of damage was done however, as the Germans used the airport the next day by dropping men by parachutes. Onkel's place is close enough, so we saw the fireworks and heard the bombing. An English plane was shot down and fell on a school building in town, setting fire and burning almost a whole block of houses. So many wild rumors were heard that people were frightened out of their wits. Everyone in the vicinity would have left farms, were it not for cattle. The farmers living nearest the airport left cattle and all. The Germans milked the cows and took care of them. To this date, April 28, Sola has been bombed fifteen times. The hotel was demolished by an English battleship two miles out to sea.

I left Onkel Lars's April 13th by train and got to Egersund at noon. Germans were on guard at the depot, on street corners, at the post office and telegraph office - everywhere. Traveling from Egersund, the bus was loaded, so I did not get a seat, but I was lucky to get a ride with Martin

Stapnes with his horse and buggy. He insisted I go on home with him, so I had dinner with them. I met Marta Stapnes who was ready to leave for Omdal. I called Onkel Petter to come and meet us. Marta was actually getting a little anxious after her scare. Six Germans were on guard, walking about her house with guns, machine guns, etc., and low flying German planes were in the sky.

May 2, 1940 - Thursday

Today is Thursday, May 2, but a holiday because it is Christ's Ascension Day. Yesterday, May 1, was also a holiday for some - Labor Day.

There was a meeting in the schoolhouse. Refugees are living in empty schoolhouses.

These are very exciting days, as intense fighting is going on at Daniba and Rørôs and Central Norway in Gudbrandsdalen. If Germany can make connections from Oslo to Trondheim by rail, they will send more reinforcements, but the Norwegians and English and French are holding them back. New troops, reinforcements, and heavy artillery has reached Norway, so we are hoping they will hurry up and make connections with troops on land and drive the Germans out.

Last Friday, about 1,000 Germans left their posts here in the south *(Egersund)* to go to Stavanger. Three boatloads of them were being sent to Bergen but were sunk on the way up.

Many of these poor Germans don't like war any more than we do but are forced out. Many did not know where they were when they got off their boat. They had no idea they were in Norway. They said they had been herded onto the boat without any idea of where they were being taken.

It's surprising how well fed, handsome, brown, and polite these Germans are. It's plain to see that Germany has given their soldiers the best they had in food, while the rest have suffered. However, their food rations here are not so hot. One sees them with a loaf of hard bread under their arms, which they cut from and eat where they are. They do love chocolate bars. They seem to have plenty of German money - paper bills, worthless, not even good in Germany, but people in town are forced to take them or nothing. This can't go on long. Most of Egersund and Stavanger are still evacuated. Sola has been bombed for the 16th time, but the Germans are using LPTA Penitentiary for their new flying place, as Sola is completely demolished - Turisthotell as well.

It was on April 8th that the Germans came up the coast of Norway, flying French and Norwegian flags, piloted by Norwegian pilots. On Tuesday morning, April 9th, they had entered Oslo, Kristiansand, Egersund, Stavanger, Bergen, Trondheim, and Narvik.

In Oslofjord, the Norwegian Battleship "Olaf Tryggvason" sank one German battleship and several troop transport ships before they were given orders by Quisling, a traitor, to stop firing. Thinking it was orders from the King, they stopped. The Germans took possession of it, but it had been put out of commission to prevent Germany from making use of it. The Germans bombed the Norwegian fort in Oslofjord continually, but they were unable to make a dent. Had it not been for all the Nazis and traitors in the country, Germany could not have made the grip it did. Traitors had furnished Germany with all the information needed to get Norway under its control after careful study and laying out of plans. The King and family was to have been murdered by one appointed by Hitler himself. This failed. Quisling was appointed, by Hitler himself, to become leader of the country. Quisling has now disappeared as have other Nazis and traitors.

Here in Egersund, the forces were not given a chance to mobilize as the town is completely controlled by German forces.

Fighting has become gruesome in Bjerkreim where Germans were shot down like flies as they stepped off buses to get in line.

In Sviland, Germans used a cheap trick. When Germans saw they were losing, they hoisted the white flag – the sign of giving up. When the Norwegians stopped firing, the Germans started firing again, killing 25 Norwegian boys.

Another cheap trick was used in Northern Norway near Trondheim. The Germans sent a telephone message to Norwegian troops controlling the Railroad saying a train with Germans was coming through. Thinking the message had come from a Norwegian source, Norwegians fired on the last two cars killing several passengers – refugees!!! Not a German on the train. They use these methods and many others like them also. Entering harbors with Norwegian and French flags shows their low-down means of warfare. Wrong cannot win in the end.

Food has been rationed more strictly. We have to have a card for sugar, coffee, flour, even bread. We get only half the coffee we used to, and half the sugar. We are allowed only 2 ½ loaves of bread per person per week. Of course, there is not a car on the roads unless controlled by Germans. Buses still run, however.

May 5, 1940 - Sunday

Thelma, Sivert, Petter, Alf Henry, and their cousin Else came over for the afternoon.

May 6, 1940 - Monday

People are still evacuated from town after a whole month. One family which has been living next door moved back to town.

May 7, 1940 - Friday

I went to town today. The bus was late on account of a German caravan which held up all traffic. I waited first at the highway, then walked onto the Lædre bridge where I waited a long time. Still no bus! Finally, a long caravan of German Petrol trucks came along and, in the rear, transport troops. The bridge was too narrow for the biggest trucks, so traffic was held up there for about two hours. I talked to German officers. After watching them at work and trying to get over for some time, I started to walk to town as I wanted to get into the bank before noon. I got clear to Lygre before the bus came. By that time, I was almost to town, having walked at least six miles. I did not get passage on the bus to home, so I had to walk back. I had company with Elisabet O., Bergliot O., and Ingeborg G. I had blisters on my toes before I got very far. I stopped at Puntervoll at Ingeborg's aunt's and had coffee and lunch. I met Karen Theodora Gordham, an old friend of my folks. Got home about 6:00. Walking time was three hours. Was I tired and sunburned! Walking distance was thirteen miles. The American dollar was supposed to be worth a lot, but I could only get the same amount of 4.50 kroner *(per dollar).*

I saw many German soldiers in town. Many looked to be 16, 17, or 18 years of age.

True story – I am reminded of the poor boy from Germany who found his father's grave in Egersund. His father had lost his life in the World War. At that time, the boy was two years old. The poor fellow, very downhearted, speaking with some Norwegians, had expressed how bad he felt about the invasion. and that he feared he would never see his mother and homeland again. The same day, he was called together with his troops to Bjerkreim to attack Norwegian troops in the mountains. The boy, hating war so badly, took off his gun belt, etc., and threw them away. Then, crying desperately, he flung himself on the ground and refused to go. He was killed on the spot by Germans.

There have been seven Germans stationed at Stapnes. They were quite nice fellows, helping with spring work when they were not busy. They lived in Tønnes Stapnes's house. Tønnes moved out to Kaia's.

Near town one day, a friend saw German troops being ordered in troop formation when one flung himself on the ground, refusing to go to war, but he was taken by the collar, shoved in line, and forced to go.

There was a battle in Bjerkreim; fighting was guerrilla fashion. As fast as German troops stepped out of buses, they were shot down by Norsemen. Over a thousand Germans fell while only five Norsemen lost their lives.

Hitler has ordered all Norwegian prisoners freed. It must be that Germany has no means of supporting them.

May 8, 1940 - Wednesday

English troops this week have withdrawn from Trondheim and Namsos. Fighting is still going on at Narvik.

Ingvald Omdal, who lives near Sola flying field, returned home to see how things were, to find twenty Germans occupying his house and school. His silverware had been stolen, and his set of best china broken. He was not allowed to take anything from the house that the Germans could use. He did get a few clothes for the children. *(The Germans)* promised that he could come back in September when the war would be over. *(Note - When school started in September, Ingvald had to hold school in a dwelling house. Germans were still living in their school on January 5, 1941.)*

May 9, 1940 - Thursday

At noon, we heard a terrible shooting out at sea. Thinking it was a sea battle, we climbed the high mountain in back of the place to see what was going on. It turned out to be five German boats shooting at mines near Stapnes and Mong. But they were such poor shots, especially on the sea, that they wasted forty cannon shots on the mine before finally sinking it. Very dumb, too, how they let bullets fly in over land. In Mong, people who went out to see were soon running for their lives, as bullets were heard whizzing by their ears. Sivert said he hid behind a huge rock and for the first time in his life, he really was scared for his life.

About two weeks ago on April 28, Sunday, a German plane fell near Birkeland in the mountains. The four occupants were burned to death as they were thrown out by force of explosions. People who went out to see the wreck said there was nothing but bones left of the victims. One motor of the plane was still good, so the boys from Birkeland took it in pieces and carried it home together with other pieces they thought they could use. Some machine guns and other weapons were still good. They are now waiting for a chance to crack down a German low-flying plane, as they fly very low over mountaintops.

One man up in the country is said to have cracked down a plane with his small gun. The plane flew so low, he got a good shot. This story may not be true, as many stories heard have no truth to them.

Planted garden - peas, beans, onions, beets. Raked a lot of rocks out of the garden, while Onkel Petter fenced it in. I shall plant carrots and more peas on Saturday.

May 10, 1940 - Friday

This morning at 3:00, the Germans invaded Holland, Belgium and Luxembourg, all of which are fighting fiercely to keep the Germans out. German troops landed by parachutes not successful. Holland has flooded certain sections of their country. Holland is also said to have shot down seventy German planes. Hitler is in command of army on Western Front today, reports say. Great activity in the air over France, with many small towns bombed. Chamberlain resigned today, and Churchill is to take his place as Prime Minister.

I cleaned house today. The rest planted potatoes.

May 14, 1940 - Tuesday

Mathilde and I went to Rodvelt. We stayed overnight for Pentecost and the Monday following which are legal holidays.

Alfred Rodvelt *(Andreas' brother)* and his wife and child arrived the other day after he was a German prisoner for three weeks at Madla,

Stavanger. He had gone to the country near Algård and Ganddal to escape a raid expected on Sandnes. While there, with Germans and Norwegians fighting in the vicinity, the house in which they were hiding was shot at by machine guns, but the shells did not go through the walls because they sat in front of the fireplace. Soon a hand bomb was thrown in, and they all had to run out of the building. The men were taken prisoners. A Norse soldier had hidden in this house. The Germans, thinking the house was full of Norse soldiers, attacked it. They apologized profusely when they saw women and children come out. A Norse civilian had shot at the Germans, and that is why they had to take all the men they saw, as they could not find the one who had done it.

May 15, 1940 - Wednesday

Thelma and I went to town by bikes. A whole battalion of German soldiers had just arrived in town. We watched them march through town. They took most of the churches, the schools, and the Stapnes Bedehus *(House of Worship)* as living quarters. Reports have it that the Germans are going to have headquarters in Egersund, as the head Commander is located here. He has his offices in the Grand Hotel. Mr. Tollefson is the "tolk" *(interpreter)*. Their ammunition storage is located here, and it is believed that they expect to attack England from here.

All Germans show very good manners and etiquette on the street. The rule now in town is that any girl who is seen out in company with a German soldier is given a good sound trouncing. They actually do it too.

We had dinner at a café. We walked into the inner dining room, as the other two rooms were filled with Germans. They soon filled this room too. Some appeared to be at least forty; others as young as seventeen. Most of them very sober-looking - not many smiles. The poor fellows don't like this any more than we do. As we walked out of the café, a German on a motorcycle with a side car smilingly offered us a ride.

After dinner, I decided to send a telegram home. I went first to the telegraph office and was refused. I went and saw the German Commander-in-Chief, who said I could, but when I went back to the telegraph office, they refused again, so I went back and told the Commander, who telephoned to find out why. It was impossible, as telegrams were forbidden out of Oslo. He was very nice to talk to and polite. Are their men handsome? You should see them. Later, on our way home, we met those same two Germans who waved and smiled. Two other Germans who were guards at the hotel entrance recognized us and smiled a greeting.

Stopped in Årrestaddalen and had coffee and lunch with Jenny *(Mong)*. She was in to see Karen *Rodvelt Birkeland's* mother, *(Jakobine Oline Åvendal Rodvelt)*. She is pretty old and feeble now. She is quite nervous about the Germans being in town.

May 17, 1940 - Sunday

Today is Norway's Independence Day which is annually celebrated in a big way, but this year all parts of Norway under German control are forbidden to celebrate. It must be observed as an everyday workday. This was quite hard for some of these patriotic Norwegians to swallow.

We worked in the garden today. We have planted peas, beans, beets, onions, and carrots.

May 18, 1940 - Saturday

Holland has been taken by the Germans. Belgium and Luxembourg are also now under German control. The Dutch royalty arrived in England. The Grand Duchess of Luxembourg left the Royal Palace fifteen minutes before the Germans occupied it. The Germans have also gone into France in an attempt to get at the heart of Paris. Fierce fighting!

This morning, shots were heard along the coast. An English torpedo boat had sunk six tank and transport ships coming from Germany to Stavanger. It is estimated at a loss of several thousand men. Three horses swam ashore, landing on Jæren. Horses were to have come to Egersund where Germans were building horse barns. Work was discontinued on that this morning.

May 19, 1940 - Sunday

Andrew was in town Saturday. He saw Germans out practicing guerrilla fighting in the Årrestad valley. The Germans have suffered great losses in Norway, as they are not used to mountain fighting, so now they are training their own soldiers in Norwegian tactics.

I went to Rodvelt last night and stayed overnight. In the morning, I took off to Sokndal on a bike tour. Sivert, Mikal, Thelma, and I got there in time for church services. Reverend Berge preached.

We saw the graves of the seven Germans who were killed on the Altmark. The graves were newly decorated with many flowers. We had coffee and lunch and rested on the way to Sandbeck, did sightseeing and went home.

May 20, 1940 - Monday

Sivert and Thelma accompanied me to the Grødem way. A friend accompanied me the rest of the way home. I had a swell time. I was not very tired after a day of cycling. Now I simply must get ahold of a bicycle.

May 22, 1940 - Wednesday

Intense fighting on the western front. Nip and tuck.

They have been planting a lot of potatoes here. Started to shear sheep today.

May 23, 1940 - Thursday

Thelma and Sivert came over for the evening. We went out and picked "hegg" *(bird cherry)* flowers. Grødem is beautiful this time of year with hedge cherry trees, apple, and plum trees all in bloom. We have had very warm weather, but it has been too dry for crops. Have had to carry water for the garden.

May 24, 1940 - Friday

Petter went to town today and sold wood, wool, etc.

Tante Anne and Mathilde sheared sheep this morning. In the afternoon, Anne and I spaded up a patch for a flower garden in front of the house.

May 24, 1940 - Grødem, Egersund

Dear Mother, Dad and All,

I suppose you have been wondering how everything is with us over here. I hope you haven't worried, as we're all OK. I just heard today that there would be air mail to the U.S.A. one of these days, so I'm writing in hopes I can get this off. I tried to send a telegram earlier but couldn't get it through. Everything is very peaceful in this part of the country. Most of the town people who have been evacuated have moved back to town, but Mathilde Grødem is still staying here. She is a great help.

We have gotten all the spuds planted and some of the sheep sheared. Next week, they are going to cut "torv" - peat. I have

Helene and Andreas Rodvelt with Thelma, Petter, Mikal and Alf Henry

planted quite a big garden of peas, beans, carrots, beets, turnips, lettuce, cabbage, cucumbers, and ten tomato plants I just got the other day which had to be set out right away. Anne and I dug up a flower bed by the big rock – in front of the house, so we're going to have flowers, too.

We have had pretty dry weather lately, but it started raining this afternoon, so I don't have to water the garden tonight.

Today I canned veal and baked a cake and cookies. I'm going to town tomorrow morning, especially to see if I can get this letter off. Tomorrow night, Tante Helene and Miss Ålvik are coming to spend the weekend. I am getting a bicycle tomorrow. It is one Sivert Mong's aunt gave them, and no one has used it for a long time. He said if I would fix it up, I could have the use of it as long as I wanted.

Last Sunday, Thelma, Mikal, Sivert, and I took a bike tour to Sokndal. We went early enough to get there in time for church. Reverend Berge from Stavanger preached. It was a nice trip.

We had greetings from Onkel Lars today by one of Larsine's boys who has come to visit at Omdal for a while. Everyone in Helleland and Sirdal are fine. I talked to Anna Østrem and Tante Valborg on the telephone the other day. I am taking a trip up the valley again June 1st.

I sure hope I can get mail again soon, as it's been about six weeks since I've had any. Someone wrote that Theodora had had an operation for goiter, so I surely have wondered how everything went. I am sure your letters are lying in New York or England. I have a lot of interesting experiences to relate when I get home.

Grandpa is the same, and Tante Anne is fine. I am sure glad Mathilde is here to help. Will write more next time. Hello to everyone.

Love to all, Sophie

May 25, 1940 - Saturday

It's raining today. Sivert has my bike ready, so I shall get it today.

I went to town with Thelma to look at dress material for her wedding dress. The wedding is now set for June 30 at Grødem. We put our bikes in at Iversons at Svå Bridge, as it rained too hard to cycle all the way home. We bought a lot of flower plants to set out. I came home about

3:00, dripping wet. Tante Helene came over in the evening and stayed overnight.

May 26, 1940 - Sunday

Else, Alf, and Petter came over in the afternoon. They all went home in the evening.

May 26, 1940 - Grødem, Egersund

Dear Theodora and Chris,

I haven't had any mail for about seven weeks now, so I surely am anxious to hear how things are at home. I had a letter then from someone saying you had had an operation and that everything went OK. This was written March 29, so I gathered it must have been immediately after the operation. I have been hoping that you have gotten along well since. I suppose the folks have written me about it, but no mail has been coming through. I hear now that we can send mail to

America via Italy and vice versa, so I'm trying. It will perhaps take a long time.

You, over there, have no doubt been spent on the situation over here. Although things have been happening in other parts of the country and in some places not so far away, we have been spared. Although we are under German command here, everything is running smoothly and much the same as usual.

I sent an airmail letter home yesterday, but it probably will take as long as this to get there. I hear boats have been sent here to take American citizens home, but I wouldn't think of traveling now. I am much better off here I think, and whatever you do, don't worry about me. I haven't been the least bit afraid since this started, except the first day when I was in Stavanger where things started popping. I got out of town in a hurry. I stayed with Lars then awhile but have been here at Grødem since. Next Saturday, I am going to Sirdal again to visit Mother's folks (Mikkel and Rakel Eikelandsdal). *I can't stay very long this time, as Thelma and Sivert are getting married the latter part of June, and I've offered to help with the baking, etc. The wedding was to have taken place this month, but they postponed indefinitely after the war broke out, but now they've decided to get it over with. They have everything ready - lovely furniture, etc. It's going to be a church wedding with a reception here at Grødem, as we have more room here. She figures on only about forty guests, but that's enough when it's going to last from 5:00 Saturday evening through all day Sunday.*

I have just gotten myself a bike. It's not new, but good. It's one they had in Mong. I paid $6.00 to get it repaired, and now I can use it as long as I'm here in Norway. I think I did good business there. Had I bought one, it would have cost me much more. One almost needs one to get around here. Now I can get to town more often. Last Sunday, a few of us had a lovely trip to Sokndal. We had a coffee pot and food along. We would have taken another all-day trip today, but we had company. Tante Helene came last night, and others came today. They have just left now.

It's lovely here in the spring. We just had a good rain, and everything is so fresh and green. The evenings are light until

10:30, really light. It's just after 9:00 now, and the sun has just set behind the mountains. It stays light longer in the evenings in spring and summer, but in winter I noticed it got dark much earlier here.

I should be getting mail from home now any day, as they say the mail has started to run regularly. I did try to send a telegram earlier, as I was afraid you'd be worried and imagine everything a lot worse than it really is. Although I got permission here at Egersund from the Commandant, all telegrams were forbidden from Oslo. I did my best, and the German officers were very congenial and accommodating from this end, but to no avail.

I keep thinking about David and how big he must be now. Are you teaching him to mind? Or is he a spoiled little rascal? I sure would like to see him. You've got to take a snap and send it to me. I suppose little Sigmond has changed a lot too. Sometimes when you are together, take a picture of them both. Of course, other snaps of yourselves will be welcomed too. People just swarm for snapshots of the family there at home.

You should see "my fine garden". I have some of everything in it. They don't usually bother with a garden here, but I just had to have some fresh green vegetables. They do not eat a great deal of vegetables except carrots, cabbage, dried peas and tomatoes.

I am still gaining weight. I cannot say how much I weigh as all weights are in kilograms instead of pounds.

I have my knit dress almost finished now. I think I'm going to like it.

People are still evacuated from town although quite a few have moved back. There were twenty-one at Onkel Andreas Rodvelt's for quite a while, but they have only three now. There are a lot of refugees still in the Omdal village. There are none left here at Grødem, except Mathilde who usually spends a lot of time here anyway. She wants to move back to town, but her dad will not let her. I think she will be here all summer anyway. We hope she stays, as she is so helpful and has a happy-go-lucky nature - always cheerful.

I have the job of taking care of Grandpa and keeping house while the rest work outside. So, I'm busy most of the day.

Grandpa is much the same as he was all winter. He takes a stroll around the dining room table occasionally, which tires him out. He thinks he has been on a long walk then and says he's ready to go home now so you understand he isn't so frisky.

You'll have to write soon. I hope you are well again, or well on the way to recovery as I know it takes a long time to recover from a goiter operation. I hope you will not have any more trouble now. Was it an inner goiter as I didn't know you had any goiter trouble before? Do take care of yourself now. Wish you could have some of the pounds I don't need.

Greet everyone at home. I shall answer Eileen's letter now. I should have gotten many letters written before the war broke out, which put a halt to all letter writing. Let me know how long it takes this letter to arrive there, also the one I sent to the folks.

I should greet you from everyone here, also all the cousins, aunts and uncles.

Love, Sophie and squeezes for David.

(Note - At this time, there is a long break in letter writing - probably due to Thelma's wedding and Grandpa's last two weeks and then the funeral.)

May 27, 1940 - Monday

I planted the flowers. It is rather a nice flower garden, if we'd only get some rain. We set out the tomato plants and planted turnips. The onions, beets, peas, beans, carrots and maize are up.

May 29, 1940 - Wednesday

They worked in the "torv" or peat today. Mathilde, Petter and Anne went in the morning. I cooked dinner. Anne came home after dinner.

Grandpa has been awful today. It made me terribly nervous. It's the only time I've cried since I've been here.

I managed to sew an apron and fix over my spring hat. Knut *(Hegdal)* and Johan came over and gabbed for a while.

May 30, 1940 - Thursday

Anne stayed home with Grandpa today. I went out with dinner *(for the others)* and stayed and helped in the torv all afternoon. Petter and I went for a walk to see Branddahl. Lovely scenery.

May 31, 1940 - Friday

I got my clothes ready as I'm going to Helleland tomorrow.

June 1, 1940 - Saturday

Petter, Knut and I got a ride with Kristian *(Rodvelt)* to town. I got a bell and a seat cover for my bicycle. I met Tyra Dybing in town, so we fooled around together. Went to Malene's Café for dinner, but there were so many Germans that ordinary town folks didn't stand the chance of getting any attention. *(The waitresses were)* too busy entertaining the soldiers. Was I mad? The waitresses are so dumb. They put themselves out for them *(Germans),* but I waited half an hour for dinner and didn't get it. I complained several times, then I walked out and ate dinner at the Hotel.

I decided to take my bike on the bus and ride the bus with Sigurd Østrem *(cousin/driver).* It was a free ride. Went for a bike ride up to Sig's in the evening. The children are too adorable. They are Tønnes Andreas - three years old and Arvid - one year old. Spent the night with the Østrem's.

June 2, 1940 - Sunday

Today is Dad's *(Tollag's)* birthday.

Fredrik is home. He is recuperating from an accident in the factory. He lost a thumb and part of a forefinger. He is a swell kid - 26 years old. After dinner, a nap - then coffee. Bergit and I walked over to their valley and saw the Dahlheim school buildings. On the way back, I went up to see Sofie Egelid. She has four children: three girls (Jens, Laura, and Torlaug), and the oldest, a boy *(Olav).* They have a lovely home - everything was nice. Ragna and Trygve *(Hetland)* and their two children *(Ivar and Torbjørn)* were there.

In the evening, Amanda *Gystøl* came down, so I went home with her for the night. When we got to Dybing, all the boys had gone to bed, so I didn't get to meet Gunder this time either. Tante Teoline was looking well, but Onkel Johan was not very well. He has been ill with rheumatism. Amanda has also been sick and is not very strong.

June 3, 1940 - Monday

Everyone had gone to work when I got up except Torvald. He works on the railroad near Egersund; Martin works on the railroad here. Jon is a carpenter. Gunder is at home. Onkel Karl *Egelandsdal* came up. He decided to go with us on a trip to Eiesland. He knows the way. Tante Teoline went to the station with me. I met Ragna and Karsten in town.

In the evening, I got things ready for the mountain trip to Eiesland.

June 4, 1940 - Tuesday

Bergit and I biked to Gya and got there for dinner. Then we took the 5:00 bus to Tonstad and hiked over the mountain to Ovedal (three hours), arriving around 10:00. I met Gabriel Åvendal – he is 90 years old. His wife (over 80) is as peppy as a 16-year-old. Johan and wife and their three children were there - very congenial people. We stayed overnight with them.

June 5, 1940 - Wednesday

We slept until 8:30. Had breakfast and started out after 9:00. We got as far as cousin Martha's and we had to go in and see her new, very modern house. They have lovely, overstuffed furniture and lovely weavings - priceless. Had coffee and lunch again. We didn't get on the way again until 11:00. Olga, Bergit, Karl, and I were in the party. We went by way of Jødestøl over the high mountains - a whole day's march. Got to Eiesland at 10:00 in the evening. Met Cousin Oskar and Onkel Ole first, in their lovely home with a lovely location. There were Oskar, Magnus, Ingrid, Johannes, Øyvind and Thor. Rakel is in Oslo, working in a café. Magnus is married and has a café of his own and a new house. They have a little boy, Olav, who is two years old. He is a darling child.

June 6, 1940 - Thursday

I spent a week with Tante Martha *(and Onkel Ole Eiesland)*. Her health is very poor, having been sick a long time. Fjotland is a lovely country and very mountainous. They have a fairly good-sized farm with six cows. Thor has a platinum fox besides a couple of silver foxes. All the boys are at home; their son Johannes was a machinist at Knaben, but he quit work up there when the Germans came.

We slept late every day, loafed and had a swell time. One day, we washed our clothes and hair in the creek. We had coffee out of doors in the afternoons. On Saturday evening we went to a "Fest".

Onkel Karl left for home alone by way of Haukom and Tonstad.

June 7, 1940 – Friday

(Note: On this day King Haaken, Crown Prince Olav, and about 400 members of the government left Norway for England where they stayed for five years.)

Took pictures of Thor's platinum fox. We had dinner and coffee down in the woods. All the neighbors came out with coffee pots and cakes, and we lunched together. *(Enjoyed)* music from a portable. In the evening, we walked out to Magnus's café. Everyone else stayed to dance, but I went home and sat up late and talked with Tante Martha. *(Their son)* Oskar's wedding to Selma is set for June 30-31 with ninety guests invited. I can't attend, however, as the date interferes with Thelma's wedding.

June 8, 1940 - Saturday

We left Fjotland about 5:00. Ingrid went with us. We took the bus to Netland and a taxi the rest of the way to Knaben, to an iron ore mine there. The mine is owned by Norway and Sweden. There are now thirty German guards to see that all of the ore goes to Germany. The mine lies very high up in the mountains. The snow lies in old drifts all year round. Friends of Ingrid *Eiesland* treated us to coffee and supper, after which a couple of friends showed us through the mine. There are twelve stories. We watched rock being crushed, ground, washed, and ending in fine powder form resembling silver. It was very interesting. We spent the night at the Café in lovely rooms. The proprietress was a young woman age 27 or 28 whose husband had died from illness resulting from mine work. The work is very dangerous. They breathe in so much metal that their lungs get filled, which finally, after about twelve years, results in death.

June 9, 1940 - Sunday

Had breakfast at the Café. We got a ride in a grocery truck to Risnes. We sat in the back and did we get dusty? Ingrid departed from us there. We set out over the mountains, crossing several snow drifts, resulting in a five-hour hike. We came out at Tonstad and had coffee and sandwiches at a hotel. We missed Tonetta. We were lucky to get a ride down, meeting Sigurd Østrem on the way, so we got a ride all the way home to Helleland.

Bergit and I both had a powerful coat of tan. Bergit's boyfriend, Alf Skåra, had just come. Pretty kjekk *(handsome)* boyfriend - a barber from Flekkefjord. *(Note: Alf became an undercover agent with a military intelligence group of Norway's armed forces. In December 1942, he was arrested, and he died in a concentration camp in Germany 2 years later.)*

Norway laid down arms today.

June 10, 1940 - Monday

Did nothing in particular. Bergit and I loafed out to Sigurd Østrem's. Spent the afternoon with Sofie Egelid. They have a lovely new home.

June 11, 1940 - Tuesday

I washed clothes, then biked over to Årrestad in the evening to Torger and Malene's to hear the news. They are in the process of having their whole house redecorated. It is looking lovely, and it will be cute when it's finished. They showed me their car and also their new bikes, as they can't get gas for the car.

June 12, 1940 - Wednesday

In the afternoon I biked over to Øgreid to see Rakel.

June 13, 1940 - Thursday

I spent the afternoon with Bertha Aarrestad. I had a conversation in English with Nils Aarrestad, Magnus's brother.

Torger came over later and walked home with me. When we got home, Olav had come home from Nærbø.

June 14, 1940 - Friday

After dinner, Torger took Rakel, the kids *(Anna Kjerstina, Jostein, and Sylvi)*, and me to Gya in his car. He didn't have permission to use his car, but he had some extra gas. He was lucky not to meet any Germans or officers.

Ragna was still home. Martin was also home from Nærbø. He is now working on German barracks. Their company of carpenters are forced to work for them. They see a lot of air activity where they work, as well as sea battles. Many ships are sunk along the coast there.

Got some cute pictures of the kids.

June 15, 1940 - Saturday

I left Årrestad at 9:00 and biked to Helleland. I didn't stop at Tante Berthe *Østrem's* longer than just to pick up my things. I arrived in town before 11:00. It was fun cycling.

Talked to Albrethson about my passport and ticket and did my errands. I had time to go in and chat with K. M. *(Kristian Mikkelsen).* I got a letter from Evelyn Oakland. It's the first letter I've received since war broke out in Norway. The letter came through Germany and Italy; it was opened in Germany. As I was ready to leave town, I met Arne Friestad, who insisted I come up and chat. I was talked into staying for dinner, and then later, coffee, cream puffs, etc. Along my bike ride home, I stopped at Halsen for a drink of water. They talked me into staying for coffee, then Petter came to meet me. He thought something must have happened.

June 16, 1940 - Sunday

Grandpa is weakening gradually; he is much worse. He doesn't keep quiet for one minute. Tante Anne is getting quite worn out.

The garden is full of weeds. The peas have grown quite high, so I cut poles and strung up the peas and pole beans. The carrots are looking fine. I set out cabbage plants. The kålrabi and turnips are fine. I carried water as it has been so dry; it has rained but once since Pinsedag *(Pentecost).* The hay fields are burning up, with many brown patches. Onkel Petter has hayed a couple of small patches of cultivated hay. The cherries are drying up. The tomatoes are coming along swell.

Thelma came over in the evening to spend a few days.

June 18, 1940 - Tuesday

Thelma, Mathilde and Anne housecleaned in two "kammers" *(small rooms).* I took care of Grandpa and cooked dinner.

June 19, 1940 - Wednesday

We cleaned and scrubbed in the living room and the front entrance. Grandpa is awfully tiring to take care of; he is driving us all crazy. I ironed a few things for Thelma and baked bread. Thelma went home in the evening.

We heard terrible shooting at sea at about 10:00 - 10:30 tonight. Later, we found out there was a sea battle out from Sola.

June 22 1940 - Saturday

Anne and Mathilde scrubbed the kitchen. I helped a little in-between cooking and taking care of Grandpa. Big battle today! Tante isn't all patience and sweetness; I put in my word too. It all started because Anne asked Mathilde what she should do when Grandpa kept yelling. Did Anne fly off the bat? Not just once.

Onkel Lars, Henne, and their driver came about 10:00 in the evening. I sure was glad to see him again. He's my best uncle. I stayed up until after 12:00.

Armistice between Germany and occupied part of France was signed tonight.

June 23, 1940 - Sunday

Onkel Lars stayed all day. We two had a stroll after dinner, looking over the gardens, etc. He took home a load of fence posts and promised to come back for Thelma's wedding. The date is set for July 6-7. I helped sew pillows and curtains.

June 25, 1940 - Tuesday

Peace between France and Italy. Unoccupied France is still fighting.

A lot of flying these days - all German planes.

I went to town. I got a permanent, went to the dentist, and then met Thelma. Thelma hired a cook and invited cousins to the wedding. Stopped at Svånes and three other places on the way home, getting home late.

When I got to the Svå bridge (which, by the way, is almost finished now), my bike had low tires. A German soldier on guard helped pump my tires full of air. Got home at 11:00.

Elisabet Omdal came over and helped Anne while I was gone.

June 26, 1940 - Wednesday

I got up at 6:40 a.m., washed a few clothes, cooked dinner, and took care of Grandpa while Anne washed clothes in the cellar. Mathilde and

Elisabet worked in the spuds. After dinner, I took my bike and went to Rodvelt *(to help Thelma)*. We baked one kind of cookie. In the next two days, we baked eight kinds of cookies for the wedding. One night, I went over to help with her wedding dress. Agnes *(Rodvelt) Rotwell* and her daughter, Asta, were there yet from Stavanger.

June 27, 1940 - Thursday

There is an awfully lot of German traffic. They drive new Chevrolet trucks - hundreds of them. I heard over the radio yesterday that all these trucks had been sunk by English torpedoes out of Oslofjord.

Germans left Egersund in an awful rush Sunday night. They started packing about 11:00 and left town about 1:00. They demanded all the cars they could get to take them to Kristiansand - headed for the "front".

June 28, 1940 - Friday

I was in to see Dr. Dybing on Monday. He had been called out of bed at 1:00 to come into town and take his car full of soldiers to Kristiansand. Fortunately, he could not get his car started. They tried also, but to no avail. He had to report in the morning to the Ortskommandantur *(local commander)*. He was charged with sabotage. He said he could easily clear himself, however.

I got Grandtante Sille to sew a skirt, an everyday dress, and let out a couple of suit skirts for me.

June 29, 1940 - Saturday

The Stavanger dock was bombed and destroyed today by the English.

Today I ironed clothes. Tante Helene and Mathilde baked lefse. I worked in the garden again; I set out the rest of the cabbage and transplanted rutabaga or kålrabi. The garden is coming along fine, the tomatoes are growing fast, the green tomatoes are large. We could be eating peas in a couple weeks or less.

June 30, 1940 - Sunday

Helene and Alf Henry *(her son)* are here yet. Nothing special to do.

July 1, 1940 - Monday

Germans arrived in Slettebø on a train with 200 horses. They stopped the train before they arrived there, and the soldiers went out in the fields and took hay and carried it to the horses while aggravated farmers could only stand by and let them help themselves.

July 5, 1940 - Friday (The day before the wedding)

I scrubbed, ironed, and pressed clothes. In the afternoon, the cook came. Later, the Rodvelts and a few guests arrived for the coming wedding.

Sivert brought lobsters which we cooked and ate late in the evening after the tables were in place. There was table room for 60 wedding guests. No one got to bed before 1:00.

(Note to self) Remember the very strange accident upstairs! Disgusting and embarrassing.

July 6, 1940 - Saturday

Thelma's wedding date. The weather is fine. The cook and the cook's helper were on the job in the morning. Elisabet *Omdal* and Thora Åse were waitresses. There are some finishing touches to do in the morning. The cooks fixed the tables and decorated with pink crepe paper, silver vases, silver candleholders, and my little cut-glass candleholders. Roses and carnations were used. The wedding cake was big with four tiers.

The guests began arriving right after noon from Stavanger and Egersund by bus and taxi. The cooks had coffee ready for them.

Thelma and Sivert Mong

The maid arrived to dress Thelma's hair and fix her veil. They also curled Helene's, Anne's and Agnes's hair. Everyone looked very nice. Thelma was a very sweet bride.

Sivert had hired two taxis to call for the

bridal party to pick them up and take them to the church. Those in the bridal party were the parents of the bridal couple *(Bertine and Tarald Mong)*, Mikal Rodvelt, Tante Anne, Jenny Mong, and Arnfin Skadsem.

The ceremony was quite different from ours *(in the U.S.A.).* No other people were in church. They (*the bridal party)* got right out of the car and walked slowly up the sidewalk to the church. Guests sat in the aisle. Reverend Feyling *(Sigmund Feyling)*, the minister, tied the knot. It was all over in less than half an hour. "Love endures all things", etc. Pictures were taken afterwards.

We had a narrow escape on the way to town. We met German trucks in a curve and had to park a long time to let the rest by. They travel so fast and take the whole road, making it very dangerous to be on the road when they come. We were in church at 5:30, home again by 7:00. The banquet was all ready and the guests were all here at home when we got back from the church. I wore my long dress and had a lovely corsage, so I really looked nice. I had two table "kavalerers" *(gentlemen)* - Hans *Olsen Rodvelt*, the baker, on one side, and Sven *Mauland* on the other. I sure was glad I didn't have only Hans, as he had too many shots and was feeling too good. I enjoyed the other one.

Of course, no one went to bed all night. Some danced, some listened to the radio upstairs, some played games. Some were inside, some outside; they kept it up all night. I took a walk at 4:00 in the morning. I had to show Sven my tomatoes and vegetable garden. People played football. There was a little too much drinking going on among the men.

Dinner 7:00-9:00, Coffee at 12:00, Lunch again at 4:00, Breakfast at 8:00. The first guests left at 9:00 in the morning.

July 7, 1940 - Sunday

It started to rain about 8:00 in the morning. Everyone had a very enjoyable time. The parents of the bride and groom stayed for dinner, and also Agnes, Asta, Sven, Petter, and Henne.

After dinner dishes were done, everyone crawled into bed and took a nap. I had a good rest, but no sleep. I had the honor of serving the bridal couple coffee and lunch in bed. Sven and I had coffee with them also.

The cook left at about 7:00 in the evening. Onkel Andreas left at the same time. The rest of family stayed until Monday. The bridal couple slept over at Maria *Lædre's*.

July 8, 1940 - Monday

Agnes and Asta left for Stavanger. Tante Helene, Thelma and kids *(Petter and Alf Henry Rodvelt)* went home in the evening. Sven *(Mauland)* and Petter *(Omdal)* just got home. Sven, Henne, and I followed Thelma home. We had a Blue Master *(cigarette?)* on the way. We sang songs all the way over. We stayed about an hour and started back. Continued singing on the way back too, until we were too tired to sing anymore. Doctored Sven's finger before going to bed.

July 9, 1940 - Tuesday

The boys left today, but they are coming back in two weeks to help in the hay.

Set out a few more rutabaga plants. Took a long nap in the afternoon.

July 10, 1940 - Wednesday

I wasted a lot of time today. Grandpa is quite impossible again, but he was pretty good during the wedding.

August 7, 1940 - Wednesday

Grandpa is still unconscious. The nurse doesn't think he will live overnight.

I helped the nurse hold him on his side while she gave him a bath.

I cooked raspberry and black currant jam.

I telephoned Onkel Lars. Tante Helene came over to sit up with Grandpa tonight.

Anna Ålvik came over to take turns waking.

Late to bed as usual - 11:30. Tante Helene and Anna waked until 3:00; then I got up and kept Tante Helene company. Grandpa was much the same as usual but would lose breath and regain it at intervals.

August 8, 1940 - Thursday

Cooked coffee at 6:30. Nurse was up at 6:00 and helped with breakfast. Anna had to get off to school, as school started yesterday.

At 8:15 a.m., Grandpa passed away quietly, never gaining consciousness.

I watched him take his last breath. The house became so quiet when his heavy breathing ceased. He had lain unconscious since Friday night, August 2.

The nurse was grand. She made funeral arrangements, helped get everything in order, ironed clothes, and helped with everything in general.

August 9, 1940 - Friday

Petter and Erling went to town for a coffin.

That evening, the nurse dressed Grandpa, and the men helped place him in the coffin. He lay in state in his room.

Elisabet Omdal and Bernt Stapnes helping in the hay.

August 10, 1940 - Saturday

The nurse did housework while I went to Svånes to get Anne's coat cut out. She had secured Martine Svånes to sew the coat. She called home after dinner, and said she was lucky to get a ride all the way home.

August 11, 1940 - Sunday

I took an afternoon nap, then went for a walk in the garden. Anna Ålvik came to dinner and then stayed overnight. The dressmaker came this evening.

August 12, 1940 - Monday

I went to town; I had many errands to do including getting flowers and food for the funeral and hire a cook. I was invited to lunch and coffee at Wilheim Dybing's. It was a dainty lunch.

I got home at 7:00 or 8:00 in the evening, *(bringing with me a)* heavy load.

August 13, 1940 - Tuesday

Onkel Lars, Grandtante Elisabeth, Grandonkel Tollef and *(his wife)* Sille, Sister Margaret, Sister Karen, Henne, Tante Helene, the twins *(Petter and Alf Henry)*, Sivert, Thelma, and Mikal came to dinner tonight. Mrs. Svånes cooked; Elisabet and I waited tables.

August 14, 1940 - Wednesday

Today was Grandfather's funeral; guests arrived at 9:00. "Frokost" *(breakfast)* was served at 10:00; services were at 11:00.

Ingvald Omdal led with a Scripture reading and talk.

Peder Johan gave a very stirring and touching talk on behalf of my Papa *(Tollag)*, my Uncle Peder, and *(the other)* families in the U.S.A. as he placed our wreath on the coffin. It began to rain.

There was difficulty getting cars, but finally we got a truck and two taxis.

We got to the cemetery at 1:00. It rained hard all the time we were there.

We had dinner at home at about 3:00. We had meat soup with dumplings, vegetable, potato, meat and tomatoes. Thelma, Elisabet and I waited tables. There were forty guests.

August 15, 1940 - Thursday

Most all the guests have gone home. Tante Helene, her twin boys *(Petter and Alf Henry)*, Mikal, Sivert and Thelma have all left. I spent all forenoon getting dinner. I straightened up the house after they left, then went down and picked the rest of the currants and raspberries.

180 German planes shot down by English.

August 16, 1940 - Friday

I bound up tomato plants with the help of Anna Ålvik who came for some berries. Later, we chopped and sawed up the pile of wood in the back yard and got it all carried in under the roof.

Sivert and Mikal helped Petter in the hay.

August 17, 1940 - Saturday

I made jam – black currant and red currant combination, some raspberry jam, and a big batch of plum jam. I didn't get done till evening. It was too late to get any clothes ready, so I couldn't go to church with Anna Ålvik as planned.

August 18, 1940 - Sunday

It rained all day. I took a nap.

Anne and I went over to see Karen Guria *(wife of Lars Bowitz Larsen Omdal)* who is in very poor health and is not expected to live long. She lies talking or muttering all the time, but not a word anyone can understand.

I met three German soldiers at the dam looking over the works. They are everywhere. Germans are said to have lost 140 planes today over England.

Oh yes. Bergliot was here for dinner. She came to visit Johan and Maria Lædre *(neighbors of Anne and Petter at Grødem),* but they had gone to Stavanger with *(their daughter)* Kjellaug. The poor child has been found to have her left hip out of place and will remain at the hospital for a long time I'm afraid.

August 18, 1940 - Grødem, Egersund

Kjære Foreldre og Søsken (Dear Parents and Siblings),

Maybe I had better write in English, so all of you can read it. This time I have bad news. Grandfather passed away very quietly and peacefully Thursday morning, August 8, at 8:15 a.m. I had wanted to write before, but there simply has not been time. We have been so busy. Grandpa got decidedly worse two weeks before he died. The last week, from August 2, he lay in an unconscious sleep, only opening his eyes a few times. He recognized Anne and me, however, the day before he died. The nurse said the unconscious condition was due to "hjerne blodning" (brain bleeding). *We don't think he felt any pain but just fell into a deep sleep. On August 2, when he grew worse, Tante Helene came over and we sat up with him almost all night. He had a bright moment once, when Helene talked to him. He woke, recognized her and sang a hymn (one verse), but fell asleep again from which he never completely awakened again.*

We had a nurse to take care of him the last week. We took turns sitting up nights with him. The nurse, Sister Karen, was like a ray of sunshine to us; so helpful and cheerful. She helped with the funeral arrangements. She stayed several days after he died, to help. The funeral was held last Wednesday, August 14th, here at home. There was a lot of work. Guests came Tuesday evening to dinner (we had a hired cook). Then there was breakfast and lunch before the services (there were forty guests), then dinner, coffee and lunch after they came back from the cemetery. I don't like this old-fashioned idea of all this eating at funerals. It seems heathenish to me, but it is the custom here.

We had a lovely little service here at home. Ingvald Omdal lead. Peder Johan also talked. I bought a nice wreath of flowers and wrote "from Tollag and family and Peder and family". (Note - Tollag and Peder were brothers who had immigrated to America, and they were sons of Peder Mikal.) *This wreath was placed on the coffin by Peder Johan with a very stirring little talk on behalf of the two families in America. There was a large group at the cemetery in spite of the fact that it rained heavily all day.*

Grandfather looked so nice; he had such a peaceful look on his face. "Han har fare vel, Det er godt han fik hvile" (He has lived well, it's good that he gets to rest). I can't help but say it is good he could go. If you had been here and seen how he was - out of his mind most of the time, you could see too, that there was nothing more for him to live for. When he had his clear moments, he was either praying or singing hymns, so he thought only of going home to God. Of course, it is very quiet and empty in the house now that he is gone, but now Tante Anne can rest too. There is nothing left of her but skin and bone after sitting up so much with him. She has slept well this week, and I think now she will begin to pick up. Grandfather was 85 years old July 29th, 1940.

They are not through haying yet, as the first part of the summer was so dry that the grass just burned up; there was nothing to start on. I guess they are about half through now. Aside from the two weeks early in June when I went to Fjotland, and the three other days that I spent at Helleland and Dybing, I've been here at Grødem all summer. There hasn't been a chance to get out of the house, even as I was always inside with Grandpa and did the cooking while the others worked outside.

I have a swell garden; we have vegetables from it most every day. They think it's pretty nice too.

This afternoon, we are going over to Omdal to the Myran farm and see Karen Guria. She is quite low. They don't expect she can live many more days. When she is gone, there will be no more old folks around here. She has been very poorly since I came last year. She is so skinny; I don't see how she could live this long.

How is Faster Berthe (Berte Gurine Mong Omdal, wife of Svend Pedersen Omdal - she immigrated to Bow, WA in 1910)? *Everybody asks me, but you know, I haven't heard a word from home since the first week in April. Have you written? If you have written, perhaps you have written too much...?*

I had a letter from Ruth Haugland by air mail. It was nineteen days on the way. She informed me that you had received my letters, so I was glad to hear that. Perhaps it is best to send by air mail now. I surely am anxious to hear how everyone at home is. When you write, for goodness sake don't write anything about the war – if you want me to get it. Her letter is the only one I have had from America written since the war began here.

Everyone here is OK. Lars, Thea and Henne were here for the funeral. Lars was here the Sunday before Grandpa died. Lars's two boys and two others have been on a bicycle tour to Oslo. Henne and his companion got back for the funeral. The other two have not shown up yet. We expect them here today or tomorrow.

Thelma, Sivert, and I want to go on a trip to Sirdalen tomorrow, but we're having so much rain, I'm afraid we won't get to go. We haven't had any summer. It has been cold, damp and rainy all through July and August. I'm still optimistic enough to think we'll have some summer weather yet.

I don't remember whether I wrote about Thelma's wedding on July 6. It was a nice wedding. So much for that, till later.

All our relatives are well. Onkel Johan Dybing is not so spry anymore. He has not been able to work any all summer. He has "gikt feber" (rheumatic fever). The boy who injured his leg last year seems to be completely well again. I was there and at Tante Berthe's three weeks ago. They wrote and said that Thorvald Østrem and his family, wife (Marta Ramsland) *and two children, Bjørg and Aslaug, were there, and since I hadn't met Thorvald yet, I jumped on my bicycle and rode over one Thursday night and stayed through Sunday. He surely has a nice wife and two lovely children. I am going to visit them at*

Nærbø this fall as soon as I can get around to it. Gudrun, the youngest girl of Tante Berthe, is going with me to Fjotland soon. This time I think we'll take the train.

I hear there are boats going to New York from Petsamo (in northern Finland), *but I have no desire to go that route, so I am just staying until the war is over. My passport and ticket can easily be renewed, the agent said.*

Love to all at home. Hope you are all well.

Sophie

P.S. Write soon. How is Theodora? I should write to Uncle Peder about Grandpa, but you can pass this letter on to them with my best wishes.

August 19, 1940 - Monday and Tuesday

I washed clothes today and ironed. Petter and Anne worked in the hay. Did some mending.

August 20, 1940 - Tuesday

Did some mending.

August 21, 1940 - Wednesday

I was to have gone to town today, but it rained so hard, we decided to wait until tomorrow. We finally got Petter to take the cake and flower boxes *(from the funeral)* outside, so they are ready to go. They should have been back to town long ago.

August 22, 1940 - Thursday

I met Thelma at the highway at 9:30. We got the boxes on-board the bus and got to town at 10:40 or so. We had coffee at Sille's; then shopped all day. We lunched with Mathilde and had supper at Sille's. I spent the evening at Elisabeth Launes'. Kaia *Stapnes* was there. I stayed overnight at Sille's.

Organization is going on in town to educate the owners of each building to put out firebombs which may fall through housetops in an air raid. Complete blackouts are going on. Factories and business houses are to be open only by daylight. Blackouts are to be all over the country, all winter.

August 23, 1940 - Friday

Got up about 9:00. Went uptown for a few errands and chatted with K. M.

as usual. Went to the bank - same 4.40 *(kroner)* per dollar.

I had dinner at Sille's and went uptown Egersund again. Another chat with the friend.

Called on Tilla Aukland, Elen Johnson's sister.

Had coffee at Grandtante Elisabeth's this afternoon.

Left town about 5:30 - had the wind behind me until I got to the Svå bridge.

August 24, 1940 - Saturday

I poked around and finally got Saturday's work done and baked some waffles. Tante Anne and Petter worked in the hay.

Went to the bazaar at Hegdal. I was lucky to win an apron and "fiskeause" *(fish ladle for fish soup).* I bought socks for Anne and Petter. I got home about 10:00. Mandius Hausan hauled hay until 11:00 in the evening. Good thing he did, as it rained all day Sunday.

August 25, 1940 - Sunday

Anne and I went to Rodvelt for the afternoon. Later we went over to Thelma and Sivert's to see their new home. Kitty Mong at Stølsvigo has a new baby boy *(named Olav)*!

August 31, 1940 - Saturday

Thelma and Sivert came over in the evening, so we all went over to Hausan. They served a delicious supper. The general topic for discussion was whether or not there is a hell. Mandius believes not. Discussion was carried a little too far.

September 4, 1940 - Wednesday

Paul Omdal and Magnhild are spending a couple weeks' vacation in Omdal.

September 5, 1940 - Thursday

Mrs. Paul Omdal *(Rakel)* arrived from Stavanger to be home for Karen Guria's funeral. She reports the bombing of Sola by the English. She told of a whole truckload of wounded and dying (some appeared to be dead), screaming, being taken into town to the hospital after an air raid. She also told of the Commander of German forces in Stavanger who was called back to Berlin to report. Rather than face the firing squad or whatever consequences offered there, he chose to take his own life here. Many similar cases have been reported over the country.

September 6, 1940 - Friday

Today was the funeral of Karen Guria. We went to the early morning services at Omdal at 10:00. We were served lunch and coffee on arrival. After services at which Nils Omdal spoke, we went to the cemetery. The coffin was taken out to Aaseheia on a wagon where it was put on a truck. Three other cars followed to town. I rode my bicycle over to Aaseheia, as I wanted to stay in town overnight. Services at the cemetery were at 1:00 after which all fifty guests went to the Grand Hotel for dinner; a very splendid dinner was served. A couple of hours later, coffee and cakes were served. I stayed with Mathilde overnight. K. M. had gone to Oslo on a business trip, so I did not get to see him.

September 7, 1940 - Saturday

All stores were closed today, arranging for rationing of all dry goods. I could not buy a thing. Johan came to town, so I had company with him going home. Mandius was also in town, so I sent the sack from Vagle home with him.

I received a letter from Olga today, and I sent a letter to home.

September 7, 1940 - Grødem, Egersund

Hello Everybody,

I am wondering if you (Mother and Dad) *get the letters I send. I have as yet received none of yours. You'll have to keep trying. Maybe some will eventually come through. I had a letter from Martin the other day written July 3rd. He said nothing about anyone at home, so I gathered you were all well. He took it for granted, I guess, that I had heard from you, as did Ruth Haugland when she wrote, so I say again: I've heard nothing since before April. So, you'll have to write all the news from then on to the present time.*

I did get two newspapers, however, the other day dated June 7th where I read about Sig Omdal's wedding. It sounded interesting. Did Pearl get married? I have heard nix from there also. If you remember not to mention the present situation, your letters will come thru OK, I'm sure.

Karen Guria (wife of Lars Bowitz Omdal) *died August 31. The funeral was yesterday. I stayed over in town with Mathilde and Lars, as I had some shopping to do today.*

I talked to Gudrun Egelandsdal today, the one who works at the Egersund Fayancefabriks Co. (porcelain factory). *She paints designs on the dishes. Astrid, her sister, works for Dr. Ranlev. They are both engaged. Maybe I'll get in on some more weddings while I'm here.*

As far as I know, every one of our relatives is well and getting along fine in every way. Onkel Johan is the same. I wanted to go up there again and pick some "tydebær" (lingonberries), but I don't seem to get away. They are so slow about getting the hay in. The oats and barley are mostly in, then they'll start on the spuds. They have a lot of spuds this year. I heard over the radio that in America people thought we were starving here in these countries. We've had plenty to this date, and I'm still gaining weight. Last winter's coat just barely reaches around me. I'm afraid to weigh myself, but I'm sure I've gained 18 - 20 lbs. since I was home.

I was at Lars Stapnes' for two days last week. I was out to Marta and Nils' one afternoon. She wants me to come and can plums for her. I've canned a lot at Grødem without sugar. I would can a lot more if the fruit jars were not so high (expensive). *Onkel Petter has so many plums.*

We are drying the peas and beans. We surely got a lot out of the garden. We are eating the tomatoes now. I surely wish we had some salad dressing to go with them. They don't use salads and salad dressings here, and I surely miss them.

Tomorrow afternoon, Anne, Tante Helene, and I are invited to the Mong teacher's place. She lives in the schoolhouse during the week. It's quite lonesome there alone. She was so nice about coming by when Grandpa was sick. She sat up with him one night and has been up several times since.

Before I forget it, Papa, can you pay my life insurance again? I could send from here, but I'm afraid it won't come through, or there might be a lot of red tape about it. Please see to it that it doesn't lapse - will you? I still have enough shillings to do for a while yet. Don't send any money, as it may only get lost. I can get along nicely over winter.

I will have to close now, as I can have company all the way home if I go now. Hello to Everyone: Tora and Sig, Pete and Margery, Margaret and Martin, Theodora and Chris, Oscar and Eileen, Melvin, Carl, and a big squeeze for David Lawrence and Siggy. I sure wish I could see those youngsters now.

Love to all, Sophie

September 8, 1940 - Sunday

I was invited to Miss Ålvik's. She entertained 14 professional women from town. She served rømmegrøt (*sour cream porridge*). The meeting, a Mission Society, was called to order. We talked about storing up treasures in heaven, many taking part in the discussion. Coffee, waffles, and tyde berries were served at 5:00. At 5:30 or 6:00 the guests left. Anna and I walked out to the highway with them.

Tante Anne and Tante Helene came over after they left. We had lunch again, and I left about 9:00.

September 9, 1940 - Monday

We took up peas today. Most of peas, which should have dried, rotted on account of the unusual heavy rainy season.

September 10, 1940 - Tuesday

I would have gone to Dybing, but it rained too hard; I decided to bake bread instead.

September 11, 1940 - Wednesday

It was still raining today, so I embroidered on my Peer Gynt Jacket. I got one side done.

I received a letter from Theodora - the first one since March. I also received an announcement of Pearl's wedding to Louis Flowers.

September 11, 1940 - Grødem Egersund

Dear Olga,

I received your most welcome letter Saturday. It surely was good to hear from you. I was almost homesick after reading about the good times you were having going places, etc.

I have been here at Grødem all summer except for the first two weeks in June. Grandfather was so sick and fussy that I felt I couldn't go away. They needed me. He passed away August 8th. The place seems awfully empty and quiet now, but we are gradually getting used to it. There are just the three of us left. I'm glad I came over (to Norway) *when I did in spite of how things have turned out. I wouldn't have missed the many interesting experiences and fun too, for anything. Everything is so different - weddings, funerals, etc. My cousin was married in July. After the ceremony at the church there was the wedding dinner - sixty guests. Of course, no-one went to bed all night. Some danced to the music of a portable out in the barn, others played games on the lawn. They kept it going all night - and here it stays light at that date until about 11:00 p.m. We went inside for quiet games and stunts a couple hours of the darkest night. Lunch was served twice during the night – Breakfast at 8:00 or 9:00 a.m., after which guests started going home. Closer relatives stayed all day, but we all took a long after-dinner nap.*

I believe the thing that gets me most (here in Norway I mean) are the lovely, long, light nights all spring and early summer. The evenings are just beautiful. In the middle of June, the sun doesn't set till 10:30 p.m. so it's practically light all night. I just had to force myself to go to bed. Norway is beautiful in the spring.

I am sorry I didn't get to take more trips this summer but am leaving tomorrow to make the rounds of all my aunts. I had one very interesting trip in June. A couple cousins, an uncle, and I had a rather long hiking trip. First, we bicycled a ways - I've purchased a bike - then went by bus and the same day walked three hours up and over and down mountains. We stayed with some distant relatives overnight and started out at 11:00 a.m. the next morning, hiking all day over mountains all the way until 10:00 p.m. that evening before reaching my aunt in Fjotland. We were almost tired when we got there. It was great fun though, and we saw some interesting country. We went home a different route, riding more of the way.

Young people are great at taking tours, hikes etc. Now that cars are not to be had, everyone has taken to bikes, and I've been along on many interesting bicycle tours (just one-day trips).

I had a letter from Theodora today which was the first letter from home since before April. I surely was anxious about her as the last letter I received said she had just been operated on, and of course I didn't know how she had made out. She sent some snaps of David. I wouldn't have known him, as he was only nine months when I left, and now he looks so big.

Was I surprised about Pearl! I had an announcement from her today. I just can't imagine her married. She sounded so happy and excited in her last letter - that was before she was married - in February. I think it surely will be fun dropping in on her when I get home. I suppose you girls are there often. Ruth B. (Bradley) *isn't getting married, is she? I've heard rumors of a boyfriend. Now, Olga - you're still sticking by me aren't you or--?*

Theodora sounded as if they had worried about me over there. That was too bad. I wrote as soon as I could, but mail is so slow. Your letter was two months on the way as was hers. She wrote exactly the same day you did. Well, I guess I'm stuck over here for a while. I'm staying until everything is over with and quiet again. We get everything we need and so far, everything is fine and dandy with us. Don't worry about us who live in this part of the country.

I have made (knitted or embroidered) *some interesting jackets and sweaters to show off when I get home. I hope I don't wear them out before I get home. I started on a sweater for Onkel Petter today.*

By the way, Olga, I cannot find any of those silver brooches, and I wanted some too. Should I get enameled ones if I don't find the kind you wanted? I'm getting enamel ones for myself. They are lovely too - pure silver underneath with enameled designs on top - the same stuff as on Pearl's coffee spoons. I have yet to go to Kristiansand; there may be some there. I shan't give up yet, however.

Greet the girls - Ruth B. (Bradley), *Pearl* (Flowers), *Edith B. and anyone who asks about me.*

I am sorry to hear Teddy Mae (Hansen) *is so poorly. Poor Clara Marie* (Boe) *Hansen* (Teddy Mae's mother). *She surely has had to take a lot.* (Note – Teddy Mae died at age 18 in July, 1940.)

And you spoke of Anne Marie *Benson getting married. Tell her I surely wish her the best of luck.* (Note - Anne married William (Bill) Suryan on October 26, 1940.)

Great your mother (Clara Boe Benson) *and family and say hello to your Aunt Agnes* (Boe) *Kinne too.*

Love, Sophie

September 12, 1940 - Thursday

I got started on Petter's sweater today.

Tante Anne and Martine baked flatbrød and lefse all afternoon.

In the evening, Elisabeth, Magnhild, Anna, Gjertine, Maria, and Lisa came over with their knitting. I served chocolate and lunch.

September 13, 1940 - Friday

Very heavy air raids were over London all week. The German soldiers here don't believe they can take England. Earlier in the summer, many Germans refused to go to England.

September 13, 1940 - Grødem, Egersund

Dear Theodora,

Another country heard from! It surely has been ages since I heard from you. The other letter you mentioned did not come through. This letter was only three months on the way. I received it the day before yesterday. I surely was glad to hear you were better after the operation. I imagine you've gotten stronger during the summer months. Thanks so much for the snaps. My, I would never have recognized the child though - he has changed so much. He is big, isn't he? He sure is a darling. I surely would like to have a hold of him. They were such good clear pictures too; who took them?

I was sorry to hear that you had worried about me. You know, I could have taken one of the special boats, but I felt it was safer staying here. And we are perfectly safe here.

It has been a rather dull summer. I have been practically nowhere all summer. I couldn't leave Anne, when she had so much to do, and Grandpa sick. I feel that I happened to be over here at the right time in spite of how things have turned out. You shouldn't have worried about me. I'm just stuck over here for a while, though I'm surely going to do a lot of visiting around now until it gets too cold to gad about.

I am hoping we have heaps of snow this winter. I enjoy skiing so much. Now that I've gotten acquainted with so many young people, we've already made plans for skiing trips this winter.

We had a lot of good times going on bicycle trips this summer. I was gone only one day at a time, however - usually Sundays. It's a good way to see the country. I am going to do the rounds to the other aunts starting this week. I've had my suitcase packed and strapped to the bike since yesterday. As I was ready to leave, it started to rain, so I thought I'd let it wait until today. It's still raining, so I'm hoping it holds up tomorrow. I'm taking a lot of knitting along and will stay as long as I like now. I started on a sweater for Onkel Petter, so that will keep me busy for some time. I have two darling sweaters, or rather one is a sweater and the other a jacket, both to embroider on.

Have the folks written, or have their letters just not come through? I'm sure they have written, but I have as yet heard nothing from Mother since the letter she sent last Christmas. I noticed on one of the pictures, that they have gotten that "much-talked-of" fence put up. It looked nice. Was that the same car you had? It looked new. I also noticed a new lawn mower. Have you or they got anything else new since I left home? You've got to keep me informed.

People are surely getting married by wholesale. It seems so strange that Pearl is married. I can't get used to it. Who's got the primary grade (teaching job) *in town? I was hoping Olga (*Benson) *had gotten in there. What is Olga doing? I had a letter from her a week ago, but of course she never says anything about herself. I heard that Anne, her sister, was getting married. Who to? Anyone I know?*

I had to laugh when you wrote about them lassoing Sig Omdal after the wedding. Who did Helen Mong get married to? Did she quit nursing, or is she going on with her work? I suppose Solveig has graduated now. Did Sig Omdal buy the Iver Peterson's place, or is he just renting?

How do the uncles like the dairy route and their new farm? That ought to keep Mynor, Palmer, and Ernest out of mischief - I mean "busy." I'll bet Aunt Ellen likes it there.

Arnold Hanson surely did well for himself. I was surely glad *to hear it. How does Lucille like nursing? I think she'll make a fine nurse. Did she ever have her appendix out? I remember she was quite bothered with it when I was home. By the way, I hope Dad pays my life insurance again - better remind him of it. I surely wouldn't like to have it dropped now. I have joined the health bureau here which is a health insurance. It's very cheap - all you pay is about $9.00 a year and you get everything taken care of in case of sickness or accident. Most everyone belongs. This country is much better organized in that respect. All old people receive a pension when they are 70 and funeral expenses paid. I was surely glad to get in on the health insurance. I hope I won't need to use it, but it is a good security.*

I received a wedding announcement from Pearl, nothing more. I suppose she was too busy to write then, or maybe she has. I just know many letters have not come through.

Well, needless to say, we are all hunky-dory. My biggest worry for the present is what to do to keep from gaining any more. I don't know how much I weigh; I'm afraid to weigh myself. I haven't been this heavy since my first couple years of teaching.

Strange enough, my money is still holding out, and then Onkel Lars told me if I ever need money to let him know. I wish you knew Onkel Lars; he's OK. Of course, you know about Grandfather's death, if the folks have received my last letters. It was just good he could go. (Little) *Bovitz Omdal's mother, Karen Guria, died about a month after. So now there are no old folks left up here in Omdal and Grødem. I heard that Faster Berthe has also passed away.*

How were crops over there this fall? There was little hay here this year, as it was too dry all spring, and then it has rained almost all summer when they should have been getting it in. A lot of people are going to have to get rid of a few of their cattle.

Well, I suppose I could just ramble on, but I think I better quit here. If this letter takes three months to get there, I'd better wish you a Merry Christmas right now, haha - let me know how long it took.

With Love to You too, Chris and David,
Sophie

September 14, 1940 - Saturday

We still had that disgusting rain today so I will wait another day *(before going to Dybing).* My suitcase is still on my bike. Petter and Johan went to town. There is now rationing of clothes, wool, shoes, and all dry goods except baby clothes. There are rumors of rationing meat, oats, spuds, etc. I sent letters to Ruth H, Olga, and Theodora.

The Germans bombed Buckingham Palace today; the Chapel was destroyed. There are continuous air raids over London. They surely can take it.

Anna and Mandius came over for the evening. General discussion of the evening was "love" - many laughs. Mandius doesn't think I'll go back to the U.S.A. If I do, only for a visit.

September 15, 1940 - Sunday

Still rainy. I slept in late and had a late dinner. Onkel Petter went to Nesvåg with Mandius. They went over there to chat with Kjellaug. Poor child - she lies in a cast from waist to ankles. She will be bed-ridden at least a year. Very cheerful now anyway. I was going to go over to Erling and Gjertine (*Omdal's*) for the evening. *(Great Onkel)* Tollef and Sille were there.

185 German planes were lost in today's battles. Second bombing of Buckingham Palace; the Queen's bedroom was wrecked. One bomb, weighing a ton, fell 27 feet onto the ground near St. John's Cathedral. Luckily, it did not explode. Men worked in spite of the danger, extricating it and driving it away, not knowing when it might explode. Had the bomb exploded where it fell, the cathedral would have been blown to bits and leveled to the ground.

September 18, 1940 - Wednesday

Practically everything is rationed now. The worst is the small portion of butter allowed each person - not nearly enough. We are fortunate who churn at home. Everyone wants to buy "bonde smør" *(farmer butter).*

September 20, 1940 - Friday

There was a terrible electrical storm in the afternoon. I cooked plum preserves - two big jars.

At about 5:00 I biked over to the Mong schoolhouse where Miss Ålvik, Tante Helene, Thelma, Lisa R. *(Rodvelt)*, and I got things ready for the bazaar which will be held tomorrow night.

I stayed overnight with Miss Ålvik. We listened to hymn singing from a New York station.

September 21, 1940 - Saturday

Thelma stopped in at the school on her way to town. She joined us at breakfast, after which I went as far as Stapnes with Thelma. On the highway, we were joined by Betzy Rodvelt. She told about the German soldier who had escaped. Two Egersund girls helped him to get away, after finding him civilian clothes. The girls are now held by German authority - outcome unknown.

I went up to Martha and Nils *(at Stapnes)* where I canned nineteen liters of plums.

I went to the bazaar after going home and changing clothes. I bought apron cloth. Petter won aprons and socks which he gave to me.

September 22, 1940 - Sunday

I slept till 10:00. Got dinner and went to "Sanitet *(Sanitation)* Fest" in Stapnes. Reverend Oanes from Egersund was the speaker.

September 23, 1940 - Monday

Baked breads and waffles; cooked apple jam.

Petter and Anne dug potatoes between rain showers. It rains every day.

Soap rationing begins today.

September 24, 1940 - Tuesday

Pulled up onions and beans to dry. Petter and Anne worked in the spuds.

October 12, 1940 - Saturday

Thelma, Sivert, and I bicycled to Sokndal.

Spent the evening with Sivert's cousins Bernt and Borghild Gyland. When we got back up from town, there were Magnus *(Svånes)* and Sigrid *(Stapnes)*.

Met Olga's Tante Inga *(Boe)*. She has a fancy workshop in Sokndal. Her special line is wool yarn. I had a very interesting talk with her; she gave me a sweater pattern.

I felt sick and vomited several times that evening and simply could not get warm. I drank only a little tea that night. I felt OK in the morning.

October 13, 1940 - Sunday

It was Confirmation Sunday today. We were at church a half hour before services, but the church was full; not a good seat left. All of the balconies were packed. There were fifty in the confirmation class. Reverend *(Tønnes)* Svånes preached. An offering was taken to help Norwegian refugees and the homeless resulting from war.

I had dinner at Gyland. After dinner, Sivert, Thelma, and I bicycled to Rekefjord to visit Fru Elle *(Marie Tønnesen Elle),* sister of Sophia *(Tønnesen)* Rodvelt. They were not home. They evidently were at a confirmation party somewhere. We got back to Rodvelt a little before 9:00. I decided to stay there overnight, as it was too dark to go home alone.

October 14, 1940 - Monday

We woke up at 1:00 at night to the sounds of shots. We thought it was only mines, as we often hear them shooting at mines to put them out of danger. They either sink or explode. I went back to sleep again. The next day, we heard about the terrible sea battle just out from Egersund near Sirevåg. Residents at Mong had seen the flames from it.

October 15, 1940 - Tuesday

Here at Gandallen and Stavanger they also saw the fiery sky from the burning ships. Sixteen or seventeen German ships in a convoy attempted to reach North Norway with new troops and supplies. Every ship in the convoy is said to have gone under, although it is very doubtful that the whole story will ever be known. Ninety-some corpses were brought into Egersund Chapel. The wounded were taken to a public hall which is now being used as their hospital. Some 500 dead and wounded are reported to have come into Stavanger; all available doctors were called to the scene from Egersund, Stavanger, and Sandnes. It is known that railway men were expecting extra trains transporting some 2000 *(Germans)*. They were expected within a few days; none arrived. The fiery heavens above the burning, sinking convoy was witnessed by many in Egersund, Stavanger, and Sandnes and as far in as Gandallen. It was also seen in Mong. It is believed to be the Norwegian Uboat "Sleipner" in service of England that sank the convoy. He cleverly worked the Uboat into fjords and shot out to sea on the convoy, preventing the German fleet from going inland. The same Uboat sank a convoy a few months earlier at about the same place. These battles have not been mentioned either by the English or the Germans.

Many Germans committed suicide in Stavanger after this sinking, as many officers and soldiers were expecting their wives and families from Germany.

October 18, 1940 - Friday

A few months ago, a boat with some 3,000 lives aboard was sunk in Kattegat. They were said to be wives and children of German soldiers on their way to meet their husbands stationed here in Norway.

It is very disgusting to see our girls dating strangers. Many dumb girls are having children by them. Will they ever learn? They even go in public with them. I don't doubt that there are many fine men, but.....

October 18, 1940 - Grødem, Egersund

Dear Theodora,

Thanks so much for your letters. Let's see, I've received three, no, four letters one after the other. There was the longest time before I got anything, but they are coming through fine now. The one you wrote right after your operation in March arrived last week. The one written in June and one from August arrived about a week before, and then I got one today written September 20; that was not as bad. It surely is good to hear from home after being isolated so long. I got Mother and Dad's letter the day before yesterday. It made good time - 13 days only. I am so glad to hear you are quite yourself again after the operation. Thanks also for the snapshots of David. He surely is cute on them, but I would never have known it was he, he has changed so. Margaret sent a bunch of pictures she had taken on their place. It surely was interesting to see how they have worked up the place, and now I hear Martin has returned from up North. I hope he made good this summer. Greet them that I have received their letters, and it is my intention to answer soon. I do hope you will send more snaps when you can, as they seem to come through OK.

By the time this letter comes through, you will be home from your trip east. I'll bet it was an interesting trip. You'll have to write and tell me all about it. How does Arnold Hansen like it at Harvard? Is the World's Fair still open? Were you there? What exciting experiences did you have? Did Einar and Ruby Knutzen go all the way with you? Say "hello" to them from me.

I was glad to hear Mother is not having so much asthma trouble as formerly. I hope she doesn't have to suffer any bad spells this winter. I was also glad to hear that Mrs. Sofie Hansen got over her operation OK. Hope she gets completely well now. Give her my best wishes for a complete recovery.

Every once in a while, my mind wanders back to school, etc. How strange it must be with Mr. Cleveland (Principal of Lincoln School, Burlington, WA) *and Mr. Towne* (Superintendent) *both gone. Who has the primary grades? It would be interesting to know. Try and gather all the school gossip you can. I was hoping Olga would have gotten in there. Is Ruth Bradley teaching the 4th grade again? Who teaches Music? Is Bertha Omdal still* (teaching) *in Edison?*

Oh yes - did you get any new clothes in New York? I have just had two new dresses made. We had a dressmaker here for four days. She also altered some clothes for Tante Anne. I was quite satisfied with them - I mean mine. I finally had that black wool dress made. The other one was a work dress - dark blue and pink checked. It has big buttons all the way down the front. I wear a blue leather belt with it. Do you know - the Peer Gynt Jacket - the blue one with the embroidery I told you about - is too small for me, but I'm sure it will just fit you, but now I suppose I'll have to knit one for Tora too, so you won't fight over them. I was disappointed it didn't fit me - but I bought yarn for another one. Then I saw some more pretty yarn the other day when I was in town, so I bought that too. So now I have two sweaters to knit. I found some cute patterns. I am almost through with Onkel's sweater - that is, I have one arm left to knit. Then, I have promised to knit a sweater for Tante Anne and one for Tante Helene, so I believe I'll have enough to do this winter too. No, I haven't finished my dress either.

We are listening to New York; we hear them most every night.

Everyone thinks you are the faithful sister to write, as I have received so many letters from you lately. I hope you continue to write often. There is not always so much news here, as things are pretty dull sometimes. I spent a few days in town this week. If I had had my knitting along, I should have stayed longer. I always have invitations to stay somewhere. I have three good standing invitations. Next Saturday, several from here are going to Vagle to Onkel Lars's. I plan to stay a month or so.

You asked about Onkel Petter a while back. He's been home all the time. I suppose Carl has had to enter military training too. I hope they don't have to do more than just train. It all sounds so awful.

Do you ever see Pearl? I dreamed about her the other night. I dreamed she was just bubbling over with excitement and happiness. Sometimes I wish I were home now, when I hear what different ones are doing around home.

I suppose the folks will read this letter too, but I shall write them very soon. Don't forget David's snaps if you have some. I would like to see Little Siggy, too. I want to get this off in the morning with Petter, as he's going to town early. Greet everyone from me - I'm still taking life easy. I suppose you hear rumors of shortages on food, tobacco, etc. over here. We are still getting plenty here. Land sakes - it's 12:00! I've got to get to bed. Write soon again. (A Big hug for David.)

Love to all, Sophie

October 19, 1940 - Saturday

Beautiful sunshiny day today. Miss Ålvik, Thelma, and I decided to go to Sokndal by bicycle. The errand was to get boots, but we were disappointed that they were sold out. We fooled around until 6:00, had coffee and lunch at a café and started home.

It's impossible to get decent cakes and bread in town *(Egersund),* but here *(in Sokndal)* there were plenty of the right kind. No shortage on chocolate either, as there is elsewhere, especially in Egersund.

Sokndal had a huge supply of wheat flour stored away, and some traitor reported it to strangers who demanded it at their disposal or else they'd take it by military force. They took it.

We got to Rodvelt where we had lunch and coffee before going on to Mong by moonlight.

October 20, 1940 - Sunday

After dinner, Sigrid, Kristine, and Magnus Svånes came over. This is the 3rd Sunday we have been together. Sigrid and Magnus are engaged, but they can't buy rings - they are all sold out. They are paying dearly for "utstyr" *(items for the home).*

Bergit paid 80 kroner *($20.00)* for just "dynetrekk" *(duvet covers)* for four feather beds - an outrageous price.

I left before dark as I had no light on my bike. Met Anna Ålvik at the schoolhouse. She presented me with an "Andakt" *(devotional)* book and accompanied me part of the way home.

It is Sivert's birthday today, so they had a party for him in the evening, but I didn't stay.

October 23, 1940 - Wednesday

It was Tante Helene's birthday today. We helped get things ready for the bazaar at the Omdal schoolhouse.

The butcher came out and shot the old horse, Polli. He was nigh unto thirty years old.

In the evening, we went to Rodvelt to the birthday party. Tarald and Bertine Mong *(Sivert's parents)*, Anna Ålvik, and Thelma were there.

October 24, 1940 - Thursday

I worked like everything to get Petter's sweater finished. I got it sewed together today.

October 25, 1940 - Friday

Few people were at the bazaar this p.m. at the Omdal schoolhouse. Reverend Oanes and Emisar Trulson were the speakers. They took in 763 kroner for missions. I won a pair of socks for Dad. Anne won short socks and long stockings, both of which I received, as they happened to be just my size.

October 26, 1940 - Saturday

Onkel Petter and I left Grødem at 9:30 on bikes for Ganddalen. Petter hauled in his fish nets on the way and got a fine mess of about fifty trout. He took them along to Onkel Lars's. We left town *(Egersund)* at 2:00, going by way of Bjerkreim. We had the wind against us, so it was difficult pedaling. Stopped at Vigeså and had coffee and sandwiches and proceeded up the Vigeså mountainous road. After climbing to the top, the rest of the way was a steep downgrade. We got to Algård about 6:30 and finally to Ganddalen at 7:30 after 5 ½ hours on the way. We surely were tired. Thelma and Sivert came on the train about 8:00. Magnhild and Jan came over. The men cooked a mess of fish for supper.

October 27, 1940 - Sunday

Slept till 9:00. It was a quiet, restful Sunday, but there was terrible traffic with trucks hauling gravel to the Forus flying field. They keep it going Sundays as well as weekdays.

In churches in Norway, the ministers are no longer allowed by German law to offer the customary prayer when they ask God's blessings on the king and his family. A step towards the ultimatum - war.

In the early evening we took a walk over to the old folks gård *(farm)*. Mr. and Mrs. Mauland were just leaving for town. After hearing news, we went home. Onkel Lars had cooked more trout for supper.

Kristoffer and Marit were over for the evening. Kristoffer is a Kodak enthusiast.

October 28, 1940 - Monday

Sivert went to Sandnes and bought shoes. Petter left for home again at 12:15. I got started on my new jacket. Petter had given me the yarn - light rust - 13.30 kroner. I have finished Petter's sweater and have promised to knit Anne's and Helene's.

Petter Omdal *(son of Lars and Thea)* is now attending business college and likes it fine.

Today is the first day of Marken *(farmer's market)*. It is usually a great attraction each year, but this year with war and so many Germans in the country, the Marken is of little interest. Strangers have taken the entire marketplace except the "torv" *(oldest marketplace)* in town.

October 29, 1940 - Tuesday

Took the train to town at 1:30. After glancing over the exhibits (not much), I went up to the hotel to call on Anna and Bergit Østrem who now manage the hotel. Anders was also there, looking for a heater for Onkel Andreas's new house. Anna was free in the afternoon. We took a walk downtown after which we had coffee and cakes.

In the evening we saw the German picture Oljeu; it was very good. We had to stand in line to get in. Inside, people knocked each other over to get to the counter to buy chocolate bars; each person was allowed two. Stayed overnight.

October 29, 1940 - Stavanger

Dear Mother, Dad, and All,

I received your last letter the 15th so it was only thirteen days on the way, which was pretty good time. I got the short letter Mother wrote last June a few days before. If you have written others, they have not come through. As you see, I am in Stavanger. Petter and I biked to Vagle last Saturday. It was a long ride, but I wanted to have my bike with me so I could go to Klepp, Anda, and Nærbø when I wanted to. Sivert and Thelma were at Vagle on Sunday too, but they took the train. They all went home Monday, but I am staying on for a month anyway. Tante Anne and Helene are coming over Friday for Bededag (Day of Prayer) *and staying over the weekend.*

Yesterday and today is "Marken" in town. Of course, there isn't so much to it this year, but there are an awful lot of people in town today. Anna Østrem is free today, so we were out this afternoon. Bergit, her sister, is also here at the hotel. The manager has been sick since this spring, so Anna got her position, and Bergit is taking Anna's old job. So that makes it pretty nice for them both. Anders Østrem is in town today. He's looking for a heater for the new house Onkel Andreas is building (in Dalen) *- you know, on his land by the Dahlheim school. I don't know whether they plan to move into it or not,* *or just rent it out. Anyway, it's a good investment for these times.*

Onkel Lars is still working, and Petter, his oldest boy is attending "Handel Skole" (Trade School) *here in town. He travels back and forth every day by train. He likes the school fine. I hope he can prepare himself for something, because he is just not interested in farming. Henne is the farmer and a good worker.*

Onkel Petter finally got rid of the old horse "Polli". He was so old, that when he lay down, he had to have help to get up. He also sold a bull and a cow. So now he has just two cows, a calf, and the young horse. I hope they have hay enough for them this winter. He got pretty good prices for them, also for his lambs and sheep which he sold a little earlier. There is also a good price for the wool, but prices on everything you buy is sky-high - food, clothes, everything.

I have yarn for a couple sweaters for myself, which I intend to knit this winter. I have knit one for Onkel Petter and promised to knit one for Tante Anne and one for Tante Helene, so I have enough work to last almost through the winter. We had a bazaar at Omdal last Friday. We won some home-knit woolen socks I'm putting away for Papa (Tollag).

I have not been up to Helleland or any of those places for ages, but I am going up when I get back from this visit. So, I expect I'll be up there somewhere by Christmas.

I suppose Theodora and Chris are home again by this time, and she no doubt has gotten my letter now. Is Carl home? Or has he also gone into training? What is Melvin doing? I never hear anything about Melvin. I take it for granted he's poking around home - I mean working, of course.

You can greet Carlton Tollefson from his Grandpa (Tollef), *and Marta Stapnes and Gjertine. I also saw his Tante - Fru Paul Omdal; she was at the Marken. She wants me to come over and spend a day with them. I shall do so another time. I have as yet not been there. Of course, I see Sille and Tolley* (Tollef) *real often, as I usually put my bicycle in at their place when I go to town. Tollef is getting old now. He doesn't do anything. Sille still sews. Grandtante Elisabeth is looking fine.*

Oh yes. We, (Thelma, Sivert, and I) *were in Sokndal a couple weeks ago. I met Olga's Tante, that is, Clara Benson's sister, and had quite a chat with her. She has a nice shop - yarn and hand work. We stayed overnight with a Sivert cousin - the one that's married to Bernt Gyland. The next day we went to Rekefjord, intending to visit Marie Elle, a sister of Sophia Rodvelt and Tom and Conrad* (Tønneson), *but they were not home. She was in the hospital in Egersund last summer and sent word that she wanted to talk to me, but I couldn't get away then, as it was just when Grandpa was so bad. When I finally went to the hospital, she had gone home. She is OK now, I understand. I have not been to Nesvåg this summer, but Onkel Petter and Mandius Omdal Hausan were there about a month ago. They are all fine over there, you can greet Sina. Hilse Bertha.*

Love to All, Sophie

October 30, 1940 - Wednesday

I went downtown in the morning - I was not able to get any money. I wouldn't risk the chance of losing a check. I don't know what to do now for money. I guess I'll have to get a job.

Bergit was free in the afternoon. We went around the lake together. I took the 6:30 train home. Marit was on the train, and Petter came home from school on the same train.

October 31, 1940 - Thursday

Town was surely full of strangers. Most of the traffic is controlled by them. Hundreds of private cars and buses have been taken from Norwegian owners, repainted, and used by them *(Germans).* Terrible traffic. Hundreds, yes, thousands of Norwegian traitors are working on the flying fields at Sola and Forus. Steady traffic goes by Onkel Lars's every day hauling gravel.

I cleaned house while Thea baked, as tomorrow is Thanksgiving Day here. We are expecting Tantes Anne and Helene tomorrow.

Onkel Andreas is building a new house in Dalen - a sound investment.

November 1, 1940 - Friday

Today is Thanksgiving Day in Norway. They *(our company)* came on the noon train right after we had eaten dinner. They told about a Fru Hadland and daughter from Egersund who had been taken by Germans because they had helped two soldiers change clothes and flee. The same two soldiers later showed up as officers. They had only spied around to see what people would do in such a case. Now, the daughter and mother of three small children are sitting in prison in Stavanger. A Sandnes girl (a waitress in a restaurant) was taken and held several weeks for talking back. She was set free again yesterday.

I am surprised to see so many girls go out with strangers.

Sven *(Mauland)* came out and spent the weekend. The ladies went over to the old folks *(Thea's parents).* Marit, Magnhild and Jan Øvestad came over, so we kept the home fires burning.

November 2, 1940 - Saturday

Everyone slept late. After dinner, we all helped to thresh. The threshing machine was on the same order as at home, only much smaller. We were nine in the crew. We had it all done in three hours after which we all washed up, changed clothes and enjoyed a good meal.

Tante Helene "took the cake" in overalls!

In the evening, Henrik came over, as well as Olga and Marie. Everyone was in a fine mood and we surely raised cane. Not much dignity in any of us. At 11:00 Sven and Henne went over and got the radio/phonograph so we could hear the new records.

November 3, 1940 - Sunday

Everyone slept late. Helene and Sven left on the 1:30 train for town. After dinner, everyone enjoyed a quiet and peaceful afternoon. Alf came over and stayed until after the New York news.

We had a look at the parts of a wrecked German plane that Henrik Vagle *(brother of Thea)* had collected. I bummed a piece for a souvenir.

November 4, 1940 - Monday

I received letters from Mother, Bertha *(Omdal),* and Margery *(Peterson)* - all written in September - they were two months on the way.

Anne, Thea, and I went to Sandnes to shop and meet Helene. We were met at the station by Helene and Agnes (*Rotwell)*. We also saw Johanna Stapnes for a few minutes. We were invited up to Agnes's sister's for coffee and lunch. After lunch, we shopped. Shops closed at 4:00 after which we went up to Larsine and Jakob Sirevåg's for a short visit. We had coffee, of course, then took the 6:00 train from Sandnes. I got to talk to Martin *(Østrem)*. The train was packed, so we had to stand most of the way. No lights were used on the train - blackout everywhere.

November 5, 1940 - Tuesday

Today was election day in U.S.A. I am glad that Roosevelt was re-elected.

Anne and Helene took the morning train home.

I knitted all week on the tangerine jacket.

November 6, 1940 - Wednesday

On Saturday night at Sandnes, some drunken German soldiers clashed with some Norwegian boys on the street. A Norseman was critically injured. It was later learned that the guilty German soldier was shot to death for drawing his sword on the street. Poor fellow. Lars said the poor fellows looked very depressed in town.

November 7, 1940 - Thursday

There has been an awfully lot of flying and shooting from Sola, Forus, or the coast. On Tuesday we saw great dark clouds of smoke rising from the Forus flying field. We heard shooting, but we don't know what happened.

Two more transport ships are reported to have been sunk out of Stavanger this week, but it was not reported on the radio.

November 8, 1940 - Friday

Wood and clothes situation: Practically everything is rationed now. Can't buy a pair of shoes, socks or even a spool of thread unless it is OK'd by officers.

People stormed the stores the day before ration cards were required. Crazy people - some bought clothes two to three years in advance. Confirmation clothes were bought for kids who are only 10 years old now.

Meat is not rationed yet, but it may not be long.

The bread, coffee, sugar, and butter just reaches. No more nice cakes with our coffee. In fact, it is quite an extravagance to drink two cups of coffee or more than two each day. We have to get used to weak coffee.

November 9, 1940 - Saturday

It's been a long time since there was chocolate or cocoa to be had. It's lucky if we can buy a chocolate bar in town. There's hardly any candy to be had.

There is practically no food for cattle, pigs, or chickens. No one gets any eggs from their hens. Prices are held down to 50 cents a kilo (16 eggs). Many will have to quit selling milk this winter - no meal *(feed)* for milk production.

People are lucky who have their own butter, as all one can buy in the stores is margarine. Some butter is very poor - made from herring oil.

There would not be the great shortage of butter, meat (especially pork), canned goods, coffee, etc., if it were not that the strangers are continually taking it out of the country. Planes loaded with butter and pork have been found wrecked in Sweden and other parts of the country. Still, they deny that they take any food out of the country. Not only that, but think of the many thousands of soldiers here in the country who have to be fed.

Another disgusting fact is the thousands of Norsemen working on Sola, Forus and Sletta *(airfields)*. They get good pay, but it's simple for them *(the Germans)* to print illegal bills. The money is good if it is used right away or invested, but it will be worthless some day or as soon as they *(the Germans)* leave the country.

November 10, 1940 - Sunday

Nothing special - it rained and blew all day so fiercely that it was good to be indoors. All of the snow is gone today.

I got my jacket (orange one) finished and sewed together on Tuesday. I am very well pleased with it.

November 14, 1940 - Thursday

I biked to Sandnes to do a little shopping. Everything is being sold out rapidly. No more of the yarn Anne wanted or cloth. I must call her up and find out what she wants me to do. I got myself buttons and a belt for my jacket, also a girdle. I went up to Martha and Martin's, but they were not home.

In the evening at 9:30, an English plane flew over Sola. Bombs were dropped, but no damage was done. All search lights were in full activity. Anti-aircraft guns also were in operation - just like 4th of July fireworks.

November 15, 1940 - Friday

I knitted new thumbs in Onkel's old Selbu mittens and did other knitting.

In the evening, fireworks began over Sola. It started about 9:00 and lasted an hour or so. Very violent explosions were heard, and fire was seen from them. It lit up the whole countryside. The many search lights, operating from the various directions, reminded me very much of the Northern Lights. Bombs were dropped on Sola, and cannons from English warships were shot; flashing and lighting up the airport, so the plane could see where to drop the bomb. One gas tank was set on fire.

When English planes flew over, they could be distinguished by the sound of the engines. Shots were fired right over the house, so splinters of shells from cannon were found all around the country as far as Bryne. At Time, a bomb fell on a barn, demolishing and killing cattle.

November 16, 1940 - Saturday

I cleaned house for Tante Thea. She baked bread and two cakes - one to take to Heiå tonight. I knitted the front pieces to Tante Anne's sweater. In the evening, we all went over to the old folks' where we sat until almost 12:00. At home, we cooked coffee and fooled around until about 1:00 before going to bed.

Many Red Cross planes were seen later flying to the scene.

At 11:00 this a.m. we heard a terrible explosion which shook the house. It was later learned that a German ship had been sunk by an English torpedo. It must have been awfully close to land, judging from the force of the explosion.

November 17, 1940 - Sunday

I slept until 10:00. After breakfast, Sven and Kristoffer came over, but I had to get ready to go to Sandnes, as I was invited to Martin and Martha Østrem's for dinner.

We had a lovely dinner and a very enjoyable day. Their son, Arvid, is 13 years old and a very handsome little fellow. They had to sit in an air raid shelter Friday night during the English air raid over Sola. They told how they *(Germans)* managed to get away with Norse food, and about the air raid alarm in Stavanger. One fellow thought there was something fishy about it as he heard no planes. He watched them load pork and butter onto the planes. When all of the loading was done, the "danger is passed" signal was given.

November 18, 1940 - Monday

The dressmaker came today. She sewed four dresses for Tante and a slip. I sat all three days, helping her with basting, hemming, snaps, etc. We worked three full days. I also sewed two shirts for Lars.

November 22, 1940 - Friday

The weather was beautiful today, so I decided to take the noon train to town. I had to wait for the train, so I talked with Martin Østrem who happened to be on duty there for that week. English planes have been over Egersund this morning; they bombed Slettebø. One of the barracks shattered, horse stables were wrecked, and 75 horses were killed. Many windows in Vigrestad were shattered from the pressure of bombs dropped nearby. No other damage at Vigrestad. The Germans blamed the Egersund people for being too careless about blackouts in the morning hours. For punishment, Egersunders must be in off of ruts *(off the roads)* at 8:00 p.m., do proper blackout, etc.

I got to town about 2:00 and went straight to the hotel for dinner. Anna was free for the p.m., but tired, so she rested in the afternoon. Bergit was on duty, so I went uptown and looked up Johanna Stapnes at the weaving school and spent the afternoon with her. When she was through with school, we walked to her apartment. On the way, we saw the schoolhouse which was wrecked by a fallen plane and afterwards was burned down on one of the first days of the war. Two or three dwelling houses were also completely demolished. I had coffee with her and saw all the lovely things she had woven at school. I decided to go to Peder Johan Omdal's in the evening. I stopped in at the hotel, so they wouldn't wait for me. Peder Johan had just come back from Omdal where he reported a big project is in operation at Stapnes. Five families have had to move away to make room for Germans who are building a fort with many barracks, eighteen new roads, etc. on the Stapnes village by the sea. Erling Omdal and Mandius Omdal are on payroll. Gabriel was forced to work for them against his own will.

I had coffee and lunch and spent the evening knitting. Ingrid's friend took me home. Jan took Johanna, as it is far from safe after dark in town.

November 24, 1940 - Saturday

Bergit and I went to the Maulands for the afternoon. Sven was home until evening, when he had to leave for Bryne to attend dinner at his cousin's. It rained all day. We had a very cozy time. Andreas drove us home. It is very difficult driving in black streets, blacked lights, etc. Bergit was very favorably impressed. She enjoyed the evening very much.

On Sunday morning I went to church with Bergliot Omdal. On the way home we went out to the cemetery where German soldiers are buried. There were several large trench graves where goodness knows how many are buried. I went home with her to dinner and to church again in the evening from which they took me home.

In the evenings at the hotel, we were always royally entertained by Frets. Such an interesting chap - a mason who works at the Sola airport.

November 30, 1940 - Saturday

I cleaned house in the a.m. Tante Thea baked bread. Petter brought his friend home from school. He is Thor Hunsbeth from Fjotland. He knows my cousins over there. Nice fellow, about as big as Petter is.

I baked waffles in the afternoon. In the evening, the boys went to a dance. We three older ones went over to Arnfin's for the evening. We had a swell lunch and øl *(beer)* for those who liked it. Got home at 2:00. Thea and I had coffee before going to bed, so I didn't retire until 3:00. However, I lay awake until 4:30.

December 1, 1940 - Sunday

Slept until 10:45. I started to write letters, but Henrik Vagle, Jr. and Sven came over. After dinner, there was a lot of cutting up. After coffee, all the boys went to Sandnes to a show.

Sven and I went over to see if Marit had come home; she was not home. We stayed awhile; it was raining so hard, I had to borrow a southwestern *(umbrella).* We had a good chance to talk. He gave me a little flashlight. It will be quite useful these dark days and nights. I didn't go back to town until the next morning.

December 2, 1940 - Monday

We all went to Sandnes where I got myself some rubber boots. The price was 14.60 kroner. Tante Thea bought me some yarn - five bunts. I shall use it for a sweater for Mother. She bought three kilograms altogether for a sweater for herself, socks, etc. Thor *Hunsbeth* went home today.

December 3, 1940 - Tuesday

I knit one arm for Henne's sweater. Bestemor Vagle came over for the afternoon.

December 4, 1940 - Wednesday

I took the noon train to Nærbø. English planes are over Sola, and there was shooting all morning. Marta and Thorvald *(Østrem)* had not received my letter, so the family was surprised to see me. They were in the midst of baking flatbread. Thorvald came home the next day from duty. He works at Opstad Forced Labor Institution. They have a lovely new home rented, but as soon as there is a vacancy, they will move to Opstad where they will get practically free rent. It is a good job.

Baked lefse and kråtekake *(a flatbread)*. Martha's mother, Ingeborg Ramsland, was there to stay over for the Christmas holidays.

December 7, 1940 - Saturday

Martha and I went to the bazaar. We met Olav (*Østrem*), Martin Gya, and Fredrik (*Østrem*). All three are carpenters at Nærbø. Swell kids, all three. Nobody won anything except Fredrik - an apron.

December 8, 1940 - Sunday

After dinner, Thorvald and I biked to Opstad. I took a snap of the place. I saw the site that was set up for cannons when the war first broke out. The cannons have been removed now. Prisoners were sentenced to hard labor. We went through the cow barn - 300 cows were being milked. The buildings were camouflaged in grey, green and black colors. We visited the school - much free-hand coloring and drawing. A moving picture machine was used in study.

He *(Thorvald)* has thirteen men (prisoners) in his charge - the carpenter group. All repairs are done by them. There is an electrical department, an agriculture department, shoe making, toy making, furniture department, tailoring department as well as those (*workers*) needed in daily living such as laundry, etc.

We came back home just before dark - there was a cold frost. Fredrik came over for the evening. Monday night we went up to the bachelors' place and listened to New York *(news)*. I stayed until Wednesday. Marta and her young daughter, Bjørg, went to the station with me.

December 11, 1940 - Wednesday

Got to Ganddalen and found the house empty. Tante Thea had gone to town to be with Olga who is seriously ill with blood poisoning at Rogaland Hospital. She had been in town since Monday. Olga's case was believed to be hopeless, but Friday when I left, they had rung Vagle, and it was reported that the doctor had now said there was hope for her recovery.

Borrowed 100 kroner from Onkel Lars.

December 13, 1940 - Friday

I took the 9:40 train from Ganddalen. Henne helped me with my bags. I got to Egersund about noon and carried my bags up to Mathilde's. Josephine *(Mathilde's mother)* asked me into coffee which I did.

I stayed at Sille's and Tollef's. *(They)* were over to Tante Elisabeth's in the p.m. I met Kristian at Mathilde's and went for a walk clear out past Lygre. Beautiful moonlit night - back by 10:00.

December 14, 1940 - Saturday

Biked home. It has been two months now since I was at Grødem. When I got there, Anna Ålvik and Tante Helene were baking flatbread. Jakob Stapnes had moved furniture up to our place, so my room was packed with junk. Everyone pitched in and moved it upstairs. They stayed overnight and left Sunday morning.

All the next week, the week before Christmas, we worked like slaves to get things ready for the holidays. We cleaned the kitchen and front room, taking one day at each. We baked bread, cookies, and coffee bread one day. I washed clothes another day and baked flatbread, lefse, kråtekake, and potato cakes until midnight. Went to town one day to get pass in order.

December 15, 1940, Sunday – Grødem, Egersund

Dear Mother, Father and All,

This time I am going to write in Norwegian. I will see if I can manage to write a letter to Theodora today also. Thanks for the letters I have received so far - I got the Christmas card yesterday. I have been lazy about corresponding, but I have traveled for seven weeks and when you are traveling like that it is hard to get a quiet time to write.

Today Anne and Gjertine walked to Stapnes to visit Marta and Nils, but I had decided that I was going to write no matter what. A while ago, they said that those over there would come here this afternoon, so I am thinking that I need to hurry up and write as much as possible before they come. Poor Kjellaug Lædre, a little girl that is only four years old - she has a plaster cast from under her arms and all the way down to her ankles, and she must keep it on for a whole year. She has already been lying down for three months, the reason is that one of her hips is out of joint.

I came back from Vagle yesterday, and I sure had a lot of fun there. We went twice to Stavanger, and the last time I stayed there an entire week. I stayed with Anna and Bergit at the hotel, and several times I visited with Peder Johan over dinner. It was three weeks ago today. I went to church with them, and later I went with them to a meeting in the evening, and they walked me to the hotel afterwards. It is not safe to walk the streets at night since everything is blacked out - and there are a lot of untrusting strangers. One of Lars Stapnes's daughters, Johanna, is there at a weaving school, and I visited her several times. Right now, she is back home, and she has promised to come to Grødem and teach me how to weave. That will be fun. I have visited the Mauland family several times. Since Anna and Bergit have every 2nd afternoon off at the hotel, we have a lot of time together. Bergit is engaged to Alf Skåra of Egersund, and he has a barber shop store in Flekkefjord. Anna is an old maid like me, 'ha, ha'. She says she wants to come with me to the U.S.A., but I don't think her mother will let her go. I did not like Stavanger this time - it is too unsettled.

One Sunday I ate dinner at Martin and Martha Østrem's home, and he asked me to greet you all and send a special greeting to Martin since he shares the same name. They have one child, a 13-year-old boy, Arvid. Martin is really busy at the railroad station; there is a lot of extra work now. They are doing well and also the Peder Johan family. Einar is working at the Stavanger station now.

I stayed a week with Thorvald Østrem at Nærbø. They have two cute little girls; Bjørg is three years old and Aslaug is one year old. They are living well (solid work). *When I visited there, I saw Fredrik Østrem and Martin Gya almost every day. The two of them are building a house close to Thorvald's place - they are great carpenters. Semine's son Olav is also a carpenter at Nærbø, but he makes windows and doors, etc. None of them are married - nice guys. Next week, Fredrik and Martin are starting to build another house in Egersund, and when that is finished, they are building a new house for Onkel Andreas and Tante Berthe in the valley. It is smart for the ones who have something to put their money into something solid. Sigurd Østrem is doing really well - he owns two large passenger buses and a truck that is in route all the time.*

Everything is so expensive now, and you need a ration card for everything - food and clothing. It will be a strange Christmas. No fruit, nuts, candy, sugar, or flour to bake Christmas cookies or lefse with. We have to be happy with food made out of stone ground flour and it is not so great with the coffee supply either. It is worse for the older people that are used to having more coffee. I will be OK - there is a lot to do, and there are so many other things to think about.

Gudrun and Astrid in Egelandsdal are going to have a double wedding. The wedding will be at the Grand Hotel in Egersund on New Year's Eve. It is too hard to have the wedding at home because of all the rationing, and also you would need a large house. Gudrun called and asked for me when I was visiting Onkel Lars. I assume I will be invited to the affair - it is going to be grand.

I received a letter from Semine's daughter, Margrethe, and they say they expect me there for Christmas. I don't know what I should do about that, because Anne thinks I should stay here. I will see.

Tante Valborg and Little Valborg have been to Lindeland to visit Ingrid. They (Ingrid and Torvald) *are expecting their third child.*

It is sad to hear that Martin is not feeling well. I think he looked very thin on the picture that I got from Margaret - you'll have to greet them from me. I hope he will feel better soon. I also received a letter from Margery and Peter - it was a surprise to get a letter from her. It was very nice to get a letter with pictures from Tora and Theodora a short time ago. It was so nice to see the small ones, how they are growing, and it was so fun to see the new children that Tora and Sig are adopting.

Weren't you surprised when Theodora called your home from New York? It sounds like they had a very interesting trip. Thank you for greeting Mrs. Olsen and Mrs. Wold. You can tell them that I live well, and I am healthy. It is very interesting to be here at these times, and I will have much to tell you when I finally come home. You won't believe, we see all kinds of things - but I have to say we haven't suffered any. We get a lot of good food - well you know it's not so many different kinds, but it's a lot of what we have, and we have enough of meat, potatoes, and fish. We canned a lot of fruit this summer, so we are managing. We will not at all starve this winter, and when summer comes, it will be better with the food again.

So, you have gotten a sidewalk around the house; it would be great to have been there to see. It is probably pretty there now. I have been very calm and have no fear - thank you for your prayers. I can feel that you are thinking of me a lot and pray for us.

I just talked to Berntine Skadberg. She had received Aunt Ellen's letter this morning.

Heartfelt Greetings, Sophie

December 15, 1940 - Grødem, Egersund

Dear Theodora, Chris, and David,

Thanks for your letter and snapshots; I received them about two weeks ago. The pictures were really very good. David is growing up so fast. His baby days will be over when I eventually get home. Not very bright prospects for me! I'm missing out on the fun of knowing the kids just when they're the cutest.

Your trip certainly sounded most interesting, and I can

imagine your surprise when you got the lucky number at the fair. I bet you were excited; I know I would have been. I wrote a letter home this afternoon in Norse and thought I'd get one off to you today too, but I just barely finished the first one when company came. They just left a little bit ago, so I started this, and just now another lady came in. She and Anne are gabbing, so I can hardly keep my mind on this.

I'm sorry to hear that Martin (Peterson) *was not so well. I hope he will soon be OK again. Was it from overstrain or overwork? He's just too ambitious.*

As I said in the folks' letter, I just got back last night after being away seven weeks. The time went so fast. I had such an enjoyable time. I spent a week with Anna and Bergit in Stavanger, and a week with the Thorvald Østrem's at Nærbø. He has two darling girls ages three and one. You remember he was home in America, about ten or eleven years ago. He has a job as a guard, I suppose you would call it, at a State Prison (not a Nazi prison). He took me there last Sunday to look around. Prisoners are sentenced to hard labor. We went through their barn with 300 cows at milking time.

A week ago, from Nærbø, I saw an air battle or part of it. They disappeared in the clouds. But when Thorvald came home, he had seen the whole thing. One plane took fire and fell into the sea. Another plane was shot down at the same time, but he saw only the one. One night at Onkel Lars's, we watched an air raid over an airport. You should have seen the fireworks - just like the 4th of July. The many searchlights lit up the whole sky like the Northern Lights almost. We were about ten miles from the scene, but people in nearby towns took to air-raid shelters or basements. There are very few of those in the country, but everyone in towns has their assigned air-raid shelters, in case. But we have to "black out" houses and everything, country and towns alike, and the days are so short now anyway. We are still on Daylight Savings so we can't roll up (blinds) *until 10:00 or 10:30 in the mornings. Streets in town are awfully dark at night. We've gotten used to all this long ago. There are a lot of other things that aren't so pleasant, but we have to take it.*

I had a little difficulty getting traveler's checks cashed in Stavanger. I found out I could get money sent by telegraph, *so I shall save the last 100 bucks in traveler's checks until later and write Yvonne to send me $50., as that is all I can get at a time. I've told her not to send any until I ask for it, and it's pretty nice to have it coming now. For each dollar by telegraph, I get 4.85 kroner.*

I forgot to thank Dad for paying my life insurance or taking out Health and Accident Insurance for me. I surely didn't expect him to do the latter; however, it is a fine security.

You'll have to write and tell all about your Christmas holidays, etc. There isn't much to look forward to here. NO Christmas goodies, no fruit except apples and a few oranges. Apples cost in American money from 10 to 17 cents apiece, and oranges about 20 cents apiece. Who can afford that? Well, just the same, I must say it is interesting to experience these things. We have not really suffered any hardships yet around here. The coffee supply is getting low. As well as I like coffee - you know me - I could give that up easily. But I do feel sorry for the many old folks who are used to coffee many times a day. They are the ones who will feel it. Of course, there is a shortage of tobacco, etc. also, which is both good and bad. I say bad for those old fellows who have had the habit all their lives. I had better change the subject; maybe this letter won't pass inspection.

I haven't had a personal invitation yet, but I understand I'm invited to a double wedding. Astrid and Gudrun Egelandsdal are getting married New Year's Eve. The ceremony will take place in the church in Egersund with dinner and reception at the Grand Hotel. Sounds like it's going to be a grand affair. I'm glad I have that long dress I got in New York after all.

You all will think me terrible for not sending Christmas cards or greetings, but I just haven't had the real Christmas spirit. I do hope you all have had a Blessed Christmas, and may the New Year bring you all the best of health and happiness.

Here it is 11:30, the lady has gone home, and Tante Anne has fallen asleep on the divan. Petter and the dog have gone to sleep too.

Love to All, Sophie

P.S. I am mailing yours and the folks' letters together. Let me know how long they take getting there. The Christmas card I got from Mother last night was about a month on the way.

December 22, 1940 - Sunday

Things are going top speed at Stapnes. *(The Germans)* are building a fort on Lars Martinson's farm. There are about 300 workers. Erling Omdal and Mandius Omdal are on the payroll. Five farms are being ruined. They haul crushed rock to fill in hollows. They are building many roads and a hospital. Three cannons have been put up and seven barracks. The English have been over and photographed. They flew over low, Kristine Stapnes said. Most farmers have moved home furnishings to be ready when Germans take things over, as they expect they will one of these days. They have taken over several whole houses while they occupy only parts of several others. They have built bunks up around walls so as to accommodate as large a number as possible.

The German Sending Station is at Stapnes. They say they speak to occupants of planes as they fly over.

December 26, 1940 - Årrestad, Helleland

Dear Folks,

It is only a short time since I last wrote, but I got to thinking I perhaps said too much, and the letter never reached you, or did it? Yesterday was Christmas Day. As you see, I am here at Årrestad. I had almost decided to stay at Grødem over Christmas, but "I simply had to come up here", they wrote from here and Dybing, so I spent the week before Christmas at home, and helped Anne bake and clean house before I left. Anne and Petter were going to Rodvelt Christmas Eve and staying Christmas Day.

Torger (of Tante Semine) *promised me last fall that he'd sell me a silver fox very reasonable. He wrote and said it was ready now, and I must come and look at it, and if I didn't want it, he would sell it to someone else. Prices have gone up this year, and he did very well on all he sold. He saved the best one for me, and in spite of the fact he had been offered 300 kroner* ($75) *for it by another party, he said he'd keep his word - I was to get it for 70 kroner* ($17.50) *or the cost of raising the animal. I thought it was too good a chance to pass up, so the deal was made. Well, this was the day I came, and when Christmas Eve came, and they were passing out packages, I, of course, expected nothing, as I had given nothing, and to my surprise, I get a big package, and what do you suppose it was? Yes - the silver fox fur. To say I was surprised is putting it mildly! I'm still pinching myself to make sure I'm not dreaming. It really is a beauty. In fact, it is the prettiest one I've seen. From Tante and Onkel I got a "Sang boken"* (song book).

Tonight, there is a fest in the Bedehus (prayer house). *I expect they will be there from Dybing, so then I shall go home with Amanda and Tyra to spend a few days there.*

New Year's Eve is Gudrun and Astrid Egelandsdal's double weddings. The ceremony will take place in the church at 5:00 in the afternoon, followed by a reception and dinner at the Grand Hotel in Egersund. There are to be only about forty guests. Monday, in town, I met Mikal Egelandsdal's wife. You know, she has been sick quite a while with TB. She was looking well when I met her in the morning, but about noon I could see she was awfully tired, so she isn't very strong. She didn't think she could go to the wedding. We had lots of time, so we went into a place and had coffee and lunch and talked. I had seen her only the one time before. I also met Agnes, Onkel Karl's youngest daughter, for the first time. She is the prettiest of all the girls, and they are all pretty. Now I have Ingrid at Lindeland left to meet. Tante Valborg has been up there with her awhile. They got an addition to the family a couple weeks ago. Now she has two boys and a girl.

Christmas Day was very quiet here, as is today also. The kids are all home here for the vacation except the three who are married. Torger and Malene live so near, they are in and out many times each day. They are expecting the stork, and they want me to stay with them until she is able to do her work again. This is their first. We are quite worried about her, as she is not very strong. We hope it will go well.

Well - now what did you folks do over the Christmas holidays? I suppose everyone was home Christmas Day. We have a little snow but not enough to ski on. We have had a cold spell, excellent for skating.

Continued the next day - Dec. 27

Sanna, Olav, and I are going over to Dybing today. We were at the "Fest" last night. There were some of Tante Teoline's boys there and some of Tante Berthe's. It was a really nice party, almost only youth, and many of them preached and spoke. Mikael of Tante Semine was one of the speakers. They all are great, and all of them Christians except two of the boys.

The family here tells me to send their greetings. I guess I forgot that Thorvald asked me to greet you also. He still uses the silk scarf you gave him for Christmas when he was over there (visiting in America).

So many of my cousins work at the railroad. Everybody here does (at Semine's), *except one who is a carpenter, and Trond Magne, who is still too young. Three of Tante Teoline's are at the railroad, Mikael of Tante Valborg, two of Tante Berthe's and one of Onkel Karl. They make good money. They are working at 'Sørlandsbanen'* (railroad between Stavanger and Oslo) *which is expected to be done in a couple of years from now. The rails are wider, more like the American railroad. The small trains are very slow.*

I read in your Christmas card that you are worried about if I received your letters. I believe I have received them all by now, they just take a while to get here. Everybody is fine and live well over here. We cannot complain, except for those in Stapnes who had to leave their homes; they have to find strength. I have noticed that in spite of it all, there will be a Christmas tree festivity in Stapnes.

Better stop now. Live well and greet everybody! Special greetings to Aunt Ellen and Uncle Peder.

Heartfelt Greetings, Sophie

P.S. It surely was nice to hear you have fixed up and made a cement walk around the house. It is nice with the white fence, I noticed on the picture. I hope Martin is much better. Hello to him and Margaret.

1941

Thriving Well Despite the Rationing
A Long Winter in 1941
Bicycle Trip and Mountain Travel
U.S.A. Enters War with Japan
Sophie Misses Contact from Home

January 23, 1941 - Årrestad

Dear Theodora and Chris,

Thanks for the letters and Christmas card. It was fun hearing from you, too, Chris. Most of the Christmas mail came last week and this week. Mother's card and letter was the only one that came before Christmas. I was beginning to think everyone had clean forgotten me, but it is just that it takes them so long to get here. You asked if I had received your last letter. If you mean the one with the three snaps of David, I did. I have more fun showing off David and Torvald Sigmund (Siggy). *I ask them if they want to see a picture of my sweetheart. When they see David and Siggy, they quite agree they are some sweethearts.*

I surely was let down when I got Margaret's letter telling about Martin. I felt better, however, after reading your letter, and I surely hope he will recover. I had never dreamed anything like that would strike in our family. I hope you write often so I can hear how he's getting along. Does he have health insurance, or how are expenses going to be met?

How is the weather over there? We're having a beastly cold winter. Last winter, everyone said it was the worst in ages, but I believe it is just as cold this year. There has been snow and frost since before Christmas. We had a swell time skiing awhile, but last week it was so stormy, all the snow is blown up into drifts. It is snowing again now, so it will soon be swell going again.

Continued on February 2, 1941

It has been quite a while since I started this, but the stork paid a visit here and it's been a pretty busy place. You see, I came up to Helleland, Årrestad, before Christmas, and this cousin of ours, Torger Østrem and his wife, Malene, were expecting, so they asked if I could stay and help, and of course I promised. This is their first child, Ove, - a boy. They are sitting pretty; he has a swell job with the Railroad. Right now, he's supervising the building of a tunnel for the new Southern Railway (Sørlandsbanen). We can see the tunnel from the house. He has 130 men working under him on the new stretch from Helleland to Ualand. (Mother knows where that is.) They have a darling house, so it is fun doing the housework. She has a woman who does nothing but take care of her and the baby and washes the baby clothes, so I really have it quite easy. I build the fire in the morning and make Torger's breakfast and put up his lunch. Then I have dinner ready when he comes home about 5:00 in the evening. It was Torger who gave me the silver fox fur for Christmas. It is in Stavanger now, being finished - you know - tanned and trimmed up. He gave his wife one too.

By the way, you asked if you should send those magazines. No; don't do it - I don't think they'll come through - I've gotten so I read the Norwegian magazines without any effort anymore. Funny, isn't it? Before, I couldn't sit down and read Norse, but it's all very natural now.

I have been wondering what you all did Christmas. I had a letter from Alma H. (Hood) *the other day. She says there is so much flu around there. There are an awfully lot of influenza cases around here too. They are really quite sick with it, too. There have been several deaths in this vicinity. One surely has to be careful when one gets a cold. I have certainly been lucky. I haven't had a cold this winter, but you should see how warmly I dress. It's been down to -20 degrees Celsius. I don't know how much that is in Fahrenheit, but I believe it's below zero. It has stayed about the same now since before Christmas - lots of snow. There's a swell hill right below the house. The snow goes right over the fence.*

We have new clothes-rationing cards. One can't buy very much on them in a year. People can't just go and buy what they want any more. It's what you need, not what you want. Women are going back to the spinning wheel. Many women spin their own wool and knit many of their clothes.

I was to the double wedding of Astrid (with Gjert Skadberg) *and Gudrun* (with Karl Thorsen) *on New Year's Eve. Both of their husband's families were from town, and since its quite impossible to get cars, they had the wedding at the hotel. It was a nice wedding and reception which consisted of dinner for the forty guests. Gudrun's husband is quite musical as are two of his friends, so they had violin and piano music and group singing and humorous readings. At about 10:00 we had coffee, cake, and cookies, and at 1:00 they served fancy sandwiches and tea. Everyone went home around*

2:00. I stayed overnight in town with Berntine Skadberg, Aunt Ellen's sister. She was at the wedding too, as Berntine is Gjert's (Astrid's husband's) *aunt. Gjert is a farmer, and Karl (Karlemann) works at the Egersund Fayancefabriks Co. The latter have a darling apartment. Their furniture, bedroom, and living room is of this really light wood. Gudrun quit her job at the factory. For a table partner, I had Karleman's brother, Arvid Thorsen, who has been in the U.S.A. for ten years. He came home for a visit about two years ago and can't get back again. We had to try out our English to see if we had forgotten it or not.*

Well, I surely hope Martin is getting better, and all the rest of you are well. Do write as often as you can. I had an interesting letter from Agnes Benson the other day, and I had three more Christmas cards and letters this last week.

Love to all, Sophie.

P.S. I heard Pearl (Urmey) *Flowers was expecting and Ruth Bradley is engaged.*

I hear we can't send pictures in our letters anymore. I wonder if that's true.

February 2, 1941 - Årrestad

Dear Mother and Father and All at Home!

I have just finished a letter to Theodora. I think it has been a long time since I've written to you as well. I guess I lost interest in this letter writing and am getting more and more lazy, I think.

How are you all at home? It was very sad to hear about Martin, and I understand that you knew already when you wrote me before Christmas, but you did not want to tell me. I learned about it when Margaret wrote to me, and when Theodora wrote, she said he was feeling better. I really hope that he will be well again. Is he still home, or is he at the sanitarium?

I'm still here at Torger Østrem's. They had a little boy on January 25th - it was their first. Bertha and her two children, Svein and Liv, were here with food - 'fløtekake' (cream cake - white cake with several layers of cream). *There have been several visitors here already with 'sviskegrøt'* (prune porridge). *Aunt Semine is much better than last year, strong and healthy;*

and Uncle Ommond is also okay as far as we can see, but he is still on a diet. It is very busy at the Railroad now - there are so many new workers on the tracks. Both Mikael here, and Martin Dybing have become railroad superintendents/ caretakers.

Two weeks ago, Semine, Ommund, Torger, and I visited Gya. It is probably the last car trip we will have this winter, as the road will be closed because of snow. Aunt Valborg looked so good, and she is quick as a girl and in a very good mood. She had received a letter from Lisabeth Halvorson (in Canada). Lisabeth had mailed it to Montana to a brother of her husband Ted's, who had mailed it on.

I got a little bit off the lines here; it is so dark I couldn't see the lines - now I have lit the lamp. They do not have electricity here. Uncle Johan Gystøl is so much better than last time - he says he has been carding wool every day, but Teoline won't give him anything for it, 'ha, ha'. Both Tyra and Amanda are home. Martin and Gunder have been sick with influenza but have now started work again. Someone is sick in almost every house. I have been so lucky, I haven't even had a cold - I must have a strong immune system, nothing is affecting me. We have had a terribly cold winter this year; the water pipes froze a long time ago.

I haven't been to Grødem since before Christmas. I was thinking of going there last Saturday, but Malene did not feel so well in the morning, so I didn't dare leave. That same afternoon, she had the baby boy whom they named Ove. Everything is well, and Tante Semine comes over every day.

How is your asthma this winter? I hope you do not take any trips this year. I heard that you went to Clara Rodvelt's wedding to Robert Elde, and I assume that it was grand.

It is so popular to spin now, and that is good, since we cannot get more clothing on the rationing card. There is not so much you can get in clothing on the card anyway. I bought a lot of yarn before the rationing, but I wish I had bought more. The wool that we receive now is mixed with rags and is pretty bad. Petter and Anne have wool from last spring, so that is great, and I have enough yarn to make socks for the boys and for Father, Sigurd Freestad, *and Chris* Hansen, *and wool yarn for sweaters for Father and Mother. Aunt Anne saved me some yarn for Father's sweater* (for me to make) *and the yarn for your sweater, Mother, I got from Uncle Lars. I have not started any of them yet. There is so much to knit, that I am not going to run out of work for a while. I knitted a cardigan for both Anne and Uncle Petter before Christmas, and I made myself a sweater vest after Christmas.*

What are you working with at home? I heard that you had a freeze, and cold weather also. How is Tora and her children? She is probably very busy now.

I still get Christmas cards; I received one the other day. Tell Bertha Omdal thank you for her card and for what she wrote. She is probably as busy as she was last year with schoolwork and other. There is a different pace here - everything moves along slowly. I can tell you that the teachers are doing much better here in Norway . They decide themselves what to do and should not be blamed for working too hard, some of them. They go home at about 2:00 or 3:00, same as the children.

I often think of Martin and how long he has to be bedridden, but I guess that doesn't matter, if he can just get well. You must write often, so that I can hear how he is doing. Do you know what? I think it hit him while he was in California gold mining. He really hasn't been in great shape after he came home from there, and he has been skinny for such a long time. We all must pray that he will be well again.

Torger asks who I am writing to. He is telling me to greet you all. He is so bad with teasing and playing around - we are pretty bad at fighting, but you know, it's just for fun. His wife is from Bryne. I better stop scribbling. Say hello to everybody everywhere.

Heartfelt Greetings, Sophie

March 9, 1941 - Gya

Dear Mother, Dad, and All,

I received your letter dated February 4 last night. I am here at Tante Valborg's now. I came up a week ago. I'll probably be here a week longer before going up to Egelandsdal. I haven't been up there for over a year.

It was interesting to hear the news from over there. I was glad to hear Martin is looking well and eats well. I surely hope he will soon begin to show improvement.

I had been at Torger and Malene's at Årrestad until last Saturday. I was there a month before the baby came (Ove) *and a month after, so she should be able to do her own work now. Everyone at Årrestad is well. Mikael is engaged to a girl from Ramsland, Minnie, a sister of Thorvald Ostrem's wife, Marta* (Ramsland). *Also, Olav is engaged to a girl at Nærbø, Berta. Olav has just quit his carpenter job, as he got a job with the Railroad. He looks after the engines, greases them, etc. Torger, Olav, and Mikael have just bought a farm up from Årrestad.*

Continuation of letter on March 24, 1941 – Egelandsdal

It's been a long time since I started this letter. I was in Gya two weeks and have been here at Egelandsdal over a week. I am going back down to Gya today and take the bus to town tomorrow. Everyone at Gya is just fine. Tante Valborg sits and cards wool and spins all day. She got a new spinning wheel. Olga and little Valborg have also learned to spin, and believe it or not, I learned myself. I carded and spun wool for a pair of half socks. Of course, it is pretty thick, but when I get to Grødem, I am going to practice more. It was lots of fun. Now, since everything is rationed, everybody who has wool is beginning to spin again, just like in the olden days.

I have done a lot of skiing this winter, as there is lots of snow. At Gya, we went out awhile every day. Here at Egelandsdal, we've gone on some long trips, but not so often. One day, Tyra and I took a trip (I guess I had better write in Norwegian).

We walked up the steep hill behind the house of the farm of Ole (Bakke), *across the first lake, then down the valley towards Hommet. We returned down to the track on the right side of the large mountain behind the house* (of Uncle Karl). *It was a nice trip. We also had a nice ski trip yesterday. It was the four of us - Tyra, Gudrun, Ingfrid Larsen,* (sister of Gudrun's husband), *and me. On this trip, we went up on the other side of the main road in the valley that Uncle Karl owns* (Joheie). *We skied across several frozen lakes and to a place that had great viewing points. From there we could see all the way to Eik and also to the lake that is located on this side of Moi.*

When we looked down in that direction, there was a deep valley, and we could see four to five farms. On our way back home, we went by Aasen. The trip took about 5 ½ hours. It was very fun skiing up and down hills and over frozen lakes and valleys. I am very brown (tan).

There is an evangelist, Meland, holding meetings here this week. They had a meeting yesterday, but I couldn't go, as I came up from Gya on skis and didn't have any other clothes.

Everybody is doing well here in Egelandsdal. Tyra's little girl, Kirsten, is almost four years old. Agnes is home recuperating from bladder trouble. She was in the hospital awhile and has to be very careful with herself from now on.

The skiing traffic has begun. They are going to have twenty skiers here over Easter. They want me to come up again then, but I've been away so long now, that I expect to be back at Grødem by Easter. By that time, I will have been gone from Grødem almost a half year (not counting the one week just before Christmas).

I got Theodora's letter the other day. I was surely glad to hear that Martin is improving. I hope he continues to get well.

How is Dan Rasar? I hope he is well again now.

You can greet Agnes Benson and Thelma Haaland and tell them I have received their letters and that I will answer soon.

I keep forgetting myself and write in Norwegian. I have so many letters to answer; I just have to get busy soon. It isn't so convenient to write when you travel around so much and get no privacy.

I was so surprised to hear that Pastor Lauritz and Mrs. (Valborg) *Rasmussen were leaving. What does he plan to do now?*

Mr. Torkel Mikkelsen (shoemaker) *died, that is Andrew Thompson's dad. It was heart failure. It was March 13th he died. There was an air raid alarm in town. He had gone to bed and had slept. The heart attack came while he was on the way down to the basement to shelter.*

Onkel Karl is working on the road. It surely is a job keeping the road open these winter days. It is almost impossible for traffic to pass.

I am going to spend a couple weeks now at Helleland and Dybing, and then I'm through gadding for a while, I think.

I am going to Haugesund and will take a trip to Eiesland, Kristiansand, Mandal, and those places sometime this summer.

Uncle Andreas' house (in Dalen) *is almost finished now, but they aren't moving in until this summer. They are going to rent the old house out.*

I'm supposed to greet you all so very much from Tante Valborg, Onkel Karl and Tante Anna. Tante Valborg spun some light gray, pretty yarn for me. I think I shall knit me a little vest out of it.

Well, tell everyone hello from me. I am still thriving well in spite of the pesky rationing. I am going to walk to Gya this afternoon; I could have taken the bus this morning but thought the walk would do me good. I could ski down, but the road is so icy, it is just as well to walk. I am leaving my skis up here until next winter.

Special greetings to Martin and Margaret. I hope you can read this mixture.

Love to all, Sophie

March 30, 1941 - Helleland

Dear Theodora,

Thanks for your most welcome letters. I surely was glad to hear that Martin is improving so satisfactorily. That, I'm sure, puts everyone in a much better mood.

Just think, here it is almost April, and it is still severe winter. The ground has been white since early December, and we had another heavy snowstorm just the other day. The only sign of spring is that the days are longer. Lakes, creeks, rivers, etc. are still frozen. Everybody's faucets are still frozen, so we are growing tired of winter and hope there will soon be a change in the weather. I have even had enough skiing this winter.

I haven't been at Grødem all winter. Egelandsdal and Gya lie quite far up the valley, so snow lies almost even with the fence posts there yet. I just came down from Egelandsdal this week. We had some interesting ski trips up there. We went way back in the mountains. It was up and down hills, over fences, creeks, lakes, and everything. Boy, was it good to come home after those runs and sit down to a good dinner.

I'm here at Østrem's - Aunt Berthe's. Fredrik and I have just come from the "Dalen" as they call it, where they have just

Aunt Berthe spinning wool yarn

built a new house. It's really the boys who have built it. It is an investment for them. They are moving in this summer and will rent out this house.

Well, you can be thankful you don't have any food rationing over there. The bread is getting darker, coarser, and heavier all the time. There is a scarcity of many things in the line of food, so we've learned to do without many things.

I turned in my return ticket the other day. He, the agent, said he'd fix it so it would be good at any date. I wrote to Washington D.C. about my passport but have had no reply. I told them to send the bill for a new passport, if needed, to Papa, as it would be difficult for me to send money over there. I have sort of been waiting for some money from Yvonne Arnold by telegraph, as they said at the bank that should go OK. I don't have very much left now. This spring I want to take that trip to Haugesund and Kristiansand too. As soon as the weather warms up, I'm going. I have gotten no new clothes this spring except a pair of shoes, and there was a lot of red tape to that. You should see our clothes rationing cards. I bought flannel for a pair of pajamas on it this winter, and it took so many numbers that now I can't get anything more until July. I have to laugh, as terrible as it is. There is a special card for shoes and household goods. You have to fill in an application blank for shoes, for half-soling of shoes, for towels, linens, curtains and such. I suppose we'll live through this too, as crazy as it is. It's a great life and a great experience, and interesting in many ways. Such things as dishes, hardware, etc. are not rationed, however. The other day I saw the prettiest coffee set and I just had to have it. Prices have doubled on most things.

When I started on this letter, I intended to send it airmail, but since I'm returning this blank check, it would make the letter too heavy, so I am changing over to this heavier paper and sending it the usual way. Just keep the check or give it to Dad, as I couldn't get it cashed anyway (I don't think). You asked some time ago if your letters came thru OK without any extra postage. They have all come thru OK.

Thanks so much for the last two snaps. It was thoughtful of you to take the cacti. I'll say, they have grown! I guess I wouldn't recognize any of the plants now. David looks so tall where he is standing with his back turned.

So, Tora decided to let the girls go back (instead of adopting them). *By the way, how is little Siggy's foot? Does he limp any? I often wonder about that. I thought on the picture that one leg looked a wee bit thinner than the other. He surely is a cute kid.*

How has Mama been this winter? I wrote home last week. It had been quite a while since I had written, but you see, when I move about from place to place, it isn't so convenient to sit down and write where the whole family sits around and jabbers, and you know, it's been so cold this winter, people stay in when they can. So, there has been very little privacy; then, too, there isn't so much to write. It's the same old mess.

Here in Norway, it is the custom to go on ski trips over Easter vacation. They rent cottages or rent a room at a mountain farm home and spend the week there. Uncle Karl in Egelandsdal always takes in skiers. They put beds in all the rooms and let them go to it. They were going to take twenty this year. They wanted me to stay over Easter too, but I couldn't see where they were going to put everyone as it was.

I figure I've had enough ski trips to satisfy me for a while, so I guess I'll go back to Grødem for Easter. I left my skis up there. All those kids are whizzes on skis; you should see them. It is rather difficult getting transportation this year, because there is so little gas. Buses are putting on wood generators for fuel. That is to say, the bus or truck runs on the gas generated from this wood. It is an expensive apparatus, but then the fuel is cheaper and, of course, wood is one thing that isn't rationed.

I am spending a few more days here and then a few days at Dybing; then I'm going home (to Grødem).

I got a permanent the other day and am very well satisfied with it. I've rattled on so long and jumped from this to that without paragraphing - you'll have a hard time making this out.

Onkel Andreas and Tante Berthe say I must "hilse" (send greetings).

Love and best wishes to all, Sophie

April 13, 1941 - Årrestad

Dear Everybody at Home,

Happy Easter! Here I am at Årrestad again and today it is Easter - I arrived here last night. I was at Grødem only one week and should have stayed there through Easter. However, Aunt Semine called and said that they were going to have a Christening here on the 2nd day of Easter, and since I had promised to be a 'fadder' (godmother) *earlier, I had to come back here again. Today is Easter, so tomorrow the baby, Ove* (Østrem), *will be Christened in the Helleland Church. Aunt Semine will carry the baby, and Uncle Ommund and Magnus* (the father), *and I, are godparents.*

The weather has not been too nice this week. It has been raining every day, but we have finally got some milder weather, and the snow is melting fast. There isn't much snow left around Egersund and Grødem, but there is quite a bit left at Årrestad and up the valley. I was only long enough at Grødem to help clean a little bit in the house and to bake something for Easter.

Yesterday, Helene - sister of Mandius Hausan, and Ingvald Holgersen from Stavanger came over for dinner. Helene told a story about when she was little and had to look after some kids - Tollag and Peder Omdal. I guess they were a handful!

I should have been to Rodvelt one day, but it just did not happen. I had not seen them since Christmas, but I had spoken to Tante Helene several times on the telephone. She had a painful foot - they say it is arthritis. Mathilde Grødem has been awful with arthritis also. She was up along the road here yesterday and could barely walk across the road. Josephine (Mother of Mathilde) *is better now, so she gets up and has started to take care of herself. She cannot understand why she has not heard anything from Inga Vatland or Gustav Grødem* (Mathilde's half siblings) *so if any of you see them, please tell them to write.*

I was able to meet Trygve Haaland (Brother of John Haaland in Bow, WA, U.S.A.) *yesterday for the first time.* Trygve had spent four years in the U.S.A.. *Lars Grødem was talking to him when I came walking by - I would not have known him if Lars hadn't told me who he was. I do not know if you have heard that old Severine of Mong died about six weeks ago. Several older ones have gone to rest this winter.*

*So how is the mood over there? I am assuming it is just as "exciting" there as it is here. I hear many around there have been called (*drafted*), and I sure hope it does not last long. It is not so good to be in town nowadays, because people in town do not know when they must run down* (to a cellar) *from an air raid day or night. I was in town several nights ago, but I did not experience anything. The coarse flour gets more and more gritty, but we can use oatmeal for many things - at least we know it is oats. But when it comes to coffee, I must laugh. It only has a little bit of coffee smell, and there will be an end to that too. It is hardest for the older people.*

I am thinking of Grandonkel Tollef; he is always asking about Karl Tollefson (in Bow, WA, U.S.A.). *You must be after him and make him write. Poor Tollef, he is so old, and Karl needs to write him. Tollef and Grandtante Sille were not at Omdal this Easter. His legs are not well enough for him to walk from the road, and you cannot get ahold of any cars these days. Torger has a car, but he must rent a taxi to take us to church tomorrow, as he is not allowed to use his car. Yes, it is a strange time.*

By the way, how are all of you at home? I'm embarrassed that I haven't answered the letters from those who have written to me. I am thinking about Bertha Omdal, Alma Hood, *Thelma Ploeg, Ruth Haugland, Agnes and Olga Benson, Eileen Peterson, and many others. It is so nice to hear from all of them, but I have traveled so much around, yes, with that I mean I haven't stayed so long in one place that I could even collect my thoughts. My thoughts have become very rusty and anyway, there isn't much to write about.*

Have you heard anything from Washington D.C.? I wrote there about my passport, and they said they were going to fix it and send the bill to you, because it is not so easy for me to send money from here. I hope that it is OK with you. I have not heard anything, so now my passport has expired. I have delivered the ticket to the agent, and he will fix that part. Well, now if just the money from Montana would come. I wrote right after Christmas and asked her to send it by telegraph, but I have not heard anything yet. I could need some money for this summer. I would love to make a bicycle trip; I have big plans, but there are so many places I should be, so we will see.

Right now, all the people in the house have gone to bed. It is late; I'll finish this tomorrow. Good night. It is pouring rain tonight.

Continued April 22, 1941

Yes, it is now over a week since the Christening, and all went well. Right now, I am at Dybing, and I've been here since Wednesday. The snow is melting little by little, but there are still big drifts left.

Little by little, they are starting to prepare for spring. Jon Gystøl, one of the boys here, has leased a farm in Rødland, and he has some nice, special sheep that he is most interested in. He is moving over right away, so Amanda has to move with him and help him run the farm. He has also hired a young sixteen-year-old boy to help. Tyra will be staying here at home on the farm. Their father, Onkel Johan, is better now, and Teoline looks much better now than when I came here.

Since I'm thinking about it right now, I just have to say - Papa - don't pay my health insurance this year because it will be taken care of here and it is cheaper. But New York Life - I would like you to keep New York Life for me until I come back home.

I was so happy to hear that Martin is getting better. I really am so thankful for that. Please say hello - give him my love. Also, say hello to all the siblings and everybody else around - Bertha, Sina, and them. Live well.

Love, Sophie

P.S. for Mother - I had closed the letter, but then I came to think of something. I was over at the Hans Sem Orrestad place at Årrestad last week, and they told me that I had to tell you hello from them. The old man, Hans, wanted to meet Christine's daughter, so he sent Ruth (his daughter) *down and asked me to come visit that evening, and I did. He told about the time he was going to drive you and the suitcases to the parsonage. Ruth only talked about Knut Jakobson Birkeland; it was Knut this and Knut that the whole evening. Ruth is engaged to him. I wonder if it will be something more with them. And this last Sunday, Amanda and I went to Gunvor at Møgedal - whom you know. She is sending her love. I had to say hello from her too.*

June 24, 1941 - Grødem, Egersund

Dear Mother, Father and Siblings,

It has been a long time since I've written you, so I'm assuming you are expecting a letter from me. It has been a busy spring, and spring came late this year. Most people around here did not get the potatoes in the ground until about a week before Pentecost (Pentecost was June 1). *We planted the vegetables the week after the first day of Pentecost. This spring the fields were frozen longer than normal, but now the weather is beautiful with warm sunshine and some great rainfalls. Everything is growing very nicely now, although it is pretty late. Last year, we planted a lot of vegetables; we had carrots and rutabagas the whole winter through, and we still have some left. We thought that was great, so we planted even more this year.*

How are you doing over there? I heard that you, Mother, had a bad turn with asthma again. Didn't the medicine that you got in Seattle help? Please continue taking it. I understand it has been very busy with all the cows you have to milk, etc.

Do you have a lot of chickens this year?

I received a letter from Theodora the other day. It took about three weeks - one week to Portugal - it was stamped there, and then two weeks from Portugal to Norway. Carl wrote a little letter and sent it together with hers. It sounds like he loves his work and flying. I also heard that you fixed up so nicely around the house; that was fun to hear. I am so curious as to how it looks now, so I hope Theodora will take some snapshots and send them to me. It would be great to be home right now. I am starting to get tired of being here, but I feel like they need me at Grødem - there is so much to do.

It was great to get all the sheep up in the mountains, but it was a huge effort to get them off. Onkel Petter, Sivert Mong, and Mikal Rodvelt herded them together up to Leland. People have lost a lot of sheep this spring. There was never enough food for them - last winter was very hard and long. It has been sparse for the cows also; everybody has scraped together whatever they could find, because of so little hay.

I should have been on a trip to Eiesland in Fjotland. They will start the grass harvest in a couple of weeks. Uncle Lars's son Petter and Sven Mauland want to come here and help with the harvest. The two of them plus Lars's son Henne were here during Pentecost for a few days. Petter is done with business school and is now working at a furniture factory, but this fall he will start working in a store at Fjotland. A friend of his, Thor Hunsbeth, from the business school, is taking over his father's store, and he has promised Petter work. They live well at Onkel Lars's house. Lars and Thea were here last Saturday and Sunday; and Tante Helene and Onkel Andreas (Rodvelt) *came Saturday night, and we had a great time together. Thea says that when the war is over, she is going to make coffee seventeen times a day. We don't get enough coffee in one week to fill the kettle one single time. How would you survive* (with so little coffee) *over there?*

A couple of weeks ago, Thelma Mong and I went to Nesvåg. We bicycled to Birkeland and walked across the high meadows - it was only an hour's walk. You need to tell Sina (Nesvåg) *Omdal that her sister Tomine* (Nesvåg) *is quick, healthy, and in a good mood. I stayed over with Sina's stepsister Gurina, and everybody there was well except for Marie* (Tønnesen)

Elle, the sister of Sophia (Tønnesen) *Rodvelt, Conrad* (Tønneson), *and Tom* (Tønneson). *Poor thing, she was in bed with inflammation of the vessels and she had been in bed for five weeks. They had both a maid and a nurse, so she was well taken care of. She was pretty sick then, and I haven't heard anything since we were there. We had a nice afternoon with her, and I have to admire her good mood and bravery.*

Elisabeth, Ole Birkeland's sister, has built a nice new house at Nesvåg - it wasn't quite finished yet. We stayed there from Sunday through Tuesday.

(Some days later)

Today is Saturday, and Anne has been to town shopping. I do not have any money to spend, so I might as well stay home. I guess I won't get any from Yvonne (in Montana, U.S.A.). *She wrote that she had gotten married, but since she had gotten a job at a school, she was going to pay me later, and I don't know when that will be. I borrowed some money from Uncle Lars, but I don't like to borrow money here. If you can send me just a little bit, I would be very thankful. I think it is possible to send it with a telegraph. It should not be more than $50 and if you do, send it to me c/o Egersunds Landsogns Sparebank, Egersund. In the fall when it is not as busy, I will try to get a job.*

Tomorrow and Sunday there will be a large festival. Thelma and Sivert are probably coming for dinner, and the next week the three of us will go on a bike trip. If it is going to happen, it must be before harvest.

A few weeks ago, I bicycled to Svinland. Tomine Egelandsdal is pretty good now but must rest three times a day. Agnes Egelandsdal is newly engaged; she is the youngest of Karl's girls and she is engaged to a nice young businessman with the name Øivind Berentsen.

Please write if you haven't already done so. It's so great that Theodora sent me all these letters. It has been a long time since you at home have written, but I assume life is very busy for you. Live well, all of you, and tell Bertha Omdal that I will write and tell her everything about the visit to Nesvåg.

Heartfelt Greetings to everybody at home,
Sophie

July 21, 1941 - Grødem, Egersund

Dear Theodora,

I know, it's been ages since I wrote. I was going to answer your letter written May 28th right away, but time flies and I don't get any writing done. We've been so busy all spring and summer. I have had only a few short trips this summer. A couple weeks ago, Thelma and Sivert along with a friend of mine and I had a week's bicycle trip up the Sîrdalen which was very interesting, but the two days we planned to hike into the mountains, it rained. We had a tent along and slept out some of the nights. The scenery was beautiful. The road up the valley runs along a swift river with mighty mountains on each side. Some places, the mountains were bare rock, but they were mostly forest clad. We spent one night with a cousin of ours named Ingrid, Valborg's daughter, who lives at Lindeland. We went as far up as Leland where we met friends of Sivert's. Here, we saw them bring home the herds of goats, milk them, and make goat-milk cheese. This was interesting, and by the way, the people happened to be related to a friend, Anne Leland, whom I went to P.L.C. (Pacific Lutheran College) *with.*

Since we have come home (to Grødem), *we've been very busy with the hay. Everybody has to help with that, because it's all done by hand, and we're so few to do it. This friend from Stavanger has been here at Grødem since the bicycle trip but is leaving now soon. Don't get excited, however. He doesn't mean anything special; he's just a good friend.*

Next week, three other girls and I - two of them cousins of Tilda Hansen and the other a cousin of Leif Burkland – are starting out on a two week's bicycle trip. (Leif changed the spelling of his last name at some unknown time. He was born in Bow, WA. His father was Ole Birkeland.) *We're taking a tent along. On this trip we will travel part of the way by boat up the coast and then go down through Telemark and down to Arendal on the southeast coast. Then I imagine we'll follow the coastline home. We will go thru Kristiansand on our way back. I shall try to look up Mrs. Carl* (Sofie) *Hansen's brother there, Bjarne Larsen.*

A week ago Sunday, I was to a party at a cousin of ours - Anders Østrem. Their baby, Ove, was baptized, and I was one of the witnesses. Aunt Berthe showed me the house (right by the church) where Mother and Dad lived when Peter was born. I also met the lady of the house where they rented. I was to greet Mother so much from her. You'll have to tell her in case I should forget to write about it when I write home.

I had a letter from Eileen and Oscar Peterson last week and was pleased to hear they had gotten a baby girl. I just imagined Oscar wanted a boy, but he sounded awfully proud and pleased. I hope Eileen and Judy Nela are both doing well.

I hear everyone is pretty busy over there - must be a lot to do around home. I suppose Mother is about overworked, too. She doesn't write anymore, neither she nor Dad, so I gathered they don't find time. I wrote Dad I needed money, so I hope it's possible to send it now. I'm on my last shekels. I could have taken a job this summer, but they needed me here. Now I'm getting so tired of this... I crave a change. When I get back from this trip in the middle of August, I'm going east of the mountains to Aunt Martha Eiesland's for a while and on my return get a job of some sort either in Stavanger or Egersund. I suppose it will be an ordinary housekeeping job - anything for a change.

I just read over your last letter. You asked how come Yvonne didn't send me the money. She finally wrote and said she was married but still was teaching. She hoped she could send some soon, but it didn't sound very promising. I am afraid I won't get it until I come back. I'm wondering when that will be! I surely wish I were home now. The food situation is steadily growing worse. I haven't had fresh meat but once in over a month. Coffee is only a substitute. Can't go over everything, but it's no fun trying to get meals with so little to do with. The flour is so poor, the bread won't rise decently. It's a great life over here now, so I really shouldn't complain, because we have enough of what there is. I'm afraid there are places where they don't get enough to eat. We'll get along somehow.

I was glad to hear Peter has a good job. I hope he can pay his debts now. Is Carl still staying with you? Tell him thanks a lot for his little letter. I shall write him another time. He sounded like the same old Carl. So, it looks as if Melvin will be marrying Wanda. What do you all think about it?

Yesterday was Tora's birthday and tomorrow Martin's. I wish I could have been with you for the occasions. I was glad *to hear Martin is really better - just so he doesn't do too much now. Don't be too long before you write and tell all about how everything is at home. Tell Mom I'm surely waiting for a letter from her, and that I get a little homesick once in a while.*

I sure wish I could see the garden at home you described to me. You'll have to take some snaps and send them. I think they'll come through OK.

My best love to all of you "der over" (over there). *Write soon. I guess I'll go to town tomorrow and get this mailed, then stop in at Stapnes on the way back to talk over our plans for the trip next week. I'm really looking forward to that.*

Love, Sophie

August 19, 1941 - Årrestad, Helleland

Hello Everybody,

I know it has been quite a while since I have written now, so this will have to be to Mom and Pop and all of you. How are you all anyway? I surely hope everyone is well, and that Martin is steadily improving. It has been almost six weeks since I've had any mail from over there, so I'm anxious to hear how you all are.

I have just returned from a three-week bicycle tour over Telemark and Southern Norway and believe me, we had a grand trip. And we got really tan! We were three girls - Kristine Stapnes, Sigrid Stapnes, and me. We slept in a tent the first two weeks, but the last week it was rainy, so we had to sleep indoors.

We traveled 71 Norwegian miles or 497 English miles. We took our time about it - we didn't do many miles each day, so we could enjoy the scenery which certainly was worth seeing. The first day, we bicycled to Stavanger where we took a seven-hour boat trip. The next day, we started to cross the mountains. Up in the highest mountains we passed "sæter" after "sæter" (mountain dwellings where local people stay with their animals so the animals can graze there) *with their "støl". Here they have their cows and goats during the summer. Here they make butter and goat's cheese and send it down to the village. We spent one night on a "sæter" where we got all the milk and buttermilk we could drink, which was a treat in these days of rationing. We crossed some mighty mountains. It was*

work pushing our bikes up those steep mountain roads. We each had a heavy knapsack strapped to our bikes. You see, we had bedding, clothes, food, pots and pans, as well as the tent along, so we sweated going up, but then what fun when we finally got to the top and could coast down. Some places we could coast for hours. In the Telemark district, the houses had a quaint style of architecture. I can't go into detail. We took four rolls of film; I hope they turn out.

We came down to the coast again at Arendal, then followed the coastline home by way of Grimstad, Lillesand, Kristiansand, Mandal, Lista, Flekkefjord, and Moi where we stopped in at Ragna and Karsten Moi's. We spent the night there, and she wanted us to stay longer, but after being out so long we were anxious to get home and get cleaned up. It rained, so that day we took the train the rest of the way. However, I thought I couldn't go by Årrestad here without stopping in and saying hello, and as you see by the heading, I haven't gotten any further. I just couldn't get away again. I got to take a bath and wash my clothes, so I felt better right away. I have been gadding about every day and visiting with Tante Semine every day. Yesterday I was there to dinner, then

Bertha came over, and I went home with her and spent the evening there. Tonight I guess I'll have to take a little trip up to see Hans Sem (Mamma knows him). He is quite old now, and Malene says he keeps asking about me. He calls me Kristine. It is his daughter, Ruth Orrestad, who is engaged to Knut Jakobsen Birkeland (in Stanwood, WA, U.S.A.). *By the way, does anyone ever see him? Does he talk about coming home? I just wondered, as he got himself engaged over there.*

And Theodora, you must greet Mrs. Will (Helen) *Knutzen so much from me and from her sister Tilda* (Mathilde) *Tryland. We were up at Vigmostad and looked her up. She was just grand to us. We spent the night with her and enjoyed her so much. I was lucky to get two pieces of weaving - one for you and one for myself and are they lovely! It's almost impossible to get ahold of such work now. The new yarn is not so good. I ordered one more if she gets yarn to weave. There is so much red tape to go through to get anything. She isn't doing so much weaving right now, she said.*

I also tried to look up Mrs. Carl (Sofie) *Hansen's brother, Bjarne Larsen, in Kristiansand, but I must not have had the correct address, as they said he didn't live there. When I got to Vigmostad, Mrs. Tryland said he had just been there on*

At Mandal

vacation but had just gone back to Kristiansand, so I missed him there too. If I had his correct address, I could look him up another time, if I happen to be down there. I liked Kristiansand better than any other city here in Norway. It is built more like an American city with wide, straight streets. Most towns have the crookedest streets; it's hard to find your way through most of them.

I bought two lovely silver brooches. One is for Olga Benson. She sent money with me, but I haven't found anything really nice until now on this trip. Then I got a smaller one. The money that you, Theodora, sent with me will just about cover the little weaving and that smaller silver brooch. Your weaving is about a yard long and about fourteen inches wide. My weaving is about 1-1/3 yards long and I guess ¾ yard wide. I'm just thrilled about the weavings. I cashed my last traveler's check, so I'm ready for the poor farm - ha! ha! I hope some of you will take pity on me and send me a little money, if it is at all possible to send anything from over there.

I was so surprised - while visiting in Grimstad, we talked to the customs officer there, Betjent Jørgensen, and spent the night at his house. Both of the girls I was with were well acquainted with this family. Now I'm getting to what I wrote

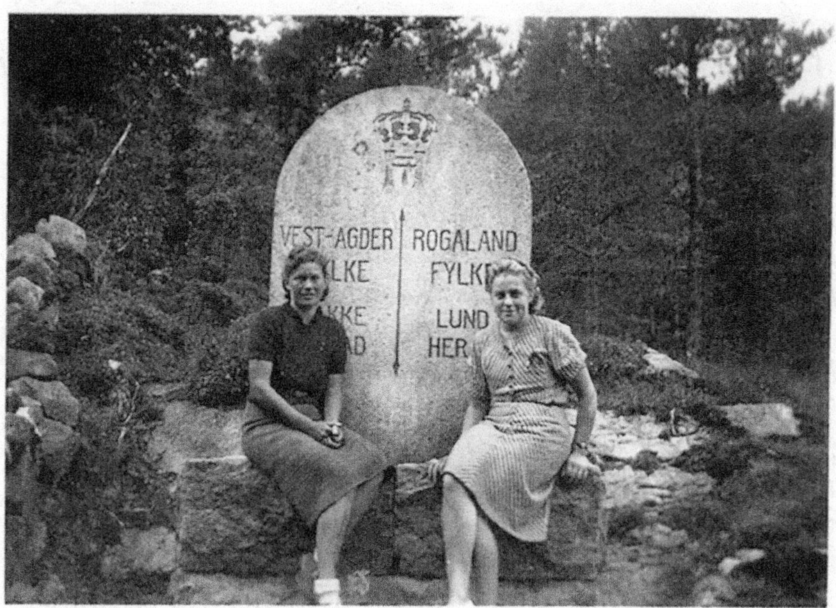

Near Tronåsen

to say. This customs officer said I could have coffee and sugar, etc. sent to me from over there (U.S.A.), *as much as four pounds at a time. A lady was there the day we were, and we saw her get coffee, sugar, and a pair of shoes. I was so surprised. He said the tariff was not much, but I wouldn't expect you to send anything (that isn't why I'm saying this). Now, he didn't charge much duty, but here at Stavanger I suppose they would, as they surely checked up on the contents of my trunk.*

I've been offered a job with Anna Østrem, our cousin in Stavanger. She is manageress of the Indre Missions Hotel. Bergit has been with her until now but is getting married this fall, so I can have her place if I want it. It would be fun and not very much work. They have had every other afternoon off all the time. I'd have lots of time to knit, and when I had a whole day off, I could go out to Uncle Lars's. I rather think I will take them up on it.

I talked with Amanda (Gystøl) *on the telephone yesterday, and she says the "tydebær" are ripe now, so I shall go up there and pick berries to take home to Grødem. I guess I won't get to Grødem until next week sometime.*

I hope Momma and Papa and all are well, and do write, somebody!

Love, Sophie

P.S. I had a letter from Pearl Urmey Flowers today. She sent a couple pictures of herself and the baby. Pearl was surely looking fine as well as the little one.

October 31, 1941 - Rodvelt, Egersund

Dear Folks and All of You,

Thanks, Mom, for your letter received about three weeks ago. I was beginning to think you had forgotten me. Yesterday I surely was thrilled when I received three American letters from Theodora, Tora, and Bertha. Thanks a lot, all of you. I haven't even answered your last letters which I received last month. The pictures you sent, Theodora, were swell. I've looked at them so much, I've almost looked a hole through them. And little David is so grown up. I thought the one in his pajamas was especially sweet. Tora, I wish you'd send some of Siggy. He must be a real live wire. I wanted to send some pictures home, but nope, it's "forbudt" (forbidden) *from this side. I guess we can be thankful, so long as we can exchange letters.*

I understand by your letters that you have not received the letter I wrote after receiving the money Dad sent. I wrote right away, but it may be that the letter didn't go through, or that it was still on the way when you wrote. Anyway, I surely received it in good order sometime in August. It came while I was on that bicycle tour, so that was a long time ago. I've surely been hanging on to it; I haven't spent much of it yet. I don't buy any new clothes. Yes, I bought a pair of wooden-bottomed shoes, and I simply must have a hat this winter. You should see the awful stockings we women have to wear. Of course, everyone wears only woolen hose in the winter here, as it is so cold. Well, the hose now are so coarse and the awfullest dark colors - but everything goes nowadays. I, at least, am well supplied with warm clothes for this winter which is the main thing. I've knit me some good warm undergarments. You'd laugh if you saw them. As I was going to say, I've decided not to take any job, as it is best to stay out of towns and cities. Food is poor, there's little fuel, and the country has so many more advantages, especially in the winter, so I thought this: if you, or someone could send me 50 bucks more, it would do me a long time. There is always the thought - if something should happen - that I couldn't get anything later on. The time may come where all communications may be stopped. If you send, send it to the same place. Then they telephone me as soon as it arrives.

As for the coffee, if you can send it at a reasonable cost, it would be very much appreciated, but not otherwise, because it isn't worth the outrageous postage you mentioned, Theodora. I understand they can send four-pound packages. Don't send anything but coffee, and if you do send, send it to me in care of: Tollbetjent Jørgensen, Grimstad. He has my address and will forward it to me. That way, I'd be sure that no one else took the package, as I trust this man. I know he is fair and honest, which is more that you can say of other customs officers I know of. If it is going to cost a lot, just forget the whole thing.

Today is Thanksgiving Day in Norway, or rather it's called

Day of Prayer. People meet all over the country this morning in churches, schoolhouses, etc. at 9:00 to pray for the country and its people. How long can this last? I'm of the belief that there won't be peace for over a year yet. I'm not planning on any "hjem reise" (home travel) *this next summer, but if I can't come home the summer of 1943, I'll be disappointed more than I can say. By that time, there won't be much left of Europe either, I'm afraid.*

I have been staying here at Rodvelt with Tante Helene about a month now. She has been sick but is much better now. When she is on her feet too much, her knee swells up terribly, so I've been helping her so she can take it easy and get well sooner. She is too heavy to do much walking. She left Wednesday for Stavanger, where she will see a doctor and get her glasses fitted again. Thelma was to come home and tend the house, but she and her husband, Sivert, are invited to a wedding this week and will be gone at least a week, as she will visit with Uncle Lars while over there. The twins, who are thirteen years old, were just vaccinated for smallpox so have missed several days of school.

Marta and Nils in Stapnes asked me to greet Mother and Dad so much. I was there several days this fall and canned plums and meat for them, and then I spent one day at Vådlen and canned meat. People are beginning to do more canning now than they have previously. Marta says to greet Carlton so much - you know, she is his aunt. She wants you to tell Karl Tollefson to write and remind Kristian (Chris) *Rodvelt to write to the old folks; they have waited so long for a letter. While in Stapnes, I got to see what changes are going on there. Aunt Ellen surely won't know the place again for buildings and roads, etc.*

Trygve, Aunt Ellen's nephew, is not so well. You know he was sick with pleurisy last winter and it went over to tuberculosis. He has been in a sanitarium all summer. A few months ago, they moved all the patients to Moi where he is now. He still is in bed with a temperature. It surely is too bad. He is such a fine fellow. I talked with his mother Sunday. She surely has gotten gray and old-looking since I came two years ago. With the suspense under which they are living and with Trygve sick, it soon shows on a person.

I talked with Tønnes Friestad in town. I was sorry to hear Øystein Friestad is sick with diabetes. I suppose they have written Sig. He still works but takes insulin and is on a diet - too bad.

I could think of more to write but can send only three sheets in a letter unless I want to pay extra. How is Martin? I suppose he has received my letter now. I hope he is doing OK. Write soon. Papa, you will have to write and tell me about the work on the farm: crops, cattle etc. They ask about everything here. I also send greetings from Grødem and Rodvelt and others.

Best wishes to all, Sophie

P.S. Tora - Don't send the postage you mentioned.

November 16, 1941 - Grødem

Dear Mother, Father and All of You!

Well, it has not been so long since I have written to you, but since I received a letter from you the other day, I have the urge to write to you again. Your letter was stamped October 18, so it took about three weeks to get here.

I hear that you did not know that I received the money that you sent in August. You might have a thought that it did not get here, but it did; and I heard that you wanted to send it again. If you have sent it for the 2nd time, I assume I will be fine through the winter; I do not use too much money. The only thing that I might need is a coat - not because I have worn out the other, but it is getting to be too small. It looks like I have put on too much weight, and the coat does not reach around me now, but I will see if I can get a seamstress to alter it. I could not have bought a new one anyway, because I need so many marks, and I do not have enough on the rationing card. So, there are all kinds of things to worry about.

The winter has arrived in full, and this morning it was all white outside. It is cold and nasty out. Aunt Helene, Jonas Rodvelt's wife Lisa, and Anna Ålvik, the teacher in Mong, were supposed to come for dinner today but the weather was too bad. We had 'fårikål' (lamb with cabbage). *Every farmer gets to slaughter a certain quota of sheep and lamb, and we slaughtered here the other day. This fall we have had enough meat, but that is because it is slaughtering season; it will be worse during the winter.*

Aunt Helene spent about a week in Stavanger and Vagle. I think she enjoyed herself, and she feels much better now. She had not been to Grødem since Pentecost, so it was time that she made the trip. Tante Anne had hidden away a little bit of wheat flour, so I made a "fløte kake" (sponge cake) *for the occasion. We will invite the neighbors over this afternoon for "corn coffee," etc. We call the coffee "Kettle Cornelius" now. Before we always called it "Coffee Lars," but it has gotten a different name now that a substitution came.*

I am not at all happy to see the snow today; I got so tired of it last winter, and we had snow the entire spring. I hope this winter will not be as tough as last winter. It has been storming this entire week; it was blowing so hard that we lost a lot of roof panels from our roof here. Marie, in Omdal, would barely go to sleep at night - she was so afraid the house was going to blow down. It was an ugly storm, but it slowed down a little bit yesterday, and last night it started to snow.

I am so happy to hear that you are doing well with all the cows. It's a large herd that you have gotten now, and I hope it all goes well with you also.

Continued on November 21, 1941

It has been about a week ago since I started this letter. The snow is gone, and the weather is mild again - it is so much better. I have gotten the coat altered. Thelma was here Wednesday and helped me alter it, so it fits really nice now. Tomorrow I will get a new hat with silver lining, and I will be in tip-top shape.

Onkel Petter and Mikal Rodvelt traveled to Vagle today. They were going to get whatever they could get their hands on (food and clothes). *I have been darning and fixing clothes all day yesterday and today, and now I am ready to travel there tomorrow.*

I had another letter from Margery and Peter the other day, and they say they are enjoying themselves. She must be in pretty good health because she has put on quite a bit of weight; she weighs 150 pounds. I weigh just about the same. I had better stop eating so much, but I have an appetite like a horse. So, you understand we are doing well; we have enough food. But I am thinking about people in the towns - the poor school children in Stavanger now must grow potatoes in their schoolyard, and the bread cards (rationing cards) *are not enough.*

It is pretty bad at the farm by the ocean closest to Aunt Helene now. I do not know if you have heard that there are barely any men left. They are captured - and we do not know for what. We have to watch our mouth. At Nils Mong's, everybody is still home; well, one is out sailing, and Herman Mong (the father of Nils) *is home, and then you know one of them has left. It has to do with the fact that there are so many that are arrested. I know many cases like that; it is very sad.* (From later reports through Rolf Mong, what happened here is that six young men from Mong, ages 17-22, one of them being a brother of Nils Mong, escaped from Norway in a small fishing vessel and made it to Scotland. Some or all of these young men volunteered for war operations on board Norwegian Navy vessels operating from the UK. Two of them lost their lives in the war effort. While they were gone, the Gestapo, in revenge, arrested six other men from Mong, most of them being the fathers of the young men who had escaped, and the older men ended up at Grini *(Gestapo prison in Norway)* or in concentration camps in Germany. One lost his life there.)

I hear there are several that receive packages of coffee from USA. It looks like it arrives OK - I wonder if it is expensive to ship. If not, and if it is somewhat convenient, it would be great to get some, via Portugal, of course. You can just send it directly to me and not through Grimstad, since they say it will arrive safe anyway. You probably think I have turned into a bad beggar, but no wonder, since there is not a lot of nice stuff to get ahold of.

Anne is sitting here cleaning nuts. We had a lot this year, and people are crazy for them. No fruit, no candy, no nuts (available to buy), *no, nothing, and if we just had good flour to bake with. We just have to be happy that we have what we need most - not everybody has this much.*

I received a greeting from Ragna in Moi. She had another boy, Vegard, in October, so now she has two boys. Olga Gya is with her. Kristine Stapnes stayed with them at Moi when she visited Trygve who is sick. She does not feel so well, and it is hard on them, as they are still in their best years. But if you think about it, there is really nothing to live for, the way the world is today. It is just sin and sorrow, and the Christians are having a hard time. It seems like they are trying to get rid of Christianity. It is hard to be a teacher now. It is good to have everything cleared with Him. It's much better to die than to keep on living a life where you can't worship Him.

It was very nice to get the snapshots of the flower garden at home - it looks so beautiful. I cannot hide that I am longing for home when I'm looking at the pictures. But we must be strong. There must be a change sometime. If you have more pictures, please send them; it is so nice to get something from over there. I am not allowed to send any pictures. I should really have sent some so you can see how chubby I am now.

Well, I better stop, take a bath, and go to bed. The bus leaves tomorrow morning at 9:30 and it is dark all the way until 9:00 in the morning now.

Anne says to say "hi". I talked to Tante Helene on the phone just a little while ago; she is feeling much better now. Anne was over yesterday and helped to bake flatbread. We baked the day before. Today they baked at Gjertine Omdal's at Myran farm. I should have been over with my knitting, but I need to finish everything I am taking with me by tomorrow morning. It is Dad's cousin, Martine, from Pintlo farm, that is baking.

Aunt Semine just wrote to me and she wants me to come and visit her. She has some wool that she wants me to spin and use for myself, but I think I'll have to wait until spring. I am thinking about staying with Uncle Lars most of the winter.

Just send mail to the old address as they will resend it to me from the post office. Please let me know if this letter reaches you. Yes, live well, have a Merry Christmas and Happy New Year.

Heartfelt Greetings, Sophie

Christmas 1941

I am at Uncle Lars's - Ganddalen - I arrived a month ago. Time has gone quickly; nothing special has happened. Oh yes, it was December 7 that the U.S.A. went to war with Japan. That was a terrible shock. Although we've heard rumors a long time, I just couldn't believe it would go that way. Tante Thea and I were in town to a birthday party at which time the news came out. It surely made me sick. I felt quite upset for a week's time, but one gets used to that too. My biggest worry was, "Will the boys at home have to go out to war?" Of course, I get no mail from home any longer, so I don't know how things are at home. I can only hope and pray that things are not as bad as we fear. Then too, I won't be able to hear how Martin is getting along. I only hope he is steadily improving.

It was that same week that I went with Anna and Bergit to Helleland over Friday and Saturday. Onkel Andreas Østrem celebrated his 70th birthday anniversary, and all his children were home except Tor, the youngest son, who was enrolled in the "Arbeids Tjeneste" *(Work Service),* and Randi Skipstad, who couldn't very well leave her small ones at home. There were about twenty guests.

I got up early the next morning and took the train to Egersund. Here I met Aunt Anne, Helene, and Thelma. We all met up at Mathilde's where we had lunch and rested up after our trip downtown. All four saw me off at the station at 5:30 that afternoon. Onkel Lars met me at the station here at 7:30. When we got home, the house was full of gentlemen guests. Tante Thea had cooked "forrektig" *(real)* coffee, and fixed lefse, and served cakes that we had baked for Christmas. Later in the evening we skated. The guests decided to go home about 2:30 a.m.

A few days before Christmas comes a letter from Malene with forty kroner in it as gifts. Twenty are from Tante Semine and twenty are from her and Torger. Tante here bought six extra cups, saucers, and plates to my coffee set. With the money received I am buying a hand-carved fruit bowl, a beauty - made at Moi.

I suppose the folks at home think that I'm very nearly starving or at least am having an unpleasant time of it. I'm lucky to have most of my relatives out in the country, and none of them are suffering any hardships. Onkel Lars is especially well fixed. They keep all their milk *(from their cows)* at home and separate it to churn. So, we have all the good butter, cream and milk we can use. They take their own wheat, oats and barley to the mill and grind it. They butcher when they need fresh meat. Now let's see how town people have it. One fourth liter separated milk a day. No cream for coffee or anything. No coffee - only this substitute Trio and other brands which is supposed to be burned grain, but contains, most likely, other harmful ingredients. Once in a great while they are lucky to get dairy butter. About all there is on the market is margarine made of fish oil etc. Some brands taste pretty fishy. Imagine how appetizing this dark, heavy, soggy, sour bread would be, and margarine, with black coffee substitute.

Where did all the good butter and fat go? Of course, much less milk is sent to the condenseries now, as naturally, due to poor fodder, cows give less milk. Farmers get no meal for them but can buy cellulose or paper which the cows eat, but if they eat too much, it is harmful.

Going back to the food situation, even potatoes are scarce in large cities or towns. Meat, needless to say, is very scarce. People, that is, good customers, are lucky to get meat once a week. There was hardly any fruit to get ahold of this summer, so those who have no direct contact with the country have very little to eat. The flour, butter, sugar, etc. dealt out on rationing cards do not reach. There hasn't been an egg on the market since summer. They stand in line four hours to get a package of cigarettes. Now there will be no more tobacco or "snus" *(snuff),* as factories are closing down due to lack of raw materials.

There is not a piece of candy on the market except some cough drops. No chocolate. However, we were with the lucky ones to get two bars apiece, rationed out on extra cards. No rice, no peas, no potato flour for thickenings, no fruit. The grocer dealt out a few apples to each family at Christmas time. Each family was allowed a small portion of cheese for the holidays. We were five persons - 1 ½ pounds cheese. No syrup and no pepper on the market. Not a can of sardines, no canned goods of any kind left. For Christmas, each family was dealt out a few cans of sardines as a Christmas present. No candles, no Christmas tree decorations.

Of course, there is not a decent brand of toilet soap to be had - only for babies. We get a B-grade which is awfully hard on the skin. No laundry soap, only poor grades of powdered soap, very strong and harmful to clothes, but what is there to do?

Now in the line of dry goods - one may need shoes. He applies. Answer: one pair a year. He needs rubber boots. He applies. Answer: records show he has rubber boots - none granted. Half soling is a problem too. Only one a year. But they get around it by just patching in the various places, perhaps taking only one shoe at a time. I need woolen hose in the worst way, but what am I to do? There is not a pair on the market. I have several good pairs of silk hose, but one can't wear them here in the winter. I have started wearing home-knit hose around the house to save on my good ones. I hope this situation changes for the better in the new year.

There isn't a yard of cotton material on market. One sees a few bolts of silk and this new "cell ull" cloth. One can't buy a strainer cloth, hankie or anything. There are plenty of rayon silk underwear and rayon hose. Not even a spool of thread is to be purchased at any price. No bedding, table linens, or curtains worth having.

Egersund, which is noted for its china factory, has very little on that line on the market - mostly loose pieces. Not a good dinner set to find now. The last one sold at 150 -200 kroner. My coffee set came to 58 kroner. 35 kroner for a set of six, but Tante here bought six extra cups, saucers, and plates for me.

Jewelry shops have practically gone out of business. One can do business only if the customer brings in old gold or silver. There is not a wristwatch to be bought. Wedding rings are a cheap metal with gold plate.

Hats are about the one and only thing not rationed and of which there is to buy. Not much choice, however.

1942 until Sophie's Arrest

Reporting to Sheriff Becomes Part of Life
Trying Times & Homesickness
Constitution Day Celebrations Forbidden
Sophie Rejects Opportunity to Return to U.S.A.

January 1, 1942 - Thursday

We had a very quiet Christmas. The family was alone Christmas Eve. The boys went out for a while in the evening. On Christmas day, Tante Thea and I went over to Bestemor Martine Vagle's for the afternoon. The town people came home with us and spent the evening. The folks, Martine and Henrik, received a lovely wrought iron floor lamp.

I myself was so homesick over Christmas I was quite beside myself, especially Friday and Saturday, but also Sunday after Christmas. I have managed to shake most of it off now. It surely is painful to be homesick, and I didn't want anyone to know it either. However, I managed to live over that, too. I hope I never get another siege like that. I think it was because everything was so quiet. We went only a few places. All Christmas "Fests" were called off due to a diphtheria epidemic which has been raging in Stavanger and other places for over a month.

I have had to report to the sheriff three times and am obligated to continue every Friday as long as this war lasts. I went through a lot of red tape to get records in order but now have finally gotten permission to remain three months at the end of which time I apply for renewal of a year's time. I should have done this when I came to the country but knew nothing about it. The sheriff is very human. He came out to the house here Monday, as he happened by anyway. The roads were so slippery with ice, he didn't think I could make it to Sandnes. It was very considerate of him.

A very depressing time was Monday, December 28th. The eleven persons from Stavanger, doomed to die as spies benefiting England, were shot to death. The City is to mourn three months. No large public gatherings allowed. Everyone is terribly upset. Tilde Mauland in town knew them all but one, so naturally they are terribly upset about it. The relatives are to receive personal effects but not the bodies.

The Germans have now called in all State cars, highway trucks, etc., which are standing ready at a moment's notice to take off for unknown places. We wonder, are they planning on deserting us? All indications point that way. Norman made them a little nervous last night. For fun, Henrik Vagle over here struck off a dynamite stick. This was answered a little later from another direction. Then a third was heard, after which the Sola air raid alarm sounded. They must have thought it was something else.

January 5, 1942 - Monday

Anna and Bergit *Østrem* came out to dinner and stayed all day. I met them at Ganddalen and followed them to the station in the evening. On the way back, I stopped in at Marit Skadsem's.

January 6, 1942 - Tuesday

I was awakened at 5:30 a.m. by terrific bombing and anti-air guns from Sola airfield, being only four miles from the airport. I was soon on my feet. Standing in the door, we witnessed the whole affair. Planes came over at regular intervals, dropping bombs and incendiaries. The response from ground was intense and resembled giant 4th of July fireworks. The bombing was so forceful that it shook the house and doors creaked. We didn't dare go outdoors during the raid, for fear of being struck by falling shrapnel shells, which we heard fall on the ground outside. Continual raids lasted until 7:45. We heard later there had been thirteen planes over Sola. One large hangar was struck and burnt up, destroying 30-40 planes. Some 40-50 lives are said to have been lost. Many lives were lost the following day when a time bomb went off while men were clearing up a wreck from a raid the morning before. Some places where bombs exploded, holes were left in the ground so large that a whole house could have been placed in the holes.

January 17, 1942 - Saturday

Mikal, Thelma, and Sivert arrived by train at noon to spend a few days.

In the evening, we went to a show at the new theater in Sandnes. The building was lovely, but the show very inferior, called "Den Forsvundne Pølsemakere" *(The Sausage Maker Who Disappeared).* We walked home after the show - it took 1 ½ hrs. to walk.

January 18, 1942 - Sunday

I went nowhere, and nobody came. Thelma and Sivert left for the city on the 9:00 train. Mikal stayed until evening when he took out the proud owner of a brand-new bicycle.

January 23, 1942 - Friday

My birthday – It was the appointed day to appear before the sheriff, but on account of a blizzard, I called him up and talked to him. He "caught on" and said I didn't need to come in, for which I was very thankful.

I baked a cream cake. Olga, Jonas, and Alf *(a friend of theirs)* were the only extras for genuine coffee in the evening. I received a lovely hand-carved fruit dish from Ragna and her sisters and brothers at Gya.

January 24, 1942 - Saturday

Tante had asked in a few friends for the evening. I had baked and decorated a birthday cake. The guests were Olga and Jonas Vagle, Marit Skadsem, and Alf.

January 25, 1942 - Sunday

We went to the horse races on the ice at Stokkelandsvatnet. Horses taking part represented Oslo, Trondheim, Bergen, and all parts of Norway. The grand champion winner was from Ålgård, a small town a couple of miles from here. It was not a very large crowd due to intense cold, etc. One couldn't stand still for even a few minutes at a time. We, Marie *Vagle (Thea's niece)* and I, walked back and forth or jumped up and down to keep warm. We stayed only 1 ½ hours, then went over to Marit's and spent the rest of the afternoon and evening.

January 26, 1942 - Monday

Today the temperature is 25 degrees below zero Celsius, but it is still. I walked to Sandnes, shopped, and was back in three hours.

January 27, 1942 - Tuesday

Today there is not quite so much frost, but such a cold wind is blowing that it is almost impossible to keep warm, no matter how much clothing one has on. Marie was over a little while - I am helping her to knit a dress.

February 15, 1942 - Sunday

Tilde Mauland and her friend Ella came out from town on the morning train and stayed for dinner. Each week someone comes out after milk, cream, eggs, meat, etc., of which there is none to buy in town.

I have been here *(at Onkel Lars and Tante Thea's)* about three months now and we have had good coffee every Saturday evening and Sunday afternoon. I have baked a cream cake every Saturday and have had fresh or home-canned meat almost every Sunday.

Today, after coffee, we all went "home" to the "Old Folks." Marie and I took out on skis. We happened to come out near the station about train time, so we went over and saw the Simonsons, Ella, and Fru Tilde Mauland off *(on the train).* The train was so packed with skiers from Ålgård that there was hardly a place for more passengers, but they managed to make room. Then we took off for the "Heiå" *(the farm the Skadsems lived on)* to see how they were there. Målfrid and Fru Marta Skadsem were still in bed. After running for some time up and down the hills, Jan *(Øvestad)*, Marie *Vagle*, and I went in and got warm milk, home-baked bread, and head cheese which tasted good after the run.

Some time ago we started a little English class. Only a few students - David *(Vagle)*, Marit, Målfrid and Magnhild, Marie *(Vagle)*, and "Gutteman" a young Vagle boy named Henrik, attend. We have some good times meeting up every Thursday evening. We didn't meet last Thursday, as there were too many sick people in the house.

I have been meeting up with the lensmann *(sheriff)* every Friday. Last Friday, Henrik took us in the sleigh again for a "good old-fashioned sleigh ride with bells and everything". This Friday we visited Larsine Omdal Sirevåg and her husband Jakob after the shopping was done.

People here were all assigned respective places for evacuation, which people seem to think will and must eventually take place.

I have knitted jackets for Mother and Tante Thea and am at present working on a vest for Gamlå *(the old woman)* here, *Bestemor Martine Vagle.*

February 22, 1942 – Sunday

Mr. and Mrs. Mauland from town, and (*one of their boys*), Sven, were here today. Andreas had just returned from a business trip to Oslo. I asked him how things looked in the city, and he said, "Pretty dark". Most all hotels were filled with "other" guests. The rooms were uncomfortably cold due to lack of fuel. The food was poor. "For dinner, two small or one large potato and fish which was not good at any time", he said. The soup was barely edible. The best part of the meal was the potatoes. For other meals, the bread was not bad, but only ten grams of butter allowed each person. Sardines and smoked herring were all they had to offer besides. The coffee substitute was served with separated milk. No, we don't know how lucky we are to be out in the country. Oh, yes - in Flekkefjord, he said, for dinner they got cooked fish and stewed kålrabi (no spuds).

This morning, Ganddalen sponsored a ski tournament. Only local residents were allowed entry. There were 25 taking part. "Henne" and Petter Omdal both entered. Henne somehow fit into both groups. He came in second in the youngest group and fourth in the other. Petter made no showing. Henne will receive trophies this week.

January and February have been a continual cold spell. It turned milder about the 14th or 15th - it has been perfectly still since then. On Saturday the 14th, Marie and I had a couple hours out on skis on the swell new snow. In the evening, Onkel Lars, Thea, and I went to the TB Bazaar. Tante won a beautiful, hand-embroidered, white linen coffee or lunch cloth and an apron. We came home, cooked "forrektig" *(real)* coffee, and sat and talked until the early hours of the morning.

March 6, 1942 – Saturday

Petter (*Omdal's)* birthday today *(Lars and Thea's son)* - 21 years old. I baked him a cream cake. I also baked rusks *(biscuits)* for them to take on the ski tour to Egelandsdal. They left today on the evening train. Marit followed them on the way, and Tante Thea followed to the station. I thought I had lost a package after I got on the train, but to my relief, Lars called long distance and said they had it.

Mathilde Grødem and Sigrid Hegdal met me at the Egersund station. I spent the night with Mathilde.

School Situation, Spring '42

About the first of March, all schools, all over the country, were closed. The reason was supposedly due to lack of fuel, but we learned later the teachers refused to join the new organization. About a month later they tried to open the schools, but teachers stood firm and refused to join. This time, all nonmembers were given walking papers. Then we heard that N.S. (*Nasjonal Samling = Name of the Nazi party in Norway during the war*) teachers would replace others, but there are so few of them, that they cannot begin to fill positions, and parents are all agreed not to send children to school if it happens.

Many principals and superintendents have been arrested and sent away to no one knows where - to frighten others into joining. Now, the school authorities of the land have given orders for schools to open with the same teachers or else be brought before the War Court, but as yet no schools have opened. Teachers are strongly organized and stand firm.

There are riots everywhere along the line where trains with teacher prisoners have stopped.

At Eastertime, all ministers were given warning that this was the last Sunday they were allowed to preach. People flocked to church from miles around. "So packed-in churches that Satan himself could not squeeze in", was quoted, but the night before, ministers had received telegrams that they could continue indefinitely until further orders from the Church Department in Oslo. All ministers who are not members of the new organization are working without pay. They also stand firmly organized and firm on their belief of right. It is a very trying time for pastors and teachers, and people do not know how long they will be allowed to hear the Word of God unadulterated from the pulpit.

(Reverend) Oanes is at Nodland. Several efforts to force him to join (*the N.S. -Nasjonal Samling, political party founded by Vidkun Quisling*) have failed.

March 7, 1942 - Saturday

I met Thelma Mong in town today, and she asked me to come home with her. Frøken *(Miss)* Anna Ålvik is moving, as all teachers not N.S. *(Nasjonal Samling = name of the Nazi party in Norway during the war)* are fired. So, I did want to see her before her departure, as no one knows when, if ever, we'll see her again. I took the late bus to Mong, and was I car sick? It had snowed and frozen over again, so the road was just like glass. It was awfully slow and dangerous walking. One could only take the smallest steps and then only at a risk, so it was a relief to relax one's nerves when we finally reached Myro. They ate "kvelds" *(the evening meal),* but I was glad to crawl into bed after heaving several times.

March 8, 1942 – Sunday

In the afternoon, Thelma and I stopped in to see Anna Ålvik who followed us to Rodvelt. Agnes (*Rotwell)* from Stavanger was there. Old Mikal (*Kristoffersen Grødem)* Rodvelt's health is very poor *(Andreas's father)*; he has some bad coughing spells which almost take his life. He is 83 but thinks clearly. I spent the night at Rodvelt. Thelma and I slept on the divan. Sivert is on a fishing trip to Ålesund and Haugesund.

March 9, 1942 - Monday

Monday, after dinner, I walked to Grødem. Arrived in time for Ladies Aid Society at Marie Omdal's. Onkel Petter came out to "Bjelkeveien" *(the road)* with horse and sleigh, so I really rode most of the way.

We are having awfully cold weather; everything is frozen up. Everyone has to carry or go after water with horse and sled. There is so little water that power stations cannot function half properly. People cannot cook by electricity nor use electric heaters; the current is too weak. When it comes on full, it is only for a few hours. The light is so poor that a kerosene light is equally bright. Everyone is praying for milder weather.

I have been meeting up with the lensmann here in Egersund every Saturday. The money I was to get from Elen's sister was taken over by another party immediately *(when)* war broke out in West U.S., Far East *(probably a reference to Japan bombing Pearl Harbor).* Could have used those 500 crowns *(kroner).*

I am planning on joining in on the Easter ski trip to Egelandsdalen, but it will be very difficult to get a place on the bus.

Sent Red Cross letter home today.

March 22, 1942 - Sunday

Tante Anne and I walked to Rodvelt in the afternoon.

March 25, 1942 - Wednesday

Anne and I went over again and helped bake "flat bread". I helped clean out some cupboards in the afternoon. Mikal Rodvelt is doing very poorly; he is very weak and waiting for the end.

March 28, 1942 - Saturday

I went to town again today. They use four buses to take passengers home on the Sokndal route.

One is lucky now to be able to buy a good magazine. Paper is also rationed now. The output of the Ukeblad *(weekly magazines)* Hjemmet *(The Home)* and Alle Kvinner *(All Women)* is very small. First there, first served. I borrowed a couple good books from a friend, Kristian Mikkelsen, - "Quo Vadis" which I read in a couple days and it was very good. Also borrowed "New York's Millionaire" or "The Four Millions" title of the other - short stories of New York life.

We are having mild weather at last, but no rain, so electricity is still poor.

I should have taken the Tonstad bus to Egelandsdal today, but there was no room on the bus. Astrid Omdal from Stavanger came out on same bus to spend Easter vacation in Omdal.

April 2, 1942 - Wednesday

Mikal Rodvelt passed away at 2:00 this morning. Tante Helene called up this morning.

April 3, 1942 - Friday

Today is Good Friday. Tante Helene and her cousin, Agnes Rotwell, came up for dinner. I went skiing in the afternoon on Onkel Petter's skis, but the snow was too new.

April 5, 1942 - Sunday

Today is Easter Sunday. We had a pork roast dinner and rice. In the afternoon, Einar and Jon Ø. came over. We had a political discussion. Martin Østrem and his son, Arvid, came over in the evening, and Marie G. and sisters.

Einar has Martin Østrem's job as telegraphist at Sandnes. Wait and see. Will it be the R or the E & A?

April 6, 1942 - Monday

It snowed about eighteen inches the Wednesday and Thursday before Easter. Friday brought bright sunshine - perfect skiing weather. Saturday it was foggy and rainy. Sunday and Monday there was more rain and lots of it. It is awfully sloppy out, so it may flood some places this week.

I was to have gone to Mong for dinner, but I stayed home on account of the weather. Sivert came up in the afternoon, but walking was so difficult that he wished he hadn't gone out. All the Omdal women came over for the evening.

April 7, 1942 - Tuesday

I intended to go to Rodvelt and help get ready for the funeral, but it rained all day steadily. Finally, at about 4:00 it held up and I went out. I went to work helping to make sandwiches until dark. I stayed with Thelma overnight.

April 8, 1942 - Wednesday

The funeral was today. The front room, filled with tables, seated about 35 at a time. 40-50 guests came. Each family that was invited brought something, so there was lots of good food and cakes of all kinds. The first serving began at 10:00 after which the funeral service was held. Several hymns were sung, and Nils Omdal gave a good talk. Tante Helene also said a few words. The bier and casket were carried out to a truck at the top of the hill, and everyone had a place either on the truck or in the one hired car. Inga Åvendal, Tante Anne, Mathilde, and I stayed home, and at 3:30 the procession returned to home, and they were served coffee and lunch again. At this table setting, many gave short talks in memory of the deceased.

I went home *(to Grødem)* as soon as we got through washing up. I got home about 8:30 p.m. Petter surely had turned the house upside down. How he can mess.

April 10, 1942 - Friday

I washed clothes, ironed, pressed, and packed to be ready to leave for Årrestad on Saturday, but began feeling myself unwell. Flu, I think it was, and I had to stay in bed a couple days. I telephoned to Tante Semine Østrem not to expect me yet.

April 11, 1942 - Saturday

Mathilde and Thelma came up in the afternoon and stayed overnight. Thelma is expecting, but when? I haven't talked with her about it yet.

There is no more flour to be sold from now on, as bakers get it all, and everyone is obliged to buy bread at the bakery. One can buy oat flour, oatmeal, and barley flour. Many people have to get along without potatoes too, so food is quite a problem. I have talked with people who have not eaten potatoes for months, only carrots and kålrabi or turnips. We have meat cards, but it is not every week one can buy on it. It is not always one can get ahold of fresh fish, either.

This poor food situation is going to result in a lot of sickness and many weaknesses among the younger generation. The butter allowed on the cards amounts to less than ½ lb. for a whole week. This doesn't go very far for a working man who takes lunch with him. I have noticed how a lot of town people are gradually losing weight.

April 13, 1942 - Monday

Mathilde stayed over, and she and I washed and scrubbed the living room and entrance.

April 14, 1942 - Tuesday

We baked flat bread all day. We are having lovely weather now. Snow drifts are disappearing fast.

April 15, 1942 - Wednesday

I got ready and left for Årrestad this morning. Anne carried my suitcase halfway out to the highway. I took the bus to town. I had to promise to come back and plant vegetables.

I made arrangements with the sheriff to report to the sheriff at Helleland from now on. I took the noon train out to Årrestad.

Little Ove Østrem is quite cranky, as he is getting his molars. He is 15 months old and is a smart kid. He surely is crazy about animals of all kinds.

I am having a soft time of it here. There's lots of time to knit and do things for myself. Torger and Malene are perfectly grand to me. I am over home *(to Onkel Ommund's and Tante Semine's)* most every day.

April 24, 1942 - Friday

I did errands in town for Malene and came home on the 2:30 train. I made an appointment to have a permanent next Wednesday.

Sanna Østrem is home on a month's vacation from nurse's training in Stavanger. She has only three months left, and she'll be through.

We had a good rainy spell about the first of May. Since then, it has been lovely weather.

Margrethe is engaged to Einar Sørdal who lives there but is a watchman on the line *(drift)* and gets good pay.

Mikael and Minnie are moving down to Vormevikt. Olav has gone back to Nærbø to carpentry.

Fredrik is engaged to Jenny and is getting married soon. He has a good job; he is a carpenter on the *(railroad)* line.

Sigurd has moved to Sokndal where he will begin a new bus route aside from his daily milk route to Helleland. He has bought a big new house for 25,000 kroner - a two-bath, three-story house. A doctor has his practice downstairs and will continue to rent from him.

Anna, Bergit, and Gudrun *(of Andreas and Berthe)* are all home again. Anna and Bergit got themselves in a little scandal and ought to be glad they escaped so easily.

May 7, 1942 - Thursday

Bertha Aarrestad made a trip to Moi to buy leather gloves but was disappointed. Although the factory is still functioning, all work is sold beforehand. There is not a glove to buy at any store or factory. But she visited with Ragna Moi and reported that her two children - Arvid age 3 years and Vegard 7 months, were sick with whooping cough and bronchitis after having just gotten over measles which she had also had. Ragna sent word she wanted me to come up and help her awhile, which of course I want to do, but will have to see what Malene says to that.

Torkel *(Thomas)* Mikkelsen passed away this Tuesday very suddenly. The funeral will be Friday.

May 8, 1942 - Friday

I went to Grødem to plant a garden before going to Moi again. I got there in the afternoon, fixed the fence, fertilized, and dug up the garden.

May 9, 1942 - Saturday

I planted flower plants and a few seeds from the year before, and red beets, turnips, radishes, lettuce, parsnips, and greskar *(pumpkin)*.

I bicycled to town and took the train to Årrestad in the evening. I spent the night at Malene's and left Sunday for Moi.

I made arrangements with the lensmann *(sheriff)* before leaving, as I must report each week to authorities.

May 10, 1942 - Sunday

I got to Moi about noon. Karsten was at the train to meet me and took my baggage. The little fellow, Vegard, looked very poorly. It really will be a wonder if he gains health and develops normally and becomes in no way handicapped. They are really afraid of losing him.

May 17, 1942 - Sunday

Today is Norway Freedom Day *(Constitution Day)* but no observance and no flags; it is forbidden, of course. A few have been out in their national costumes.

Ascension Day was also observed as any other Sunday. Children's service in the morning and Children's Day Sports in the afternoon.

Everything is going fine. The children are improving. I am enjoying myself lots but there is not much to do. I sleep until 8:00 every day. Today, as I was about to get dressed about 9:00, Ragna came with a breakfast tray, so I crept under the covers *(feather bed)* and enjoyed my "coffee" in bed, after which I lay and read the "Scarlet Pimpernel" until about 11:00. Soft! Eh? Wot? I finished the book later in the day. It was not a bad book. I read two others last week "Det Blåser Fra Dauingfjell" *(1934)* and "Ingen vei går utenom" (1935), *(collectively called, in English, The Wind from the Mountains)*. Both were very good by a Norwegian author *(Trygve Emanuel Gulbranssen)*.

We have had steady good weather since Easter, except two or three days of rain about the first of May. The rain did wonders, but we need a little rain again now.

I had a chance to go home via Sweden and Spain. The police department telephoned, but I answered, "not interested", as it seemed like taking too much of a chance - so I am still waiting, but I felt a pang of homesickness the other night when I got on a train and saw an American trunk labeled "New York". The owner was a young man who was leaving for the U.S.A. May he reach home safely.

June 7, 1942 - Sunday

I came down from Moi after spending four weeks with Ragna. Little Vegard is improving, so Ragna is going to try to get along alone. A terrible restlessness has come over me, so I must have a change of environment, even after this month's stay. Moi is a lovely town and the most interesting for its size that I have been in, but strange enough, when everyone are strangers, it gets to be lonesome.

June 18, 1942, Årrestad, Helleland

(This letter was hand-carried out of Norway by a relative who took it to Sweden and mailed it from there)

Dear Mother, Dad and All of You,

How are you, one and all? I surely have been wondering how things are over there. How is Martin? I have been thinking mostly about him. I do hope he is regaining his health and the rest of you are all well. Are any of the boys out to war? I have been trying to make myself believe that none are and consoling myself with that. Is there any state of alarm there along the coast? You see, we hear rumors, as I suppose you do about us over here. Everything has been very quiet here for a long time, that is, right around here. We don't know what is going on north or east of us.

I received Mother's and Martin's letters shortly before the mail was stopped. I answered both, but too late, as they came back. That was about the first of December. Since then, I have had no mail. I got Aunt Ellen Peterson's letter too.

Elsa, a daughter of Tønnes Friestad, is mailing this from Sweden. She is leaving in a few days to be married there. Whether she is planning on living there or not, I don't know. If so, you can send me letters through her. Find out from Al and Sig Freestad (Tønnes's brothers in the U.S.A. - they changed the spelling of their last name). *They have also received letters through her, I am sure. I am going to see her tomorrow, and if she is going to remain in Sweden, I shall send with her money so she can re-address your letters and send them on to me. You will have to address the letters to her then. See? No doubt you have been wondering how we are faring over here. I must say, we are doing very well under the circumstances. We have had plenty food - of its kind - all the way - that is, we who live on farms, but when I've been in town and have seen what they live on there, I'm mighty thankful to get back out on a farm. The country people helped the town folks as long as they could, but there is such strict control now, that it is almost impossible. There has been a scarcity of potatoes all spring. I* have talked with folks who have lived on only rutabagas and fish for dinner for several months - not a spud. It isn't because they don't have the money to buy, but there just isn't anything else to resurrect in town. And - the bread - you should see the bread. It's heavy as lead and sour and soggy, as well as bitter - that's the bark in it. When you try to slice it, it sticks to the knife. Sounds appetizing - what? I know I don't eat much of it. We eat "flat brod" (flat bread), "potatoe kake" (potato cakes), waffles of oat flour, and lefse of that "wonder" flour (which is not so bad) instead of bread.

All our relatives are well. Tante Valborg isn't quite as frisky as she has been. She thought it was an awfully hard winter without coffee. She is getting old, you know (69 years), and is used to strong coffee three to four or more times a day. She was quite nervous last I saw her (about three weeks ago).

At Dybing (I was there last Sunday), Tante Teoline and Onkel Johan (Gystøl) are fine. At Tante Berthe (Østrem's) and here at Tante Semine (Østrem's), they are all in the best of health. Semine had a letter from Martha Eiesland yesterday. Things are OK there too.

At Rodvelt, I suppose you know by now, that Old Mikal

Valborg, Berthe, Semine, Teoline – sisters of Christine Egelandsdal Peterson

Rodvelt passed away just before Easter. I helped serve at the funeral April 8th. Young Mikal is in Kristiansand in the Arbeids Tjeneste (Work Service) *which takes the place of the "Exis" or Compulsory Military Training. He will be there and home again soon.*

At Grødem, everything is going its usual tempo and style. Onkel Petter didn't send his sheep to Liland this year. He is keeping them home, and I think he is wise in doing so. It has been so cold this spring that many sheep have died up there. In spite of the fact that this is the middle of June, it isn't summer. It has been so cold since crops were put in that they are growing awfully slow. At some locations, the potatoes are just coming up.

I spent most of last week at Grødem, and now Onkel Lars telephoned that they were coming down this weekend, so I'll have to peddle my way down again this weekend, too. I spent three months with Onkel Lars last winter.

*I haven't seen any Nesvåg people since last year, but Thelma had met Gurina (*Nesvåg) *and Marie* (Tønneson) *Elle, who was so sick last year, a couple weeks ago. They had told her to tell me they were expecting me out again. So, you can greet Sina* (Nesvåg) *Omdal and tell her that it sounded as if things were OK there. There had been a lot of Nesvåg people in Mong to a meeting.*

Sigurd Østrem has moved to Sokndal. He has a regular bus route from Sokendal to Egersund, as well as other trucking.

Has Aunt Ellen Peterson *heard that Lars* Stapnes *(and family) have moved to Svånes? I suppose she has heard that Trygve, their son, passed away between Christmas and New Year's. It has been hard on them. Believe me, it is not much fun to be chased out of your own home. Selmer Stapnes' family* (father of Petter Stapnes in Bow, WA) *have also moved to Svånes.*

The seven from Mong have not returned home yet. They have been gone about nine months now. The teachers who left did not come back. Those who remained have now started teaching upon request after a three month's "spring vacation". The "real" teachers and preachers are working without pay. As far as I know, Ingvald Omdal is back on the job.

Did you receive the Red Cross letter I sent about three

months ago? I am patiently waiting for a reply. Please make an effort to send a few lines, so I can hear how you all are and how things in general are.

Elen Johnson's money went in the wrong hands. When her sister, Tilla, got her letter, she went directly to the bank, but it was too late to save it. I wonder if she knows about it. As for myself, I'm getting along OK; I am earning a little here and there.

I hope you didn't look for me on that last boat. I just didn't have the courage. The Police Department telephoned and notified me that they'd help me make arrangements, but I said, "No thanks. I prefer traveling in peace times!" I hear now they made a safe return trip. I hope next summer I'll be back with you. I had a spell of homesickness this winter and it has been gnawing some this spring, too.

It's after midnight and getting dark. I can hardly see the lines anymore.

Greet Bertha and Sina and everyone - friends and neighbors.

Please greet Carrie H. (Carrie Stapnes Holt) *and Sina B.* (Sina Larsen Stapnes Birkeland) *from Sigrid Stapnes. Also, Kristine Stapnes tells me to send a greeting to Aunt Ellen* (Ellen Stapnes Peterson) *and Martin M.* (Martin Martinsen's) *family. She* (Kristine) *and Sigrid are both sitting right here, busy sewing. I stopped by their sewing room. Larsemann* (nickname for Lars Stapnes) *is a Second Mate now.*

Sending greetings to everyone from Semine. If the others knew I was writing, I'm sure they would have sent greetings too.

Love to all, Sophie

P.S. When you answer, send the letter to Elsa Friestad - Grundsund, Sverige, Sweden; she will forward.

July 10, 1942 - Friday

I have been another month at Årrestad.

I spent the last Sunday in June at Grødem. Tante Thea and her son Petter spent the weekend there. Tante Helene came Saturday evening. She took the bus to town and the train up. On July 4 and 5, Tante Thea, Tante Helene, and Marit came to Årrestad (they came Saturday evening and stayed over Sunday). Marit stayed until Monday and met Jan and

Magnhild and went to Moi. Magnhild *(Marit's sister)* and Jan Øvestad are just married and are in the market for new furniture.

Sigrid and Kristine Stapnes *(friends, not sisters)* were up a few weeks ago. They picked lilies of the valley and had coffee and lunch out on the hill in the warm sunshine.

I received lovely dress material from Sigrid the other day with the promise to sew it also.

Today I spent the afternoon in the "Dalen". I made plans for a bicycle trip to Sokndal tomorrow.

I saw Bergit *(Østrem's)* trousseau. Anything so complete have I never seen before. She told of her experiences in Flekkefjord.

July 12, 1942 - Sunday

I had a fine bicycle trip to Sokndal. It took a little over four hours. The weather was lovely for a change. I spent the night with Signy and Sigurd Østrem. I was served a lovely breakfast in bed Sunday morning. In the afternoon, I bicycled to Grødem. I only got as far as Rodvelt, where I spent the night. I came to a place in the pass where T. had blasted out the way and had stopped all traffic for 24 hours. They had worked all Sunday to repair it, and it was just finished as I came by. Fifty men were getting ready to leave. Experience showed they used too much dynamite. In case of invasion, the same will take place.

August 29, 1942 - Saturday

I spent three weeks at Grødem helping with the hay. It has been very poor hay weather - very little sunshine, very cold weather. I haven't worn a light summer dress until now, the 29th of August. In many places the hay rotted. Petter was very lucky to get the hay in without getting it spoiled… that is, the thick hay. He had good help too. Mathilde for three weeks, myself for three weeks, Lars for one week, and others a few days at a time. Anne is getting more and more hopelessly pokey. She never gets anything done.

(Note – In the later writings, we know that Sophie was arrested on October 17, 1942 while preparing for her Onkel Lars's 50th birthday party. You will read more details in several of the following entries.)

Letters from Liebenau Internment Camp

Jail, Prison, Internment for Sophie
Prison Letters from Sophie to Family
Sophie Yearns for News from Home
Sophie Treated Well
American Red Cross Packages Appreciated
Sophie Hopes to Return to Norway for Christmas

Mit Luftpost Nach Nord Amerika

Interniertenpost! Taxe perçue 40 Rpf

Mr & Mrs Tollag Peterson

Bow,

U.S. CENSORSHIP EXAMINED By 497

TETTNANG (WÜRTT) 22.4.43-20

Ort: Washington (State)

Gebührenfrei!

Land: U.S.A.

O/0853

Absender: Name: Sophie Peterson

Gebäude: Josef's Haus **Stock:** 2 **Zimmer:** 58

Internierungslager Liebenau Post Tettnang (Deutschland)

U.S. CENSORSHIP EXAMINED By 497

After a short stay at a jail in Stavanger, Norway, Sophie was transferred to Grini Prison Camp, a Nazi Concentration Camp in Bærum, Norway, where she was kept for about seven weeks. She was then transferred to the Liebenau Internment Camp on Lake Constance, close to Meckenbeuren in southern Germany near Switzerland. Liebenau Internment Camp was used as an assembly point for prisoners who were being considered for exchange. The following letters were written by Sophie to friends and relatives, sent from the internment camp.

December 18, 1942 - Liebenau, Germany

Dear Theodora,

I just got here a few days ago, so this is our first opportunity of sending mail. I like it much better here than where I came from (the Grini Gestapo Prison). *We are treated kindly, get plenty of food, are allowed to be outdoors all we want during the day, and can go hiking most every day. Here there are sewing rooms, a library, and language classes every day, so the time passes very quickly. I am sending for more clothes and my knitting. We are to receive packages free of charge from Norway. Letters may also be sent free of postage. Inquire about it for yourself and answer soon. I am in the best of health. I hope Mother, Dad, and the family are all well. Is Martin well again? I hope so. Is Melvin married? What is Carl doing and all the others? Greet my friends and tell them to write. Hello to all the family and in-laws.*

Christmas Greetings to All, Sophie

December 18, 1942 – Liebenau, Germany

Dear Folks,

You don't know how anxious I am to know how you all are. I hope you are all well and everything else is OK. After being interned near Oslo about two months, we were brought here on the border between Germany and Switzerland. On a clear day we can see the Alps. Our journey took five days - three days by boat and two days by train. We are on a lovely estate with about 600 internees. We are being treated very kindly and are given good food and many privileges. The Red Cross treats us to a lovely food package every week. So please, please don't worry about me and don't feel sorry for me because I am rather enjoying this new adventure. Did you receive my Red Cross letter dated last March? I shall write often now. Please inquire about the quickest way of sending me mail. Write soon and often and tell all the home news. All our relatives in Norway are well, and I can greet you from them all. How is Martin? Love and best wishes for a Merry Christmas and a Happy New Year.

Greetings to all - Sophie

December 20, 1942 – Liebenau, Germany

Dear Thelma!

Thoughts go back to the last time we met. I thank you! How is the situation at your place and how is Rolf, your baby boy? I very often think of you all back in Norway. It was very unexpected for me to celebrate Christmas at this place, because when we were at Grini we expected to go back home. Well, we had to travel - and it happened so fast.

Now we've been here a week. We are ten from Norway. It seems one has to take whatever comes along and can't do anything about it. We have enough food, a warm bed, and can do almost what we want. I wish I had some knitting wool. I have written to Grødem to ask for different things. I hope they will send something really soon.

We have nice weather, not so cold, no snow and on a clear day we can see the Alps in Switzerland. We are located only a few hours from the Swiss border. I have been to church three times today. We are also going to have a "Juletrefest" (Christmas tree party), *they say.*

Best regards to the Rodvelts. Please write soon. You may send letters free of charge. Use message: (Internierten Post) instead of stamps.

Sophie

January 1, 1943 - Liebenau, Germany

Dear Folks,

I wonder what you folks are doing this New Year's Day, and I'm wondering what this New Year will bring. I hope it does bring peace. Many people expect to be released this month - some going home, others exchanged or transported. How long I'll be here, I don't know. If there is another transport, I may go with it - to New York, of course. But if I do, I shall let you know ahead of time. What do you think I should do? I'll not be allowed to go back to Norway until after the war. I am satisfied being here for the time being. The American Red Cross packages which we receive each week help so much. I have not heard from Norway since I came here almost three weeks ago, but mail takes so long now. These have been very strange Christmas and New Year's holidays for some of us, but we have now seen how some of these other countries keep Christmas. I hope this finds you all well. I am waiting for my package from Grødem, so I'll have some knitting to do. Not so much to do here.

Love and Best Wishes to All, Sophie

January 2, 1943 – Liebenau, Germany

Dear Tora,

I wrote to Theodora last month, so now I'll send you a line. I have just written to the folks again. I am so anxious to hear how things are at home, but I suppose it'll be ages before I get any reply. I hope you are well, all of you. Little Siggy, I suppose, is quite grown up now. I surely would like to see everyone again, but I'll have to be satisfied to remain here for a while yet, I suppose, although one never knows. There is talk of a transport. I wonder if I should sign up. If the war should last much longer, I'd be better off coming home on the transport, I guess, but in case I do I'll surely let you know. We are treated well here and allowed to feel quite free, although there isn't much to do but read library books and go for walks. Each week we look forward to the American Red Cross packages. Write soon. Hello, Sig (Tora Freestad's husband). *Greet Al and Hanna Freestad* (Sig's brother in Arlington, WA, U.S.A.).

Love, Sophie

March 11, 1943 – Liebenau, Germany

Dear Folks,

I hope you have been receiving the letters I have sent from time to time. I've been here three months now, but the time has passed very quickly. The weather has been grand, so we spend a great deal of the time outdoors either going for walks or just sitting around in the gardens knitting and reading. We are quite undisturbed from the outside. We receive our Red Cross food parcels regularly which we certainly do enjoy. I hope you are all well and everything is OK at home. I wanted to write a letter to Melvin and Wanda Peterson (Sophie's brother and his wife) *upon hearing they were married, but as you know, these cards and letters are limited, but as soon as I can, I shall write them. Until then, give them my best regards. There are so many things I would like to write and ask about, but space does not allow. Friends and relatives in Norway are good about writing often. All are well to this day. I'm beginning to look for a letter from you also. I am in good health and in good humor. Greetings all. Romans 8.*

Love Sophie

March 25, 1943 - Liebenau, Germany

Dear Mother, Dad, and "Sosken" (Siblings),

This is my first opportunity of sending you air mail, and I hope it is not long in reaching you. Now there will be air mail service each week; isn't that grand? However, I hope you have received at least some of the letters I have been sending from time to time since December on. I hope this finds you all well, and especially do I hope Martin is quite well. I am in the best of health myself. My letters will be short, as you see, but you may write as long letters as you like and as often as you like, so I hope you do write often and tell about all the things I have missed out on these four years I've been away. Relatives and friends in Norway write often to me here. They are all well. Also, Aunt Ellen Peterson's people in Stapnes write. I had a letter last week from Kristine Stapnes. I also heard from Sina Omdal's people in Nesvåg. The relatives felt very badly about my sudden departure last October 17. Except for the first two months, I have had no reason for complaints about anything. We have plenty of good food, comfortable rooms, and as much freedom as can be expected. We receive Red Cross food parcels each week. The weather is grand, so I am spending much time outdoors. The Lord is good. He takes care of His. Greet friends.

Love, Sophie

April 22, 1943 - Liebenau, Germany

Dear Mother, Dad and All,

I hope you have received the last two letters which were supposed to have been sent by air. Things are going much the same as usual. After Easter, however, there will be a big change. Quite a number of internees are leaving for a camp in France where they will join other members of their families; husbands, brothers or sons (Liebenau internment camp was for women). *I am satisfied to remain here. Sunday is Easter. Teddy and Esther* (the Norwegian girls), *and I have baked a cake and fixed a little extra for the holidays. We are receiving eggs for Easter which will be quite a treat, not having seen hen fruit for quite some time. There has been very little news from Norway lately; nothing from Grødem for many weeks now, but I am waiting every day. Anna Østrem wrote last week - everything was alright with them. Onkel Lars's boys, Petter and Henne, are spending Easter Holidays in Fidjeland Mountains in Sirdalen, skiing. Here we have lovely spring weather. All the apple orchards round about are pink with blossoms. It is beautiful. I hope you will write soon and tell all the family news. Best wishes to neighbors and friends.*

Love, Sophie

May 19, 1943 - Liebenau, Germany

Dear Mother, Dad, and All of You!

I haven't written for a few weeks now. I hope this finds you all well. I have received nothing from you yet, but since it is over five months since I started writing, I am in hopes of hearing soon. I am very well myself, only a little anxious for a change. We are only nine Norwegians left. One of our friends was released and left for her home near Oslo the other day. I have news from Norway regularly and had a lovely package from Grødem a few weeks ago. Anne and Helene wrote they were all well and very busy. Lars and Thea write that they are fine and the same goes for relatives at Helleland, Årrestad and up the valley. They all ask me to greet you when I write. From Tante Martha I have heard nothing yet. Kristine Stapnes writes that they are living with Kaia and Otto. Berntine Skadberg and family are OK. I know Aunt Ellen will be interested to know. I had a letter from one of Peder

Omdal's girls – they are all well. It sounded as if Ingvald was working in Stavanger. Grandmother Rodvelt is the same. (Note – Grandmother Theodora Rodvelt had died March 29, 1943. News traveled slow about this.) *I have heard nothing from Nesvåg. If it is possible and not too great an expense, could you try and send me some underwear? Can't get them here or from relatives in Norway.*

Love, Sophie

June 2, 1943 - Liebenau, Germany

Dear Mother, Dad, and All of You!

Congratulations on your 59th birthday, Dad, and (Brother) *Peter on your 40th! I would like to write separately to Peter, but my quota is so small you'll all have to share the same letters. But remember, I can receive any number of letters, so I hope you are all writing. Today it is exactly four years since I left home. I never dreamed then that I should stay away so long, nor live through all these experiences which I have had the last few years. If I live through it, and I shall if the Lord wills, I shall be richer for it. I hope you are not worried about me, as I am very well and in good care, have had my health all the time, a lot to be thankful for, and have plenty to eat. If only the people in Norway had it half as good as I. There is so little food to get there. They had an excellent herring fishing season this spring. I had a letter from Tante Anne yesterday. They were busy with spring work. She fully intends to accompany me home when I come. She's fed up with working and slaving on that farm with hardly any help. She's worn out. Thelma and Sivert Mong have an eight-month-old boy named Rolf. Have you inquired with the Red Cross about sending me anything? If it is at all possible to do so, I need underwear most and walking shoes. If it's too expensive, never mind. Looking each day for a letter from you.*

Love, Sophie.

June 24, 1943 - Liebenau, Germany

Dear Mother,

Of course, you won't get this for your birthday, but I am writing so you will know I am thinking of you on that day and am hoping you are having a pleasant birthday in spite of all the unpleasantness in the world and about us. I wish I were there to bake a cake and help to celebrate the day with you. I hope you will have many more birthdays to come and that at this time next year there will be peace in the world and I at home again with you all. I am still anxiously waiting to hear from you. I wonder why they don't come, or don't you write? A friend here, who came when I did, has received many letters from her people in California, so if you answered my letters, I should have had them long ago. Have you inquired at Red Cross about sending the underthings and shoes I mentioned? My pajamas are also getting quite lacey. I shall save some of my mending for an exhibit someday. However, I am glad as long as there is thread and material to mend with. I had a letter from Bertha Aarrestad. They seem to be in very good spirits, working hard and hoping for the best. My love to all the family.

Sophie

July 1, 1943 - Liebenau, Germany

Dear Mother and All of You!

I wrote just last week, but, as we have a new address, I thought I'd let you have it as soon as possible. I have had no luck with the other address. If you have written, I have received nothing. Each day I say to myself, "Surely there must be something for me from America today", but I'm disappointed every time. Other letters are only five weeks on the way from over there. Why don't yours come through? I am in good health, only suffering a little from eye strain. I shall go to an oculist one of these days. I can greet you from Lars and Thea. They are living peacefully but in a state of expectancy, hoping for the best. The boys, Petter and Henne, are at home. I had a card from Stapnes a few days ago. Everyone seemed to be well and living at home - no more evacuations yet. On Saturday we Americans are giving a 4th of July Garden Tea Party for the other internees. We are about 400 now. So, we are more than busy chasing around getting things ready for it. It's fun for a change, and the time passes so much more quickly when we have something to do. I do hope everything is OK with everyone. I don't dare to think of what may be happening.

Love, Sophie

August 6, 1943 - Liebenau, Germany

Dear Folks,

I had just written you this a.m. to thank you for the lovely parcel received yesterday and dated March 11 - May 10. But today I received your letters; Mama's from May 1, sister Theodora (Hansen's) *from May 14; and Thelma's* (Mrs. Edwin Haaland in Bow, WA Edison Lutheran Church) *from April 30. Today I am the happiest person in the Camp, I am sure. It is so good to hear you are all well and that Martin is much improved. I see I have two new nephews Stanton* (Button) of Oscar and Eileen Peterson *and Marvin* of Melvin and Wanda Peterson. *I understood that none of the boys are in the Service - am I right? You didn't mention Carl.* (Note - Brother Carl Peterson, in the second row, just behind the dog, had been in the service for about a year at this time.)

The parcel was fairly banged up and showed signs of being repacked at Geneva. I don't know if anything has been lost. It was open when I got it. These are the contents, so you can see yourself, as so many things get lost in the mail these days: 1 pair of panties, 2 pair of cotton hose, 1 pair of anklets, 3 hankies, coffee, sugar, raisins, bouillon cubes, 4 noodle soups, vitamin tablets, 2 pencils, toothbrush, comb, wafers, chewing gum, 3 soaps, and 1 candy bar. The clothes articles were most appreciated as we have plenty of food. Lately I have also received a few things from Norway, so I think I shall manage until I get back to Norway again. I would say don't send any more parcels, as things may only get lost. All I need really now is a girdle and shoes, but I'll manage somehow. I have lots of yarn from Norway, so I have plenty of things to knit. Grandma Theodora Rodvelt died after a stroke on March 29 (Helene asks me to write you this). I am writing Molly about it too. I had a letter from Østrems at Årrestad today. I can greet you that they are all well, and the same for Grødem and others. Do write often. Greet neighbors and friends.

Love and Best Wishes to You All. Keep smiling.

Sophie

August 26, 1943 - Liebenau, Germany

Dear Theodora,

I hope the folks have received my reply to the first letters received. Since then has come your first letter dated April 16, and others from Ruth Bradley, Mrs. Donner, Gladys K., and this a.m. one from Tora dated May 8. It is wonderful to hear from you all again. I only wish letters wouldn't take so long on the way. Send "Transatlantic Air Mail" as I do. I wrote home and sent thanks for the lovely parcel, but I guess it is to you I owe the thanks. Whenever I write to any of you, you know it is to you all, as my quota doesn't allow but four letters per month, divided between Norway and you, also eight postcards, but they are only for Norway. I hope others will write, but I can't promise to answer. If you send another parcel, be sure it is well packed. What I need worst are shoes and underthings, but I believe I asked for that some time ago and you have perhaps already sent them. Of course, I could use some yarn, as that which I am working on is not for myself. I need toothpaste and bobby pins as well, but I won't die if I don't get them. I sent your coffee, raisins, and soap to Norway. I know they will be delighted with such luxuries. I am so happy to know all are well at home, as that is the main thing. I am healthy and am kept quite busy. After coffee now we are going hiking, and those who wish may go swimming. I shall take a book along and read while they splash. Give my love to all.

Lovingly, Sophie

September 16, 1943 - Liebenau, Germany

Dear Theodora,

Your letter, dated July 21, arrived today, less than two months on the way. I hope you will always send by airmail, then I can expect to hear from you more often. Now I have received three letters from you. You said you had sent several parcels, but as yet I have received only the one that I mentioned in earlier letters. But you should use the address I give you on this folder as there are so many Liebenaus in this country. Some of my letters have been to no less than four Liebenaus before coming here. Parcels sometimes are worn out that way before arriving at the right destination. I was happy to know all are well. I guessed as much about Carl. Is he too far from home to visit? (Note - she probably thinks he is still at training camp.)

I'm wondering if we'll be here for Christmas again. We Norwegians have a petition in to return to Norway, but I don't believe it will be granted, so I expect we'll be here until the war is over. Over fifty are being transferred to Belgium to avoid overcrowding here. Since classes have begun, I am quite busy with Spanish and German and attending various lecture courses, all conducted by fellow internees, of course. I am also assisting with the English teaching once a week. Tell the folks that Tante Anne has written that Grandonkel Tollef (Omdal) *is slowly failing in health and could not get to Omdal this summer. As far as I know, others we know in Norway are OK. I'm in best of health. You can send snapshots, I hear, so I would love to have any you can send. Write often. Give my love to all at home - David, Chris, his folks Carl and Sofie* (Larsen) Hansen, *and other friends.*

Much Love, Sophie

September 21, 1943 - Liebenau, Germany

Dear Sister Tora,

I was pleased to get your first letter dated May 8 last week, but I was surprised to hear you had moved to Skykomish. Did you sell your houses in Everett? I am sorry to hear Siggy's foot is not yet corrected. Poor kid. Of course, you must do what you can for him. I surely would like to see all my nephews and nieces now, and the rest of you as well. I wish you could send me some snaps. It is about a month now since I received Mother's and (Theodora) *Teddy's letters, so every day I'm looking for more. I wonder if you couldn't send by "Transatlantic Air Mail", same as I. I hope you are all well as I am, but I expect you are busier. However, I keep quite busy.*

Sergeant Carl Peterson, Sophie's Brother, U.S.A. Army

Today I've been picking up apples (*there are large orchards outside the grounds*). *Tomorrow is laundry day. Three of us volunteer to do the laundry for this floor every other week. I prefer doing something to lying around. Goodness knows we get enough lazy habits here. We have a very fine library which I surely enjoy. One can always read - good educational books too, which I otherwise would never find time to read. Regular classes are starting up again next week. I am one of the assistant English teachers* (*charity work*). *Class meets only once a week. I am tutoring two others in English, and I am taking German lessons every other day. So, you see, time does not drag too much. But I do hope this terrible war soon ends so those yet living may return to their loved ones. Much love to you, Sig* (Freestad) *and Siggy. Give my love to all at home.*

Sophie

September 23, 1943 - Liebenau, Germany

Dear Mother, Dad and All,

I hope this finds you all well. Here it is fall again and I am still here. I dread the thought of another winter here, but perhaps I am better off here than in Norway anyway. Another lady from Norway is free this week but I don't envy her the trip. She goes to Bergen. I have had hardly any mail from Norway this month. On the whole, there has been very little. Something is holding it up. I wrote to Theodora last week. I hope she received it. She said you were sending parcels; I have received only one as yet. I hope you have not been sending food, as that is quite unnecessary. Perhaps you should wait and see if I receive the others before you send more. In fact, it isn't necessary to send any, although there are many things in the line of clothes I could use, but I can always manage somehow. I made myself a pair of shoes this week. You'd laugh if you saw them - they are only for inside wear with grass soles and pieces of material. One learns a lot from an experience of this kind. We are not so exact about clothes, just so it is something clean, mended and warm. I am lucky to have my knitted outer garments. Some have gotten clothes from the Red Cross but not I. I had expected that Carl was in the service, so I was not surprised.

Best Wishes and Love to All, Sophie.

P.S. Please use the address I give you.

October 6, 1943 - Liebenau, Germany

Dear Martin and Margaret,

I received your letter of June 17 last Sunday as a few of us had just sat down to our usual afternoon coffee on the terrace. The news about Carl gave me quite a shock, but at the same time I had felt that you were holding something back. We can only hope and pray for his safe keeping. It doesn't help to worry, and I don't want anyone to worry about me, as I am quite OK in every way. In less than two weeks it will be a year since my internment, and I can't say that I have ever felt better physically, thanks to the American Red Cross for their wonderful help. But I often want to kick myself for getting stuck over here when I could have been of some good another place.

Tell Theodora I received her package last Saturday containing the yarn, slippers, chocolate bars, and present from Selma. The list was gone this time too, and the package had been repacked somewhere along the way. I wish they would use the address I give you, as there are so many other Liebenaus. I will write again next week to Mother. I hope Mother doesn't worry too much. I am glad they are doing well on the farm. I surely wish I were back there with you all again and hope the time is not so far away now. We are having beautiful weather for this time of the year, and each time I hear the white geese going over I think of Carl.

I am kept very busy with lessons, etc., so time passes quickly, but I had hoped to be back in Norway for Christmas. Give my love to all the family and my friends.

Love, Sophie

October 14, 1943 - Liebenau, Germany

Dear Sis,

I received yesterday a copy of your telegram, forwarded from Geneva. It was twenty days from Geneva; a pleasant surprise and good to have such recent news that all is OK. Your package arrived October 2, and I am especially grateful for the yarn and slippers. I am afraid some things were missing as the parcel was badly broken, and the list of articles was also missing. These were the contents - five skeins of yarn, slippers, knitting needles, six candy bars, peanuts and

Selma Omdal's gifts. Please thank her for me for the hankie and framed scripture passage which happens to be one of my favorite verses. The peanuts were the first I've had in four years, so you can imagine how I enjoyed them. Your letter written June 19 arrived today, exactly one month after your air mail letter which you wrote July 21. Since you asked me to write what I'd like you to send me, I'll tell you what I need most: pajamas, bobby pins, a few yards of print material, underwear and any plain shoes - I have asked for shoes before as I need these badly. I surely would like a knitting book, and others I see have received them, but they may have been sent directly from the shop. I was quite upset when I heard from Martin where Carl is, but there is nothing we can do but trust that the Lord will be with him and spare him as He has spared me until this day. How about Uncle Peder (Peterson's) boys, (Palmer, Mynor and Ernest), and how is Arnold (Hansen)? I am glad to hear that Mother is keeping well. Thanks again for the telegram, parcels, and everything. Write when you hear from Carl.

Love to All, Sophie

October 17, 1943 - Liebenau, Germany

Dear Theodora,

Today I have just received a letter from Gya with snapshots taken on Tante Valborg's 70th birthday. All of her children and grandchildren were there for the occasion. They all look fine in the pictures. I wish I could send them to you, but I am afraid it is not allowed. The old man who has always lived with them, you remember, died just on that day. They had had an anniversary celebration on Onkel Karl's 60th birthday in Egelandsdal. All are well there now, but they have had scarlet fever, and one of the boys was very low for a whole week but is OK now. Mikal Egelandsdal's wife, Tomine, seems to be well again. Grand Onkel Tollef Omdal I hear, is quite low. The coffee, raisins, and soap you sent me in the first parcel, I sent to Grødem and it got there just for Onkel Petter's birthday. You can imagine how they enjoyed the coffee. I should greet you so much from Petter and Tante Anne. They have had a stormy and wet fall in Norway, but here we are enjoying a lovely fall. In Gya, they were having a time getting their *fifteen "mål poteter"* (measurement of land equaling 3.8 acres) *harvested. Only Ole and Mikael Gya are home, the other two are working out, and only the youngest girl, Valborg, is home. I was awfully glad for the house slippers and yarn. I have the jumper half made already. What do you hear from Carl?*

Love, Sophie

November 19, 1943 - Liebenau, Germany

Dear Mother and Dad and All,

I was delighted with the package which came yesterday - the third one now, and this one was less than three months on the way. Others have taken longer. Everything was there, even the list this time. They're doing better. I was more than pleased with everything. The shoes fit fine as do the other things. Just think, it is nearing Christmas again. I hope this will be the last one here. I am glad I'm kept busy. It makes the time pass more quickly. It is getting cold and wintry. We had a little snow, but it didn't stay. Last week there was a party for the camp. We are still about 400. Two Dutch and English girls and I did the whole baking. We received quite a recognition for it, and we each rated a present from the Camp Captain. Personally, I don't care any about these parties and didn't go, but everyone got their share of the goodies anyway. We Norwegians and a few Dutch spent a quiet, pleasant evening together. One of these Norwegians is from Portland, Oregon and is fairly well acquainted around Burlington and most of Washington, for that matter, having traveled many years as an evangelist. Three others are, or rather were, in the same work, one having lived In California. The other two are from Minnesota. Well, thanks so much for everything, and I hope this finds you all well. My thoughts are much with Carl. Do you hear anything from him? Could he write to me? Best wishes for a good Christmas, and may we have a happier one next year. Greetings to all.

Love, Sophie

November 19, 1943 - Liebenau, Germany

Dear Teddy,

I was glad to get your letter dated August 24. You can't write too often to suit me, but I would like to get one from Mother too, now and then. So, you finally got my old ancient history letters after all. I hope you have received more recent ones by this time. I am writing at least two each month, if not more. I received Bertha Omdal's letter, mailed August 23, and would like to answer it too, but if she doesn't get one it is because my quota won't reach. I hope she will write again anyway. I had such a nice letter from Onkel Lars in Norway. You see, I was picked up from his place on his 50th birthday a year ago. There was a big dinner party that evening, and I was taken away in the midst of the preparations. It was a sad parting, believe me. He wrote to me on that same day a year later. I had the sad news that Grandonkel Tollef (Omdal) *has passed away. Onkel Lars didn't give the date, but the funeral was October 9.*

Tante Valborg and Tante Teoline will be pleased to hear you have visited their daughters, Lisabeth (Halvorson) *and Maria* (Halvorson, at Squamish, British Columbia, Canada.) *I was glad to hear that I can soon expect another parcel. You know, we are just like a bunch of kids looking forward to our parcels. I hope it is all intact. I wish you would say in your letters what you are sending, so I can check up on it when it comes. I expect to finish my sweater this week and am very pleased to have the house slippers. Two other girls and I are doing the baking for a camp party this week. We will be baking three days. We are still almost 400 enrolled. I'm sorry I can't write more. Greet Bertha and Sina Omdal and of course everyone at home and your own family and friends. Love Sophie.*

December 1, 1943 - Liebenau, Germany

Dear Theodora,

Your letter of September 28 and the snap of David (Teddy's son and Sophie's nephew) *arrived yesterday. 'Twas a sweet picture and so big he is, only I must have one now with him standing up so I can see how tall he is. Please send some of yourselves and from home too. I wish Tora and the others would too. I surely would enjoy seeing them and the kiddies.*

I received Bertha Omdal's second letter and one from Agnes Benson from August 20. Please tell them how I enjoyed their letters, but I am sorry I am not able to answer them. I enjoyed the copy of Carl's cablegram. I hope he writes often.

It was mentioned in one of the letters the other day that Ole Birkeland (in U.S.A.) *had died. I had just had a letter from Norway the other day from his sister Elisabeth asking me to forward her greetings to her relatives. I shall write to Gurina Nesvåg and ask her to break the news to her. Gurina sends greetings (through her letters to me), especially to Aunt Sina and other relatives, while Marie (*Tønnesen) *Elle sends her love to Sophia (*Tønneson) *Rodvelt and brothers Tom and Conrad (*Tønneson). *Marie Elle seems to be quite well again. So many things I should like to write, but one can't even get started on one of these little forms. Should you continue to send me parcels, I could use sewing thread, mending cotton, bobby pins, talcum powder, toothpaste, a ball or two of white crochet cotton, circular knitting needles, notebooks for lessons, and a square yard of material so I can make a little tablecloth (the latter considered a luxury here). Use your own judgment. Oh yes, girdle size - waist 28 inches, hips 37 inches. I hope I'm not asking for too much. These are only things which cannot be obtained here and many things I've learned to do without. I hope I don't break you up in business. I should mention that even here in Germany we are enjoying Anacortes salmon every week which comes in our Red Cross food parcels. Best wishes for the New Year and love to you, yours, and the family. Thelma Rodvelt Mong sends her best regards.*

Love, Sophie

December 30, 1943 - Liebenau, Germany

Dear Teddy,

*Your airmail letter of November 18 reached me Christmas Eve, and you don't know how welcome it was coming just on that day. I know I would have been very blue had I not gotten anything. I am enjoying the three snapshots which accompanied the letter. They are some sweet kids, all of them. Little Judy (*Peterson*)* (daughter of Oscar and Eileen) *is a darling, isn't she? I had a letter from Tora two weeks before Christmas and had just answered it when I got your letter* *saying they had just moved. I suppose it will be forwarded. I'm glad this Christmas is over. We spent the days very quietly. Christmas Day we Norskies had a supper party together. The Christian morning service was led by our camp captain. The next day the Lutheran pastor held a service. However, most of the people here are Catholics, and they have their masses as often as they like. One night we (on this floor) entertained ourselves with a silly program, and tomorrow night is the fancy dress ball, but I'm not going. I hope to enjoy a quiet evening for a change, if not too many others have the same idea as I. We received American Red Cross food parcels. It was not so different from those we get every week, but they are always nice. Mail from Norway is very irregular and old. Today I had one from Gystøl's from Dybing. They are all well and send their greetings. The last letter from Grødem was from September. I'm sure there are letters on the way. Give my love to Mother, Dad, and the rest of the family, as well as Chris, David, and all.*

Much love, Sophie

P.S. Just got your letter dated December 6. It surely was nice.

January 13, 1944 – Liebenau, Germany

Dear Mother, Dad, and All,

I am writing to you instead of answering Theodora's letter of December 6 which reached me just New Years' Eve. It surely was nice to receive letters from home on Christmas and New Year's Eve. I am glad each time I hear you are all well. I have been very well all the time. I have been going to the dentist once a week lately. We have free service. It's a good hour's walk each way, and it is good to get out now and then. I received Pearl Flowers' letter of October yesterday and a Christmas card from Hanna Freestad today. I enjoyed their letters and hope they will write again - longer letters, although I cannot promise to answer. I had a card from Onkle Lars the other day but have had no Christmas mail from any others in Norway. The mail service is very poor now. Red Cross clothes were distributed this week to those in need. I got a pair of everyday shoes, a towel, and a couple of underthings. I keep the black oxfords for Sunday wear. I hope you had a nice

Christmas. You know, it is bad enough as it is, being scattered as we are, but it could be much worse, but next Christmas it will surely be different. I was so sorry to hear about Dan Rasar. Remember me to Goldie (Adema) *Rasar. We are having a very mild winter. I made a lovely long-sleeved sweater of the yarn you sent. Thanks for everything; it's all appreciated. I am looking forward - like a child - to the next parcel.*

Love and Best Wishes to All,
Sophie

January 27, 1944 - Liebenau, Germany

Dear Mother, Dad, and All,

The last letter I wrote was on January 13. I have been expecting something this week, but as yet I have had nothing from you since New Year's Eve. Pearl's and Hanna's letters are the only other American letters I have received this month. From Norway I have had many letters lately. All seem to be well, but I understood Tante Anne feels herself quite worn out and very tired. She would like to get off to Vagle on a vacation, but it isn't so easy to get away. Torvald Gystøl from Dybing is married to Konstanse, and Tante Semine's kids are getting married right and left. The three youngest are engaged, Sanna to Harald Peersen, Margrethe to Einar Sørdal and Trond Magne to Alida. All relatives ask me to send you their greetings and Thelma Rodvelt Mong especially. Things are the same here - nothing much happens. No transports to other camps or otherwise, and there seems to be no hope of an American transport either. So here we sit, 400 women, some not too congenial. It's a dog's life many times. We used to live on rumors, but experience has taught us to believe nothing we hear and only half of what we see. I am glad I have other things to occupy my mind. I understand German quite well and read it now, but speaking is more difficult. I enjoy Spanish, but started learning it later, so have not gotten quite as far with it. I am hoping you are all well. Parcel has not arrived yet. Write often and tell friends to write.

Love, Sophie

Sophie's Release and Later Communications

Newspaper Articles Announcing Sophie's Release
Sophie Sends Relief Packages from America to Norway Relatives
Letters From Fellow Prisoners
Letters to Sophie From Norway with News & Heartfelt Thanks
Letter From Brother Carl Still Serving in Europe

Sophie Peterson Tells Rotary Of Nazi Internment

Miss Sophie Peterson, daughter of Mr. and Mrs. Tollag Peterson of route 1, Bow, and a former teacher in Burlington schools, who was among American citizens repatriated aboard the motorship Gripsholm, which arrived March 15 in New York, was a most interesting guest speaker when she appeared yesterday before the noon meeting of Rotary club.

Miss Peterson was introduced by President H. Van Tinker, who also introduced Mrs. Louis Flowers, Jr., of this city. Mrs. Flowers, who had accompanied Miss Peterson on her trip to Norway in 1939, had returned home prior to the invasion of Norway, while Miss Peterson, on a year's leave of absence from her duties as primary instructor at the Burlington grade school, remained for a longer visit.

Miss Peterson was sent to a concentration camp at Grini, near Oslo, Norway, at the time of her internment in October, 1942. She described the living conditions at the camp as very bad, and said there was very little to eat. Four thousand men were prisoners at the time she was there, mostly Norwegians who had displeased the Nazis. All were under the control of the Gestapo, whose word is law in Norway. She told of people dying of starvation in the cities, especially in northern Norway, while the people in the country were able to eke out a better existence. A great many men were sent out of the concentration camps to Germany for "slave labor." Finally, the women and others were rounded up and taken to the dock. They had no idea where they were going, nor did they even know they were being shipped away. They ended up at a German concentration camp at Liebenau, near the Swiss border.

Here, she said, conditions were much better, and the internees were under the supervision of the military, rather than the Gestapo. There was no particular work for them to do, except to keep their own quarters and barracks cleaned. The camp had been converted from

(Continued on Page Six)

Sophie Peterson

(Continued from Page One)

a convent, and they were able to attend classes, where they could study almost any foreign language, science and other subjects. She was interned there for 14 months. The food was poor, she said, very poor, but parcels were received weekly from the International Red Cross, which "were lifesavers to us." However, men quartered in the big concentration camp, especially the political prisoners, did not fare as well, though she could not go into detail. The many war prisoners working on the farms around the concentration camps in Germany seemed to receive better treatment.

Upon returning to the United States, she was astounded at the amount of food here; and she never sits down to a table, she said, but she thinks of Norway and the concentration camps, and the men who had to do hard manual labor and looked like corpses. The Norwegians, the speaker continued, are not "giving in;" they hate the Germans. However, they are forced at present to abide by German rule, as the Germans are much too strong for any resistance.

Miss Peterson could not voice enough praise for the International Red Cross for the work they had done in Germany and other countries. "They did everything," she said, "that they could possibly do."

Just a small percentage of the people in Norway are "Quislings," she revealed. However, those who are, are forced to cooperate with the Germans in order to get food and prevent the suffering of their families. In Berlin one and one-half years ago, she saw no evidence of bombings, she said. However, she did not think the morale of the German people was now as high as they would lead us to believe.

She had had no idea she was to be repatriated, and when her name came up, she was very happy. The repatriates, who were sent by train to Lisbon, were shipped through France. The trip, which ordinarily should have taken one day, took five, and for two days on the trip they received no food from the Nazis. All they had to eat was food they had saved from their Red Cross parcels. As they crossed through Spain and Portugal, everywhere the train stopped, the people cheered them and wished them good luck.

Upon arrival at Lisbon, they were taken directly to the Gripsholm, and getting on the boat, she said, was just like entering a new world. Everything was clean and fresh, and there was an abundance of fresh food. Many became ill from eating too much. The trip across the Atlantic was uneventful and they sighted no submarines or war vessels. She could hardly describe the thrill of seeing the Statute of Liberty in New York harbor after five years away from home.

Walter Mercer was chairman in

charge of
meeting. F
talk, Bob
the high
made an a
meet Frid
field, and
of the Red

SKAGIT WOMAN, PRISONER OF GERMANS NEARLY FIVE YEARS, IS RETURNING ON GRIPSHOLM

A Skagit county woman, Miss Sophie Peterson, 38, daughter of Mr. and Mrs. Tollag Peterson of Bow, will be aboard the motorship Gripsholm when it docks in Jersey City about Wednesday of this week. Miss Peterson is among the 524 Americans being repatriated from France and Germany. A former Burlington grade school primary instructor, she returns from an internment camp situated near the Swiss border in Germany, after an absence of nearly five years.

Her family at Bow had no intimation of her approaching repatriation, and said that her last letter contained no hint of her impending return. Their hopes were first kindled when a news broadcast last Tuesday told of the sailing of the Gripsholm from Lisbon with her homeward-bound passengers. The first confirmation that she was aboard came Friday when they received a telegram from the Red Cross, which was followed Saturday by a wire from Congressman Henry Jackson.

Plan Happy Reunion

Her return will bring a happy reunion with her relatives here, who besides her parents include two sisters, Mrs. Chris Hanson of Burlington and Mrs. Tora Freestad of Samish Island; and four brothers, Pete of Port Orchard, Martin and Melvin of Bow, and Oscar of route 5, Mount Vernon. A fifth brother, Sergeant Carl Peterson, is serving overseas with the army engineers in England.

Miss Peterson had left here in June 1939, accompanied by Mrs. Louis Flowers, Jr., of Mount Vernon, and Mrs. Flowers' sister, Miss Verna Urmey of Ketchikan, Alaska (now Mrs. Ronald Schaumloffel of Tample, Texas), to visit relatives in Norway.

Mrs. Flowers and Miss Urmey returned to the United States at the end of the summer, Miss Peterson wishing to remain and enjoy a Norwegian winter. At the outbreak of the German-Anglo war later that summer, when other citizens were returning to the United States, she decided to remain, rather than risk crossing the submarine-infested waters, believing the war would soon be at an end.

Seized in Norway

She was taken prisoner by the Germans in October 1942, being transported to the internment camp in Germany in November. No word was received here of her internment until late the following February, when she wrote, her family said, telling how she had been taken from the Norway home of her father's brother as they were preparing a birthday party for her host, and how they had later written her, saying what a sad party it had been.

In her succeeding letters, she wrote she was receiving good treatment, and was instructing English in the camp, receiving in return lessons in foreign languages, including German. She was also help-

(Continued on Page Six)

(continuation of newspapeer article) ed (helped) by baking in the camp kitchen. Miss Peterson received her early education at the Field grade school and was graduated from the Burlington high school. She was granted her teaching certificate following her graduation from Pacific Lutheran College at Parkland and has been instructing since 1927.

"We are not sure when she will arrive," her father stated, "but we have contacted the Red Cross, who will keep us in touch with her until her plans are made and she is able to return home."

THE PRAYERS OF MANY WERE ANSWERED, IT WAS LEARNED FRIDAY WHEN THE FOLLOWING MESSAGE WAS RECEIVED IN A TELEGRAM FROM OUR CONGRESSMAN HENRY M. JACKSON;

"State Department advises me Sophie Peterson now enroute to United States aboard exchange liner Gripsholm. She may be contacted on her arrival by writing or wiring to Gripsholm Repatriates, American Red Cross, c/o Postmaster, New York City, New York."

The Gripsholm is expected Tuesday. Air Mail letters and wires sent today will reach Miss Peterson. Let us give her a big welcome home by writing. She will have plenty time to read as she travels westward 3000 miles.

April 10, 1944 - New York City

(Angelica had been an internee with Sophie at Liebenau Internment Camp but had also been released.)

Dear Sophie,

So sorry I did not see you anymore, but from the Red Cross I learned you were met by your friend (in New York); lucky girl you were. I wonder how your trip was and if you had some friends with you; write to me please? I often think of you. I cannot live with my niece anymore; her cousin is going to live with her, so I started moving right away into my old store "Wema marketing", living in a room nearby. To tell you the truth, I wish I was with my people in Holland, but it was not going to be that way it seems. I have a few friends in the store who are very nice to me, but I still feel lonesome now and then. I hope you are happy and in good health as I am. Lots of luck and greetings with love.

Angelica

May 4, 1944

Letter from Esther, Sophie's fellow internee, to Bertha Aarrestad.

(Note - Bertha would often write to Sophie when she was at Liebenau Internment Camp. Esther corresponded with Bertha after Sophie was released.)

Dear You, Bertha Aarrestad:

Takk for sist! (Thank you for the last time we met – a typical way to greet someone in Norwegian.) *Now, as Sophie has no chance to write to you, I'm taking the liberty of sending you a card. It was very sad that she left, but I can tell you that she arrived well at the destination. I haven't heard directly from her, but my twin sister wrote that Sophie traveled through our town and they got to meet each other, and everything was well with her. I can just imagine how happy she is that she is among her own again. Several of us must continue to stay here since only a few got to leave. We must be patient because maybe it will be our turn next. Dear Mrs. Aarrestad, it would have been so nice to hear from you again. Sophie was so nice and shared the letters from you, and you would not believe how I loved it and felt that it came from someone who belonged to me. The way you write gives us a way to laugh – it kind of wakes us up, and we had so many fun times together over your letters. Please greet all my friends in the area from me. I wonder when I will see them again. If not here on earth, we will one day gather together around the throne of God singing about the Lamb that freed us with his costly, precious blood. As each day passes, my faith is precious to me, and I praise the Lord for His great gift. We have a beautiful summer here now, and we are doing quite OK. We know how unsure our life is and often think of how fragile life is, but we are allowed to believe that below us are the eternal arms* (from Deuteronomy 33:27 in the Bible) *and nothing happens unless our Father allows it. I hope that everything is well with you there. Please let everybody else know about Sophie's wellbeing.*

Heartfelt Greetings, Esther

May 19, 1944

Five friends shared space on a one-page letter sent from Liebenau, Germany

Dear Sophie,

We were thrilled to receive your letter yesterday. Thanks. It made me homesick. No, I have not received the one you sent from New York., and we did want to know about your trip. It may come yet. So glad you can enjoy being with your loved ones again. Surely God is good. A few left on a sick transport last week, Miss Snape, Sunderland, Norvak, the Countess, Freddie & Souse and their mothers and a few others. Otherwise, we continue as usual. Yes, Ida sent your parcels to Norway. I wonder if they arrived? She received your parcel and has written you. My brother's address is Boring, Oregon. My sister is Mrs. Hendrickson, Seattle. We miss you a lot. I hope I can see you soon. Lots of love – Edith

Dear Sophie,

I am glad you are home, but we miss you so much. I hope you have heard from my folks. I have no news later than December 2. Have sent greetings to you through them. Celina has written you. I have made a blouse from your blue jacket. A.

Sophie,

Your letter was a great treat. Also, yours from France. Please write my sister: Mrs. Ray S., Napa, California. So glad for you dear girl! Little mail now! We are so lonely often. Have been busy knitting, etc. Rumor of transport next month! Weather cold yet. Love, from Rena

Hello Dear Old-time Partner:

How delighted we were to get word from you at last. Joy had written me telling of your almost miraculous meeting together. We're in the same place, same jobs etc. Dear Mrs. N. is with us no more. Teddy and I miss her so much. We were privileged to help her get ready. This is Teddy's paper, so I must also give her a chance though I could write heaps more. I rejoice with you, that you are home again. Love, from Esther

Dear Sophie,

It seems like a dream to think of you home. Miss Emninson had her operation and looks and feels 20 years younger. Perry was released. Weale, Smiths, and Jose are all well at home. Brother-in-law has vacation too. Martin's address is Idaho Springs, Colorado. Just heard from him. Lots of love – Teddy

June 29, 1944

Letter from Esther, Sophie's fellow internee, to Mrs. Bertha Aarrestad

Dear Bertha,

I received your letter June 15. It was so nice to receive a letter from you. I can also inform you that I received a nice long letter from Sophie a while ago. She is the only one of our special friends that left whom we have heard from. She could not praise enough how happy she was to be back home with her loved ones. Everything is well with her and everybody there. It is busy for her because they want her to come along and hold speeches everywhere. And it does not matter how much she protests, because they just come and insist that she participates. I understand that this is nothing that Sophie enjoys, but I do not doubt that she can accomplish it. I will never forget the first time I met Sophie – it was actually in the prison in Stavanger – she and I happened to be in the same cell. We comforted each other and shared good and bad together as a distraction. After that, we were at the same place until she left us. Yes, we are so incredibly happy for her. Maybe one day our turn will come - there are seven of us left now. Today the weather has been ideal - other days pretty raw and cold. I read in your letter that it is now nice and green where you are. May God have His good hand over all of you there, and His will be done through everything. His goal is the salvation of the soul – and it is great to learn that this happens again and again. Heartfelt Greetings, Esther

February 22, 1945

Letter from Carl Peterson, Sophie's brother serving in WW2 - Europe

Dear Sophie,

Yes, I am safe and sound. To tell you the truth, I was sort of anxious about myself for a while, but don't worry, I'm OK.

So, Ernie is still in England. I'm going to drop him a line and find out how things are going with him. And Palmer is in the South Pacific! We will probably go over there when this is over. I hope they give us a break in the States. They ought to. You can't tell what they will do.

I'm glad to hear Martin, Margaret, and baby Jeanne Maureen are getting along fine. I wish I could get around to writing more often. I really feel ashamed. Even when I do, I can hardly think of anything to write. I tried to answer a few of Teddy's questions in my last letter. I hope she understands it the way I wrote it - if they didn't cut it out.

I'd surely like to see Torvald and David in school. I'll bet they are a handful. I wish I could send them a couple Jerry bayonets to hang on their belts. They'd probably chase all the rest of the kids off the school grounds.

Well, I didn't do much Christmas day either. We only worked half a day.

*Yes, I received the L.D.R. (*Lutheran Daughters of the Reformation) *present. It helps a lot in keeping my writing material straight. It was usually scattered from the top to the bottom of my bag.*

I think I lost some packages in that German breakthrough. They went through our A.P.O. and we couldn't even send

any letters for a while. So, if I haven't written and thanked whoever sent me packages, tell them I was at a disadvantage. Thank them anyway for me.

Now that I think of it, ask Dad to send me a couple good pocketknives if he can. I lost my G.I. knife and can't get another.

Hope to see you soon.

Lots of Love, Carl

May 11, 1945 – Vagle

Letter from Tante Berthea (Thea) Omdal

Dear Sophie,

Thank you for the last time. Today I will write you a few words to let you know that we, and everyone around us, lives well; and that we hope it is the same with all of you. Yes, we have gotten peace, peace on earth, after five long, dreadful years that we will never forget. Tears are shed both in sorrow and joy.

The recent days have been very nice with sun and summer. I have thought of you more than once and wonder how everything is over there. Right now, I wish I had you next to me. You have possibly been tried hard and experienced a lot since you left us that day. That day will never be forgotten, and now we feel that we have arrived at a different kind of world, and it is like both heaven and earth are alive again. Yes, it is hard to explain well enough; the Norwegian flag is waving all over, and people are rejoicing and screaming with happiness.

Yesterday evening we went to the railway station at Sandnes and together, with many others, we met the prisoners from Grini. There was music, song, and speeches - and the joy was so huge that it cannot be described. Rasmus Forus was one of those that came yesterday, and the prisoners were carried on a golden chair (metaphor) *They were the first of the prisoners coming home, and there are extra trains every night. The joy among the people is so high – it is like heaven on earth is moving.*

We are grateful for your greetings that we received from Sweden from Lars Herman Omdal. Everybody at Grødem and Rodvelt are doing just fine. I hope you understand my writing.

Everyone at home is sending you greetings, and there is also a greeting from Lars, Petter, and Henne.

Tante Berthea

May 11, 1945 – Vagle

Letter from Henne (Henrik) Omdal

Dear Sophie!

I'd like to write a few words at the same time. Yes, you would not believe what a great joy we have here. I have been to Stavanger a couple of days now and saw when the English arrived and there were also some from Canada - they are very nice people. It is almost impossible for them to get through the crowds. On Wednesday a lot of them arrived in Sola, but yesterday many also arrived in town (Stavanger) *and it was almost impossible to move around. About eighty prisoners arrived and the joy was enormous. Yesterday they disarmed the German Navy and there was an ocean of people watching. I spoke with a soldier from Canada yesterday, and he was very nice. Today I am going to Sola to see how things are out there. All the girls that had relationships with German soldiers are getting their hair cut short* (as punishment – to shame them). *We sure experience strange things nowadays. I hope you can come here again when there is real peace, as we know that the war with Japan is not yet over.*

I hope you understand what I have written, and please greet everybody I know, but it is mostly for you.

Greetings from me, Henne

May 24, 1945 – Flekkefjord

Letter from Gudrun Østrem

Dearest Sophie,

The church bells have rung for peace in Norway, and we are again a free country. We can speak, walk, and do whatever we want. After five years of imprisonment, we can breathe out and fill our lungs with clean Norwegian air. It is unbelievable, almost too good to be true that we were let go that easy. The time that the peace arrived makes it extra special - here in a beautiful Norwegian spring. The hills are green and filled with songs of birds, and the clean Norwegian flag sways from every house. The first days I was so incredibly happy, we sang and hugged each other.

But in the middle of the joy, a painful sadness snuck in, Sophie. I have a very sad message for you. Alf Skåra died in a German Concentration Camp. He was, as you probably know, sent to Germany. I am not sure if it was before or after you got sent. For two-and-one-half years he had been sitting in prison and tortured in all possible ways. He was never meant to experience the day of freedom; he died for his country. It is so painful to think about how he must have suffered. Can you believe how he must have longed for home, for Bergit and for little Alf, whom he never got the experience to meet? But God needed him more. It is very hard for Bergit, and now she is left with a little boy. She looked so forward to have him come home, and she had taught little Alf to say the word "Papa". It looks like she is doing somewhat okay, but she will not accept that he died, and somehow, she still lives with the hope that he will return. Out of five people from town that were in Germany, there is only one that is still alive. So, in the middle of the joy, there is a lot of grief. We will let you know more about how Alf died when we know something; a lot is still not clear.

Except for that, all of us are living and doing well. Everybody is healthy. However, about this time last year Sigurd's daughter Britt, their little sunshine, died at only one year old. She died of tooth cramp. It was very tough on them.

Only mother (Berthe) *and father* (Andreas) *and my brother Alf* (Østrem) *are home right now. Tor is a student at Electronic Technical School in Stavanger, and I have ended up in Flekkefjord - I am hired in a larger company as a typist. I have been here almost a year now. Anna, you know, is with Bergit* (Skåra) *and will probably stay with her going forward. It is quite fun when we three sisters* (Gudrun, Bergit, and Anna) *are together in the same town.*

It is quite strange to be able to write to America again, and to you, Sophie. I have so many times thought about you and wondered how you are doing. We had heard a while ago that you had returned home. You really were caught in the middle of it, and you can probably write a whole book about it. It would be very interesting to hear you talk about your experiences.

I hope everyone around you, Aunt Christine and Uncle Tollag and all of your siblings - Peter, Martin, Tora, Oscar, Theodora, Carl, and Melvin, are healthy and well. Greet them from me.

Right now, we are all hoping that there will be more food and clothing coming into the country. So far, it has been pretty sad. But we shouldn't complain, as we haven't starved, although we have been missing a lot. It is different with clothing; it has not been possible to buy anything for several years now. I am as poor on clothes - on all kinds - as I can be. Dear Sophie, do you think you can sell me some clothes? I do not care what it is, but I mostly need summer clothes and maybe a summer coat. I was thinking that you were not able to take all the stuff that you had earlier brought to Norway. It might be rude of me to ask, but I am in so much need of clothing. These times have taught us to grasp all options, and I will pay you well. If you can and want to sell me something, would you please be kind and write to the person that keeps your clothes and say that they can send it to my address here in Flekkefjord? I don't even care what it is, I am appreciative for anything. As soon as it is possible to send packages from America, please think of me and send me some pretty clothes. Of course, I will send you money. I will quietly look forward to it.

Anna will probably write to you one of these days. I really wanted to write to you in English, but I am afraid I would make so many mistakes - after all, you are a teacher. I would like to visit you in the U.S.A. I would do whatever, if I only could visit you and your family. I am sitting in the office and writing you, as I have nothing to do just now. The next time I write to you, I shall write more in English.

I hope to receive a letter from you by return of post. Yesterday I was talking with my mother (Berthe Østrem from Helleland) *over the telephone and she asked me to remember her to you.*

With Kind Regards, Gudrun Østrem

P.S. It is hard to feel joy over anything right now, thinking of Alf who died in enemy country, far away from his home and the one that he held dear, but we wish and hope that he is in a better place.

August 5, 1945 – Årrestad

Letter from Bertha Aarrestad

Dear Sophie and Everybody!

A heartfelt thanks for a sign of life - sent to Torger Østrem (son of Semine and Ommund). *We have waited for a letter, and we could not write to you because we had lost your address. Many thanks for the last time. However, at that time it was in a muffled and restricted Norway, but now we are free. Now we can speak and write freely. It is great - and hard to believe.*

Thank you so much for all the cheerful letters you wrote from the time you were in Germany. Greet Esther if you write to her; she was very nice, and she wrote to me when you could not.

At the railway station, next of kin received both kicks and yelling as they showed up to wave goodbye to their own that had been arrested and were being taken as prisoners. Terrible times, and thankfully, we still have all of ours. Bergit Østrem has lost Alf, her husband - he died of hunger and cold in Austria. It is terrible for her. Her sister, Anna, is taking care of her. Bergit has a little boy who is named Alf. You would not believe how we cheered when the prisoners were released, but many of them never came home. The ones that came home are marked for life.

All is well with us now, but it has been a horrible time with a lot of stress and work to make things stretch with the few things we had. We, here in the countryside, have been doing pretty good when it comes to food - it is worse for the people in the cities. Thank goodness for all the help we have received, for instance, from Denmark and Sweden. Fabric for clothing was a huge problem - we have not been able to get ahold of even one meter for the last five years. I have fixed and turned old clothes inside out - I just cannot do it anymore. I wish that we could dress in something new, however. Funny enough - people are pretty well dressed for Sundays and so. The worst have been shoes, especially for children. It really has not gotten any better yet and I hope it will soon change. So far, we have received some extra crackers and a little bit of coffee - about 200 grams for each adult, two kilos of wheat flour each, and a little bit of chocolate. That is all that we have gotten, it is not much. But in the cities, they get a few packages -we do not get any here in the countryside. However, we should not complain now when we have peace.

Will you be coming here soon? We have been thinking of you almost every day since you left us. And I am sending you lots of greetings from my children; Liv and Svein, and my husband Magnus.

How is your health? Sanna is in Farsund, working at the hospital. Margrethe is married to Einar Sørdal and expecting in September. Mikael and Minnie have one boy, Tor Olav, and are expecting another soon. Rakel is at home and lives well with her family. Olav and Berta have a little girl, Anne Elise.

The days go fast and the years too, and soon we are old. You know, I was an old aunt when I wrote to you in Germany, but now I feel like myself again. The distance between us is far - but let us remember the mercy of the throne and put ourselves, our people, and our country in His hands.

I wish your brother (Carl, serving in the U.S. Army Corps of Engineers) *could come up here* (from Europe) *and visit us.*

Quisling is acting very insulted in his prison cell. They will not let him have a knife or a fork to eat with. He says he is going to complain to King Haakon VII. He has lost a lot of weight. Yes, there are a lot of crooked cowards among the quislings. You should have been here and read all those minutes from the courtroom hearings when they were being tried.

We are so happy when we see all the allies around us - it is so much better. However, the allies think we are somewhat cold and reserved towards them. What they do not realize is that we are so used to not saying what we mean – or to have any opinions – we just have not gotten over it yet; maybe we never will.

Please greet everybody you meet from us, and your school children. We are so happy every time we see some Americans, and every time we hear about the boats that are arriving here with food. The children here are asking about when they will receive oranges, grapes, apples, and many other things. They definitely have not been spoiled these years.

I do not know anyone that has been forced to cut their hair, but it was quite bad in Stavanger. I just wonder how they could behave the way they did. There are so many stories that you could have written about – you used to collect that kind of information.

My writing paper is so bad, as you can see. I just hope the controllers (post office or government control) *forgive me that my letter is so long. But since it is my first letter for several years, I hope they will let it pass. It will not be long until I write you another one.*

Soon we will start the harvest. Thankfully, everything we now produce is for ourselves, and that is much nicer. Before, we had to deliver everything to the greedy 'worm', but we hid quite a bit for the Norwegians. If not, many would have starved to death.

*Well, you are going to have to write to me soon. Aunt Teoline (*Gystøl*) from Dybing has been sick with rheumatic fever, and I wonder if she will be completely well again. Amanda (*Gystøl*) is home and takes care of her. Torvald and Konstanse have gotten a daughter, Tora, this spring. Except for that, everybody is well, also Andreas at Dalen, and at Gya and Egelandsdal. Tyra is married to a nice man, Jakob Gyland, from Time. So, time passes - live well and I hope you understand this writing.* (Note - in February, 2021, Tyra is still alive and alert at 101 years old.)

Greet all of yours from us.

Heartfelt Greetings, From Bertha Aarrestad - Helleland, Norge

August 5, 1945 – Årrestad

Letter from Malene *(Aarrestad)* Østrem

Dear You, Sophie!

A heartfelt thank you for the letter that I received yesterday, August 4th. It was great to hear from you again. We have thought about writing for a long time, but we did not have your address. We are all well here - we have been spared from a lot of horror and are all still alive. Life has been good through it all.

I suppose you have read about how gruesome the Gestapo has treated people in this country. The priests and everybody that belongs to church have been taken, also many others here in our country. You know we have been very scared. But our family here and our family at Helleland have been spared, except for Alf Skåra, who was taken three months after he got married, and he was killed in Germany. He leaves behind a little boy who will never see his father.

Olav and Berta Østrem are married now and they live at Nærbø, and they have a little daughter, Anne Elise. Olav is the member of the Home Front, so he is wearing the King's uniform. Margrethe is married to Einar Sørdal and they live at home because it is impossible to find a house now in Egersund. He is working at the railroad station in town. Sanna is working as a nurse at the hospital in Farsund. Rakel is always in a good mood and is surrounded by those four wild kids, Anna Kjerstina, Jostein, Sylvi, and Olav, as you probably remember. Everything is well with Bertha Aarrestad, *and she is also writing a letter to you. Trond Magne lives at home; he works at the railroad during the day, the same kind of work as Torger has. I'm told to send greetings to you from Semine, and Ommund says that I need to write you and tell you that you need to come back soon, so that we can wish you the best and say goodbye in a better manner. We all saw you the day you left* (arrested) *on October 17, 1942 - we saw how they covered your hand* (on the train) *when you were waving to us. We got so disturbed when they called from Vagle and told us you were on the train. I called Ualand and got ahold of Torger, and Torger called Ragna at Moi. We were so afraid that we would never hear from you again. They told us that you were taken. We were very surprised when we received the letter that you had managed to smuggle out when you were on your way to the unknown. It was a sad time for all of us here. I received the letter December 18th - someone had posted it in Kristiansand.*

You won't believe how big my boys, Ove and Sigbjørn, are now. The little one is almost two years old. Ove says that he has not forgotten his 'Sia' (Sophie). *I have taken a picture of them so as soon as it is developed, I will send it. The youngest one has completely white curly hair, and everybody that sees him thinks he look so much like his dad, Torger.*

When will you be back and collect all your things?

Everything here is rationed but the salt is easier to get ahold of than before, and all is going toward better times, now that the war is over. You will not believe the feeling of peace that rests over us in Norway now. Everybody is so happy except for all the quislings and the Nazis that are awaiting their punishment. I must stop now. Everyone here is sending you greetings - Rakel with family, everybody at Ommund's, and at Mikael's house - Minnie and children, Tor Olav and Ingveig. Next time I need to write more. Torger also has a letter that is coming with this one. Live very well.

Heartfelt Greetings, Malene and the boys

August 7, 1945 – Helleland

Letter from Torger Østrem

Hello Sophie!

Thank you for last time! It was so good to hear from you. You will not believe how many times I have thought of you since you traveled past Ualand on way to Grini (Nazi Prison in Bærum, Norway), *but thank God it still went well. I need to tell you something strange I dreamt one night. I dreamt that you had traveled from Germany and home to America, and then eight or nine days later I read in the newspaper that Gripsholm* (ship) *had gone to America with American prisoners and I thought that I was absolutely sure that you were on board. So, if people asked if I had heard from you, I said that you were on your way home, and so you see that what I dreamed became true!*

It was a very hectic time the first week after the capitulation. I wasn't home neither day nor night for almost a week, but it was a great time that I will never forget. The roles have changed, the prisoners are free, and the quislings are behind locked doors. We had them fairly prosecuted for their wrongdoings, but the government has been giving the Nazis very light punishments. The reason for the light punishment is widely believed to be that some of the high-up authorities - parts of the government - do not have a clean conscience themselves when it comes to treason. All of this creates stress and uproar among the people.

All our family did pretty well. There was not a lot of food, clothing, or shoes, but soon that will be better. The sad thing is that everything is now very expensive for a normal worker and we cannot get everything needed on a rationing card. At Eiesland in Fjotland, Aunt Martha's boys, Oskar, Magnus, Johannes, Thor, and Øyvind, had worked for peace. They stayed several days up in the high meadows to pick up weapons that had been thrown down from (English) *airplanes.*

You will not believe the hunt that went on in Stavanger the days right after the war. They cut the hair of 'German girls' (Norwegian girls who had dated German soldiers were ostracized and shamed in this way). *Swarms of half-grown boys and men with scissors, running in and out of the houses, hair in their hands, audience clapping. It was crazy. Thank goodness none of our people were clipped.*

Will you be back to Norway soon? When it is easier to travel, we expect that you will be coming back here again. I do not have my car anymore, and who knows when I will get a chance to get a new one. Maybe you can bring one when you are coming...

Everybody around here sends their greetings. I just wish the war in the Pacific Ocean would stop; at that point things would be better all over. Johannes Gursland has stayed with us for four to five days now. He is working at the railroad, a safe job. He is also sending his greetings to all of you.

How is it with the book that you were going to write about the capture? When you finish it, please send one to me.

Heartfelt Greetings, Torger Østrem

August 13, 1945 – Egersund

Letter from Gudrun (Egelandsdal) Thorsen

Dear You!

Thank you for the last time. I suddenly felt like writing to you, although you probably get a lot of letters from Norway now. I believe you are curious to hear about us, since you knew your way around so well. It will be great to see you again when things get settled and it is easier to travel. You left so fast, but I am happy you did, because if not, maybe you would not be alive. There were a lot of terrible things that happened after you left. But I must admit that we have been lucky, all of us. We are all alive, and we have not been without food for one day. It has been a lot worse in the larger cities.

Bergit Østrem lost her husband (Alf Skåra) *in Germany; the only one in the family that lost their life. It was terrible with food during the war but worse was clothing. The ones that did not have anything to trade with (or a ration card) were not able to get anything of what they needed. Most of the people in the countryside* (farmers), *had most of what they needed. We have had to turn old clothes inside out to redo them, and getting shoes was a big problem. A few shoes were sent to the store from America a while ago, and a lot of people were in line the whole night to get some.*

We live close to the new Railroad Station at Eie and will be moving to Nyeveien (in Egersund) *soon. I do not know if we had Anna Karin when you were here. She is now a little over three years old and we have gotten a little boy also, Arild Stein. He is three months. Yes, time flies. Agnes and Øivind Berentsen have a 1 ½ year old boy, Hans, and Astrid's boy, Kåre, is three years old. Tyra is now married and has a really nice husband, Tønnes Tunheim. We went home for the wedding at Sankt Hans* (mid-summer eve). *You would not believe how fun it was.*

We expect you to come back to Norway soon - and we are thinking you need to pick up all your things. How are all your siblings and your parents? Are they all still alive? Karlemann (Karl Thorsen) *is home in Egelandsdal chopping wood; it is supposed to last us until Christmas. It is hard for people to get firewood for the winter.*

Please do not get too mad at me, but do you think you could send me two or three spools of thread? It is totally hopeless for me to get ahold of some, and I have nothing to trade with; preferably black or white because I sew everything we wear.

It is very warm these days - an especially warm summer. I went swimming today, and I am so lazy and sleepy right now - so that is why this writing is so bad. I hope you send me some words back, and I will try to write you and tell you about all I know. Please greet all of yours from me.

Love and Greetings from Both of Us, Gudrun
Nyeveien, Egersund, Norway

August 17, 1945 – Hinna, Stavanger, Norway
Letter from Sigrid Stapnes
Dear Sophie!

Thank you for the last time. It is both good and bad that

you went home to America so early. You should have been in Norway all this time; but you had to experience so much of the evilness of the Nazis. Well, I was happy when I heard you were on your way to America; and especially when I heard that you had arrived there. I believe that the excitement must have also been enormous over there when the war was over in Europe and in Norway. They felt a lot of joy in Europe, but it cannot measure up to the joy that we felt in Norway. We were expecting the worst in the last days, and full of fear of what could have happened. But then, May 7th, 1944, as we were on our way to work, the message came that the war was over, and Norway was again a free country. What we felt in that moment and all the time forward to June 7th, when King Haakon VII came home from England, cannot be described. One pastor said that if anyone could understand what we felt, it had to be the angels. The first thing we did at the Sewing Room was to tear down the picture of Quisling, and then it was just joy and happiness. The work was over for that week. The streets were full of people shouting HOORAY, laughing, and singing the King's song and the National Anthem throughout the day and the night. I am wondering where all the Norwegian flags came from in such a hurry! Of course, I went home as fast as I could - I had to get home and experience everything.

I was in Egersund the day when most of the Nazis were arrested; and that very same day the first prisoners from Grini and other prisons were on their way home. I traveled to Sandnes on the same train that carried the prisoners, and you would not believe the joy at each station when families were reunited with their loved ones. Just this trip alone was a thrilling experience, but it was also very sad for all those who did not get to connect with their loved ones again. I lost my oldest brother, Leif, on February 21st of this year. English airplanes sank the boat that he was on - they were on their way between Stavanger and Bergen when it happened.

We lived at Brunes the entire time, and we were able to move home again June 25th. It was very nice to go back home, even though the house was quite trashed. It actually got quite better just by being cleaned. It is incredible how those Germans could dirty it up and live like that year after year. We had to get new floors before we could move in – the rest had to come little by little, and it is hard to get building materials, as there are so many others with things that need to be rebuilt. When I went home on vacation, the house was upside down, because there were carpenters fixing the kitchen and putting in new windows and doors. However, at the home on the farm, very little was ruined. Out in the pastures where we kept the cows, there were quite a few mines – but the Germans have now removed them. There is quite a bit of barbed wire left, but it will be removed this fall. All the cannons will be left, because they will be able to be kept on the battery. We are tired of seeing soldiers, but they will probably be coming a few times a year to look after that.

We are happy that it is getting brighter in so many ways. Saturday, we read in the newspaper that we can soon buy white flour and bread - probably in September, and we look so forward to that. The bread we have is horrible – as I am sure you remember. We also read that soon we will be able to buy shoes. It has been quite difficult with not getting shoes, especially for the children and workers, and we also have a problem with clothing. We have a couple pairs of shoes at home, but almost everybody here uses wooden shoes when they are working, but even those are hard to get ahold of – strange, because we have had so many of them in Norway. And of course, most people have a few sheep, and from the wool we can get so many things like socks, sweaters, dresses, underwear, and suits for the children. They had to learn to spin; it was something that only the older ones knew how to do - so if you did not know how, you just had to learn. To sell the wool was not the best, because it just went to the Germans, and we had to weave woolen blankets for them – single and double threaded. Working for the Germans by weaving blankets was not really a choice, because there was no other work, and we had to live.

We did okay – we had most of what was needed, and if we did not have something, there were other people to get it from. It was better in this part of the country than other areas in Norway. Leif commented many times that he had seen how they lived between Oslo and Bergen - and we all know that it was not better far north, either. I am not counting all the people that bought whatever they wanted on the black market and did not care how much it cost. At home, everybody had their farms, so even though the farms are small, we had enough food. And then, of course, we got all the fish that we needed. There was not much of butter and sugar. Here in Stavanger, it could be weeks before you saw butter. Often, they woke up in the morning, ate a couple of pieces of that almost black bread, drank a cup of surrogate coffee with nothing in it, brought a couple of pieces of dry bread to work, and when they came home, they ate the same food again. It would often be a whole week before they had anything for dinner.

So, you can understand that the hospitals were overfilled, and other sicknesses, like TB, were spreading fast. At home, they had enough so that they could help many. Leif, who sailed between Oslo and Bergen throughout the entire war, brought a lot of rationed food with him along the coast, and delivered it to people he knew as well as people he did not know. If the Nazi Government had known, he would have been shot more than once. You probably know that we are not the ones who had it the worst – I am so grateful, because it all went well.

I am still working in Sandnes, sewing, and I live at Hinna. Now and until Christmas, I am only going to make dresses. After New Year's, I am going to Oslo to learn how to draw and cut out dresses, women's suits, and coats. I am also taking a drawing class in the evenings. After that, I am going back to Sandnes to learn how to sew coats and women's suits. I must do all of this before I take the exam next summer. I need to take this exam to be able to open my own Sewing Room, and a right to have my own students. And then, I can do this wherever I want in the country. I am tired of being here now, because I do not have any girlfriends here. I look forward to traveling to Oslo, as I know a lot of people there. Kristine Stapnes is there, and so is (my sister) *Jenny. Jenny is quitting nursing school in Ullevål. She will start Mission's School in September – that will probably take one year. After that she will go to Paris to learn French, and from there she will be sent to Madagascar as a teacher. Harriet Stapnes and Sigurd Stapnes* (my siblings) *are at home now, and Ingrid,* (another sibling), *is working in an office in Egersund. It is very hard on us that we lost* (our brother) *Leif. Except for that, we are doing pretty well. At the Sewing Room, we have a lot of work. It is quite strange that after five years of war and with no import of textiles, people with a lot of money could buy quite a bit of fabric during that time - and they have stored quite a lot of it. Except for that, we redo a lot of old clothes.*

Last summer, we went to Birkeland for a student reunion. The previous time I was there, you and Kristine Stapnes were there also. It was fun to meet a lot of these people that I knew before, but it is also sad, because there are so many from there that have died in Germany – some that I knew very well.

On my vacation, Kristine and I went to visit Helga and Magnus Svånes in Sokndal. They will probably leave for Canada next year. That was the only thing I did this vacation, but last year I went to Sirdal for one week. For a long time, it has been almost impossible to travel. Some are brave and travel more, but most people just go on short trips. At the end of the war, one could not travel by train or boat, so one had to trust the bicycle, but not everyone has a bicycle. I need to get my own bicycle back in good shape – so when you come back, we can make a trip through Hardanger and Setesdal. Yes, because I expect you to come back. No one was able to say goodbye to you, or maybe you had enough of Norway when you were here. Many have returned home now that the war is over. We live and hope to see you again. Take really good care of yourself.

I am not sure if the address is right, but Kristine used this one.

Heartfelt Greetings from Sigrid.

August 19, 1945 – Grødem

Letter from Anne Omdal

Dear Sophie and Everybody!

Thank you so much for the letter and the card that we received a few days ago. I must say that it is a joy to get a letter from you and hear that you are all doing well. And we are also doing well. At first, I was thinking about sending you a telegram, but I was not sure about the address. Then I heard that Ingvald and Lars Omdal went to Sola and sent a letter to you via the English (soldiers), *so then I knew that you knew that we were all alive. I did send a letter - I hope that you received it. Agnes* (Rotwell) *wrote it for me.*

You had asked how we are doing, and I will say that it is getting better. It has been very tough for many, especially in the cities and in the larger cities as well. There has been very little bread, meat, and milk, and this last year, almost no potatoes. It is getting better with bread flour, but we still get it rationed. Twice we have gotten one kilo of flour. We got one kilo that had to last five weeks, and it is going to be more difficult when winter arrives.

You are asking if the Mongs have come home. Tollak Mong died in Germany. Sigvart and Hans (a cousin of Berntine Mong, Sivert's mother) *came home Tuesday, and Sverre* (married to Kitty, Sivert's sister) *has come home from Grini. Hans at Stølen died in England. Kristine and Hans* (J. Mong) *at Tuen are dead. Have you heard that Alf Skåra who was married to your cousin at Helleland died in Germany? You also asked about Anna, housekeeper for Mandius – she is married now - she married last fall to Kindervag Sirevåg.*

Mandius Hausan told me to let you know that he is now walking barefoot. You are also asking how many cows we have. We have three cows and one calf; and we have not delivered any for slaughter. You also asked about the Germans at Stapnes. They were moved to Slettebø a few days after the peace, but now they have probably left. So, it is quiet after the storm. You also asked if we need anything – and I do not really know how to answer, because we are in need of everyday clothing, and for myself – I could use some undershirts.

Thelma and Sivert Mong had a girl, Brit Helene, two weeks ago. This is just a few words written in haste. I will write again soon. Greet Ellen and my brother Peder (Peterson) *and thank them for the card. Greet everybody from us too.*

Anne Omdal

August 20, 1945 - Vagle

Letter from Tante Berthea *(Vagle)* Omdal

To all of you over there –

Thank you so much for the letter that we received a few

weeks ago. It was so touching to hear from you, that I could not stop my tears from running. We have waited for you all to experience the peace, the big joyful day that we have already received. We have been listening to the radio every day, but August 15th in the morning at 8:00 we heard that the same night at 1:00 that peace was a fact. They rang the church bells in Oslo. They also had one minute of silence to remember to think of the fallen; and all the flags were raised. I was just about to eat breakfast at the time, but when I heard what had happened, all I could do was think of you and I was so happy that you were going to experience the same joy that we had, and not that long after. I bet there is a lot of joy over there now, and especially for those who have not lost anyone. We are very curious about you who have such a large family, and if all are still alive. Most of all I am thinking of your brother, Carl Peterson, who is in the U.S.A. Army. Now, when the war is over, we do not need to be afraid anymore about writing.

I have heard that your mother, (Christine Peterson), has been very sick, especially before you returned home. Be very happy while you have her. Bestemor (Martine Vagle) is no more. I will write about her next time.

We are just cutting the corn and have had beautiful weather for many weeks, but right now it is so dry, and we need rain, mostly because there is not enough food for the cows outside.

Lars is doing the same kind of work as before, and both boys, Petter and Henne, are home. Petter is about to go in the army, and it is all okay now, as the war is over. We have received coffee and all kinds of things; and we can also buy as much flour as we need. We have had enough food throughout the war, and no worries. We have never lived as well as those days, because we could not sell anything. So please do not send any food - we have enough of everything, and all is getting better. We got back the woolen blanket that you borrowed, and it is just as good as new.

In August 1944, we received a greeting from Sweden, from Henry Hansen, that you were safe at home. I have not written back to Sweden to thank them for the greeting. Mr. Andreas Mauland is driving his car now - it stayed with us the entire time and the Germans did not get ahold of it. They were here several times and looked at it, but Andreas had unscrewed so

many parts that they could not take it. But now he is driving himself. He drove off from us (here) *yesterday.*

Everybody lives well everywhere. Little Marit Vagle at home has grown so big, you would not believe it, and soon there will be another one. Helene Rodvelt visited us this summer and the twins, Petter and Alf Henry, also. They were here in Stavanger when Crown Prince Olav was visiting, so they got to see all kinds of things. Petter and Henrik (Henne) *have been to Grødem, but we have not. Thelma Rodvelt had a daughter, Brit Helene, at the beginning of August, so you won't believe how joyful everyone is because of it.*

Do not send me any money back. But if you want to send something, send me some fabric for an everyday kind of dress because we have not been able to buy anything since you left. We also could use Sunday shirts for the boys and toothpaste. It probably will not be long until there are more things coming into the country again.

Please greet everybody we know. Your Mother and Father are greeted from everybody at Vaglemoen. Greetings from everybody at home and the Maulands.

Can you send me a white and a black spool of thread and some elastic? And my whisk is broken; I really need a new one so that I can make fløtekake (cream cake).

Tante Thea (Omdal)

Sunday, September 16, 1945 - Vagle

Letter from Marit Skadsem

Dear, Dear Sophie!

A heartfelt thank you for the last time and thank you for the greeting that came in the letter to Tante Thea and Onkel Lars! You would not believe how nice it was to hear from you again. We have thought of you often since the last time we were together, and we talk about you so many times. I will never forget the day that we heard you were going to get back home to America. I was both incredibly happy, but also sad. I was happy for your sake, because I knew how you longed to be home and to see your own during the war, and especially during your time in Germany. At the same time, I was sad, because I thought that maybe we would never see you again. It moved us all when you wrote from Germany and said that you were longing to be back in Norway. We looked forward to and had hoped that you would come back here before you went back to America. We have heard that the American States will pay for a free trip to Bergen for everybody that has been in a German prison, but I think it sounds a little bit strange. It would have been incredibly nice if you could have come to Norway one more time.

*I have heard that Henne Omdal received a letter from you, and that you have heard from your brother, Carl (*Peterson*). We have talked a lot about him, although we have never seen him, because we knew before you wrote to us from Germany that he was in England and was going to join* (the war effort) *in Europe. I heard that he wanted to come to Norway, but most of them* (allies) *are probably in Oslo. But there has been a lot of Englishmen in and around Stavanger. There has been less Englishmen in Sandnes; but in Ganddal and out here in the countryside there is not one single Englishman.*

*So, Målfrid (*Skadsem) *and Marie (*Vagle) (eventually to be Marie Kvidaland) *speak pretty good English now. They have been out with the* (English) *soldiers and dancing sometimes. I can speak a little and understand a little, but not enough that I can have a normal conversation. If I do, I just feel pretty dumb.*

Can you believe that the war ended in such a surprising way for Norway? You know, all the time, I expected for us to be invaded, and that we would experience fighting on Norwegian ground. And it was close, too - the troops had already gone on board, and everything was ready. But the capitulation came, and we got peace. It took a long time before we finally realized that we had peace. The Germans were very smart and followed the orders, so the army left with no problems, and I think that most of them were happy that the war was finally over.

You probably think that it has been horrible for us here in Norway, but that is not the case - it has been almost like when you were here. And we should not complain - it was always worse for those who lived in the cities. However, they managed to get out to the country and get a few things to make things better. But, if the war had not ended last spring, it would have been horrible, because all the grain and flour storages all over the country were just about empty; and there were no potatoes in the cities or the countryside at that time of the year. And I was fearful about how it would be when people in the cities came to us in the country, and we would not have anything to give to them. But thank goodness, the war was over before it went that far. There are now big changes in so many ways. We can buy white or coarse bread – whatever we like, and the rations have been removed. We have gotten so much grain into the country; they have been writing about it in the newspapers. We now have coffee and many other things, so we are drinking coffee and really enjoying it.

It was much worse up north in Norway, and it was pretty bad before the peace finally materialized. The Germans burned and ruined absolutely everything before they pulled back. What the people up there have had to experience and still must suffer is something that only the one who has experienced it can understand. Also, all of those who have been arrested in Germany - no one can describe what they have experienced, and it is a blessing that some of them came home alive. It is great that we no longer need be afraid of Gestapo; it was weighing all of us down. It felt like we could not feel joy for anything, even if we in many ways were doing okay. It is like it is easier to breathe – as if the air is so much lighter and cleaner. Many of those who turned old and grey during these years are feeling young again since peace came. And we have had the nicest summer that anyone can remember, with sun and heat that we are not used to – at least not several months in a row.

The traitors are being dealt with and have received their punishment. Finding the right punishments has been a challenge, and many agree that the punishments have been too mild. Others and I are against that penalty – we do not understand that it can be right to take a life. It reminded us too much about a Government that we all hated and fought against. And as you know, in Norway it has been a long time since we have had that kind of penalty. I believe it would have been better if the worst of the criminals just got life in prison. A lot is written about it in the newspapers, but as we know, most of the people are for the death penalty, and one of the torturers has already been shot. I am happy that we do not have any traitors in the family and also not among friends.

*You are asking about Bestemor (*Martine Vagle) *and Bestefar* (Henrik Vagle), *and I assume that you know by now that Bestemor is not around anymore. She died August 17th of last year; so now it has been about a year ago. It was a sad time for us and the rooms at home seem so empty now - we notice it more and more as time passes. It was pneumonia, bronchitis, and a bad heart; and it was a blood clot and gangrene in one of her legs that ended her. Tante Thea and Tilde Mauland stayed with her and cared for her during her last days. She was so pleased with the idea of dying, so she was at peace, and didn't care to live any longer. She said: "I am so old and tired and worn out – I cannot work anymore, and when God wants to greet me and let me come home to Him – that is so much better. It will be the way He wants it; if He wants me home now, I'm okay with that, and if He wants me to live a little bit longer, I'm okay with that, too". And here is one of the last things she said, "You all need to come home to God, He will greet you all and He will not push anyone away – I hope we all can meet in heaven". She was totally clear to the end – only the last few days and nights she was gone a little bit. And just before she died, she was clear again. She smiled with her whole face like the sun, and then she bent her head, and then it was over. Bestefar Vagle is fine, just like before, but he was very marked by grief, especially right after*

Bestemor died.

*Except for that, we are doing well. Mother (*Martha Skadsem) *was very bad last summer with sciatica – she was in bed for a whole month; but she is much better now. The beautiful summer weather this year has done her well. You see, it has been a large workload on me, being the only woman at home when mother was sick. The way it is now, she can watch the stove when we find everything she needs, and she can do the dishes every day. That helps me a lot, and I have more time to take care of the clothing, wash clothes, fix and sew the old clothing, and then I can also rest a little bit in between.*

This summer, I visited Oslo and Lillehammer. You would not believe what a great trip it was. (My sister), *Målfrid, has had an office post in Sandnes, and now, after the vacation, she started working at a lawyer firm in Stavanger. Martin,* (my brother), *has been working at home all summer, and Henrik is working at home with us. Magnhild and Jan* (Øvestad) *live well, and little Eldbjørg is a busy little girl who is turning three years old October 18th. Jan is done with his military duty.*

*Today, we celebrate the lives of the fallen in Norway. There is a memorial service in all the churches in the country, and the names of each one who lost their life during the war will be read and honored. I believe there is about 8,000 names and that is quite a lot for a small country like ours. Yesterday, the urns of 400 that died in England arrived in Oslo and they had a large memorial that was broadcast. Today, every radio program has a memorial for the fallen. Mother, Tante Tilde, and Onkel Andreas (*Mauland) *went to church today, and afterwards they went to a place here close to Høyland where a large monument was raised as a memorial to those who were killed fighting Gestapo right before the war ended.*

Onkel has been allowed to use his car a little, although this spring he was very bad with sciatica. Except for that exception, almost no one is allowed to use their personal cars. But it will soon be better, because more fuel is coming into the country. On top of that, much more merchandise is coming into the country, faster than we dared to hope.

I could probably sit here a whole week and write to you if I were going to tell you everything – and I still would not be done. You probably listen to the Norwegian broadcast from England on the radio, and maybe you also listen to the broadcast from Oslo. We, at Ganddal, have been very lucky – all the radios from Ganddal were returned except for seventeen. The Germans ruined all the radios in the cities and the ones they did not ruin they sent to Germany. So, you can see that there are many without the apparatus (radio). *New radios will not be in the stores until Christmas, I have heard.*

This paper is not good for writing, but I hope you can understand this letter anyway. It would be great if you had time to send me a few words sometime. I would love to hear how the trip from Germany was for you. You have started to work as a teacher again, isn't that so? I have a few pictures that I would like to send you another time.

*Take care and greet all of yours. I am sending you greetings from everybody here at Maulands. Marie (*Vagle*) just finished Home Economics School this summer. I am also greeting you from everybody at home and everybody you know here.*

Heartfelt Greetings, Marit Skadsem

September 18, 1945 – Flekkefjord

Letter from Bergit *(Østrem)* Skåra

Dear, Dear Sophie!

*Thank you so much for the second letter that my sister, Gudrun (*Ellingsen*), has received from you. You wrote that you also sent a second package to her, so we are expecting it one of these days; we are waiting and are very excited. She paid nothing at customs for the first one, because we have a man living on the first floor in the house where we live, and he is working as a custom's assistant. So, we get the packages through him and do not have to pay any custom at all.*

Oh, Sophie, how happy I am that you got to go home to your own and that you are in good shape. You would not believe how much I was thinking of you when you were back at Grini, arrested, away from all of yours, and among strangers. I will never forget the Christmas that we were told that you were sent to Germany, and my beloved, unforgettable Alf was arrested in Kristiansand. It was the first Christmas after we were married, and we looked so forward to it. But it was going to be grief, instead. I suppose you have heard from Gudrun about my misfortune. Who could have believed this?

I had some connections with Alf when he was in Germany, but only through other prisoners, because he was not allowed to write. Because of that, I knew that he was alive, and as late as in May, I got a message that he was over in Sweden, and he was supposed to come home the week after. It turned out it was only a rumor. You would not believe my joy while preparing the house, baking cakes, getting all the clothing of little Alf finished because he was going to wear a white suit the day Papa came home. I was so excited that I couldn't eat, had so little sleep, and I became very thin. Instead, I received this huge grief from the priest that my darling Alf was dead in Germany. My grief for Alf can almost not be described, I miss him day and night. It is so painful, and I am so full of sorrow. My life is finished forever, but I will hold and keep myself strong for the boy and live for him. He was born June 22, 1943, so he is two years old now. You will not believe how beautiful he is - he looks a lot like his father. When he was born, we sent a telegram to Grini and Alf received it one hour before he was sent to Germany. So, it must have been hard for him to leave at that point. The date of his death is unknown. Some say he died Christmas 1944; others say February 1945. He died of dysentery. He was suffering bad in the end, and just could not take the strain, poor Alf. If I just had a grave to care for, but I do not even have that. He did not get to see his boy, not even a picture.

Sophie, I must ask you for help; do you think you can help me? And please know that I would appreciate it. But first, I want you to know that I want to pay you. Could you buy me a thick winter coat? I only have a thin summer coat, and it is so cold in the winter. I would really like a fur coat, but it is impossible to find it here in Norway. It must be black because I only dress in black now. Can you also help me with a white silk blouse with long sleeves and a black silk skirt that I can use for dressing up? All my clothes are so worn. But I want to pay for everything. I use size 42-42½ in clothing.

I would have loved to have traveled to America now. It is such a joy to hear that your brother, Carl (Peterson), *is still alive - what a great gift of God. A heartfelt greeting from me and my little boy* (Alf). *My sister, Anna* (Østrem), *will write you later and I plan to write you a lot. Can you help me with the package as soon as possible and write me how much it costs so I can send you the money? I think I will get it custom-free since I know him so well* (the man who lives on the first floor). *I wish you everything well, dear, dear Sophie, and I thank you. I am so happy that you got home to your family. Except for all this, we are doing pretty well here at home. They are all supporting me in my grief.*

Heartfelt Greetings, Bergit Skåra

September 20, 1945 – Årrestad

Letter from Magnus and Bertha Aarrestad

Dear Sophie,

Heartfelt thanks for the letter that we received yesterday, the 19th, mailed from Washington September 11th. That went quick and easy. It was so fun to hear from you; it was almost like having you right next to me. Also, nice to hear that you received our letters too.

I cannot believe you visited my first cousin Lisabeth Halvorson, in Canada – that must have been a long trip. Tante Valborg Gya is much better now, but it is doubtful that she will ever be strong again. We have just had Tante Martha from Eiesland visiting - she comes every fall. She is good at talking, as always, and she has so much to say. They are all doing well. She has a boy, Johannes, who is working at the railway as some kind of installer. He visited us not a long time ago, a nice boy.

Yes, isn't it strange that all of us have done so well. How lucky we are that we never have gone to bed hungry during these years. Another thing that has helped us is that we were taught to appreciate little and to work hard. We do not strike, even if we don't make much working. God's blessings have been over our work, and we have been able to help many with food, those who did not have much. Isn't it strange - some have God's blessings and some have dark clouds over them - and lucky are those that have the first. I often think of my Bestemor, Rakel Serina Salvesdtr Eikelandsdal (mother of Christine Peterson), *and the last years that she lived. She was bedridden most of the time, but she prayed morning and evening for her family. She mentioned each of us by name - the ones she remembered - and asked for God's blessings over our lives and our work. I have been so blessed by her prayers.*

All of us are doing well; no one has suffered, everybody is still healthy, yes, even if often it was hard to deal with the nerve strain. That is, however, my weak side. How do you handle it? I have had so much nerve pain in my head, and during the war I could not get the tablets that helped me, but I hope it will be better soon. Mother (Semine) *and Father* (Ommund) *are well. My sister, Margrethe (*Sørdal), *is still on her feet, but she is expecting any day now. Malene and Torger also are living well, as are Rakel and Abraham* (Øgreid), *and Mikael, Olav, Sanna and Magne. Everything is fine at Gya and at Egelandsdal. Ragna* (Moi) *with Arvid, Vegard and Kirsten, and Olga* (Øveland) *with Torlaug, and Valborg from Moi visited us and are also doing well. I saw Anna* (Østrem)*; she was visiting Mother together with Bergit's little boy, Alf Skåra. Bergit herself was at a vacation center for widows and prisoners. Yes, if you know Bergit, you know she was never prepared for life's traumas, and did not expect things like this would happen to her. She lived for life's joy and happiness. Let us hope that God will turn this into a blessing for her. I have heard that Anna is now a Christian.*

We are done with the harvest, and we had great weather - which really helped because there are no workers to find. We are alone, Magnus and I, but with good help from our nearest family we got everything in, and we really had a good harvest. We do not have that 'green worm' anymore - you know, I wrote about it to you when you were in Germany - you know, the 'worm' that ate everything for us (the German soldiers). *We had to deliver them everything, but most of the time, we gave them as little as possible.*

Thank you for your will to send packages, it is just great. Hopefully, it will all reach us. Malene (Østrem) *has not seen any packages yet – but a lot has arrived at Stavanger. There are a lot of American packages that have been delivered out, but they have gone to the ones who have suffered the most during the war. They are first in line – those who the Germans took from house and home and burned everything they had. You would not believe how they have suffered. So, we do not expect to receive anything yet. The cities are first in line, they just started to deliver the packages in Stavanger. We will make it, though we do not exactly like that people in the countryside are put last in everything, but we just must take it and be happy that the war is over. I am sure we will get some clothes to wear soon, and we also have wool that we can work with. If I receive a package, I will let you know right away – I promise, and I look forward to it.*

The Nazis are sucking on their paws thinking of good memories from the past. Quisling does not have a great future, but he is still alive. I am sure you are listening to the radio just as much as we are. I remember that when you saw all the jokes in the magazine, you always laughed, so I will cut some out and send to you. If you write to Esther (a prisoner with Sophie at Liebenau), *please greet her from me. We wrote each other after you were gone, and I owe her great thanks because she kept us informed about you. We all want you to come back here again and please come soon and bring some others with you. I would love to meet your brother, Carl. I will bet he has a lot of experiences to tell about.*

Time goes, and so do we. It was so fun to hear what a great time you had at school. What fun it would be to travel to you; I have started to dream about a trip to America. It has to be some time when I 'grow up' - as the children say when it is something important .... but who knows? I'm writing so fast, and I suppose you have a hard time breathing as you are reading this because you see I'm cutting off the sentences so that I can write as much as possible. I hope you understand it all. You talk about scribble, but what you write is much prettier than what I am creating. I am sad to hear about your Mother and asthma. Greet her very much from us. It would be great if she may possibly be able to see us again, and we could see her. (Bertha is her niece.) *Well, if not here, we will meet again in that place where no one evermore will be separated. Greet them all - every single one - from us. And you, Sophie, must read the prophet Joel, chapter 2, verses 18-27. At the end of April, I again had to ask God for a better future for us in our country, and at that time we didn't know about the peace* (end of the war); *we were fearing an invasion. I wanted an answer, and I got a direct answer – peace came a month later. I think it is like that now.*

Heartfelt Greetings from Magnus, Bertha, Svein, and Liv

September 24, 1945 – Grødem

Letter from Anne Omdal

Dear Sophie,

You must excuse me as I am embarrassed that I have not replied and thanked you for the letter as well as the package that we received a few weeks ago. The parcel arrived in good shape, and we thank you for everything. My brother, Petter, asked me to greet you and thank you for the pants and the shirt; and I thank you for the dress fabric, the spools, the soap, and the chocolate. I am not going to thank you for the coffee because you know that we do not care about that one - ha ha - you probably remember when we used the last little crumbs of it. Also, thank you for the letter that we received on Saturday. I did not see that you received the letter that Agnes (Rotwell) *sent. I also read in the letter that you sent two packages – they have not arrived yet; and the ones at Rodvelt have not received their packages either. Many people are expecting packages, and I assume they will be coming on the Stavangerfjord* (Norwegian ocean liner).

Last Sunday, I read the letter that my sister, Helene (Rodvelt), *had received from you. They had a Christening, and the little one looks so much like Bertine Mong* (Sivert's mother). *Both Bestemors were in wonderful moods; it was great fun. The child is named Brit Helene. All of Sivert Mong's siblings were there with the families, plus Sverre and Tor, together with Steiner. It was great to be together with them.*

Jenny Mong, Sivert's sister, was married to Torvald Retland Saturday. He is a "Jærbu" (someone living close to Jæren) *from Sandnes - he is a nice guy with a large farm, so she will be very busy working. The wedding was held in the house of Berit and Lars Mong. Helene was there and babysat the child. She was watching her at Sofie and Kristian Rodvelt's house. I am so happy that Thelma could participate as she has not done much this summer – she had to be bedridden for four weeks and was on a very strict diet for five weeks. It was worse this time than last time. Except for that, everything is fine.*

Peder Rogstad is sending a greeting; he asked about you and told me that I must tell you how he was doing during the war. He was one of the escapees - he had to escape last year around the 17th of May. It is crazy, and there were many like him. He was at home when a Gestapo car drove up, but he got out and managed to hide in a cave of a rockslide between Gya and Gystøl and lived there from May until December 23rd. After that, he went home, and they hid him there until the war was over. However, his wife ended up at Grini where she stayed until the war was over. The Gestapo had taken her in and questioned her about him, and she said he was not home. But when they went and asked their oldest daughter, she said 'yes' he was probably home (although he had managed to escape). *And with that, she* (his wife) *was finished* (arrested).

Kristian Birkeland (son of Jakob) *is dead - he was tortured to death in the jail in Stavanger. You would not believe how upset they were at Birkeland. They caught Vatland, and he was in Grini* (prison) *for a year. The other one at Birkeland managed to escape. Johan Birkeland* (son of Jakob) *and his two sons, and Berent Fidje, the husband of Ingeborg Aase Birkeland, lived in another rockslide in the place that we call The Meadows. They lived there for over a year, and it is a wonder and God's blessings that it has gone so well. A son of Aakre was shot on the street; it was terrible. He was involved in a group that smuggled ammunition.*

*I do not know if you understand this scribble - I will write more about this another time. I am sitting here writing as the dinner is cooking. I should have written yesterday, but Tante Sille (*Omdal*) and her step-daughter, Gjertine, came here for a while, and last night there was someone else visiting. It is quite busy here - Petter has gone to work since we are done with threshing. They have started to work on the 2nd railway station building - he is the only one up here that has gotten the extra work.*

It is great to go downtown again; buses are going every day all day. On Wednesday, I went downtown, as I had a doctor's appointment, and then I went to the bank and exchanged all the old money bills for the newer ones. I am happy that we are some of those that do not have too many, because those who have a lot of them are losing sleep over it.

I still have not sent any letters to Peder (their brother in Bow, WA), *so please greet them, and greet your Father* (Tollag), *and Mother* (Christine) *from Sille, Gjertine, Marie, and Mandius, and please know that many others are asking me to greet you.*

Well, take care, and again thank you for everything in the package. I also want to thank you in advance for the packages that I know are on their way but have not yet arrived.

Greetings from us two, Tante Anne and Onkel Petter

September 30, 1945 - Grødem

Letter from Anne Omdal

Dear Sophie,

It is Sunday today, and everything is quiet. It is raining and it is grey, grey, grey. I wanted to write to you and tell you that at Rodvelt they received your package on Friday, and it was all intact. Thelma did not get hers, and neither did we, but we are expecting them this week, because the Stavangerfjord (ship arriving from the U.S.) *has arrived in Bergen, so the packages are probably there now. Everything you sent to them sounded so good, and everything fit them well. They had already tasted the coffee. "It was very good", said 'gamlå'* (the old woman) *so the coffee grinder will be worked hard now.*

Helene and Andreas Rodvelt were at a funeral at Gyland yesterday, because Sivert, Martina Gyland's husband, was buried. Now she is sitting there helpless and alone. God's will is hard to understand. The youngest of the girls who lived at home is now married. A son is married as well and lives at home. So, it is not going to be so easy for her.

It will soon be the fall season, and the summer is almost over. It has been sunny and warm until a few weeks ago. The summer did not arrive until early July, but when it first came, it was so nice, and I cannot remember ever experiencing any summers like it.

We had a nice week when we harvested the hay. Mathilde Grødem was up here a month and my brother, Lars, a few weeks and Sivert Mong also a few days - so everything went fine. Tell your Father, Tollag, that we harvested at the high meadows this year. We made three haystacks close to Gravdal, and I thought it was more fun now than when I was 20 years old. We had so much rain and it was so cold at the beginning of the summer that we did not get as much hay at home as normal.

You would not believe how the girls up there ran to the river and bathed - up to three times a day, and they got me to join in, too. I have borrowed your swimsuit. and if you want to sell it, I will buy it. If not, possibly we could do some trading – because as we approach easier times, there might be something I have that you might want. I must admit that I also borrowed your raincoat a few times last year. I had to go to doctor appointments in a period of five weeks, and I thought if anyone gossips about me wearing the raincoat, I'd be the first to tell you. I had blood poisoning in my right hand and, thankfully, we were almost done with the harvest - you cannot believe how painful it was. It was luck that it went as well as it did, as I have never been so sick in my life. The first week I stayed in bed; after that I had to go to town every day to see the doctor or they would put me in the hospital, and I didn't want that. I stayed with Tante Elisabeth (Omdal). *I took the last bus into town and stayed until the next day. If we had gone to the doctor earlier, it would not have gotten that bad.*

So, at the same time, the horse was sick. The veterinarian came up and visited three times and performed a large hoof operation. It all went well, but it almost took eight months before we could use the horse again.

You will have to let your father know that Kjos Hansen is one of those who was arrested, and I have to tell you that I feel really bad for his old man.

I wish well for so many. I think it is really sad that you have gotten so skinny. You just must come back and travel up to Liland *and drink some goat milk and eat some goat cheese.*

Sven has been to the sanitarium in the east part of Norway this summer; he and Tilde traveled by airplane. This summer, when Petter and Henne Omdal were here, I forgot to ask about him. If they have not told you, don't say anything.

You asked me if I want to come back with you to the U.S.A. after you come, and I have been thinking about it as never before. It is nice to see that you are thinking about making a trip back to Norway again. It looks like I am the only one that is living with hope that you will return. It was hard to separate the way it happened. So, the fact that your father (Tollag) *has talked about it is also a joy. You know that I would love to take the trip and come with you, but I have not worked for the Germans, so I am not rich, you know.*

It is Monday, and I must stop for now. I am sending this letter with Tante Sille; she is going to town today. She has been home for about two weeks. Right now, I am making dinner and I am frying trout. Can you remember the last evening before you went to Vagle? I'll bet you have experienced a lot since then.

Greet your father (Tollag) *and mother* (Christine) *and also* (my brother) *Peder and Ellen (*Peterson). *I don't know if you understand this scribble. Heartfelt greetings from us, and thank you again for the package, it was all needed.*

Anne and Petter

October 8, 1945 – Mong

Letter from Thelma Mong

Dearest Sophie!

Thank you for the last time and a heartfelt thousand thanks for the package that I received yesterday. You would not believe how needed it was - the wonderful flannel, the spools, and all the other. Yes, you would not believe that there is not much to get in Norway now. The Germans, you know, have plucked everything from us, so we have to do with almost nothing, and it will be a while until we can get more. The worst of all is not getting shoes. Rolf is three years old now and he has had two pairs of shoes since he was born, and as mentioned, right now has nothing to wear. It is sad, because it destroys your mood when things are like this. Because of this, it would be nice if maybe you could buy some new or used shoes over there, and you will be paid back with interest.

I suppose you have heard that we have gotten a little girl. Her name is Brit Helene after both of her grandmothers. She is two months now and she is the 'peace' baby. She is such a good baby these days, and that is very helpful, because I am loaded with work. Everything is so difficult with clothing, and because of that, everything is double work.

*You will not believe how many times I have had America fever; I am longing terribly – there are so many that are taking off now. I think you know Olaf (*Svånes)*; he and his wife are traveling with the first boat now.*

I just hope that you will come back sometime. How are you

doing? It was such a horrible trip you had to take, and we are all so happy that you stayed alive and are healthy. I guess things will be better after a while.

Jenny Mong, Sivert's sister, got married September 22nd to someone (Torvald Retland) *from Sandnes. There were 95 guests altogether, and the wedding was held in town at her sister Berit and Lars Mong's house. Kristian Mikkelsen is also married to someone from Sandnes. People have gotten married like crazy now after the war.*

Well, I guess I need to get this letter ready and send it. Miss Ålvik is sending her greetings - everything is well with her. She is treating the children just like before - ha, ha.

Last year, for the confirmation, I borrowed your blue dress - the one with the flowers - because I didn't have anything to wear. Do you think that I could buy it from you, so that I have a nice dress for special occasions? It would be great if I could; it was a blessing with the snap buttons because we have not had anything like that for two years. Do you have white fabric-covered buttons? If you ever have two or three extras, maybe you can think of me. I really don't want to beg, but I just want to let you know how sparse things are here now.

November 11th is Father (Andreas Rodvelt's) *60th birthday and we are having a little party. I wish you could be with us having coffee and white cakes. You would not believe how strange it was the day we went downtown and bought white bread and white rolls - it was like a dream. And it was so fantastic with peace that day - a day I'll never forget. We went into town by boat from Mong almost every day and on May 8th, a crowd was standing at the marketplace in town listening to the church bells. When the Norwegian and American flags were raised... yes, we were all crying. What a strange time - let's hope that it will last for a while.*

On Wednesday, Mother (Helene Rodvelt) *and Inga Åvendal are traveling to Stavanger to visit for a few days; it has been a while since she was last there. I will send you a picture of Rolf when I go downtown - it was taken last year on his second birthday in Stavanger. He has grown since you saw him last.*

I will have to stop now with this messy letter; you must excuse me. I will write more later. I hope it reaches you. I once again thank you from the bottom of my heart for the package. It arrived like it was sent from heaven - a thousand thank yous.

Take care and be heartfully greeted from us, all four of us. Everybody in the house asks me to greet you so much.

Thelma, Sivert, Rolf, and Brit Helene Mong

October 8, 1945 – London, England

Letter from fellow internee at Liebenau

My Dearest Sophie!

I think you will be surprised to receive a letter from me. I am Ida, your old Liebenau companion! How are you dear? I have been thinking of you very often and wonder how you are getting along. You know, we stayed in Liebenau until the sweet end - until the French came and liberated us. My dear, that was a glorious day! Did we have a good time after our liberation! It was really worthwhile! All the Germans are scared and just weeping, and the Wache was taken prisoner, the nuns remained, the foreign office was cleared out and they were all taken to prison and afterwards put on the land to work. We just went sightseeing every day and the French made parties for us nearly every night. Mrs. Froom took the Pay Masters office for her work although she had a difficult time with all those females who absolutely ran loose. The camp was taken over by a British colonel and 6 weeks later we were all repatriated. The Americans went the beginning of August. Liebenau is now a place for French children to recover. All those people who were left in the camp are sent to Biberach. Mrs. Johnson who wants to go back to Norway is among them. Maybe by now she is back. Her friend Anny came to England with us. I am training now to go abroad again with the British Relief for Abroad. It is all under the U.N.N.R.A. I am learning to drive a truck now. Linny is also here in London. Elizabeth is back in Amsterdam but is here on a visit now. Oh, you know Sophie, that my sister is here now too? It is my married sister who was in Russia. After a very hard time in Siberia, she managed to come here; she does not know where her husband is. She is working here now, and later we are planning to go to South Africa. From my mother and other sister I never heard any more. How is your family? Is everybody alright? Are your brothers home now? I wonder if they are still in London. I see so many Americans here. If they are, tell them to come and see me and say hello! Are you still thinking of going back to Norway? O dear, I would love to see you once again. I wonder if that would ever be! Do you hear from the other Norwegian ladies? Please give them my love when you see them. Well dearest Sophie, write to me please! I would very much like to hear from you! Lots of love, Yours, Ida

October 14, 1945 – Dybing
Letter from Tyra Gystøl
Dear Sophie!

Thank you for the last time! It was so nice to hear from you. Thank you so much for the package that I received from you; it was great! I received the dress, the coat, and everything else. I really did not have any dresses. Tante Ane (Gystol) *Seland died last winter, and I did not have anything that I could wear to the funeral - so I didn't go. I have needed a black dress and now I have one – the thing I needed the most. And I also received the coat, skirt, blouse, thread, soap, coffee, and everything else. I thank you so much for everything - we needed it all. The dress, coat and the blouse fit me perfectly. The skirt was a little bit too long, but I can fix that. The coffee was so good - we made some today, but the rest we will hide away until Christmas. Things are so much better now; we have gotten white flour and white bread and you won't believe how much we ate the first day. It was so very good - soon life will be back like the old days.*

There are a lot of Nazis, stripped of their citizenship, that are still walking around loose. They should be behind locked doors and more so. They are still free and so bold, but I expect that it will be tougher for them now as it gets darker at night. The Nazis are having it way too easy; they should be locked up and shouldn't see the light of day for many years. The Norwegians are too kind to them, but I am sure a change will come.

My mother is much better now, she is up walking and gets outside every day. She had rheumatic fever, but they expect her to return to normal. Her legs are still stiff because of arthritis.

This winter I went to school for pediatric nursing, so now I am a pediatric nurse; see the attached picture of me. Later, I will send you a picture of me in my uniform. My plan is to be a midwife, but I have not been accepted in the school yet.

I am happy to hear that everything is well with you and especially with Carl who has been in the war - and that he received honors. It is such a blessing that it all went well; it really shows that he has some of the old Viking blood in him.

Everybody here greets you - my mother (Teoline), *my father* (Johan), *and all my siblings - all of us at home here in Norway.*

Heartfelt Greetings, from Tyra

Tyra Gystøl from Dybing, Helleland, Egersund, Norway

October 25, 1945 - Grødem

Letter from Anne Omdal

Dear Sophie and Everybody,

Thank you for the packages that we received in good shape. There should be a package that you sent containing shoes, but we have not received that one yet. You must take a break; do not send more, you are wearing yourself out, and you probably take from what you yourself need. I regret that I said anything when you asked me what we needed. I was in such a hurry that I cannot remember what I said. All this must cost you a lot; but I know that if we get to live long enough, we are going to pay you back.

They took away restrictions on the wool now, after they thought we had delivered it all, but we still have something left. We will try to send you a kilo of wool yarn. We are still not allowed to spin with only wool, but we have so much of it. Saturday, we got new clothing rationing cards; however, there is really nothing that I want to spend money on. It is all poor quality and too expensive.

Here is what was in the packages we received. In mine was the blue fabric, coffee, a slip, pants, socks, spool of thread, darning yarn, prunes, a jacket, soap, and hair pins. In Petter's package was a cotton pullover, coffee, soap, and shoelaces. Thank you for everything and greet your brother, Martin (Peterson). *Thank you. I just hope you did not take it from yourself. The blue jacket looks really good on me. Father* (Peder Mikal Omdal) *always said that when something looked really good, it was church clothing and it is, especially when it's measured up against what we are used to now.*

There have been some things in the stores this whole time, but it is the fishermen that take it all. American rubber boots have arrived, but the fishermen take them all as well. They should have no regrets; they did all they could to provide food and they also fished some herring for the Germans. Sivert said that last winter he made ten thousand kroner, and that was just in one year. Mikal Rodvelt works with Sivert and has also made a lot of money. He might have to serve in the military as of next month - for a whole year.

Helene and Inga Åvendal have been to Stavanger and Vagle, visiting. The idea was that I was going to go with them, but it is not easy since Petter is working. I have not been to Vagle since you left, and Thea Omdal has not been here since the Confirmation at Rodvelt. It is difficult because of the travel restrictions. Last year, Mandius Hausan was not allowed to travel to Anna's wedding.

Did you know that Anna has gotten a (baby) *boy? It all went well but it was close at the hospital in Sandnes. I talked to Ingrid Garpestad, who was with her as she got up from the bed in the middle of the night, and worried she was not going to make it - she had miscounted - so the doctor was helping recalculate; they had a lot of fun with her, both the doctors and the nurses.*

I forgot to write and tell you about the packages that came from Germany - we have received them both. One had coffee, soap, cocoa, raisins, two towels, and stretch pants. I might have forgotten something; it is a miracle that it made it here. We did not get the letter and realized something was wrong with the package when it arrived. Petter searched for you through the Red Cross and he got an answer, but it took a very long time. The police and Gestapo were up here, and Petter was quick to ask about you, but it was all very secret. I did receive a letter from you, but I think you did not get all of mine. I sent you some dark grey, quite thick yarn; did you receive it? I asked you a few times (by letter) *when you were in Germany, but you never answered me. I could not think of anything else to send you, but hoped you could knit yourself some socks, maybe for some of yours* (loved ones at home), *if you had nothing to do.*

Well, I must stop now. You are probably tired of reading this scribble. Greet your father and mother and everybody I know. Tell your father (Anne and Petter were his siblings) *it would be nice to see his letters again, unless he has forgotten how to write.*

Heartfelt Greetings and Thanks.

Love, Petter and Anne

October 25, 1945 — Egersund

Letter from Gudrun *(Egelandsdal)* Thorsen

Dear Sophie,

You must excuse this bad paper.

Thank you so much for the letter that I received a week ago. I was so happy when I received the letter, because I did not think that my letter had reached you since I was not sure of the address. I would have responded to your letter as soon as I received it, but I was disturbed by the children. It is quite a bit of work now with two small ones (Anna Karin and Arild Stein).

I really appreciate that you are sending a package to us. You will not believe how Anna Karin is waiting for the shoes that I have talked about, and I have to say that they are really needed, because the ones that she has are just a pair of fabric shoes with a rubber sole, that we managed to buy at the store with the rationing card, so I hope that these fit her. It will soon be better here. At least we have enough food. We have wheat flour and other flour, so there are no problems getting food, and it will soon be better with clothes as well. I have to say that the Americans have been fabulous with all the packages containing all kinds of things that almost every household has received. No one is starving now. Agnes got a package today from a brother-in-law with clothing for their son, Hans. I am so excited to receive your package. I hope that some time I can do something for you.

Hopefully, you will be back to Norway soon. You need to pick up your skis that wait at home at Egelandsdal. Mother (Anna Egelandsdal) *is in the hospital right now; she has an ulcer, but they will release her, and she will be coming home on Monday. Astrid's husband, Gjert, is working as a customs inspector right now, and he is helping with receiving the American packages. He said that yesterday he saw a package from you addressed to one of the Østrem's, so I just want to let you know that the packages get here. I am not going to write more this time, but when I receive the package, you can expect a long letter from me.*

Please say hi to all of yours. Many greetings.

Gudrun Thorsen

October 25, 1945

Letter from Tante Thea Omdal

Dear You and All of You Over There,

Thank you so much for the letter we received yesterday with news that you are all well. You must excuse that I haven't written you and answered that I received the packages. The days have been so busy, that in the evening I am so tired that I have not been able to write. But today, I will get serious.

We live well now, but Lars has been very sick this summer; he was bedridden for six weeks. So, it has been very busy. However, he is well enough to go out in the barn and care for the cows. Yes, it is sad when someone is that sick. He has had water on one of his lungs, and it is odd that older people can get anything like this because it is mostly young people that get this. Henne has taken his place at work, and he gets paid pretty well - 18 kroner a day. Petter is home and takes care of the outside. The only thing we have left now is threshing.

We are all thanking you so much for the packages that we have received. Do not send us anything more. I do not know what I could send you back. I guess I will have to wait until there is something that I can buy here. We have received three packages, and you are probably curious about if we got it all. My package contained dress fabric, two pairs of socks, one slip, one pair of pants, coffee, soap, thread, shoelaces, prunes, elastic, and needles. Petter received two pairs of pants, one shirt, coffee, and soap. Henne received two pairs of pants, two shirts, soap, and coffee. You have just done too much - it has been a lot of work for you to buy and ship it all. You must have been concerned that things did not fit. Petter's pants fits him perfectly; also did his shirts of finest quality. It has been easier to buy food lately, so we just hope that it will soon be easier to get clothing as well. People are going crazy when we receive packages, because there has been so much less clothing than food.

This fall is beautiful, mild, and sunny. I have heard that your brother, Carl, is still not back home. It is sad that he will not get a chance to travel to Norway now, but if you wait until next summer, both of you should come. We have more than once talked about when you will be back here again. We all like to believe that we will meet you again. Yes, I have shed many tears for you since you left us. I heard that your mother was very sick before you came home - she must have had a lot to worry about. You must be happy that she is feeling much better now.

Little Marit Vagle is bigger now, and the other day Olga had a little boy, Henrik Vagle. We were happy that something happened because we have thought so much about him. He is Henrik #10 in this family.

*Last time I wrote to you I told you that Mother, (*Martine Vagle), *is not with us anymore. It feels very empty now that she is not here. She died on August 17, 1944; it has already been a year ago. She was bedridden for only three weeks. It was the heart; it was so weak that she sat in bed day and night because she felt she could not breathe. In the end, she got a blood clot. It was my sister Tilde in Stavanger and I that cared for her - I ran back and forth. Yes, it was very sad to see her being in so much pain. The last days we had to bring in the doctor with the injections. We did everything we could. We wanted her to be better, but she said that she was so tired she just wanted to rest. All she said was that she was going to travel first, and then we must come later. It is very sad to write about her now. Everybody says that Mother was such a nice human being and so kind. I am sending you a picture of her, so now you can see if you recognize her.*

There is not so much news to tell you other than that all of us are well. Helene and Inga Åvendal were here for a short visit; they came from Stavanger Sunday night and left again Monday night. They live well over there. Andreas (Rodvelt) *is celebrating his 60th birthday November 11th and they want us to come over. But I do not think we will, because Lars must be really careful. I have not been there since the twins* (Alf Henry and Petter Rodvelt) *had their Confirmation because I'm not supposed to travel much. This summer I have been dressed up twice; Andreas (*Mauland) *drove us to church on the Memorial Day for the fallen, and one Sunday we went on a road trip. I will wait until you are back in Norway again. Yes, we do live and trust that we will soon see you again. I will write you again soon, but I must stop now for this time. Greet your mother and father and siblings.*

Greetings from all at Moen (short for Vaglemoen), *Tante Berthea* (Omdal)

P.S. Don't send more coffee.

November 4, 1945
Letter from Randi (Østrem) Skipstad
Hello Sophie!

Thank you for the last time. And many thousand thank yous for the incredible package that we received from you. It gave us a lot of joy; I almost do not know how I can thank you enough. Here is how we shared the contents. The yellow silk blouse and the light pink dress fit me perfectly and I will try to sew/use the blue fabric from the disassembled dress. Josefine was given the pretty light blue (item) *with white, the brown skirt, and the red knitted jacket, and all of this fit her so well as if they were made for her. Bertha got a light green skirt, the green blouse, and a pair of stockings. Hjørdis will get the undergarment and a couple of stockings. The spools of thread came just at the right time. I had just finished using all that I had, and now I am unraveling so many edges on curtains and napkins - everything I have - and half a bed cover that has gone the same way. So, you cannot believe how happy I was when I opened the package and right away two spools rolled out, and then one more and another one after that. It was more than I had seen through the whole war, and it is such a good quality too. Also, thanks for the wonderful piece of soap, the grey safety pins, and the stockings - it was all great because we can put everything to use. I really wanted a new blouse to wear for Christmas, and I was going to sew myself a skirt and a vest - knitting is so slow for me. But then I got this yellow blouse from you and now I have no more sorrows. Again, I must thank you so much. It was so well received for us who are so many - now we are six - we were only five when they took you from us. The youngest one is also a boy; his name is Jan Reidar and he is two years old. So, I have been fully loaded with work the entire time.*

I would have loved to see you again, Sophie; we did not even get to say good-bye. It was a horrible time for us, like a nightmare. It was even worse for you, who had to experience the war way too close for comfort. Also, for poor Bergit who lost Alf – and that was the last time I saw both you and him. We never know what life brings. Last year I heard you were safely home in America, and it was great news.

A lot of packages have arrived from America with clothing, but they only get delivered to the cities. We, here in the countryside, do not get anything unless someone is sending it to us privately.

It has been at least three years since I have been able to buy one meter of cotton fabric, so it is amazing how people have still managed. But I assume many of them have used old sheets (to make clothing with), *especially if they had more sheets than they needed. Hopefully, things will be better going forward, although if you have something later you are not going to use, we would be very grateful.*

Please greet your mother and father and all your siblings from us. I am supposed to greet you and thank you from Joseph, Josefine, Bertha, and Hjørdis. Little Kjetil asked me the other day if the package we received came from the lady that visited us together with Tante Anna (Østrem), *so it seems that he still remembers you. It is way too long since we have seen you and it would be great to see you again.*

Today, Anna came up to visit me. She and Bergit (Randi's sisters) *were home for just a little while with our parents* (Berthe and Andreas Østrem), *then Bergit went back to town to take little Alf to the Skåra family. That was when Anna came here - the wind was so cold, and she was pretty frozen when she arrived.*

Thank you very much and greetings from: Randi Skipstad, Helleland

November 5, 1945 – Årrestad

Letter from Bertha Aarrestad

Dear Sophie!

I have now received your package. It was mailed from Bow September 25th, and I received it here November 3rd. It had to travel far, but we are just so happy that it made it. Rakel's package came at the same time as mine. Heartfelt thank you - saying thank you sounds so little, but I can only thank you now through letters. Do not wear yourself out with these packages and with all the work and preparation that you are doing - to have them packed and shipped? I will write down what was in the last package so that you know if we got everything. Listen here. Three types of fabric, four packages of shoelaces, three packages of soap, one package prunes, one package of rice, one chocolate, one comb, two pairs of socks, two underskirts, one pair of pants, four white spools of thread, two black, and one shirt. I cannot tell you what of this that I love the most. For shoelaces, we have had to use paper, the comb is made of iron, the soap that we have used smells like excrement. It was fabulous with the white, wonderful soap; and the prunes tasted so good. Yes, thank you so much Sophie, I hope that we can pay you back one day.

It moves really slow here these days with all sorts of things. There are no changes when it comes to clothing, it is non-existing. We, here at Helleland, have not even seen a rag; the stores are empty. The newspapers are bragging about all of the merchandise that has arrived in the country, but where is it? I read in the newspaper that a lot gets stolen from the American packages. Here, many have received packages, and nothing has been stolen. People have turned bad now after the war; it is very sad that it is going that way. But all is well with us and we are healthy. However, I have such a bad nerve pain in my head, it is very bothersome. I cannot deal with the cold air. I used to have a cream that was really good, but they make it in the U.S.A. I have not been able to get ahold of it for several years so I hope it will soon be available again. Do you have any knowledge about it? It's called Mentholatum.

Margrethe (Sørdal) *just had a little boy, Leif Trond Magne, so now Mother* (Semine Østrem) *is taking care of children again. Mikael got a girl, Ingveig, so the family is growing and that is good. Besides it all, everything is well, and we are not suffering in any way, although we are hoping for better times when it comes to merchandise. So, it is going better everywhere.*

I went to Dybing the other day - Aunt Teoline felt pretty good. Amanda is sitting with the old ones, and her sister, Tyra, is with Ragna Moi nowadays. I guess there is no change there yet.

How are all of you? Do you hear anything from your brother Carl? How is it with you - do you live on rations like us? It would be so great to see you again. I bet you are struggling with the schoolwork now. How is your health? How did you cope in Germany? I wonder if you got my last letter.

Quisling is now dead, and he got what he deserved. It is like waking up from a nightmare. We just cannot believe that we got through these years. I am so disgusted when I read about how the Japanese treated their prisoners. They were even worse than the Germans. How can people be so horrible?

Greet everybody from us. A heartfelt thank you from Liv, Svein, Magnus, and me. Write soon.

Greetings, Anna Bertha Aarrestad

November 21, 1945 – London, England

Letter from former prisoner

My Dearest Sophie,

Received your letter and was ever so glad to hear from you. I only write you a few words, for I am packing and am awfully busy. I am off to Germany within three days. We are going to Cille, that is a camp in the North of Germany. The work will be very interesting, and we shall have to travel quite a lot. Sophie, I will write to you from the camp and hope you will answer me there. Yes, it also was very difficult for us to settle down again, that's why I am off again. Linny is here in London and I gave her your regards. Elisabeth is in Holland at her old job, so is Pat. Do you intend to go to Norway still? Sophie, I sure would love to see you again, for you know I like you very much. Dear friend, give my best regards to your family and the best of luck to you.

Yours, Ida

November 30, 1945 – Grødem

Letter from Anne Omdal

Dear Sophie,

Thank you so much for the letter we received two weeks ago and thank you for the package. We received it on October 25th. We have not written you any letters because Petter has said that he wanted to write also, but it does not look like that will happen. I had just sent a letter the day I received the package. The package was in good shape - it contained two sets of underwear and coffee. I must admit that I cannot remember exactly what else was in that package. It was not opened, and it did not cost us anything in duty/customs. There have been incidents where the receiver has not gotten everything that was shipped to them. A lot is written about this in the newspapers now, so I think stealing from packages will stop soon. Johan Lædre's sister, Helene, has sent so many packages, and they have received everything except for one kilo of coffee. It looks like they most of all search packages for coffee.

On October 30th, we went to Stapnes for the Silver Wedding of Marta and Nils Stapnes - I wish you could have been there. On November 11th, we went to Rodvelt for a birthday party, as Andreas Emil Rodvelt turned 60 years old. Agnes, Alfred, Asta, Edith, Else, and Bertha Rodvelt Askildsen *arrived from Stavanger. It was lively because, you know, where Bertha is, there is life.*

My sister, Helene (Omdal Rodvelt) *and Astrid came Saturday night, so you know it became an evening just like the old times. On Sunday night, we went down to Åseheien in the beautiful moonlight, and we visited all of the houses, and in the end, we went to Pintlo. They had just received a package on Saturday from one of Lars* (Herman) *Omdal's boys* (Roy) *from Bow, Washington. It was three dresses and a dress suit, and it all fit them well. Martine Omdal asked me if I knew who Lars Herman's son Roy is married to.* (Note - Roy Ernest Omdal married Ione Fortier on June 21, 1941 in Bow, WA.) *Gjertine Omdal asked me to ask you about Karl Johan* (Tollefson) *and Hattie* (Henrietta). *I think he should have written a letter.*

I talked to Helene Rodvelt on the telephone; she said they had a letter from you yesterday. I have heard that Carl is back home. I am sure that you all were in a joyful mood at that time. I understood in the last letter you wrote that you have all been worried. It had been a long time since you had seen each other, and I am sure both of you have experienced quite a bit. Are both of Peder's boys, Ernest and Palmer (Peterson), *back home from the service? You will have to greet them so much. I still have not sent them a letter but need to get serious and send one for Christmas.* (Note - Ernest (Ernie) served in England, and Palmer in the South Pacific.)

You asked if we needed shoes. I was not going to ask you to get me any, but it has been so hard to get ahold of shoes. So, I think I will ask you for a pair of Sunday shoes, size 40. I have looked for shoes for three years but still have not found any. There have been some Swedish shoes available, but they get sold out really fast. Last summer there were also a few American shoes. People sat in line from 4:00 Sunday afternoon - they were going to start selling 8:00 Monday morning. Some were playing cards to kill time, but at 11:00 at night, they were chased home by the police. Petter's shoes were a bit tight, but he can use them with thin socks. Thank you again for the package and for all the soap. I have almost forgotten that things like that still exist. I have cooked soap from seal oil. One time I cooked from animal fat, but I thought it was too good for soap, because others didn't really have fat to cook with. Many cook with seal oil, and you cannot believe how horrible it tastes.

It is Friday night, and Petter is on his way to town. It is getting close to Christmas - short days, and busy. Petter is still working, and they will not be finished by Christmas.

Please greet everybody and especially greet Carl - welcome home. Sorry, I do not know if you understand all of this. Do not let anyone read this scribble. You over there, please greet everybody! Siri of Peder, everybody in Omdal and many, many others are sending you greetings. Good night.

Heartfelt Greetings, Anne and Petter

December 7, 1945

Letter from Thelma Mong

Dearest Sophie!

Thanks for being in touch lately, and a heartfelt "thank you" for your letter and package. I'm sorry to hear you haven't received my letter which I sent right after I got the first package from you.

Well, I really don't know where to start. All that you sent me is so useful and appreciated. I almost cannot believe it's true. I am so pleased, indeed. First, the prunes. We have hidden them! They will be used at Christmas time. By then we will enjoy genuine prune porridge once again! Also, thanks for all the underwear, not to forget the wonderful slip, and let me be honest – the one I had was gone a long time ago, worn almost into pieces. I think you easily understand that we haven't had any clothes or fabric to buy in five years. In fact, it's quite curious that we have got anything at all.

We received your package this Saturday and its content is very useful to us – it's worth much more than money. So, Sophie, you've done a special and a good deed, like a mission towards me. You may think yourself – there's nothing to buy in the stores, and it may be a long time before we get anything....

The pink cap is wonderful, and it is brand new, and also the silk bands/ties not to forget the lovey baby dresses. One of them has a drawing - now I've almost finished sewing at that one. It's so lovely to have something pretty to work with. I must also thank you so much for the shoes for Rolf - they fit him, and we appreciate them highly. In my other letter to you, I asked you to try to find a pair of shoes for him, since he at that time didn't have any shoes at all. However, by now he has got a new pair of shoes via our State Ration Card, and now I feel very rich.

You may easily understand that I was a little bit shocked when I discovered the comb in the package. Also, you would certainly have been shocked if you had seen the comb I had before - it was of iron. It was as hard for my head as flint stone. Yes, we have endured much during all these hard years.

I sent a photo last Saturday of Rolf. I wonder if it will reach you.

Well, it's soon Christmas. This year there will surely be very special festivities as we have peace on earth. We are very happy for that. Also, we have heard on the radio that people in Norway will have a lot of good stuff before Christmas - oranges, rice, dried fruit, treacle, and many more things we haven't had for many years.

This is going to be a short letter - I will write more next time. I do hope you and yours are doing well.

We have got frost and cold weather, and it has been snowing here for the first time this winter, so we are getting some feeling of Christmas.

I wish you all the best, and again - thank you so much for everything you sent us. You're an angel!

With kind regards and wishing you a Merry Christmas and a Blessed New Year.

Brit Helene, Rolf, Thelma and Sivert

December 9, 1945 - Grødem

Letter from Anne Omdal

Dear Sophie,

Thank you for the letter that we received Tuesday. Mandius came from town and said, "Here, you got a letter from our friend".

It must have been a joyful day when you were all together again, and it would have been great to have been together with you. I cannot believe that you wrote already the first evening - you must have been so tired. You talk about God's gifts and blessings, and it is wonderful to experience things like that. Not everybody thanks God and gives Him the honor that they have been so well protected. It is a strange time and almost like a spiritual experience, and like the Lamb, both body and soul. We live in a time where it sometimes feels like Satan will strangle us, and he is not sleeping; he is working overtime. When Sigvart Mong (neighbor to Sivert and Thelma Mong) *returned home from Germany, he was very disappointed in the weakness among the Christians. Hans at Mong has gotten really hardened after the trip to Germany; no wonder, after everything they have experienced.*

You should have been here and met with Arne Friestad again. He had a visit from Prime Minister Einar Gerhardsen from Oslo, who held a meeting in the Gotemplerlokalet. The two of them had been together both at Grini and later in Germany. The Prime Minister represents the Worker's Party (Norwegian Labour Party). *It has been a lot of work with the election of a new government, and last Monday was the local election. We are really curious how it will turn out.*

You were talking about the fur coat and the letter that you say you sent from Germany. We have not received it, and Torger has probably not received it either, since we have not heard from him, so you need to write him again. Petter is talking about sending it (the fur coat) *to you, it has to be with certified mail, but we will do what you think is best. There were some skeins of grey yarn in the package that we sent to Germany, but I understand that you never received it. There were four types of yarn that we sent and several women's magazines. Did you get those? You told me that the last package you received had been opened.*

*Yesterday, Gjertine (*Omdal), *and Marta, and Nils Stapnes went to Stavanger for a Silver Wedding celebration for Paul Martin and Rakel Omdal. Marta's was at the end of October. And the first day of Pentecost, we went to Myran* (the farm at Omdal where Lars Bowits Larsen Omdal lived) *with Gjertine and Erling. We partied until late night. Karl Johan Tollefson's was also the same year if I do not remember wrong.*

You sent me so many spools of thread, and I have shared them. We get spools of thread now, but it is very poor quality. We also get coffee now - fifty grams each week. It is not much, compared to what we were used to before the war. Last summer we got fifty grams twice each week, but it was so bad that many have not used it. It was some that was stored in England during the war that the military did not use. The tobacco is released also, so now they can get as much as they want, and that is a good thing. Mathilde Grødem has gotten several things from America; among the things she got was a fur coat. She is laughing, as she will never wear it. She says she might give it to the Finns.

I never did go to Vagle. Helene and Inga Åvendal went there, and they also went to Stavanger. Lars Omdal has been ill this summer (with MS), *but I assume they already wrote to you about that. Helene talked to Sven at Vagle; he is feeling much better now.*

*I realize you have sent another package; we are thanking you - you could be so tired of all the work. This afternoon I wrote Peder and Ellen (*Peterson). *I had not written earlier, and I am embarrassed, because we had a post card from them in*

August. Helene went Christmas shopping in town yesterday. I was supposed to go with her, could I just have gotten out. The stores have not gotten much money from me during the war. I assume they are getting in something extra for Christmas, but I have not gotten my hopes up. Can you believe that it is only two weeks left until Christmas? I am so happy that we are going to experience freedom this year. I am saying thank you for the old year and greet everybody with "Have a Merry Christmas".

Heartfelt Greetings from Us Two, Anne and Petter

December 9, 1945 - Vagle

Letter from Onkel Lars Omdal

Dear Sophie,

I am writing to tell you that all is well here, and I hope that all is well with you too. I have been thinking of writing for a long time, but I think it is difficult to write, so it seems like it just does not happen.

First of all, thank you for all the letters and packages. Do not send more now, because as time goes by there will hopefully be more to buy here. Underwear is the hardest to get ahold of. They sell some very low quality and also some made out of seal wool. But I cannot use it - it falls apart just looking at it. The Germans took all our wool. Although we have enough now, it will take a while before the factories can start producing again. Until then, they are trying to get rid of all those low-quality garments – bringing it all out to the market. We have been promised some of better quality next week, but it will probably be expensive. I am sure that you are spending a lot of money on us over there as well. One day, I hope to pay you back.

Yes, we all live and hope that we will see you again. For the longest time we were hoping to see your brother Carl here, but we heard through Marit Skadsem, who has just received a letter from you, that he has come home. With all he has experienced, we are happy he got away without any scars on body or soul. Several Norwegian Americans have been able to visit family here, and it would have been great to talk with you again and learn about everything from the time you left us. The base in Germany was probably long and hard to get through.

We received greetings from you through the Swedish woman saying that you were safe at home. We are happy everything went well in the end, and that you are on American soil again. Let us know if you want us to send some of your stuff – you have clothing, jewelry, a diary, a lot of pamphlets, a money note for your old car, and much more.

We hope you soon come back and bring someone with you. Petter Omdal wants to go to sea (become a sailor), *but Thea does not like it, so we will see. Henne took my place in the factory - I am not going back yet, maybe this spring - I have enough with the farm at the moment.*

I better stop now. It feels so awkward to write. I have not written any letters since I wrote to you in Germany, so you see that I do not get much practice. Greet your mother (Christine), *father* (Tollag), *and siblings (*Peter, Martin, Tora, Oscar, Theodora, Carl, and Melvin), *and your Uncle Peder and Ellen (*Peterson) *with family (*Tilda, Palmer, Mynor, Ernest, Myrtle, Esther, and Marie). *Have a Merry Christmas and a Happy New Year.*

And here, at last, a friendly greeting from your Uncle Lars.

December 9, 1945 - Vagle

Letter from Tante Berthea (Vagle) Omdal

I am just attaching a few words to Lars's letter. Thank you so much for the package. It arrived with the Stavangerfjord (Norwegian ocean liner that sailed between Norway and the United States) *and its contents were fabric for dress making, two pairs of undergarments, a shirt, an undershirt, soap, a spool of thread, shoelaces, toothpaste, brushes, combs, and a whisk. It arrived just in time; it is almost Christmas and I am about to start baking. They fight over the contents in the package and dress us in one piece of clothing each. The shirt fits Henne perfectly, and nothing was too big.*

Although merchandise is coming to the country, most of it goes to the military troops. In some places, people are in big despair, almost naked, and just barely covered. You must have spent a lot of time and effort shopping and shipping. But we will make sure to return the favor later. Thank you so much for everything you have sent us.

It is almost Christmas, and this year we will celebrate in peace. After five years with restrictions, we will celebrate Christmas with peace and song.

We live well, although there have been some common colds going around. The weather has been beautiful this fall, but today it is raining. Rain is good, as we need electricity.

I heard that Marit Skadsem received a letter that you wrote, and that your Mother has been sick, and that Carl is back home. I know you all are so happy that he is with you again, and I am sure that he has experienced a lot. Greet everybody and have a Merry Christmas. Greet your mother and father and greetings to yourself.

Heartfelt Greetings,
*From Tante Thea (*Berthea*)*

January 1, 1946 – Egelandsdal

Letter from Tyra (Egelandsdal) Tunheim

Dear, Dear Sophie!

We wish you all a VERY Happy New Year. I received the package from you yesterday. Everything was so genuinely nice. It was so wonderful to touch and feel something that you, all the way in America, had touched before me. And it was all so carefully and beautifully wrapped.

Mother made rice porridge last night - New Year's Eve. We have not had rice to make porridge with; and we took some of the prunes you sent and made a dessert for today. Of the chocolate, everyone was able to get a small piece each. So, you know - we ate, we talked, we thought about you and your family. It was a good time. And then, all the beautiful curtain fabric, spools of thread, and all the other things. You must write to me and tell me how much it cost. I suppose it is possible to send Norwegian money to you. If I just knew of something that I could buy you instead of money. But the worst is being able to think of something, and I am sure it cost you a lot of money.

Father had a letter from your mother, and it sounds like you are all doing well. Are you home now? Or do you have school? We are all doing well here. Kirsten is out skiing. We do not have a lot of snow, but the weather is beautiful and cold. Mikal is here visiting, and he asks me to greet you with all of his heart from him and his family.

Well, we decided not to buy that farm at Helleland – it was too expensive. But now I think we might move to Moi, and that will be great because then I can meet with Olga and Ragna. I cannot leave Mother alone, so I will not leave until I get a girl (maid) *to look after her and help in the house. My health is not the best right now, and I probably will not see improvement until this spring. At that time, I hope it will be better.*

Kirsten wanted to write something to you; but she writes such large letters, so I guess it will have to be later. Can you believe that this year we could bake bread and cakes for Christmas? And we were each able to get one kilo of oranges, and you won't believe how wonderful that was.

You need to come for Easter and go skiing. Sigmund has built himself a cabin on top of the hill from the house. It is very nice. You have to come, and we will have so much fun. Your skis are here. I used them last year, but this year I will leave them alone.

Mother, Father, and everybody here tells me to greet you. How many of your siblings are married now? Again, thank you so much for everything you have done and for all you have sent me. I really desire to repay you for everything and your hard work to pack it all. A thousand thank yous for everything.

You must write and let me know how you are doing. My husband is sending his greetings. I hope with all my heart that all is well with you, Sophie, and we would love to see you again.

Heartfelt Greetings, from Tyra Egelandsdal Tunheim

January 15, 1946 – Moi

Letter from Olga and Jonas (Øveland)

Dearest Sophie!

I wish you a very healthy new year. I hope this year will bring more peace to the world than ever before. We are reading in the newspapers about the atomic bomb, about new disagreements, and strikes. People have gotten so greedy; they do not care about anything anymore. But maybe this is how it is after a war and before things get normal again.

Here in Norway we think that the trials for the Nazis are

going way too slow, and the punishments are too mild. But, thankfully, they are being punished and judged by the law, and they get what they deserve. If people were to judge, it would have been bad for many of them, because the hate would have won over common sense, and I am sure you know about that. Yes, you, poor Sophie, have experienced a lot during these years and have seen how hate can grow where there is no conscience. I am so glad that it is all over, and now it just feels like a bad dream. I am happy it went as well as it did, because Jonas (Øveland) *was working with the Home Front the entire time - I didn't know anything about it until the end of the war. However, I knew he had a radio, because I got to listen to the news every day. But that he sent messages, and had connections with England, I, thankfully, had no idea about. People were amazingly good at working underground.*

Sophie, thank you so much for everything that you sent us. We received your package Friday. It was way too much for you to send to us all. It was great to receive, but it is just way too much for you to send to all of us, having such a large family here. The skirt and vest fit me perfectly; and everything else, too. I did not have to make changes on anything. And I am wearing these good and warm clothes every day, because it has gotten so cold now with snow and ice. Our daughter Torlaug's suit fit her perfectly and it's so nice and warm. Now, as she is so busy walking all day, she wants to wear the "merikadress" (America suit). *My shoes were a little bit big. However, they fit Jonas's sister so well that I gave them to her. She really needed them, so it all worked out in the end. They were too small for my siblings. She greets you and thanks you very much.*

I have a woven pillow and a wooden bowl that I want to send to you as a little memorial and a thank you. I want you to give one of the things to Oscar's wife, Eileen Peterson so that she has something to remember me for. You might not be able to use it over there, but it is a real Norwegian thing, so I hope it will be fun for you to get.

Here at Moi, everything is good. Last Sunday, Ragna's little girl Kirsten Synnøve was Christened. They named her after themselves. Karsten is so proud, now that he has gotten a daughter, that he almost is not to be spoken to.

*Mother (*Valborg*) was visiting a little bit on Sunday; she needed the coffee bag you know, ha,ha. Yes, you will not believe how happy she was when she got coffee again - "just like a new human being," she says about herself.*

It has been really busy, because my brother, Ole (Gya), *is getting married next month. Her name is Asgjerd - she was working as a maid at Gya last summer. She is such a great person, and she is good with everything, so I have to say he is very lucky. And it is great that she and Mother get along so well with each other, since they spend a lot of time together.*

My mother greets you and she thanks you so much for everything and for the coffee. Thank you so much for everything you sent us, it is just not enough with a thank you. We hope that you will come back again, and we want you as our guest, unless you are scared about coming to Norway after all that has happened. Live very well and greet everybody at home.

Heartfelt Greetings, Olga, Jonas and Torlaug Øveland

February 16, 1946 - Årrestad

Letter from Malene Østrem

Dear Sophie!

Thank you so much for the letter we received yesterday, it was so nice to hear from you. We understand that you have been very busy, just like you were when you were in Norway. Everybody is asking for you – you should have stayed a few more years - everyone feels that they needed more time with you. Since your Mother (Christine) *does not feel well, I understand that you have your hands full. Our boys are often talking about you. Ove says he is sure he will recognize you and says he wants to go to "Mirka"* (America) *to see "Sia"* (Sophie).

We have had a quiet and peaceful Christmas celebration. Torger dressed up as a Julenisse (Norwegian Santa/Elf), *and the boys, Ove and Sigbjørn, were very excited when he gave them each some presents. They thanked him and ran over to me and turned around and looked at him again. The celebration was special this year with good food, oranges, and chocolate. The children had never experienced anything like it before.*

We received the letter from you from Lisboa, Portugal. It was mailed January 5, two years ago.

Torger has sold your fur, but he is promising you a new one much nicer. Torger says that I have to greet you and tell you to let him know when you are coming back to Norway, and he will give you his nicest fur and drape it around your neck. If time allows, he will send it to you before that. At one point, you mentioned about being back by 1948 and if we live, that will be great.

Ole Gya got married today - he married the maid that worked for them after Valborg got married to Albert Espeland and moved away. I have seen her, and she looks like Ole. Torger said that he would never have believed that Ole ever planned to get married.

You will not believe what a mess it has been in Egelandsdal. Gunnar is sick with tuberculosis and it is pretty serious. He had been feeling bad since last summer and saw the doctor just a week ago. It is too late for any other treatment, so he is at the sanitarium now. Worst of all, he has transmitted it to a girl he was seeing, and she is very sick and has been admitted to the hospital. Everyone in Karl's house is being checked. Anna is being sent to Stavanger for x-rays. It is believed that the infectious disease comes from Karl's family, and another farmer, Ole Egelandsdal, had to take his whole family to Stavanger to be checked. His children have been in school together with Kirsten, so now they are very worried about her. Ole Egelandsdal's wife has been sick with erythema nodosum (a painful disorder characterized by tender bumps under the skin). *She has been in the hospital for a month now. Everybody in Egelandsdal is scared – they live so tight together and have visited Karl's house, so it is no wonder they are worried.*

I have gotten ahold of a very nice hand-painted wooden tray for you that I want to send you for your birthday. However, at the moment, we are not allowed to ship anything out of the country. As soon as things change, I will send it. I would love for you to use it when you serve your friends coffee.

Heartfelt Greetings, Malene

The following letter was not dated. It may have been weeks after the previous one.

Letter from Malene Østrem

I just thought that I want to write you a few words. You would not believe how much they have added to the house of Semine and Ommund. The plan is that Mikael and Minnie will take over the farm; he is moving in this spring. They have added another living room, kitchen, hallway, and two dormers. And they have added new windows all over the house, big ones like we have. The older ones are going to live in the new house. Martin Gya has built it, as you might know. I will take pictures from all sides this summer and send them to you, that way you can see the 'castle' as we call it.

Trond Magne is home on leave from the Air Force today; he is stationed at the Sola Airport. A lot of trains pass by - three "to" and three "from" Stavanger all stop there. Also, there are four trains between Stavanger and Oslo.

You would not believe how great it is to not have to see the ugly German trains – I am sure you remember them. Torger enjoys working on the railroad line/tracks now. It was a huge pressure when he worked for the Germans – they could never be safe. I really hope that we do not hear anymore from the iron heels (Germans) *although there are still several at Slettebø. The government has promised that they are leaving in March. I hope that is right; they have been in our country long enough. They* (Germans) *are still proud and large, but I have not seen any since early last summer when I went into town. I was only in town twice last year, so you know, I do not travel a lot. There is almost not anything to do in town, since there is nothing to buy - not even as much as a handkerchief.*

*Karl, Tyra, Karstein, and Sigmund Egelandsdal were all healthy after the last doctor's appointment, but I have not heard about Anna. I will let you know when I hear more, or maybe Anna Bertha (*Aarrestad*) has already told you.*

Live so well.

Greetings, Malene

May 21, 1948 – Norge

Letter from Bertha and Magnus Aarrestad

Dear, Dear Sophie!

Please let me wish you all the best - you really surprised us all. My thoughts will be with you in June when you are getting married to Birger Johnson. I just wish we could reach out and touch your hand and squeeze it really good; or be a bird with light wings and fly over the ocean and land and spend the day with you and your family. Joy and peace with you in your new home. And we are so happy that it is a Norwegian that you met. Can you please send us a picture?

Yes, you have a life with many strange, rich, and maybe sad memories to look back on. Not many get to experience such a Norwegian trip as you did. So, maybe you will be nervous about making the trip again? But we hope to see you soon, and we hope that in the year 1948 we will see some American visitors. And you are so welcome here, together with your husband Birger. You have been very sneaky not telling us anything about this, but I understand that you must have been busy, because I have been looking for letters for a long time.

Can you remember when I wrote to you in Germany about the green worm that ate all of our grain and you wrote back to me "wonder if maybe Johan on the other side of the ocean might have some advice for that". It was fun because the green ones did not understand anything that we were writing about. It is so great that that time is over, even though there are still sad things.

Live well my dear. And a thousand hurrahs for the bride and groom. Write to us and tell us about your wedding.

Greetings from everyone here - Liv, Svein, Magnus and Bertha

Heartfelt Greetings, Bertha

ADDENDA

Wartime Memories from Relatives

My Family Members Involved in the Resistance during WWII:

by Liv Aarrestad Stapnes

Bergit Østrem Skåra was a first cousin of Sophie's. Her husband, Alf Skåra, was active in the Resistance during the war. He worked as a barber in Flekkefjord. They had been married for only three months when Alf was taken and sent to Germany to a concentration camp. Bergit was pregnant, and Alf received the message about her pregnancy when he was in captivity. When the war was over, Bergit thought he would be coming home. A fellow prisoner who survived said that he had died right before the war was over. It was an unbelievable heartbreak. Their son was named Alf – we used to call him "lille" *(little)* Alf.

Margrethe Østrem was also a first cousin of Sophie's. Her husband, Einar Sørdal, worked at the Railway Station in Egersund. His assignment in the Resistance was to steal a camera from the Germans travelling on the train. The Germans came to Rjukan wanting the Heavy Water for atomic testing in their war industry. Einar managed to get ahold of the camera when the Germans were inside of the Railway Station. He hid it in his small apartment (this was before Margrethe and Einar were married). The Germans suspiciously turned his apartment upside down but did not find the camera. Einar then biked it to Flekkefjord and left it with the Resistance Group there. He played his part in stopping this plan that the Germans had – at least we know they didn't manage to make atomic weapons, thankfully! Einar received a recognition from the King of Norway after the war (a war medal given for bravery). I, Liv, have seen this camera with my own eyes at Uncle Einar and Aunt Margrethe's home.

My own father, Magnus Aarrestad, was captured one night while all of us were sleeping. The Germans walked straight in – we normally didn't lock the doors in the countryside. My grandmother, Lise Aarrestad, who lived in the neighboring house had locked her door and the Germans shot their way in. They had learned that someone in the village was a member of the Resistance Group. Therefore, they took all the men with them to a barn at Hæstad where they had them stand up against a stone wall the entire day being interrogated at gunpoint. None of them revealed any information that would have damaged the Resistance Group. The farmer who was hiding members of the Resistance Group in a cave out in his fields and helped them with food, etc., was extremely scared. He was afraid that someone would tell and that he would be caught. But no, they kept quiet! My father came home in the evening unharmed. Thank goodness! Later, one of these men was hunted down by the Germans and he took his own life in fear of having to reveal what the group was doing. His name was Edvin Lundevold Aakre. There is a monument in Egersund as a commemorative of him.

My Memories of Sophie

by Liv Aarrestad Stapnes

It was a great joy when Sophie came visiting! She came all the way from the 'promised land', America! She stayed with my Uncle Torger and family at Buhammeren (Årrestad). One Christmas Eve, in 1940 – I was 4 years old and my brother Svein was 5 ½ and Sophie came to see us at Årrestad. Uncle Torger was dressed as "Santa" and we children did not know that it was him. He asked with a low and unrecognizable voice – "Are there any nice children here?" Svein was very brave and he said "yes". I was very scared and not at all sure if I had been good enough to get a Christmas gift from the "bag" that Santa was carrying. I was just about to start crying in fear. Sophie noticed, and she comforted me, and I saw that she was holding back laughter. This made me brave enough to walk over to the Santa and receive the Christmas present. I shook his hand and made a bow *(form of a thank you acknowledgment).* I can still see it in my mind, Sophie's nice smile and that she enjoyed herself watching Santa and us children.

The Worst Day of my Mother's Life (April 9, 1940)

by Håvard Østrem Peersen

My mother Sanna (a first cousin of Sophie) was born in 1919. She was the third youngest of eight siblings who grew up on Orrestad farm in southwest Norway together with their parents, Ommund and Semine Østrem. In 1939 Mom left Orrestad and went to Stavanger, Norway to train as a nurse at the city hospital. After the war, she started as a nurse at Dale Psychiatric Hospital in Sandnes, close to Stavanger. There she met my father Harald, who was studying law and had a summer job at the hospital. After Dad completed his education, they married and moved to Oslo where he got a job. Not long after, they moved to Førde, and some years later to Sogndal, both small towns in the midwestern part of Norway. Dad died in 1985, at the age of 62. Mom lived on as a widow for nearly 30 years and died in 2014, at the age of 95.

Even though in the 1960's we traveled to Orrestad every summer holiday and visited Grandfather Ommund and Mom's siblings, we somehow lost contact with the Egelandsdal part of the family (my grandmother had six siblings). Sophie was unknown to me until Randi Kiester contacted me via Messenger in August 2020 and wrote about Barbara, Karen and Teresa and their Sophie Project. Randi also sent me an old black and white photo of Sophie together with Mom and her younger sister Margrethe which I had not seen before. The photo shows the three young women standing arm in arm with Sophie in the middle, all of them revealing expectant facial expressions, unaware of the horror that was to come.

Through the contact with the above, I have had the pleasure of becoming acquainted with a part of the family tree that has been unknown to me, and one of the mysteries in my life has been resolved as well. Even though both Mom and Dad went through terrifying and traumatic experiences related to World War II that affected them afterwards, this was never a topic of conversation in the family when I grew up. The day before Mom was to be buried, my sisters and I talked to the priest in charge of the ceremony about her life and we said: "We think our mother faced events during the war that she never told us about". The priest nodded. "I call those who experienced World War II the 'silent generation,'" he replied. "Many of them underwent horrific incidents, which they never told anyone."

However, in her last living years, Mom talked some more about her war experiences, including what she experienced on April 9th in 1940, the day that Germany occupied Norway. "I had a day off and lay still in bed, free from duty. At half past seven the Headmistress came into my room and said, 'Wake up Sister Sanna; Norway is at war'. Shortly afterwards I heard the horrible sound of German bombers flying over at low altitude. It is the worst thing I have ever experienced."

When I think of what Mom told me about these years, it strikes me that her stories often were about people she knew, who were arrested by the Gestapo only to disappear without her knowing where they ended up, sent to one of the concentration camps in Germany or maybe executed.

Among these stories was first and foremost the one about Sophie, Mom's cousin and friend, who she told had been arrested and sent to a camp in Germany. But Mom could not provide me with specific details, neither about what Sophie should have done or where she had been sent. (After the United States became involved in the war in December 1941, it was no longer safe to be a U.S. citizen in Norway, not even in the remote Helleland area.) I searched records containing the names of the Norwegians who were sent to camps in Germany, without finding anyone who could fit the descriptions that Mom had given. Now I know why. As an American citizen, Sophie is not listed in overviews of Norwegian prisoners of war in WW2. The mystery about Mom's disappeared cousin was resolved for me, but sadly, too late for Mom.

Others of Mom's stories were about patients who suddenly disappeared even though they were not healthy, including a doctor who disappeared without anyone knowing where he had gone, and two sisters at the age of 17 who worked in the hospital's kitchen and were sent to Grini, the Nazi's concentration camp in Norway, and then disappeared without anyone knowing where they had gone.

Mom also experienced one of the dramatic war events in Norway up close, namely the sad ending of Operation Freshman, an event that partly took place on the hill just opposite Orrestad farm.

In February 1943, the heavy water plant in Rjukan that Hitler needed for the making of atomic bombs, was made useless by a British-Norwegian sabotage operation. This operation became a legend in history, also portrayed on popular film including "Heroes of Telemark", directed by Anthony Mann in 1965 and starring Kirk Douglas and Richard Harris.

Less known is the fact that there was an earlier attempt at sabotaging the plant in late 1942 which ended catastrophically. This failure is known in history as "Operation Freshman." On the night between November 19 and 20, two British bombers, each towing a glider, penetrated Southern Norway. Each bomber had a crew of six, and each glider carried seventeen young soldiers. The plan was to release the gliders some distance within the coastline. Then they should land at a specified location on the massive mountain plateau that lies between Helleland and Rjukan, whereupon the soldiers would make their way to the factory under cover of winter darkness. However, everything went wrong. One glider crashed at Lysefjorden about 100 km north of Helleland, while the bomber managed to return to Great Britain. The line that held the other crew together broke, and the glider crashed into Benkafjellet, the hill just opposite Orrestad farm, about 7 km away. Three of the soldiers on board died instantly. The fourteen who survived were taken by German soldiers, brought to Egersund and executed the next day. The bomber crashed in a land area nearby and everyone on board died. German soldiers who arrived at the scene of the accident just threw their bodies into a swamp.

In the days that followed, armed German soldiers searched for possible survivors on the farms in the surrounding area, including Orrestad farm. Mom was home while this was going on. "We were gathered in the courtyard while German soldiers searched the house, the barn and the hen house," she told me. "Some of the soldiers aimed at my father with their guns. 'I can see that you guys have brought weapons with you today', he calmly said to the soldiers."

Mom used to smile while telling this. I think it is because she remembered her father acting as a strong protector of his family during this dramatic and potentially dangerous event.

Memories

by Randi Kiester

When Rakel and Mikkel Egelandsdal were old, they shared a house together with their son, Karl, and his wife, Anna, and their children in Egelandsdal. They had their own small quarters, one room at the south end of the house. Karl, their only son, was running the farm, and lived with his family across a hallway, at the north end of the house. The hallway was not heated, and most food preparations were done here, as Rakel's kitchen was in the back part of that hallway. The kitchen had slate-covered mud floors. Sometimes she also cooked on the wood burning oven inside the living room. Upstairs there were two larger rooms for sleeping. The children shared beds; two children, sometimes three in each bed. They slept on hay mattresses, and the hay got changed out each summer. The elders slept downstairs in their living rooms; it probably kept a better temperature. Other than for sleeping, the loft was used for storage, especially nicer clothes used for church, weddings and funerals. In about 1922, they built a newer, larger house, using materials from the old. This house still exists. Mikkel died before they moved into the new house.

My great grandmother, Rakel Serina, was used to work, and her hands did not easily rest in her lap. She would help her daughter-in-law Anna with certain chores in the house and on the farm. She often walked the kids to the schoolhouse down by the road (my mother said they had school about two weeks every month, as the teacher traveled to teach at other smaller schools in the countryside). Following behind the children, Rakel would pick up twigs for firewood for the oven in the kitchen and carry them back home in her apron. Time was never wasted. For the cows, she would collect a certain kind of grass, tying it up into a tight ball, probably some kind of a special treat.

I have learned that they made cheese, some stinky old cheese that they kept in a jar covered with a cloth at the foot end of Rakel's bed, deep in the hay madras. I believe it may have been in later years, assuming she stayed more often in bed, and therefore, the temperature was perfect for the cheese.

My mother, Gudrun, remembers that her grandmother was scared of thunder and lightning. She believed that doomsday would come with lots of thunder. Religion and superstition often went hand in hand, and especially this part of the country (southwest coast) was known as The Bible Belt since way back. The Bible Belt also had a strong pietist movement. I believe their faith was strong. My mother would refer to my grandfather, remembering him singing hymns. They often housed preachers, who drifted and preached from farm to farm and were highly respected.

My grandfather, Karl, was a farmer. They kept a horse, cows and sheep, and had two new pigs every year. They slaughtered one pig for Christmas and one later in the spring. He put out snares to trap grouse, and if he caught more then they needed at home, these would be sold at the market, and sometimes, especially around Christmas time, Grandfather would bring cookies, oranges, and raisins back for the children. Karl trapped grouse for food, but also for the feathers. In wintertime the snow sometimes had a thin layer of ice, hard enough for a light child to run on top of, but it would break if a grown man tried to walk on it, and he would sink deep, maybe to above his knees. In this situation my mother, Gudrun (age 7), and her sister, Tyra (age 9), were sent to fetch the birds from the traps that were scattered around the mountainside, a great distance from the farm. They both knew how to kill the birds by wringing their necks, then strap them around their waist with a rope. My mother told me that by the time they had fetched them all, the two girls came sliding back down the mountainside, 35 birds between them, the birds sticking out like a tutu.

In the evening, after work, Grandfather sat inside by the fire and carved wooden shoes that he sold at the market. He also made broomsticks and kitchen tools for the same purpose. The kids would use the wooden shoes and hand knitted socks in the winter but ran around barefoot in summer. They all learned that the shoes had to be perfectly lined up inside the door, all with the heels parked towards the wall. Anna was loving but strict - she had nine kids to raise, and they knew to listen. There was not a lot of time to play; everybody helped out from a pretty young age. She kept the house impeccable, sewed, spun and dyed yarn, wove blankets, and knitted warm clothes for the family. In the little stream close to the house, Anna washed clothes and cooled the milk. They also fished here, sometimes catching fish with their bare hands.

When the kids lost their milk teeth, they hammered them into the wall of the outhouse.

On the way back from church (at Tonstad) and my mother's Christening, the sled tipped over, just enough so that my mormor (Norwegian for "mother's mother") Anna, dropped the baby (Gudrun, my mother). It was February and cold, and there was lots of snow. It happened right below the farm, where the ground slopes down to a small stream. The baby, who was wrapped well in warm blankets, rolled down the slope, but stopped just before the stream. It all went well, but she often was called by the nickname "sneens datter", the daughter of the snow.

When my mother and her siblings prepared for their confirmations, they had to travel to Tonstad from Egelandsdal. This could easily take a whole day. They owned one bike, and each of them used the bike for this purpose as they came to age. First, they biked to Espetveit (about 10 miles), then walked four miles down the steep hills to Tonstad to the church. At the return they spent the night at Espetveit where their cousins lived.

These things happened to my parents during World War II -

My parents, Gudrun and Karl Thorsen, were forced to leave their newly established homes twice. The first home was a small house they had rented, the second home was an upstairs apartment in a larger house.

Both times, a German officer walked in and asked them to leave. They moved into a smaller cabin on the edge of town (Egersund), where they had a view to Varberg, a smaller mountain shielding the town and the inner harbor from the ocean.

On top of Varberg, the Germans had a "battery" of soldiers and guns directed at the enemy planes and boats and ready to be fired at any time. "Enemy" airplanes approached (Australian under British command). The Germans hit one of the planes, and the plane was swirling and heading towards the cabin. My very pregnant mother grabbed my 2 ½-year-old sister, Anna Karin, and my 5-year-old cousin, Aasa (*Thorsen Rødland*), opened the latch to a storage area beneath the floor and went down, shielding the kids from what seemed like a certain hit from the plane. However, the plane crashed further back, and they were unharmed. You can read more about this happening here: *https://www.aftenbladet.no/lokalt/i/mR234l/takknemlig-australier-ga-maleri-av-flyangrep-til-egersund?fbclid=IwAR2NmLuEoBaRdppgG1ITGrX_KuimmnRQIoj6MNNUh8cp7qyF2ygJhLYOR1s*

My father, Karl, and my uncle, Gjert (married to Astrid, my mother's sister), went out fishing from Ystebrød, on the Island Egerøy. This was illegal, due to illegal transportations to England of Norwegians hiding from the Gestapo. My father and my uncle had just pulled up their boat and were gathering their fish as they saw a whole troop of Germans approaching in the distance. Germans were often fast on the trigger, especially in a situation like this. Luckily for the two of them, a thick fog rolled in from the ocean at the same time, and they managed to get away without being noticed. By following the outer perimeter of the island, they walked back to Skadberg where my uncle and aunt were living.

Geographical and Topographical Aspects of the Egersund Region -

Including Omdal and Grødem – and how it affected the livelihood of the people and transportation.

By Rolf Mong

In most of the areas where Sophie lived or travelled during her stay in Norway around 1940 – like Omdal, Grødem, Stapnes, Mong, Rodvelt and Egelandsdal – the *green* areas were – and still are – mostly very small, even after an enormous number of rocks had been removed from the soil. Through the years, this area has accumulated only thin layers of soil for vegetation and cultivation, yet enough for a farmer to settle down some places like Omdal, Grødem and Hegdal. Only in a few places in the region are there flat areas and alluvial plains.

Egersund has a very mountainous and rugged landscape with huge boulders, deposits of slide rock, steep slopes, narrow valleys, stones, moraines, numerous ponds and lakes, creeks and rivers, waterfalls, as well as small fjords, etc.

Sparse population in the rural Egersund region had been typical for generations. Small hard-to-work farms with steep terrains were quite normal. The average farmer and his family had a few cows and some sheep, and they usually cultivated potatoes and maybe some corn. Often the corn crops failed due to bad weather. This indicates that it was a really hard life for many people of rural Egersund - right until the 1960's. Life changed in Norway in the 1960's when people in rural areas moved to town, as some sold their small farms to get a job and work in some kind of small industry or business.

Before 1937, the road (Americans would call it an

Near Stapnes - Sophie may have ridden on this bus. Used by permission from Grethe at the Dalane Folkemuseum in Egersund, from the book Årbok for Dalane 2000–2001. Published by Dalane Folkemuseum, Egersund in 2001

access road) from Grødem to the main road was narrow and winding and barely usable even for a horse and carriage. The people used their feet and had to carry goods on their back or use a horse. In wintertime, a sledge would be an option – on the bad road or on ice. After 1937, the old "track" was improved as much material was to be transported from Egersund to Grødem when the electricity company started building the Grødem Power Station.

From 1917 there has been a regular bus route between Sokndal and Egersund. It was not much hampered by the German occupants when they arrived in 1940, but soon fuel became a problem. Bus departures became fewer and bus motors had to be rebuilt to use wood as fuel.

We know a lot about how Sophie travelled during her stay in Norway during 1939-1942. She had many relatives beyond the Egersund area. She used the train from Egersund to Ganddal near Sandnes in the northerly direction to meet and stay with her father's family, and she took the train eastward from Egersund to Helleland or Årrestad to get in touch with her mother's family there.

Around 1940 train services all the way to Flekkefjord were more of a local character - stopping at many very small places along the line. The Orrestad station (at Årrestad) was very typical with a small shed where travellers could hide while waiting to board, in case of heavy rain or snow.

As bus services were reduced during war time, everybody used their bicycles. Sophie Peterson tells about trips by bicycle to Sokndal – it must have taken about two hours to get there from Grødem. If she wanted to visit family in Stapnes, she could walk the 2–3 km or use her bicycle. In Norway as a whole, people took to their feet much more during the war.

Photo used by permission of Rolf Mong

History of Omdal and Grødem

By Rolf Mong

The place Omdal near to Egersund is a small mountainous and rugged area, not easy to farm, and where the people had low income around 1900. Most of the people at Omdal were close or extended family, and at that time there were eight homes/farms with more that sixty people belonging to the place. In addition, as in many places in Norway, some other people, mostly very old widows or widowers, lived there periodically with family from time to time. So, nearly seventy people needed food there, and many needed some kind of work. Oh, yes, Omdal was indeed a poor rural area – and many of its people eventually left for America.

Omdal Farm

The small Omdal farm "Der Ude" always was decribed as *"Petterstykket"* – "Petter's piece of land" – by family members at Grødem and Omdal, named after Peder Mikal Pedersen Omdal. This piece of land consisted of slightly more than one acre cultivated area. It was a very small and steep farm surrounded by fences made of stones. However, there were a lot more acres of outlying fields in nearby hills and mountains, shared with several Omdal neighbours. Until the early 1970's there was an old barn to keep the hay in.

Around 1907 there was an Omdal man from the extended Omdal family

House of Jonas Pedersen Omdal at the farm called Hausan at Omdal. The barn was built right against the house.

House of Tollef Pedersen Omdal, later of Martine and Elisabet Omdal (sisters), at the farm called Pintlo at Omdal

circa 1920 - This view of Omdal pictures in the foreground, with hay barn on the left side, the farm originally owned by Peder Mikal and Taline Omdal, and later by their daughter Anne Marie Omdal. The farm in the middle belonged to Peder's brother Elias Pederson Omdal, and later to his son Nils Emil Omdal.

who ran a small shop in Egersund. Because of different problems, alcohol, etc., the business didn't work well, and he needed a lot of money to get going. Peder Mikal Pedersen Omdal and a few other Omdal residents gave bail to the guy. However, the "businessman" was declared bankrupt after some time.

Peder Mikal Pedersen Omdal lost his money and his farm, "Der Ude", at this point. As Peder Mikal had no money, the family was saved by Peder and Taline's son, Tollag Olaus Severin Omdal Peterson (then living in Bow, WA, U.S.A. since 1903), who bought another farm at nearby Grødem for them, being himself the owner of this Grødem farm until 1923. Peder Mikal Pedersen Omdal with his wife Taline and their youngest kids, among them Anne Marie and Petter Theodor, moved and settled at Grødem, a place approximately one km downhill from Omdal.

House of Peder Mikal and Taline Omdal and family

Several years later, Peder Mikal Pedersen Omdal's third-born son, Lars Mikal Omdal, born 1892, got the opportunity to buy back the farm "Der Ude" for a reasonable price, and he received deed of conveyance by auction on 10 Dec.1912.

Lars Mikal Omdal married Berthea (Thea) Vagle from Vagle in Høyland, Sandnes. They settled at her place and started farming at Vagle. At the same time, he was the owner of the Omdal farm "Der Ude". Not a good situation.

As Vagle and Omdal are miles apart, Lars Mikal Omdal sold his Omdal farm to his sister, Anne Marie Omdal, on 10 March,1933. She owned it personally and ran it until she died in 1976.

The family had moved to Grødem where there was a relatively newly built farmhouse, erected in 1897, and a farm which had belonged to Johan Jonassen Grødem. The family's new home measured 80 square meters. It contained six rooms, with the kitchen and basement under half of the house. A new cowshed and stable were constructed in 1917, and a barn built in 1918. Many years later, on 7 Oct. 1923, Tollag conveyed the house and farm to his brother Petter Theodor Omdal Grødem.

The name Grødem means "the place with much stone or rocks". The terrain, also today, is quite steep. At that time, it consisted of approximately four acres cultivated area and large pastures or outlying areas in hilly terrain, along with some wooded areas. These were shared with the Grødem neighbours.

The children of Peder Mikal Pedersen Omdal and Taline were, in order of birth, Tollag Olaus Severin, Peder, Helene, Lars Mikal, Anne Marie, and Petter Theodor. Tollag moved to America in 1903, being married to Christine Egelandsdal since 1902 (she and their son Peter immigrated in 1905), followed by Peder in 1905. Helene married Andreas Emil Rodvelt in 1914, Lars married Berthea Vagle in 1919, and the two youngest, Anne Marie and Petter Theodor, never married. These four and their families stayed in Norway.

Anne Marie Omdal and Petter Theodor Omdal Grødem

Anne Marie Omdal was born at the steep and tiny farm "Der Ude" at Omdal on 10 Oct. 1896. "Der Ude" means the farm "Out There". She went to primary school at Omdal. Anne Marie helped her parents and worked at the two small farms of the family – the one at Omdal on which she was born, the other at Grødem where her family moved to around 1907 or 1908.

Petter Theodor Omdal was born 19 Sept 1899. He also attended school in Omdal. He took over the Grødem farm formally in 1923, when his father Peder Mikal Omdal was 68 years old. So, in the next years Petter Theodor and his sister Anne Marie lived together with their parents until they died. Taline died 25 March 1929, and Peder Mikal passed away on 8 August 1940.

Daily Life at Grødem

In 1956 Anne Marie and Petter Theodor had these animals at the Grødem farm: four cows, a calf, a horse, and around sixty sheep. The main income came from keeping sheep, but also some from making butter. They didn't keep animals at Anne Marie's Omdal farm. Anne Marie or Petter Theodor had to walk or use a bicycle to get to the highway, and then use a bus to get to Egersund for shopping or to sell their butter.

The two farms were not easy to run because of the terrain. In addition, Petter Theodor and Anne Marie were not the most structured persons in the world. They often started late in the spring to do what had to be done at the farms. That indicates harvesting and making hay took a very long time for them.

I've always thought Anne Marie and Petter Theodor seemed to have far too much to manage. They had to keep an eye on all the sheep and lambs which were away in the hills and outlying areas during the entire summer, cows had to be put away on pasture every morning and brought back in the afternoon, grass had to be cut mostly by hand, and often the hay was carried on the back to the barn, etc. Sometimes they surely must have felt overwhelmed by work – then, quite often, Petter Theodor picked up the telephone to call for a hand. Thus, family living at Rodvelt, Mong, Vagle, and elsewhere were asked to come to help. Some left their work immediately and travelled to Grødem as soon as possible.

The family members who were their best supporters and always ready for help after 1945 were my parents, Thelma and Sivert Hovland Mong, but also Petter Rodvelt and his brother Alf Henry Rodvelt. During summer, Marie Kvidaland and to some degree Petter Omdal and Henrik Omdal from Vagle also helped a lot from time to time.

Grødem farm where Anne Marie and Petter Theodor lived surely was a place many Omdal family members met – some coming from places nearby, some from Egersund and Stavanger, or they came from the U.S.A. Numerous photos have been shot in front of the house as people sit on the old steps made of stone.

Anne Marie was a kind woman to everyone. However, she was often stressed by something. Usually, she preferred work outside the house - mending a curtain in the kitchen or changing a tablecloth was normally put aside. During hay-making season she often offered canned fruit, made by herself, to the people helping them, either working at Grødem, or at her Omdal farm. From time to time she pointed out - it was her farm.

Most of the time Petter Theodor was in command at Grødem, but sometimes he was in rough discussion with his sister about what and when and how to do things. He always was quite busy and administering some kind of project – looking after the lambs in the hills, cutting grass near the farmhouse or at outlying fields, slaughtering a sheep or lamb, trout fishing, hunting for birds and animals, logging for firewood, etc. There was much work to do, but he didn't always have a plan for the day.

In spite of many discussions during a week, Petter Theodor and Anne Marie were very dependent on each other. Anne Marie spent almost a year with Sophie and Birger Johnson in the U.S.A. in 1957, and Petter Theodor was left alone. It was a really hard time for him, and to most people he said she "probably would never return to Grødem".

Petter Theodor had great interest in planting fruit trees, so he had a big garden filled with trees for apples, plums and pears. He even did a lot of grafting. In autumn they picked up most of the apples to eat or to give to the animals. I remember very well from my childhood one of the two living rooms completely covered with apples. Now, many, many years after, I can still imagine the strong smell of hundreds of apples covering the tables and floor of that room.

Petter Theodor was a kind-hearted man, but also full of fun or tricks. Once, he surprised visitors and family after he had been out hunting. Well, he came back from the hills and entered the back door and went straight into the living room with his boots on and rucksack and rifle. Then, he opened the rucksack and out popped a hare, still alive. Think of the mess to catch the wild animal! There's also a story from around 1960. Petter Rodvelt and Henrik Omdal were helping Petter Theodor to repair some doors in the house. At one point, Petter Theodor went upstairs to pick up some nails. After much waiting, the "carpenters" shouted to Petter Theodor to return with the package of nails, so they could continue and finish the job, but he didn't show up. At last, Petter Rodvelt went upstairs and found Petter Theodor lying at a bench reading in an old Bible he had found there.

Anne Marie and Petter Theodor's neighbours, Johan and Maria Lædre, lived only 20 metres away. In everyday life they had very much contact and went in and out of each other's houses. Once, a son of Johan and

Maria, John Harald Lædre, tells me his mother had made cookies. Maybe Petter Theodor had smelt what was going on, and suddenly he came to Maria's kitchen. Looking at the lovely cookies on the table he asked: "Is it possible to eat these cookies?" John Harald Lædre then answered, "We have made them for the hens, but you may taste if you want..."

After 1970, life for Anne Marie and Petter Theodor became very difficult, and it wasn't easy for either of them to slow down the farming and start relaxing. They were getting older, and health problems started. Anne Marie encountered heart problems, and Petter Theodor had an accident as a rusty steel wire got into an eye, making inflammation and blindness in that eye. Later on, he was kicked by a cow or the horse at the other eye, and became so-to-speak, blind. He continued to live on the farm with much help of his sister Anne Marie and others.

In September 1976 Anne Marie had an appointment at the regional hospital in Stavanger. A taxi took her from Grødem to Stavanger, but on her way to the hospital she died of a heart attack. Date of death: 9 Sept. 1976.

Now Petter Theodor was left alone at Grødem. It was a hard time for him to have lost Anne Marie and to be almost blind, so after a few days family members managed to get him a place at a home for elderly people in Egersund. Only a few weeks afterwards he passed away. Date of death: 18 Oct. 1976.

Omdal and Grødem Farms – what now?

As Anne Marie and Petter Theodor had gotten older and needed more and more help, selling the farms to get an easier life was never a question. So, when Anne Marie and Petter Theodor passed away, nothing was arranged for what was going to happen to the farms. After some time, Petter Rodvelt, Alf Henry Rodvelt and Sivert Hovland Mong decided to buy and take over the Grødem farm. At the same time, they wanted Anne Marie's Omdal farm to be sold to a neighbour in Omdal. However, in 1977 Alf Henry Rodvelt died suddenly of a heart attack. At that point, Petter Rodvelt and Sivert Hovland Mong ceased their efforts to buy the Grødem farm. The Norwegian State took over the farm, and later on it was sold to Egersund Treplantningsselskap in Egersund. They have done a lot of planting trees and making trails in the mountain areas.

Thelma and Sivert Hovland Mong - my parents and their love for Grødem

Thelma, my mother, was born in 1917, and she was the first surviving child of Helene Pettersen Omdal married to Andreas Emil Rodvelt in 1914.

Helene's sister and brother, Anne Marie and Petter Theodor, lived at Grødem. From her earliest years, Thelma visited Grødem along with her parents – by horse and wagon, by bicycle, or just by walking the approximately 6 km. It was a long walk for small feet. At Grødem, she also met her grandparents Taline and Peder Mikal. She was the first grandchild of Taline and Peder Mikal's in Norway and must have received lots of attention and care. She got stars in her eyes when she talked about Grødem.

Around 1937 she introduced her boyfriend Sivert Hovland Mong to the family at Grødem. So, through more than forty years, Thelma and Sivert had great relationships with family there – they had even had their wedding at Grødem, instead of making celebrations at her home at Rodvelt. They married in July 1940. At that time, Grødem was only accessible from the highway by a narrow gravel road with lots of winds and twists, ups and downs. Why they chose Grødem is not clear, but we know Grandfather Peder Mikal was quite old and had poor health - that could be the reason.

Through Sophie Johnson's lovely letters from Grødem to family in the U.S.A., both before the German occupation and during wartime, she is often mentioning Thelma coming over to do something in the house – sewing or mending or doing something else for them. These helping hands of my mother continued as long as Anne Marie and Petter Theodor lived, even though she was busy with her three kids and the farm in Mong.

My father Sivert also got along very well with his new family at Grødem. Since after the 1950's he practiced both farming in Mong and worked partly as a carpenter, he was highly appreciated at Grødem. During all the years he must have spent a thousand hours cutting grass, making hay, picking potatoes, butchering, and doing repairs on buildings, etc.

There is a most private saying in our Mong family which goes like this: "When Anne Marie or Petter Theodor phoned for some kind of help, Sivert left what he held in his hands at once, picked up his bicycle, later on his motorcycle, and set course to Grødem".

Omdal and Grødem Kvinneforening
Women's Society of Omdal and Grødem
"Ladies' Aid"

By Rolf Mong

As Norwegian missions expanded mainly to Africa during the latter part of the 18th century, people in Norway were asked to support missions and missionaries in faraway countries with prayers and finances. Thus, a lot of women across the country, mostly in rural areas, banded together to form local clubs or societies to back missions.

Det Norske Misjonsselskap – The Norwegian Mission Society, based in Stavanger, has always been Norway's main mission organization, founded on the Lutheran Church of Norway. The Women's Society of Omdal and Grødem belonged to this organization, but sometimes they also offered small amounts of money to other mission organizations.

Unfortunately, we don't know what year "Ladies' Aid", which is the name Sophie calls this group of old and younger women, formally named Women's Society of Omdal and Grødem, was established. Most probably it was functioning well around 1900. Also, it's unclear who had the specific idea to form the group of women, but it seems that Ingeborg Helene Nilsdatter Omdal, born in Mong in 1859 and married to Elias Pedersen Omdal, had been a key person from the start, and continued until her daughter-in-law, Elisabeth Marie Omdal, took over the management of the group in the 1930's.

Elisabeth Marie Omdal, born in 1891, managed the group of women for many years. She was the wife of Nils Emil Omdal, and they lived at the farm "Der Oppe" at Omdal. As her mother-in-law was, Elisabeth Marie Omdal was also well respected, and along with her husband Nils Emil they continued the religious work for some years – until the late 1970's when there were only a few residents left at Omdal and Grødem.

Another woman who was actively involved in the group was Taline Omdal. We find her in every old photo of Omdal and Grødem kvinneforening (women's group). To clarify, Elias Pedersen Omdal's brother was Peder Mikal Pedersen Omdal who married Taline Tollaksdatter Mong in 1883, and they were parents to Tollag Olaus Severin Omdal, Peder Omdal, Helene Omdal, Lars Mikal Omdal, Anne Marie Omdal, and Petter Theodor Omdal.

From the 1950's, "Ladies' Aid" had close contact with a missionary from the neighbouring town of Stapnes; her name was Jenny Stapnes. She served in Madagascar for many years. Jenny Stapnes often reported about her work in the local newspaper as well as in mission magazines. Reading about all her different experiences in that far away country was of special importance for the women of Omdal and Grødem, since they knew her personally. Also, it was of great importance for the work of the women to welcome Jenny Stapnes to attend their meetings when she had longer periods of time back home in Norway.

At this stage we don't have any notes or material from the earliest years to accurately describe the work and activities of the Society, nor who all the ladies were and how many there were, nor how much money they collected and forwarded to the mission through the years.

However, we are sure the women of Omdal and Grødem met in each other's homes during afternoon or evening, once a week, or each fortnight, or maybe once in three weeks to make small things for the annual fund-raising raffle. In the earliest years they would bring wool to be carded, a spinning wheel, knitting, etc. Later on, they brought mostly items of knitting or needlework to work on for an hour or two.

Usually, all the self-made things were put together and offered at an annual raffle at the Omdal schoolhouse where people gathered from Omdal and Grødem, but also from neighbouring places like Hegdal, Stapnes, Lædre, Mong and Rodvelt. Some even showed up all the way from Egersund. One could say that from the 1930's and far into the1950's, the raffle at Omdal always was considered a local happening. Every seat at the schoolhouse would be occupied as people were waiting to buy raffle tickets. Usually there was not space for everybody inside, so many youngsters, both girls and boys, would be attending from the entrance hall or from outside. Often, they would be joking and having some fun there – maybe after enjoying a beer in a nearby shed. However, the youngsters always spent a lot of money buying tickets – and they won a lot. But it all started with some singing and a speech based on a verse from the Bible and prayer – then members of the "Ladies' Aid" started selling raffle tickets and one could hope to win something produced by the women.

I personally experienced the raffles at Omdal as a boy in the 1950's. Usually I walked with my mother, Thelma Mong, all the way from Mong to Omdal, always making a stop at Grødem to chat with Anne Marie Omdal and Petter Theodor Omdal, my mother's aunt and uncle. Usually, Anne Marie would join us walking uphill to the schoolhouse. Sometimes we would travel with my mother's brother, Petter Rodvelt, in his car.

I will always remember all the objects one could win at the Omdal raffle. Most of them were hung from a rope along the walls so everybody could see – and plan how much to spend... There were lots of nice tablecloths, some small and some bigger, lots of socks in all colours and sizes, colourful aprons, towels etc. etc. On a table in front of everybody, one could enjoy the sight of several cakes, sometimes a kransekake (wreath cake), or boxes with all kinds of fresh and canned fruit. Usually, I won an item or two – in most cases – grey socks too big for me...

During a meeting of "Ladies' Aid", somebody would usually be reading from the Bible, and they would be praying for their own work and for the missionaries abroad. Also, they would normally sing a song or two either from a song book or the psalm book. The ladies usually were quite anxious to get news from the mission and the missionaries, therefore somebody would be reading from mission magazines like "Norsk Misjonstidende" or "Til Jordens Ender" – both magazines were issued by The Norwegian Mission Society.

Last but not least, we should not forget the importance of a cup of coffee, a piece of cake or lefse with gomme (to spread on lefse), and also all the women's chat about what's going on in Omdal, Grødem and beyond – the social dimension of the meetings.

People in this Book Who Immigrated to Washington State with Immigration Dates

Aase, Berentine (1913) – married Arthur Boe

Birkeland, Ole Nilsen (1896) and Sina (Stapnes Larson) (1906)

Boe, Anton (1888) and Ellen (Stapnes) (1889)

Boe, Clara Theresa (1901) married Berent "Big Ben" Benson (1884)

Haaland, John (1904) and Edla (Hood) (from Finland)

Holt, Oscar and Carrie Larson (Stapnes) (1917)

Jacobson, Hans and Bergitte (Birkeland)

Johnson, Ben C. and 1. Ellen Seglem (1914), 2. Sophia E.

Johnson, Rasmus Stapnes (1872) – married 1. Gjertina (Haaland), 2. Johanna (Lonn), 3. Anne (Mong) (1900)

Martinsen, Martin (1906) and Carrie Aase (1907)

Mong, Nels or Nils Tobias (1909) and Emma (Knudson Århus) (1910)

Omdal, Berte Gurine (Mong) (1910)

Omdal, Lars Herman (1903) – married Jenny Johnson

Omdal, Lars "Little" Bowitz (1909) and Selma Omdal (1910)

Omdal, Louisa Marie (Omdal) (1907) married Andrew Johnson (1888)

Omdal, Nils Tobias (1903) and Sina Marie (Nesvåg) (1904)

Omdal, Peder Martin (1909) and 1. Inga Marie (Stapnes) (1910), 2. Anne Gurie (Stapnes) (1919), 3. Clara Marie Boe (Hansen)

Peterson, Peder (Omdal) (1905) and Ellen (Stapnes) (1910)

Peterson, Tollag (Omdal) (1903) and Christine (Egelandsdal) and son Peter (1905)

Rodvelt, Chris Marius (1905) and Elisabeth Marie (Omdal) (1910)

Stakkestad, Sig (1922) and Agnes (Bjørklund) (1923)

Stapnes, Petter (1920's) – married Alice (Torkelsen Hadland)

Tollefson, Karl Johan (Omdal) - married Hattie Johnson

Norwegian Pioneers of the Samish Flats/Bow Area

The first pioneers from Norway to arrive in Skagit County were Gus Wolden, who arrived in the early 1880's, and his first cousins Anton Boe, arriving in 1888, and John Boe. They settled in the area known as the Samish Flats on the Samish River near the town of Edison. They may have been attracted to the Puget Sound area because of its similarity to the mountains, sea, and fishing in southwest Norway.

The Boes and Wolden began by clearing land and starting farms. They corresponded to relatives back in Egersund and a migration began which included more than a dozen interrelated families.

Some of the other earlier arrivals in the Samish Valley were two Norwegian fishermen, Rasmus and Andrew Johnson, who came in the late 1880's after fishing for a time in Lake Superior. (Note – Rasmus Johnson was Sophie Peterson (Johnson's) father-in-law.)

The single women who came soon found employment in the homes of earlier pioneers and were well thought of as faithful workers. They learned the American way of food preparation and homemaking quickly. They baked bread, canned fruit and berries, and prepared meals for the harvest and threshing crews.

The Norwegian Pioneers seemed to have a strong urge to better themselves in America – the land of opportunity – and to become a part of the American people. However, their "roots" were never forgotten; they were proud of their homeland and their love for the country of Norway was communicated in many ways.

Partially quoted from Arne Johnson and Gordon Omdal (Families Who Immigrated to Edison-Bow, Skagit County WA from Southwestern Norway)

Relatives Who Immigrated to the U.S.A. Founded Edison Lutheran Church in Bow/Edison, WA

The first known Lutheran service in the community was held in the home of Mr. and Mrs. Anton Boe on November 4, 1891, at which Clara Boe (later Mrs. Peter Omdal) was the first to be baptized among the early settlers.

The original constitution named the church "Edison Norsk Evangelisk Lutherske Menighed" (Edison Norwegian Evangelical Lutheran Congregation).

The minutes of the January 1931 meeting include the first reports by females. "Bertha Omdal (later Johnson) gave a report on the Sunday School and Selma (Mrs. Bovitz) Omdal gave a report on the "Ladies Aid".

Minutes of Congregational Meeting are recorded in Norwegian from the beginning through the annual meeting held on January 5th, 1934. The last minutes in Norwegian were signed by the then Secretary, Bovitz Omdal.

At the January 1938 meeting, the Congregation approved a change from Norwegian Language services every other week by holding them only on the last Sunday of each month. In 1939 Pastor Rasmussen was given authority to decide when to have Norwegian services.

Seven Omdal brothers and cousins attending Edison Lutheran Church

Back row - Peder Martin Omdal, Nels Omdal, Lars Herman Omdal.
Front row - Karl Tollefson, Tollag Peterson, (Little) Bovits Omdal, Peder Peterson

Edison Lutheran Church women's singing group in 1922 - Back row: Ellen Johnson (Ben), Celia Anderson (Nels), Anne G. Anderson (Herman), Johanna Hood (Eric,) Edla Haaland (John), Carrie Martinsen (Martin), Christine Peterson (Tollag), Middle Row: Louise Johnson (Andrew), Emma Mong (Nels), Jenny Ruth Omdal (Lars), Selma Omdal (Bovitz), Bina Hood (Ed), Mrs. Simon Bruget, Serina Benson (Al), Ellen Peterson (Peder), Front Row: Sina Omdal (Nels), Valborg Rasmussen (Pastor Lauritz), Anne Gurie Omdal (Peder Martin), Hattie Tollefson (Carl), Mrs. Oscar Myre, Annie Anderson (Eli)

Edison Lutheran Church in Bow, Washington. Lifetime church of Sophie and her family

Edison Lutheran Church men's choir in 1921

1921 Male Chorus Taakeluren (Talk in megaphone in fog at sea)

Back row from left: Bert Knutzen, Albert Benson, Jacob Stakkestad, Nels Mong

3rd row: Ben Johnson, Andrew Sather, Tollag Peterson, Pete Peterson, Nels Mong

2nd row: Lars Omdal, Bovitz Omdal, Pete Omdal, Anders Anderson, Melvin Erickson (Bellingham)

1st row: Carl Tollefson, Nels Anderson, Oscar Myhre, Eli Anderson, Martin Martinson, Sören Anderson

Helena Anderson

At Edison Lutheran Church

Names of people in preceding picture

Egelandsdal Family Pictures

Rakel Serina Salvesdatter (Bjørnstad) and Mikkel Karlson Eikelandsdal, parents of the seven Egelandsdal children: Valborg Gya, Martha Eiesland, Teoline Gystøl, Berthe Østrem, Christine Peterson (Sophie's mother), Karl Egelandsdal, Semine Østrem

Liv Aarrestad Stapnes remembers being told by her aunt, also named Rakel Serina, that Rakel Serina prayed for all her descendants, and that, with tears in her eyes, she quoted a verse from the Bible: "… how often would I have gathered thy children together, even as a hen gathereth her chickens under her wings, and ye would not!" (Matthew 23:37)

1925 Valborg and Tollef Gya Family – Back row – Ragna, Mikael, Martin, Ole, Lisabeth. Front row – Little Valborg, Ingrid, Tollef, Tor, Valborg, Olga

Valborg Gya with six of her kids - Martin, Olga, ???, Tor, Ole, Mikael

Ole Gya, unknown, Little Valborg Gya, Karsten and Ragna (Gya) Moi

Valborg Gya with sons Tor, Mikael, Ole, Martin

Gya farm

Home and family of Martha and Ole Eiesland at Fjotland

Grandchildren of Martha and Ole Eiesland

Teoline and Johan Gystøl in front with six of their kids left to right - Amanda, Jon, Martin, Tyra, Torvald, Gunder

Torvald, Martin, Jon, and Gunder Gystøl

Johan and Teoline Gystøl with three grandchildren (Johan Gystøl, Tora Gystøl, and Sigrun Egelid), with Karl Egelandsdal and Valborg Gya in back

Andreas Østrem standing on the right side, Berthe peeking from behind, and other family members

Berthe and Andreas Østrem with family members

Wedding of Alf Botolf and Sigfrid Østrem.

For pictures of Christine (Egelandsdal) Peterson & family, see Omdal/Peterson Family Pictures – Page 335

Karl and Anna Egelandsdal family - Back Row: Sigmund, Gunnar, Gudrun, Mikal, Agnes, Karstein. Sitting: Tyra, Astrid, Anna, Karl, Ragna

Tyra, Ragna, Astrid, Agnes, Gudrun, daughters of Karl and Anna Egelandsdal

Egelandsdal house and hay barn

Karl Thorsen below, with Gunnar, Gudrun, Astrid

Karl Egelandsdal with children - Agnes, Gunnar, Gudrun, Ragna, Sigmund, Karstein

Semine and Ommund Østrem with all of their children.

House and barn of Anna Bertha and Magnus Aarrestad.

Margrethe (Østrem) Sordal, Sophie Peterson, Sanna (Østrem) Peersen

Rakel (Østrem) and Abraham Øgreid with their children from left to right – Olav, Anna Kjerstina, Jostein and Sylvi

Omdal/Peterson Family Pictures

Tollag and Christine Peterson with young Sophie and Peter

First seven children of Tollag and Christine (Egelandsdal) Peterson - Peter, Torval, Sophie, Theodora, Oscar, Tora, Martin

Family of Tollag and Christine Peterson; Back Row: Torval (1911-1932), Sophie (1906-1988), Peter (1903-1950), Tora (1909-2005), Martin (1907-1981), Front Row: Oscar (1913-1963) Theodora (1915-1994), Tollag (1884-1965), Christine (1881-1962), Carl (1918-2010), Melvin (1921-2004)

Christine and Tollag Peterson in their field in Bow, WA. Their sons helped on the farm, mostly raising cattle, but also growing sugar beets, cauliflower, peas, and wheat. The land there was exceptionally fertile. Their son Melvin eventually ran the farm with his wife, Wanda, and she grew strawberries commercially for a while. Wanda Peterson still lives on the farm as of November 2021

Tollag and Christine (Egelandsdal) Peterson with family
Front row: Oscar, Christine, Carl, Melvin, Theodora
Back row: Martin, Torval, Tollag, Peter, Tora and fiancé Sigurd Freestad.
Sophie is in Montana at her first teaching job

Sophie Peterson

Christine and Tollag Peterson

1958 Sophie Peterson Johnson, Barbara Peterson, Anne Marie Omdal, Karen Peterson

Siblings: Carl, Martin, Melvin, Theodora, Tora, Sophie

Peterson Family:
Back Row: Birger Johnson, Sigurd Freestad, David Hansen, Tom Fuller, Judith Peterson Fuller, Stanton, Melvin, Marvin; Middle Row: Sophie, Jeanne, Tora Freestad, Nancy Hansen, Carl, Alice, Dennis, Roger, Wayne, Wanda, Cheryl, Teresa (in front of Nancy Hansen), Barbara, Karen, Keith; Sitting Down: Margaret, Martin, Christian Hansen, Theodora Hansen, Tollag, Christine (holding Kathryn Hansen) Oscar, Eileen, Paulette

1990 – Family of Tollag & Christine Peterson - Standing: Oscar, Carl, Melvin, Martin; Seated: Tora, Theodora (Teddy), Tollag, Christine, & Sophie

Peder Mikal Omdal with wife Taline in back, and family - Anne Marie, Petter Theodor, Lars Mikal, and Helene; Missing are two sons in America: Tollag Olaus Severin (Omdal) Peterson and Peder (Omdal) Peterson

Caption: From back left: Palmer Peterson, Esther Peterson Boe, Ernest Peterson, Myrtle Peterson Allgire, Mynor Peterson, Tilda Peterson, Ellen Peterson, Peder Omdal Peterson, Marie Peterson

Front row: Helene and Thelma Rodvelt, Taline and Peder Mikal Omdal. Back row: Andreas Rodvelt, Anne Marie Omdal, Petter Theodor Omdal Grødem

Helene and Andreas Rodvelt with Thelma, Petter, Mikal and Alf Henry

Peter, Lars, Thea, and Henrick Omdal

Anne Marie Omdal, wearing Carl Peterson's Agrichem cap, and Petter Theodor Omdal

Standing from left - Nils Emil Omdal, Ingvald Eliasen Omdal. Sitting from left - Peder Mikal Omdal, unknown, unknown

Family Memories from America to Preserve and Pass On

By Wayne and Bunny Peterson

Wish I knew the year. I suspect it was about the time when Grandma and Grandpa made the move from the big house to the little house on the other side of the road by the slough, just south of the barns. The location, of course, is directly under the big hay barn. The cows used it for shelter, and it's where they ate hay and quenched their thirst at the large water trough, all the while waiting for their turn to be milked in the milk barn

Pictured: My father Melvin Peterson and his father (Grandpa Tollag) working side by side in Bow, Washington.

which was adjacent to Worline Road. You can tell how high the mixture of straw and "cow pies" would get by the darkened color of the support poles. I do remember doing just what is pictured, only I think the manure spreader was a newer model.

I do have fond memories of Uncle Carl stopping by on Sunday afternoons to read, in its entirety, the Sunday paper. Also, I remember more than once sitting (or should I say squirming) with Grandma at a Ladies' Aid meeting.

We had a root cellar where we cleaned, candled and stored the eggs before taking them to market. Once, and I repeat only once, was I fooling around when I should have been working. Grandpa came down the steps into the root house and found me horsing around instead of cleaning the eggs for market. He grabbed me by the ear and set me down. Then in a few simple words scolded me and told me to get to work. It caught me by surprise, because he was always gentle and kind with a hint of a smile. But he was all business when there was work to do.

Other times I would follow him out the lane across the slough to watch him cut the weeds down along the fence line. I was always amazed at how he would turn that scythe upside down and sharpen it with the stone.

It's been mentioned already about breakfast at the little house. What fond memories of walking down to see the wafting steam of the hot mush sitting on the open windowsill forming a crust on the top layer. We each got our portion, and then Grandpa would take the kettle, pour a little cream over what was left and partake with us. I'm not sure if I remember this table prayer more from Grandma and Grandpa or from Bunny's aunt. Anyway, I do remember it even if I don't pronounce it correctly!

I Jesu navn gar vi til bords
At spise og drikke paditt ord
Dig Gud til aere, oss til gavn
Sa far vi mat i Jesu navn. Amen

Grandma didn't say much, but I always felt warm and cozy around her. Then again, maybe part of it was the old wood stove/oven. We still have the rocker she used in raising her children. The small cross she wore is still with me. Teething marks have forever dented it.

Did everyone get a Bible from Aunt Sophie? Mine was a zippered King James. I can't remember what year I received it, but I still have it. Grandma, I was told, prayed for each of us kids. Sophie was an extension of those prayers.

I treasure Grandpa's Bible that was found at our church here in Arizona. I think you've all heard that story. There are indentations on the outside leather where I can only imagine him carrying it as I place my fingers there.

Ever have one of those WOW experiences? Some of you have heard the story of "Grandpa's Bible," but for those of you, especially my many cousins, who haven't, let me share one of ours:

The Sunday before attending my mom's 90th birthday celebration *(By the way, Wanda was 99 years old October 2, 2021),* Bunny and I were in our Bible study class in our Baptist Church in Glendale, AZ. A lady handed us a Bible which she had just found above a cabinet in our classroom and said it had the name "Peterson" in it so she wondered if it was ours. The unfamiliar Bible had the name "Tollag Peterson" hand-written inside. Hmmmm......that was Grandpa's name, right? But, knowing he lived his life in Bow, WA, from age 19, we considered the possibility that it was not Grandpa's.

At home we googled Grandpa's name. Only one Tollag Peterson popped up. Meanwhile, we asked sister Cheryl if she might have brought Grandpa's Bible down to Arizona – the answer was no. She had not seen it or known of it.

Bunny's sister checked with Ancestry.com and found there are hundreds of thousands of Petersons in recorded American history; but only ONE Tollag Peterson.

We took the Bible with us to Bow and checked Grandpa's naturalization papers and all those present agreed the signatures matched that in the Bible.

There is so much more to this story. Numerous verses were marked by Grandpa. I'll mention one passage since it just happened to be the verses we were studying – Heb 10:23-25, "Let us hold fast the confession of our hope without wavering, for He who promised is faithful. And let us consider one another in order to stir up love and good works, not forsaking the assembling of ourselves together, as is the manner of some, but exhorting one another, and so much the more as you see the Day approaching."

We are convinced that having this Bible placed in our hands is no accident. God continues to speak to us today. And for the many in our family and friends, He is using Grandpa's Bible. It's no surprise that Grandpa also marked John 3:16-17, "For God so loved the world that He gave His only begotten Son, that whoever believes in Him should not perish but have everlasting life. For God did not send His Son into the world to condemn the world, but that the world through Him might be saved."

We hope this story means as much to you as it does to us.

Let's not lose sight of a day forthcoming where we purpose to gather together for fun and fellowship.

By Marvin Peterson

One special memory of Grandpa and Grandma Peterson was in 1947 or 1948, when our family moved to our new home on Worline Road in Bow, Washington, where Polly and Larry *(Wilhonen)* now live with our Mom, Wanda. I was four or five years old, and it was a short move down the road from our old, small home. Indeed, our family switched houses, as Tollag and Christine's kids had all gotten married and left the big house. My Dad was the only one who remained to help on Tollag and Christine's farm - so we were granted use of the big house. My dad Melvin was the youngest child of Tollag's, and our family was growing with three kids - me, Wayne and Cheryl, and with Polly on the way. I remember the move vividly as I was allowed to sit on the family truck on some furniture as we made the big move with Tollag and Dad in charge.

After the move, I spent a lot of time in Tollag and Christine's house when my parents were at work or doing other things or when they wanted to get rid of me. I enjoyed eating the mush Grandma made, a gooey mess of oatmeal mush with fresh cream and a lot of sugar. She also made a lot of lefse, potato cakes and krumkake, usually with Mom and Aunt Sophie - all of which I liked. Also, I remember Grandma cooked lutefisk several times, which tasted horrible. I recall that several times when Grandpa was home, he sat in the small living room reading the paper and his favorite magazine, Newsweek. It may be weird, but what sticks in my mind is that I liked going to the bathroom in their house, because when I was finished, Grandma always came in and lighted a match, from a special bathroom match container, to get rid of the stink.

Growing up, I had plenty of chores to do. Grandpa had two large Belgian horses to plow the field, and Wayne and I were allowed to sit on them, briefly, before the real work was done. It was not until 1950 when the family could afford a tractor - a John Deere Model B. At that time Grandpa and Dad loaded up the Belgians and sold them to someone on Samish Island. I remember, since I rode along with the truck all the way to Abe's Point on Samish Island (the site of the current MacGregor mansion). In the 1940's, Grandpa's farm was only half-cleared of forest, and while Dad was busy with the cows, Grandpa spent much of his time with the slow process of removing the trees. He had a large ax, a very large lumber saw, and many cases of dynamite to blow up the stumps. We kids were not allowed in the area when dynamite was in use, and Grandpa lit the fuse and retreated quickly to safe ground. I remember one day in the early 1950's when I returned from school, that during one explosion a large tree root flew through the air more than fifty yards and struck and broke Grandpa's leg. It wasn't a major break and, being a stoic Norwegian, he laughed it off and life went on. After the major logging was done, Wayne and I spent years picking up sticks, and more years driving the tractor and farming the land.

Tollag and Christine also had two large chicken houses which produced a lot of eggs. When Wayne and I came home from school, we helped collect the eggs with large wire baskets and took them to the root house where they were stored and prepared for the weekly egg man. Before the eggs were put in the shipping containers, we had to clean them with sandpaper brushes to get the chicken shit off.

The last thing I remember about Grandpa before going off to college was his expertise in scything. Between our two houses, alongside the slough bank, there was a large area filled with grass in the springtime which Grandpa loved to cut with his scythe. He was quite graceful and moved quickly through the field. The bad news is that Wayne had a cow, Clarabelle, who was quite curious. As Grandpa was in the middle of scything, when he reached back, Clarabelle's hind leg was caught by the scythe and it neatly cut off a major tendon. Grandpa was saddened by this. Clarabelle survived, but went through the rest of her life with a very severe limp.

I believe I was in college or in the Army when Grandpa and Grandma died. They were always kind to me, and I don't recall ever getting into trouble with them when I was young, through grade school and high school, but this may be caused by my selective memory. I don't recall any time either of them expressed any regrets about leaving their family and friends back in Norway. Aunt Sophie was the prime intermediary with the remaining family in Norway.

As long as Grandma was alive, my Dad made me go to Sunday School, to which I agreed. But unlike Wayne and Cheryl, I was never a true Christian, but nevertheless I enjoyed being brought up in a true Christian family.

By Polly Peterson Wilhonen

I remember Grandma Peterson letting Katy Omdal and I build tents over her clothesline in their back yard. She would bring us homemade bread cut into bite sized pieces with jam. I have fond memories of following Grandpa home after doing chores in the barn, to eat wonderful oatmeal. I have tried to duplicate the taste, but to no avail. I talked to dad about this, and he wisely told me that you cannot duplicate a memory.

By Barbara Christine Peterson Schutte

During our young years, Grandma and Grandpa Peterson would pick us up for Sunday School. I have fond memories of trying to balance our Sunday School offering of a dime or nickel on the rope handle that was positioned in the back seat for the purpose of stability when needed (a built-in mechanism in the older cars before seat belts). It was great competition to see whose dime would stay on the rope handle the longest!

I do not remember having toys to play with at Grandma and Grandpa's. However, they would often reach to the top of the hutch and present me with their small card file of Bible Verse Memory Cards. I remember it being special to play with those cards! Grandma taught me how to dry dishes proper. "Hold the towel with both hands while drying – thus not having to touch the item you are drying". Occasionally during the winter when the water was frozen on the slough near their home, dad would take us kids down the road to enjoy some sliding or skating on the ice. We (Carl Peterson family) lived just ½ mile down the road from Grandma and Grandpa's in an old farmhouse (built in 1902) that dad bought from Aunt Sophie (and Birger) and was transported from their property on Farm to Market Road to dad's property on Worline Road in the year 1954.

By Jeanne Peterson Youngquist

Grandma and Grandpa Peterson immigrated to America after getting married in Norway and having their first child, Peter, there. Sophie, the next of kin, was born in America in 1906. My father, Martin Peterson, the third born, was mentioned often in Sophie's writings. Before marrying Mom in 1939 (while Sophie was in Norway), he fished in Alaska and then spent time as a merchant marine. I'm not sure where he contracted tuberculous, but it required him to be a patient in Seattle at the Firland Sanitarium for three years.

Because Mom needed to work to keep up payments on the house and farm, I, at five years old, went to stay with my Uncle Birger and Aunt Sophie (Peterson) Johnson. I stayed with them during the week for three years and spent the weekends with my mother, Margaret, at home. Sophie had taught school in Burlington before World War II and in Edison after the war. She and Birger did not have children of their own. I guess I was the closest they came to having a child.

When I stayed with Birger and Sophie there were things I especially remember. At five years old I got great comfort sitting by the stove in the corner of the dining room with my dolls, coloring books, and other important things for little girls. I also would sit by the big almost-jukebox-size console radio and try to listen to The Lone Ranger, Abbot and Costello, The Whistler, and The Shadow Knows. Sophie didn't like me to listen to the latter scary programs, probably because she would often have to come upstairs to comfort me. I slept all alone in a huge bedroom with its own room-sized closet and another big closet close by with a portion sloped over the stairway. That closet just outside my bedroom door was fun in the daytime, but at night this five or six-year-old was sure that was where bears hid as well as under my really big bed. Sophie would often have to comfort me with a Bible story or two.

(Note – this house was sold to Sophies brother, Carl, in 1954. Carl had the house moved the few miles to his property on Worline Road in Bow. Carl and Alice raised their five children in this house - Carlene, Barbara, Keith, Karen, and Teresa. Carl continued to live in this house after Alice died from cancer in 1978 until his death in 2010.)

Grandma Christine and Grandpa Tollag eventually lived between two of their sons' homes. Melvin and Wanda and their kids were living in the homestead home and my parents, Martin and Margaret, and me on the other side.

I remember Grandpa used to pick up his neighboring grandchildren every Sunday for Sunday school - Polly, Cheryl, Wayne, Marvin and me. Thank you, Grandpa. I remember Marvin had hard questions for our Sunday school teachers.

We spent quite a bit of time with Grandma Christine. She made preserved Norwegian meats. I remember Rolla Pulsa, an interesting sausage she made and hung in the cool room outside behind the kitchen. She would provide a midmorning and midafternoon Scandinavian spread of breads, including flat bread, hardanger, lefsa, goat and other cheeses, and pickled items. When we cousins stopped in, she would always offer us "Peeknotbuddar and yam sannvitches." I was Yeennie, with her bit of an accent. She didn't talk a lot, but we know she spoke and understood English very well. We would often interrupt her while she was reading her Bible in the front room or working on a patchwork quilt.

Quilt! That reminds me of the fun we had in their backyard, with Grandma's bag of clothespins, the clothesline, and a pile of her blankets. We made tents out of all those blankets. We had such fun. I don't remember if we ever slept in the tents, but we spent a lot of time there. The four of us, Polly, Cheryl, Wayne and I were about the neighborhood together a lot. Marvin was home reading James Bond and lots of other books. Aunt Wanda would at least on one occasion send him out to get some fresh air, locking the door behind him. His interest in James Bond might have led him to study Political Science at PLU and into his career, a real-life James Bond adventure. After serving in the Army in Vietnam in 1968-69 as a counterintelligence agent, he later worked for the U.S. Government in various nuclear safeguards and nuclear intelligence positions. The highlight of his career was working for the State Department in Vienna, Austria from 1990 to 1997, where he was the Senior Science Counselor serving as the liaison between all U.S. intelligence offices (CIA, DIA, NSA, and DOE and State intelligence) and the International Atomic Energy Agency (IAEA) in support of their nuclear safeguard inspections in Iraq, Iran and North Korea.

I am thankful for my happy memories of growing up next door to my grandparents and cousins. I cherish the times spent and the memories of those days.

Sophie's Life in America

Upon Sophie's return in 1944 to the rural area of Bow in the Skagit Valley near Burlington, Washington, U.S.A., she resumed her profession as a primary school educator, teaching at the Edison Grade School. She married Birger Kon Johnson, an American-born son of Norwegian immigrants (Rasmus Stapnes Johnson from Stapnes, Norway and Anne Berentsen Mong from Mong, Norway) on June 1, 1948, at Edison Lutheran Church. She and Birger lived on the Farm to Market Road in Bow - very near to Edison, in the State of Washington.

She was a very special sister, aunt, and friend to many. We have fond memories of Aunt Sophie hosting family gatherings on occasion, with lots of good food to share and enjoy. She involved herself with the Edison Lutheran Church and the "Ladies Aid", also known as ELCW. She was a teacher at heart and is remembered as a teacher in Sunday School who could tell Bible stories so that the characters seemed to come alive. Many remember receiving a Bible as a gift from Sophie in celebration of a special occasion or milestone in their life. Her gifts of handiwork - crocheting fine doilies, knitting and such - are special keepsakes to many.

Sophie was instrumental as she joined with her siblings in organizing gatherings uniting relatives from Norway that had immigrated, some to the Bow-Edison area and others to the Squamish Area in British Columbia, Canada. These connections would provide ties to the families for years as they exchanged locations at which to congregate. The first cousins of Sophie's and her siblings that settled in Canada were Lisabeth (Gya) and Ted Halvorson as well as Maria (Gystøl) and Martin Halvorson. Memories of these reunions are valued.

We do not remember Sophie verbally sharing much about her experiences in Norway during the era this book records. It seems that the memories were too painful to talk about. She did say that while in the Grini prison she often had only carrots to eat, and water. She quietly lived life with dedication to God and a servant's heart, which is epitomized within the communication received from family in Norway that are preserved within the pages of this book.

Sophie's beloved father, Tollag, was in her care in her home when he passed away in 1965. Her mother, Christine, when challenged with angina, is remembered being in Sophie's care as Christine would lie on Sophie's couch and revert to her native language of Norwegian as they shared conversation. She lovingly cared for her husband, Birger, who passed away March 9, 1980, of Parkinson's Disease.

She returned to visit her beloved family in Norway several times. She, Birger, Theodora, Chris, and David traveled on board "Bergensfjord" from New York on June 7, 1957. A trip in 1983 with her brother, Carl Peterson, was enjoyed and recorded in another of Sophie's detailed and cherished diaries.

Sophie's earthly life ceased on May 28, 1988, due to heart complications. However, through her writings, she continues to inspire and encourage; and we are thankful Sophie preserved this for us to appreciate.

With "Heartfelt Greetings", loving memories, and thankful hearts,

Barbara, Karen, & Teresa

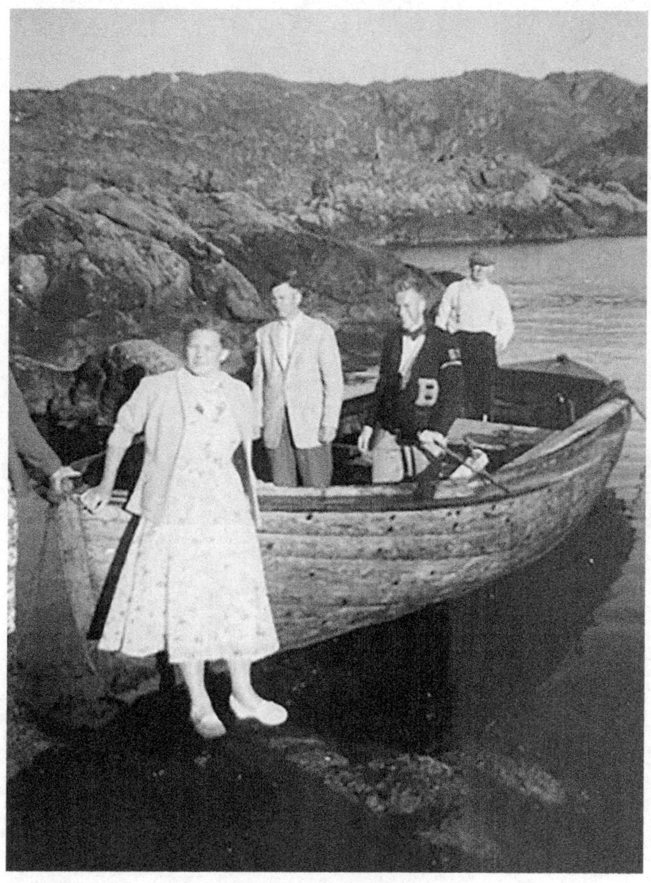

Sophie, Birger, and nephew David Hansen; visiting Norway in 1957

Special Recipes from Sophie & Others

Skagit Valley Herald **FAMILY**/Food

Sophie Johnson slides a wooden spatula under a piece of lefse to keep it from sticking as it sizzles on her griddle. Each piece is cooked on both sides then transfered to a towel where it cools and crisps. Mrs. Johnson coats hers with butter and sugar and cuts it into serving-size pieces.

By KATHLEEN HOSFELD
Family Editor

EDISON — In the warmth of rare winter sunlight streaming through her kitchen window, Sophie Johnson rolls out a tradition.

Leaning over a board covered with a clean, floured feed sack, she rolls out balls of potato dough with a textured rolling pin.

The dough is rolled up on a stick, which helps transfer it to a 14-inch wide round griddle. It sizzles softly, and she loosens it gently with her fingers and a spatula. A deft flop and the other side sizzles.

The whole round is transfered to a clean towel where it dries slightly.

Later she will coat it with butter or margarine, sprinkle it with granulated sugar and cut it into serving-size pieces.

Mrs. Johnson is carrying on an age-old Norwegian tradition by making lefse, a staple food in many Scandinavian households, particularly abundant during Christmas.

There are many ways to make lefse, said Mrs. Johnson.

One Better Homes and Gardens cookbook reports that in Norway, there are as many recipes for lefse as there are Norwegian cooks. Cooks several miles apart will have entirely different recipes for lefse.

Potato lefse is found in eastern Norway (Better Homes and Gardens Classic International Recipes 1982) while the flour and other recipes are found in the rest of the country.

Norwegian immigrants, such as Mrs. Johnson's parents and her late husband's parents, came directly to Skagit County, bringing their various recipes.

Many of them settled in the Bow-Edison area, as did her parents, she said.

And although many of them came from the same regions, their recipes for lefse vary widely.

Norwegians have used lefse many ways. Pieces are sometimes wrapped around bits of food, such as meatballs. Or fresh lefse can be served crisp like crackers.

Others like lefse soft, buttered and sugared as Mrs. Johnson does, are filled with gjetost (goat cheese) and sour cream.

Still others top them, crepe-style, with lingonberry preserves and whipped cream.

"In Norway they would bake lefse for days," she said. "They wouldn't use any oil in the recipe. And they would stack them in tall stacks. Sometimes they would last for months."

Mrs. Johnson's mother was the traditional lefse supplier until her death in 1962. Mrs. Johnson picked up where she left off.

"You know Norwegians have to have their lefse at Christmas," she said.

She makes potato lefse.

"I usually cook them (potatoes) the night before," she said. "If you work with warm potatoes you just get a runny mess."

She mixes four parts riced potatoes with one part flour, a quarter cup of oil, a tablespoon sugar and a teaspoon or less of salt.

"It's best not to make too big a batch or else the dough gets too soft," she added.

Those who frequently make lefse like to use the lefse griddle, lefse rolling pin and lefse dowel. These are available in many hardware stores and kitchen specialty shops. An ordinary large griddle, rolling pin and any large dowel can also be used, however.

For complete lefse recipes turn to page 18.

16 – Skagit Valley Herald   Wednesday, January 30, 1985

Various lefse recipes create regional favorites

Continued from page 15. **Following are some of the many recipes for making lefse:**

FLOUR LEFSE

2 to 2½ cups all-purpose flour
1 tablespoon sugar
1 teaspoon salt
¼ cup butter or margarine
1 cup buttermilk

In a mixing bowl, stir together 2 cups of the flour, the sugar and salt. Cut in butter or margarine until mixture resembles coarse crumbs. Add buttermilk; stir until just moistened. Cover. Chill at least one hour.

Turn out onto a lightly floured surface. Knead in enough of remaining flour to make a stiff dough (8 to 10 minutes total). Divide into 8 portions; shape into balls. Cover and let stand 10 minutes. On a floured surface, roll each ball to a circle 10 inches in diamter. Roll around rolling pin, transfer to a hot lightly greased griddle or skillet. Cook over medium heat four to six minutes or until light brown; turn once (should be limp).

Cover with plastic wrap to prevent drying out. Repeat with remaining dough. Makes 8.

HARDANGER LEFSE

2 cups buttermilk
2 eggs
½ cup sugar
1 teaspoon salt
1 teaspoon soda
¼ cup margarine, melted
4 to 5 cups flour

Mix buttermilk, eggs, sugar, salt, soda and margarine together. Add flour a little at a time. Chill dough. Taking an egg-sized piece at a time, roll out on a floured surface into a thin circle. Wrap lefse around a wooden dowel, transfer to a hot lefse iron or flat grill. Cook turning once, until light brown on both sides. Cool.

Wet lefse under cool water. Stack on a plate placing paper towels between each one.

Let rest 20 minutes.

Melt one cube butter. Spread on each lefse. Sprinkle with cinnamon and sugar. Fold in half and cut into 2-inch diamond shapes. Serve or freeze for later use.

POTATO LEFSE

3 or 4 potatoes
¾ cup cold water
3 cups rye flour
1 cup wheat flour
extra flour for kneading

Peel, wash and dry potatoes. Grate them into a large bowl. Add the water, salt and the flours, and mix well. Let the dough stand covered overnight.

The next day, on a flour-covered board, roll out the dough very thin. Cut it into circles about 6 inches round. Place the rounds at least 1-inch apart on a greased baking pan. Bake at 400° for 6 minutes. Then turn lefse and bake it for 6 minutes more.

Makes 12 pieces.

Kim Thomsen / Skagit Valley Herald

Potato lefse made by Sophie Johnson.

SOPHIE JOHNSON'S POTATO LEFSE

4 cups riced potatoes, chilled
1 cup flour
¼ cup oil
1 tablespoon sugar
1 teaspoon salt or less

Boil, peel and rice potatoes the night before. The next day combine all ingredients in a large mixing bowl. Mix well. Form dough into ¾-cup balls.

On a covered and floured board, roll out dough very thin with lefse rolling pin.

Transfer to lefse griddle. Cook turning once, until lightly browned in spots. Remove from griddle and place on clean towel to cool.

Spread with creamed butter. Sprinkle with sugar. Fold in sides to make the circle a square. Then fold the square in half. Slice in 1-inch wide pieces.

Kråtekaker

Recipe origin is from Sirdal Norway, shared from generation to generation, from Irene Tunheim. (Thank you, Irene!)

- 100 grams melted butter
- 2 eggs
- 1 liter buttermilk
- 1 teaspoon baking soda
- 3 teaspoons baking powder
- 500 grams sugar
- About 1.5 kilo flour (hold back a little bit for rolling out the dough).

Mix baking soda and baking powder in some of the buttermilk. Add lightly whipped eggs, the rest of the buttermilk, and the melted butter (cool a bit). Mix in sugar and flour. Work dough lightly in a machine or by hand, not too much or the dough will become rubbery.

Divide the dough into about twenty 150 gram segments. With a rolling pin, (preferably textured), roll out to a round shape, about 15"-17" diameter. Cook on preheated griddle, medium high temperature, on both sides until there are light brown spots. Transfer to a towel to cool and crisp.

Before serving, moisten lightly the entire Kråtekake (both sides) and leave it on a towel a little bit before smearing it with a mix of butter and powdered sugar. My mother used to hold the crisp Kråtekake under the running water faucet JUST A FEW SECONDS to get the right amount of moisture. Make sure that all parts of the Kråtekake gets wet.

Fyrstekake – The Duke's Cake

A Norwegian Recipe

Prepare: Preheat oven to 350 degrees, grease a 9" round layer cake pan or pie pan.

DOUGH:

- ½ pound butter
- 2 cups flour
- 2 teaspoons baking powder
- ½ cup sugar
- 1 egg
- ½ teaspoon almond extract

FILLING:

- ½ pound of scalded almonds, ground
- 2 cups powdered sugar
- 1 teaspoon flour
- 1 egg white
- 1 teaspoon rum or brandy extract, or a few drops of lemon.

Mix dry ingredients, butter, and eggs quickly by hand. Divide dough into two parts and roll out. Cover bottom of pan evenly with one half.

Mix all ingredients for filling, spread over bottom of dough. Take second part of dough, cut into ½" or broader strips with cookie cutter and place lattice-wise over the filling. Flute edge as you would for a pie. Bake 350 degrees F. for 50 minutes.

Kvæfjordkake (The World's Best Cake!)

Kvæfjordkake cake or Verdens beste in Norwegian is a sponge cake baked with meringue, vanilla cream and almonds. The cake is named for Kvæfjord, a municipality in Norway.

- 100 g (3 ½ ounces or scant ½ cup) butter or margarine
- 1 ¼ dl (1/2 cup) sugar
- 4 egg yolks
- 1 ¾ dl (2/3 cup) flour
- 1 teaspoon baking powder
- 1/4 cup milk
- 4 egg whites
- 2 ¼ dl (1 cup) sugar
- ½ dl (3 ½ tablespoons) sliced almonds
- 1 package (4 oz) rum or vanilla pudding mix
- 3 dl (1 ¼ cup) full fat milk
- 3 dl (1 ¼ cup) whipping cream

Preheat oven to 180 degrees Celsius (350 degrees Fahrenheit). Beat butter and sugar until light and fluffy. Beat in the egg yolks, one at a time. Sift the flour with the baking powder and add alternately with the milk. Pour into a greased 20 X 30 cm (8 X 12") pan. Beat the egg whites until stiff but not dry. Gradually add the sugar and beat until stiff and glossy. Spread over the cake batter. Sprinkle with almonds. Bake 20-25 minutes until light brown. Allow to cool, then cut in half to make two 8 x 6 pieces. Prepare pudding according to the package directions but use only 3 dl (1 ¼ cup) milk. Cool. Whip the cream and fold into the pudding. Spread one cake layer with cream, then top with other cake layer.

Krumkager

- 1 cup butter, melted
- 2 cups sugar
- 4 eggs and 2 egg yolks, beaten
- 1 cup light or heavy whipping cream, unwhipped
- 1 teaspoon ground cardamon
- 4 cups all-purpose white flour

Cream butter and sugar. Add beaten eggs and beat again. Add cream, then gradually add flour sifted with cardamon. Drop approximately one tablespoon onto a hot krumkager iron and bake until lightly browned on both sides. Remove from iron and immediately roll into a cone or cylinder.

Wonderful Spice Cake

- 1 cup butter or margarine
- 2 cups sugar
- 4 eggs, yolks & whites divided
- 4 cups cake flour
- 4 teaspoons baking powder
- 1 ½ teaspoons cinnamon
- 1 teaspoon allspice
- ½ teaspoon cloves
- ½ teaspoon salt

Cream butter and sugar together. Add 4 egg yolks, one at a time, beating well after each addition. Sift together the cake flour, baking powder, cinnamon, allspice, cloves, and salt. Add alternately with milk. Fold in 4 stiffly beaten egg whites. Bake in two 9" square cake pans in a 350-degree oven 40-45 minutes. Excellent with a lemon frosting.

Sophie's Swedish Pancakes

- 3 eggs
- 2 cups milk, (or 1 cup milk and 1 cup half-and-half)
- 1 cup white flour
- ½ teaspoon salt and 1 tablespoon sugar (optional)
- 7 tablespoons melted butter

In a large bowl, beat eggs until light. Add milk. Gradually add dry ingredients and beat until smooth. Stir in melted butter. If time allows, let rest for one hour, then stir well and pour a small amount of batter onto a small or medium-size hot skillet – just enough to thinly coat the bottom of the pan. Brown on each side and keep warm in oven until ready to serve with maple syrup.

Sophie's Chocolate Chiffon Cake

- 2 eggs
- 1 ½ cup sugar
- 1 ¾ cup sifted Soft-As-Silk cake flour
- ¾ teaspoon soda
- ¾ teaspoon salt
- 1/3 cup oil
- 1 cup buttermilk
- 2 squares unsweetened chocolate, melted

Heat oven to 350 degrees. Beat egg whites until frothy. Gradually beat in ½ cup sugar. Beat until very stiff and glossy.

In another bowl, sift remaining sugar, flour, soda, and salt. Add vegetable oil and half of the buttermilk. Mix at medium speed. Add remaining buttermilk, egg yolks, and chocolate. Beat 1 more minute. Fold in beaten egg whites. Bake 30-35 minutes in layer pans or 40-45 in an oblong pan.

Whole milk may be substituted for buttermilk in this recipe.

Bibliography

Families who Immigrated to Edison-Bow, Skagit Co. WA from Southwestern Norway
Compiled by Nina Anderson Larson, July 1999

The farm Dyldo at Rodvelt in Eigersund. FAMILY HISTORY 1400-2000
By Åsa Sande, Rolf Mong, and Bjørg Torill Waldeland, January 2000

Slekten etter Andreas Martinius Pettersen Rodvelt og hustru Elisabeth
By Åsa Sande, Rolf Mong, and Bjørg Torill Waldeland
Slektsstevne Egersund August 1996

The Daily Chronicles of World War II
WW2days.com

Norway-World War II
Britannica.com

World War II – The Royal House of Norway
Royalcourt.no

Hetland Skipreide 1 450 ÅR
Petrus Valand og Olav Heskestad

The Bible.

Wikipedia.org

Index

Index created by Karen

Made in the USA
Monee, IL
17 September 2023

42832628R20226